GARDENS in CHINA

GARDENS in CHINA

PETER VALDER

TIMBER PRESS
Portland, Oregon

Pre-title pages Lake in the garden of the Taihua Temple,
Western Hills, Kunming

Frontispiece View through a doorway, Zuibaichi, Songjiang

This page A terracotta plaque in the Forbidden City, Beijing,
showing lotuses, arrowhead and herons

Contents pages Yuquan Shan and the Western Hills viewed
across the lake at the Summer Palace, Beijing

First published in North America,
the United Kingdom, and Europe in 2002 by
Timber Press, Inc.
The Haseltine Building
133 S.W. Second Avenue, Suite 450
Portland, Oregon 97204, USA

ISBN 0-88192-555-1

A catalog record for this book is available from
the Library of Congress

Editor Ariana Klepac
Designer Stan Lamond, Lamond Art & Design
Produced by Phoenix Offset
Printed in China

Acknowledgments

Needless to say, the writing and publication of this book would not have been possible without the support and assistance of a great many people. I am particularly indebted to Allan McNeish, who accompanied me on several trips to China, rescued and guided me on endless occasions when I have proved incompetent in dealing with my computer, and carried out investigations on the Internet on my behalf, as well as making many helpful suggestions and offering general support. Likewise I am most appreciative of the assistance of Richard Clough, who twice accompanied me to China, read the manuscript and, with his experience both as a landscape architect and collector of books on horticultural topics, offered much good advice. Particular thanks go, too, to Gilbert Teague of Florilegium for agreeing to be the principal publisher and allowing me such a free hand, to Stan Lamond for doing such an excellent job with the design, and to Ariana Klepac for editing the text and facing up to my idiosyncratic style with equanimity.

Of the many people in China who assisted me I would especially like to thank Professor Zhang Zhiming, Tan Jie and Mr Niu in Beijing, Li Xingfu in Kunming, Su Yidong in Dali, Tin Jianhong in Lijiang, Zheng Fang in Luoyang, Dong Jihong in Ningbo, Zhang Longchun at Putuo Shan, Li Yimin in Guilin, Mr Chai in Shanghai, Yong Zhenhua in Suzhou, Jiang Jin in Ji'nan, Mr Xu in Nanjing and Bush Jiang in Yangzhou.

In Australia I am particularly indebted to Tang Luhua, who has provided translations and transliterations, as well as unravelling many of the complexities I have faced when grappling with the Chinese language. I am indebted also to Dr Liu Yang of the Art Gallery of New South Wales for guidance in coping with Pinyin orthography, to Terry Smyth for obtaining on my behalf the meanings of names of sites in Yunnan from her friends at the Kunming Botanical Institute, and to Ross Steele for assistance with the French language. My thanks go, too, to Antoinette Duncan and Margaret-Anne Mayo, who have been totally without fault in organising my travel arrangements.

In my research into Chinese gardens I have been most grateful for the advice of Dr Frances Wood at the British Library in London and for the guidance provided in Paris by Mme Monique Cohen of the Bibliothèque nationale de France. In Sydney I am especially indebted to Anna Hallet and Miguel Garcia of the Library of the Royal Botanic Gardens Sydney, and my thanks go, too, to all the librarians elsewhere who have been helpful, particularly those at the University of Sydney, the University of New South Wales, the State Library of New South Wales, the Australian National University and the National Library of Australia.

Permission to reproduce illustrations from Osvald Sirén's *Gardens of China* (figs 1.32, 1.34 1.39, 5.40) was kindly granted by the Östasiatiska Museet, Stockholm, and for providing photographs I am indebted to the British Library (figs 1.4, 3.92), the Bibliothèque nationale de France (figs 1.5, 1.7, 1.8), the State Library of New South Wales (figs 1.9, 1.14, 1.31, 5.46), the National Gallery of Australia (figs 1.21, 3.61, 4.5), the Library of the University of Sydney (fig. 1.3), Richard Clough (figs 3.84, 3.85, 4.31) and Terry Smyth (figs 6.25, 6.26). The remainder of the photographs are my own.

Contents

Introduction

While many excellent books have already been written about Chinese gardens, on the whole they have dealt only with the imperial gardens and a limited selection of gardens of retired officials and scholars. Rarely are the fascinating courtyards and gardens of temples, shrines and mosques mentioned, or the evocative enclosures of imperial tombs and ancient burial grounds, let alone the parks, botanical gardens and arboreta, most of which have sprung up since 1949. Thus, while it would be almost impossible for anyone to write comprehensively about the gardens of so large a country, it has been my aim to bring to notice, in one book, a wider range of Chinese gardens than has been done previously. More than 200 sites of horticultural interest which I have visited are described and, in all but a few instances, illustrated in colour.

Like many gardeners of my generation, my interest in China was fired by the adventures and discoveries of the famous plant-hunters of the 19th and early 20th centuries. I had long hoped that some day I, too, might be able to go to the west of the country and see something of the fascinating native flora. However, owing to the turbulent times prevailing in China during the early part of my life, it was not until 1980 that an opportunity arose for me to do so. In that year I was invited to join a small group of camellia enthusiasts whose principal aim was to visit Kunming to see

Figure 0.1 Apricot and *Prunus triloba*, Zhongshan Park, Shenyang

11

Figure 0.2 *Camellia reticulata* 'Shizitou', Bamboo Temple, Kunming

cultivars of *Camellia reticulata* (fig. 0.2). I asked whether it would be possible for Emei Shan to be included in our itinerary since, having read everything I could find about western China, I had come to the conclusion that, at that time, this must be the most easily accessible of the famous collecting sites, having a stepped path to its summit, up which pilgrims had been trooping for centuries. And so it came about that, as well as visiting Guangzhou, Kunming, Chengdu and Beijing, I was afforded the opportunity of seeing rhododendrons, camellias and many other Chinese plants growing in the wild. I also saw a few gardens and had the stimulating experience of having to contend with the Chinese culture of the time.

I did not return to China till 1994, when I undertook a trip to investigate and photograph wisterias, about which I was writing at the time. This involved visiting a large number of gardens and, for the first time, I was exposed fully to the reality of Chinese garden design (fig. 0.3). Those used to herbaceous borders, lawns, rose gardens and suchlike usually find coming to terms with Chinese gardens challenging, as they are the product of a culture with philosophical and cosmological bases very different from those of the West. In this I was no different from most Western visitors. Initially, for instance, I found the frequent use of rock as the principal structural component, the presence of strangely shaped individual stones, and the prominence of name boards, poetic couplets and other inscriptions to be somewhat at odds with my concept of a garden.

Between 1995 and 2000 I made eight more trips, principally to see and photograph gardens and garden plants. All this was made possible by the opening up of most of China once more during the last 20 years. And it has been the introduction of efficient air and rail services, the construction of an ever increasing number of expressways, the abundance of taxis in the cities and larger towns, the building of modern hotels, the ready availability of guides speaking foreign languages, the presence almost everywhere of people with at least some grasp of English, and the restoration and opening to the public of a large number of temples, gardens and other historic sites, that have enabled me to undertake a survey on a scale that would not earlier have been feasible for a person of my situation and means. And, although it was their plants which first drew me to Chinese gardens, during these visits

Figure 0.3 A garden on Ruyi Islet, Imperial Summer Villa, Chengde

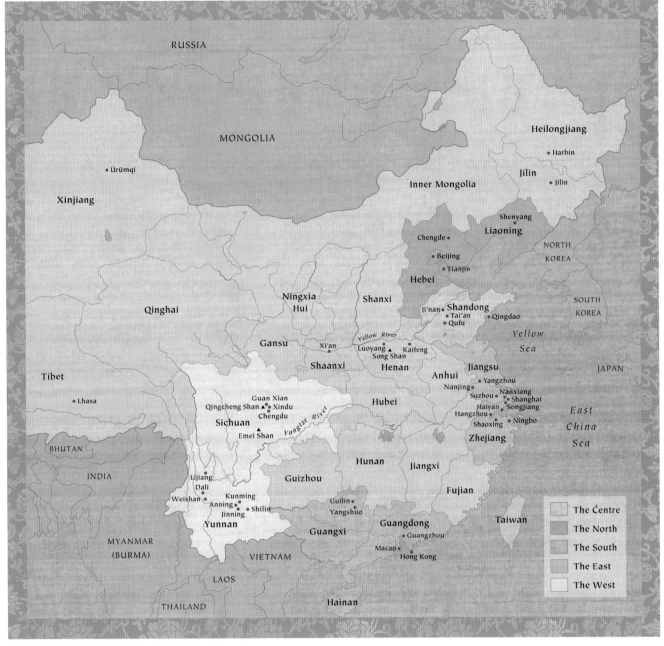

Figure 0.4 Map of China showing the five regions described in this book

I became more and more interested in the gardens themselves and gradually came, like others before me, to appreciate them for what they are—the end product of between three and four thousand years of garden history and a fascinating expression of the culture of a great civilisation.

I was greatly helped in this by reading what other Western visitors have had to say about these gardens. Hence, in order to place my own descriptions and opinions in context, I have chosen to begin this book with a chapter devoted largely to a survey of those of Western visitors who have gone before

me. As far as I know, this has not been done previously and it is my hope that it will provide an appropriate introduction to the rest of the text. However, I must point out that, for the period from 1860 on, I have relied principally on those who have written of their experiences in English.

As far as the structure of the book is concerned, the remainder is divided into five chapters, each dealing with the gardens of one of five regions—the centre, the north, the south, the east, and the west (fig. 0.4). This arrangement has been suggested by the tenets of ancient Chinese cosmology in

Figure 0.5 **Garden viewing, Huagang Park, Hangzhou**

which each of the five elements—wood, fire, earth, metal and water—became symbolically correlated with everything else in the universe which could be fitted into a fivefold arrangement. For example, wood became associated, amongst other things, with the east, spring and green; fire with the south, summer and red; earth with the centre, yellow and, at one time, a very short season interpolated between summer and autumn; water with the north, winter and black; and metal with the west, autumn and white.

Lengthy descriptions of the best-known gardens have been given by many earlier authors, so I have often tended to be relatively brief about these in order to devote space to those about which information is not readily accessible. Also, while little attempt is made to discuss the architecture of the buildings, walls, walkways and bridges which form an integral part of most Chinese gardens, I have frequently included comments on the plants present, as I believe this aspect of the subject has not received the attention it deserves. I have rarely, however, gone into detail concerning the history and symbolic significance of these plants, as I have earlier written at length on this topic. Also, in order to place the gardens in their setting, I have provided a little information about the provinces, cities and towns where they are found.

As a general rule, for the transliteration of Chinese characters I have used the Pinyin system throughout this book except for the citation of authors and the titles of books and articles where the original romanisation has been retained. In order to avoid confusion I have also retained long-established usages such as the Yangtze and the traditional transliterations of the Cantonese pronunciations of the Fa Tee Gardens, Hong Kong, Sun Yat-sen and Chiang Kai-shek. As far as the names of gardens and temples are concerned, since Chinese characters often have no exact English equivalents and translators vary in their interpretations, in most cases I have given the name of each site as both a Pinyin transliteration and an English translation. Even so, Pinyin transliterations are based on pronunciation and do not allow the reader to be certain of the original characters which they purport to represent. Similarly, translations are usually literal and give no indication of the literary, religious or other allusions which are often present in the original names. Added to all this are the complexities of Pinyin orthography. While the

correct spelling of the Pinyin romanisation of a character is not a problem, uncertainties arise when it comes to capitalisation and the joining or separating of syllables. In this regard I have attempted to follow the Basic Rules for Hanyu Pinyin Orthography devised by the Commission for Pinyin Orthography, State Language Commission, P.R.C., an English translation of which is given as Appendix I of the *ABC Chinese-English Dictionary* edited by John DeFrancis and published in Australia by Allen & Unwin. These rules, unfortunately, are not sufficiently detailed to enable all decisions to be made with confidence, so some of my courses of action may be regarded as being wide of the mark. Nevertheless I have tried to be consistent.

References are cited by author and date, the full reference in each case being listed alphabetically under the authors name in the Bibliography and References. I have also included an abbreviated chronological table of the Chinese dynasties in order to avoid giving their dates every time they are

mentioned. As far as dates generally are concerned I must point out that, as a result of there being a variety of sources and methods of dating, there are considerable variations in Chinese dates. However, I have done my best. For the dates of dynasties and the reigns of the various emperors I have used Ann Paludan's *Chronicle of the Chinese Emperors*. Also, since the Chinese emperors had many names, I have followed Ann Paludan's example and used the names by which they are best known in the West. Up to the Yuan dynasty these are usually their temple names, for example Huizong of the Northern Song dynasty. The Yuan emperors, on the other hand, are generally known by their birth names—Khubilai Khan for instance—and the Ming and Qing emperors by the names of their reigns—e.g. Kangxi and Qianlong.

The photographs depict things as they were at the times of my visits, rain or shine. It should be understood that at the present time, on most days in many parts of China, the atmospheric pollution is such that, even when it is not cloudy, the sky is grey (fig. 0.5). Also I have not always been able to conform to the convention, followed by most garden photographers, of ensuring that depictions of gardens do not include people. In China one might wait forever to achieve such an aim. However, just as written descriptions, poems, paintings, woodcuts and photographs have recorded Chinese gardens in the past, I hope this book will be seen as a record of Chinese gardens at the turn of the 20th and 21st centuries. I hope also that it will stimulate others to develop an interest in these gardens and that it will be useful to those visiting China. It must be remembered, however, that in no other country at the present time is change proceeding at such a pace, and that the descriptions which I have given are of the gardens as they were at the times of my visits.

CHAPTER 1

Through Western Eyes

In China records have been being made of gardens for well over 2000 years. They are mentioned in official histories and gazetteers, shown on maps and plans, described in literary works and depicted in woodcuts and paintings. However, only during the past 300 years has any detailed information about them become available in the West. Perhaps the earliest reference we have is that of Marco Polo, who claimed to have visited China during the time of Khubilai Khan, the first emperor of the Yuan dynasty (1279–1368). As well as mentioning various cultivated plants, he gave an account of Hangzhou in which he mentioned the lake with its islands, the gardens and the splendours of the palace. Admittedly he acknowledged that his description of the palace was second hand and that by the time of his visit it had fallen into decay. Also, although he said he went there frequently, it must have been shortly after the city—which had been the capital of the Southern Song dynasty (1127–1279)—had been captured by the Mongols, when one might have expected it to be in a much less exciting state than he would have had us believe.

Figure 1.1 **The Pavilion of Admirable Fragrance, Gongwangfu, Beijing**

Figure 1.2 Tree peony,
Wangcheng Park, Luoyang

wise in 1643 in his *Relatione della Grande Monarchia della Cina*, and appears to be the first European to have mentioned the wintersweet (*Chimonanthus praecox*); and Martino Martini who, in his *Novus Atlas Sinensis* of 1655, seems to be the first to have noticed the tree peony (fig. 1.2). Michael Boym's *Flora Sinensis* appeared the following year—the first European book devoted exclusively to Chinese plants (Bretschneider, 1880). However, apart from da Cruz's brief account, none of these publications gives us any idea of what the gardens in which these plants grew were like. As a result perceptions of Chinese gardens remained largely fanciful, having arisen from their depiction on imported Chinese decorative objects.

Subsequent Western descriptions did not become available until after Europeans reached China by sea during the Ming dynasty (1368–1644). The Portuguese anchored in the Pearl River delta in 1513 and arrived in Ningbo a few years later, establishing trading posts in both places in the 1530s. Amongst the few Portuguese records of Chinese gardens and garden plants, the earliest appears to be that of Gaspar da Cruz, who visited southern China in 1556 and whose observations were recorded in 1569 in the first European book devoted entirely to China since that of Marco Polo (Boxer, 1953). In Guilin da Cruz saw the small gardens of magistrates and obtained a second-hand account of a very large garden within a walled compound occupied by a kinsman of the empress. This, it seems, had many fruit trees, large ponds for the raising of fish, and gardens for flowers and herbs, as well as a wooded area where the owner kept deer, wild boars and other beasts of the chase. Other fragments of information came from Gonzalez de Mendoza (1588), who mentioned a variety of cultivated plants; Alvaro de Semedo, who did like-

Although his journals did not become generally available until much later, the earliest first-hand descriptions of Chinese gardens which I have come across are those of the Italian Jesuit Matteo Ricci, who was in China during the late Ming. For instance, in 1598 he was taken by friends to see the Duke of Wenguo's garden in Nanjing. He described it as the most beautiful in the city, labyrinthine in nature and requiring two or three hours to traverse. He praised its towers, terraces and other buildings, and recorded the presence of caves, an artificial hill made of rocks, loggias, steps, pavilions, shelters, fishing places and other 'galanteries' (Clunas, 1996).

The Ming were eventually overthrown by the Manchus who established the Qing dynasty (1644–1911). Observations of the destruction wrought by the Manchu army as it moved south were made by Johan Nieuhof (1665), who accompanied the Dutch East India Company's embassy to the first

Qing emperor, Shunzhi, in the years 1655–57. He also described and drew an example of extraordinary rockwork which he saw in northern Jiangxi (fig. 1.3). It looks like a giant version of the sort of thing you still see in gardens today. He saw similar artificial rockwork in the emperor's palace in Beijing.

Nieuhof's brief descriptions were followed by Sir William Temple's lengthy essay 'Upon the Gardens of Epicurus: or, Of Gardening, in the Year 1685' (Temple, 1690), in which Chinese gardens received a brief mention in a paragraph he wrote about irregular design. He had not been to China and, according to Ciaran Murray (1998), it seems probable that his pronouncements were based on reports he got from Dutchmen who had seen gardens in Japan and his own observations of depictions on artefacts. Nevertheless he had hit upon the general idea when he claimed, concerning the gardens of the '*Chineses*', that 'their greatest reach of Imagination, is employed in contriving Figures, where the Beauty shall be great, and strike the Eye, but without any order or disposition of arts, that shall be commonly or easily observ'd'. He also showed perception in remarking that they were 'a People whose way of thinking seems to lie as wide of ours in *Europe*, as their Country does'.

Since the European traders were allowed little freedom, almost the only people to succeed in getting far into China at this time continued to be the Jesuit missionaries. With their competence in the European arts and sciences they managed to ingratiate themselves with the emperors, presumably hoping that, if they could save their souls, the rest of the vast population would follow suit. However, in spite of the valuable assistance they provided in scientific and other fields, they met with little success. Nevertheless, in their letters and journals sent to the West they were the chief source of information about China at that time. For instance, J.-F. Gerbillon, who was in China in 1688–91, was of the view that beauty in China 'consists in a great Propriety and Imitation of Nature as Grotto's, Shellwork and craggy Fragments of Rocks, such as are seen in the wildest Desarts' (Du Halde, 1736; Moyriac de Mailla, 1780).

Next came Matteo Ripa, a Jesuit who lived in Beijing from 1711–23 and saw the imperial gardens there and at Chengde. The Qing emperor Kangxi (reigned 1661–1722) had built a

Figure 1.3 Rockwork in northern Jiangxi. FROM NIEUHOF (1665), COURTESY OF THE UNIVERSITY OF SYDNEY LIBRARY.

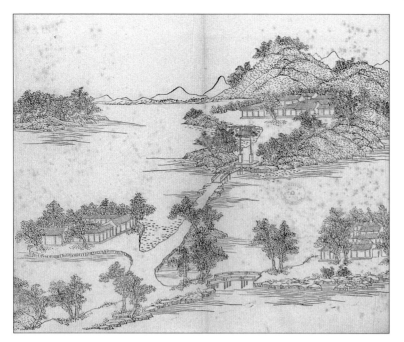

Figure 1.4 **View of the lake at the Imperial Summer Villa, Chengde, looking north and showing the causeways leading to the three principal islands.**

TAKEN FROM A COPY OF THE KANGXI EMPEROR'S POEMS DESCRIBING THE SUMMER RESORT, AN ILLUSTRATED COPPER ENGRAVED EDITION BY MATTEO RIPA, POSTFACE DATED 1712. THE BRITISH LIBRARY [19957 C.4].

by means of art, endeavour to imitate nature. Thus in these gardens there are labyrinths of artificial hills, intersected with numerous paths and roads, some straight, and others undulating; some in the plain and the valley, others carried over bridges and to the summit of the hills by means of rustic work of stones and shells. The lakes are interspersed with islets upon which small pleasure-houses are constructed, and which are reached by means of boats or bridges. To these houses, when fatigued with fishing, the emperor retires accompanied by his ladies. The woods contain hares, deer, and game in great numbers, and a certain animal resembling the deer, which produces musk. Some of the open spaces are sown with grain and vegetables, and are interspersed with plots of fruit trees and flowers. Wherever a convenient situation offers, lies a house of recreation, or a dwelling for the eunuchs. There is also a seraglio, with a large open space in front, in which once a month a fair is held for the entertainment of the ladies; all the dealers being the eunuchs themselves, who thus dispose of articles of the most valuable and exquisite description.

country residence—the Changchunyuan (Garden of Exuberant Spring)—on the outskirts of Beijing, and had also constructed a modest palace at Chengde. Here he had laid out an extensive park in which there were 36 'scenes', to each of which he gave a four-character name. Ripa and four other Jesuits went there in 1711, together with Chinese painters who had been engaged to draw the 36 scenes. He recorded that Kangxi 'usually resided there from the beginning of May till the end of September, with an escort of about thirty thousand men, besides a great multitude of people who resorted thither for the love of gain or pleasure'. He described the park and court life there and later produced copper engravings of the drawings made by the Chinese artists. These were presented to Kangxi, who used them to illustrate an edition of his poems on the 36 scenes, a copy of which arrived in Britain perhaps as early as 1724 (Jacques, 1990) and is now in the British Library (fig. 1.4). His written observations, however, did not become known in Europe until 1832 when his memoirs were published in Naples, an English version following a few years later (Ripa, 1844). Had Ripa's memoirs been published on his return to Europe he would have been the first to provide the Western world with a detailed first-hand description of the Chinese garden. He appears to have based his remarks principally on the design of the Imperial Summer Villa at Chengde and the Changchunyuan. Amongst other things he noted the contrast between the straight lines and symmetry of European gardens and the layout of those of the Chinese, who:

Another to visit Beijing around Ripa's time was John Bell, a Scot who was there with a Russian embassy from 1720–22. During this time he visited the Changchunyuan three times and described a courtyard with rows of forest trees, gravel walks, canals, plots of flowers, and a garden with artificial rockwork, shaded by old bent trees and with water running underneath it. He went on to say: 'this garden, and many other things in China, display the taste of the inhabitants for imitating nature' (Bell, 1763). Bell also mentions Mr de Lange, a member of the Russian embassy who went to the Imperial Summer Villa at Chengde in 1721 and expressed the view that it was 'infinitely superior in beauty and magnificence to the Palace at Pekin or Czchanzchumnienne [Changchunyuan]'.

Since Ripa's engravings appear to have attracted little attention and since his writings and those of John Bell did not appear until later, it was left to the French Jesuits to provide the first detailed descriptions of Chinese gardens to become generally available in Europe. These appeared in the *Lettres édifiantes et curieuses écrites des Missions étrangères par quelques Missionaires de la Compagnie de Jésus*, published in Paris in 34 volumes from 1702–76, which was followed by the *Mémoires concernant l'Histoire, les Sciences, les Arts, les Moeurs, les Usages, etc. des Chinois par les Missionaires de Pé-kin*, which appeared in 17 volumes from 1776–1814.

Most notable of these was Jean-Denis Attiret's letter of 1 November 1743 which appeared in the *Lettres édifiantes* in 1749, an English translation following in 1752 (Attiret, 1752). In this letter Attiret gave an evocative word picture of the Yuanmingyuan on the outskirts of Beijing. Beginning in 1709 this garden had been constructed on the site of the ruins of a Ming country villa by Kangxi for his son, who succeeded him as the emperor Yongzheng (reigned 1723–35). Subsequently it was extensively enlarged and developed by Qianlong (reigned 1736–95), with the result that it became one of the largest and most remarkable gardens ever built. Like Ripa and the imperial gardens in Kangxi's time, Attiret was in the unusual position of being able to offer this description as he had been engaged as a painter by Qianlong and, in the course of his duties, saw every part of the Yuanmingyuan and also at least some of the Forbidden City—one of the few Europeans ever to have done so. While, as Sirén (1949) puts it, 'he has not begrudged his imagination and his rather facile pen a certain margin', this letter appears largely accurate and remains the first substantial account of an actual Chinese garden to reach the European public.

Attiret's description shows great similarity to Ripa's account of earlier imperial gardens. It also accords well with the paintings made by Tang Dai and Shen Yuan, somewhere about 1744, of the principal 40 scenes of this garden, which eventually found their way to the Bibliothèque nationale in Paris (fig. 1.5). Having seen other gardens created about the same time in and around Beijing and those of the Imperial Summer Villa at Chengde, it seems to me that he has given as good an introduction to this type of garden as one could wish. In fact much of what he said applies to Chinese gardens generally. For this reason it seems sensible to quote here some passages from the English translation of his letter. For

a start he recorded that hills had been raised with a great number of valleys and pieces of water between them and went on to say:

> They go from one of the Valleys to another, not by formal strait Walks as in Europe; but by various Turnings and Windings, adorn'd on the Sides with little Pavilions and charming Grottos: and each of these Valleys is diversify'd from all the rest, both by their manner of laying out the Ground, and in the Structure and Disposition of its Buildings.

He noted that the paths were paved with small stones and that:

> The Sides of the Canals or lesser Streams, are not faced, (as they are with us,) with smooth Stone, and in a strait Line; but look rude and rustic, with different Pieces of Rock, some of which jut out, and others recede inwards; and placed with so much Art, that you would take it to be a work of Nature.... The Banks are sprinkled with Flowers; which rise up even thro' the Hollows in the rock-work, as if they had been produced there naturally. They have a great Variety of them, for every Season of the Year.

He made further comments about rockwork in his description of the buildings, almost all of which were only one storey high with their bases raised up above the ground. He wrote: 'You go up to them, not by regular Stone Steps, but by a rough Sort of Rock-work; form'd as if there had been so many Steps produced there by Nature'. He also mentioned bridges, which 'generally wind about and serpentize', and the roofed walkways which led from one building to another. These were either open on both sides or had a wall on one side in which there were openings of different shapes. Concerning these walkways he was moved to write:

> But what is so singular in these Portico's or Colonnades is, that they seldom run in strait Lines; but make a hundred Turns and Windings: sometimes by the Side of a Grove, at others behind a Rock, and at others again along the Banks of their Rivers or Lakes. Nothing can be conceiv'd more delightful: they have such a rural Air as is quite ravishing and inchanting.

Figure 1.5 (right) Luyuekaiyuan (Carving the Moon and Chiselling the Clouds), one of the 40 scenes at the Yuanmingyuan painted by Tang Dai and Shen Yuan c.1744.

CLICHÉ BIBLIOTHÈQUE NATIONALE DE FRANCE, PARIS.

Figure 1.6 (left) Doorways, Pianshi Shanfang, Yangzhou

He also observed another of the features (fig. 1.6) which visitors to Chinese gardens cannot fail to notice, saying that there were

> no People in the World who can shew such Variety of Shapes and Forms, in their Doors and Windows, as the *Chinese*. They have some round, oval, square, and in all Sorts of angled Figures; some, in the shape of fans; others in those of flowers, Vases, Birds, Beasts, and Fishes; in short, of all Forms, whether regular or irregular.

He also mentioned pavilions half on land and half jutting out into a lake, waterfowl, menageries, brightly coloured fish 'of which the *Chinese* are most particularly fond', a miniature town with markets and shops where fairs were held for the amusement of the court, and an area set apart as a farm arranged to express 'a rural Simplicity, and all the plain Manners of a Country Life, as nearly as they possibly can'. And while he pointed out the contrast between the informal arrangement of this garden and those of his home country at the time, he went on to write:

> But then there is this Symmetry, this beautiful Order and Disposition, too in *China*; and particularly, in the Emperor's Palace at *Pekin*, that I was speaking of in the Beginning of this Letter. The Palaces of the Princes and Great Men, the Courts of Justice, and the Houses of the better Sort of People, are generally in the same Taste. But in their Pleasure-houses they rather choose a beautiful Disorder, and a wandering as far as possible from all the Rules of Art. They go entirely on this Principle, "That what they are to represent there is a natural and wild

View of the Country; a rural Retirement, and not a Palace form'd according to all the Rules of Art"…. When you read this, you will be apt to imagine such Works very ridiculous; and that they must have a very bad Effect on the Eye: but was you to see them, you would find it quite otherwise; and would admire the Art, with which all this Irregularity is conducted…. All is in good Taste; and so managed that it's Beauties appear gradually, one after another.

It is interesting that, unlike many of the Westerners who followed, Attiret should have so readily appreciated the nature of the Chinese garden. Those of us who have visited similar gardens might find it hard to agree with his creation of the impression, which was reinforced by subsequent writers, that what was represented there was 'a natural and wild View of the Country'. However, it seems to me that he and others of his ilk must have become attuned to the Chinese concept of the 'oneness' of man and the universe, in which no distinction is made between nature and artifice. In fact, in his letter he even went so far as to say 'Since my Residence in *China*, my Eyes and Taste are grown a little *Chinese*'. It seems appropriate to mention here, too, that, as Stuart (1990a) points out, nature and artifice have always mingled in Chinese gardens, with artifice in fact predominating.

Attiret's letter was followed by the writings of P.M. Cibot, who went to China in 1759 and died in Beijing in 1784. These appeared in the *Mémoires* between 1777 and 1786. While

Figure 1.7 (left) Chinese greenhouse, exterior view.

FROM *SERRES-CHAUDES DES CHINOIS, ET
FLEURS QU'ILS Y CONSERVANT* (REÇU EN
1777). CLICHÉ BIBLIOTHÈQUE NATIONALE
DE FRANCE, PARIS.

Figure 1.8 (below) Chinese
greenhouse, interior view.

FROM *SERRES-CHAUDES DES CHINOIS, ET
FLEURS QU'ILS Y CONSERVANT* (REÇU EN
1777). CLICHÉ BIBLIOTHÈQUE NATIONALE
DE FRANCE, PARIS.

most of them are about cultivated plants and horticultural procedures, they are of particular interest as he seems to have been the first person to refer to mention of them in the Chinese classical literature and to comment on their history and symbolism. Especially notable is his account of Chinese greenhouses (Cibot, 1778), and presumably he was also responsible for making or commissioning the accompanying watercolour paintings which are now in the Bibliothèque nationale (figs 1.7, 1.8). These ingenious structures were used in northern China principally for protecting frost-sensitive plants in winter and for forcing plants into bloom for the New Year. The most substantial of these greenhouses were made of brick and from outside looked much like typical domestic buildings, but had paper-covered windows stretch-

ing from ground level to the eaves on the southern side to trap the light and warmth of the sun. Straw mats were rolled down over these in the evening to conserve heat and rolled up again in the morning. Inside, the floor was sunken and surrounded by benches for the plants. In the more sophisticated examples there were built-in arrangements for heating, otherwise heaters were brought in when necessary and even containers of boiling water to maintain humidity.

In addition, like Attiret, Cibot sent to Paris an essay on Chinese gardens (Cibot, 1782). Once again, avoidance of symmetry and the importance of naturalness, irregularity and wealth of variety were stressed. He noted, too, that it was not only the emperors who succeeded in 'bringing back the countryside' to their gardens, but also rich citizens. He commented on the use of water, rustic bridges, buildings of many types, rocks, fossils, pebbles, grottoes and much more. And with his special interest in Chinese garden plants, he recorded information about their use and their relationship to the changing seasons.

Cibot's essay, however, is of particular interest as, to the best of my knowledge, it contains the first summary in a Western language of the history of Chinese gardens—an achievement which has certainly not received the recognition it deserves. Just as he had done with the plants, Cibot delved into the Chinese literature for his information and was able to provide a survey of developments from pre-dynastic times to his own day. He mentioned the hunting enclosures of the early rulers and the enormous parks of the emperors of the Qin (221–207 BC) and Han (206 BC–AD 220) dynasties, pointing out that, with their palaces, lakes, hills, birds, animals and plants, these creations were microcosmic representations of the universe. As an indication of the immensity of these enterprises, he recorded that the Han emperor Wudi (reigned 141–87 BC) had employed 30 000 slaves to care for his domain. In describing all of this, Cibot's tone was somewhat censorious, and he recorded that Wudi's successors up to the 7th century continued to indulge in excesses, including the use of greenhouses for the production of out-of-season flowers and fruits. He went on to mention the extravagant garden of the Sui emperor Yangdi (reigned 604–617), where leaves and flowers of silk were used to supplement those provided by nature, before describing the gardens of the Tang dynasty (618–907). He also recorded that, at this time and during the following Song and Yuan dynasties, more and more different ornamental plants were being cultivated.

In spite of his disapproval of the excesses of early times, he recognised that it was from the past that the Chinese garden style of his day had evolved. Interestingly, when he came to the Ming his tone changed, as he had become aware that the principles of design which he had come to admire in the gardens he saw had been developed during this period. The essay is interesting, too, as it includes information supplied by a Chinese, whom Cibot called Lieoutchou, on the nature of the Chinese garden—an English translation of which was given by Sirén (1949). Lieoutchou is reported to have said that the planning of the Chinese garden involves 'the ability to arrange the "mountains," the clumps of trees and the streams in such a way as to reveal the beauty of Nature, enhance its effect and offer an infinite variety of shifting views'. Cibot thus delivered to the West a glimpse from a Chinese point of view of a topic to which Chinese authors have devoted much attention and which, from early last century, has engendered much comment in the West.

Another claiming to give the views of a Chinese informant was William Chambers, who had been to Guangzhou in the1740s in the service of the Swedish East India Company, and who subsequently published his essay 'On the Art of Laying Out Gardens among the Chinese' (Chambers, 1757). He did not mention any specific gardens or include plans or drawings but based his opinions on the small gardens he claimed to have seen and material obtained from conversations with Lepqua, 'a celebrated Chinese painter'. His general remarks about the design and diversity of scenes in these gardens seem reasonable. They include his statement that their aim is to imitate nature 'in all her beautiful irregularities'. However, while his descriptions of the use of rock and the building of rock mountains and caverns seem realistic, those of 'scenes of horror' seem fanciful and unlike anything in existence today. Likewise his account of large gardens seems unlikely to have been based on anyone's actual observations, involving as they do meadows filled with cattle, rice fields running out into lakes, and the erection of mills and other hydraulic machines, the motions of which enliven the scene. It is probably fair to say that, compared to those of the French missionaries, his writings were in large part imaginative and served only to confuse the Western record of Chinese gardens.

Meanwhile the behaviour of the foreign powers in their trading and other activities had not pleased the Chinese authorities and, in the year preceding the appearance of Chambers's essay, an edict was issued allowing Western merchants to trade only in Guangzhou and only with a limited number of authorised merchants. As a result the country was in effect closed to almost all foreigners other than the French missionaries and the Russians. Since the demand for tea, silk, porcelain and other Chinese products remained high, and since China did not seem interested in importing anything from the West, serious imbalances of trade began to develop. As a result a series of embassies seeking amelioration of these conditions was mounted in the years that followed, and it it was from those who were involved in these that additional information about Chinese gardens came.

The first of these was Lord Macartney's unsuccessful embassy to Qianlong in 1793. A factor which appears to have contributed to the failure of this embassy to achieve any concessions was Macartney's refusal, as the representative of George III, to kowtow to the emperor. During their journey, however, he and other members of his party were able to make various observations, particularly about the Yuanmingyuan, where they stayed on the outskirts of Beijing, and the Imperial Summer Villa at Chengde, where the emperor received them. Macartney did not have a great deal to say about the Yuanmingyuan and, unlike earlier visitors, who had been enthusiastic in their praise of what they saw as the designers' ability to imitate nature, he failed to give his unqualified approval, as his following remarks attest:

> Although you ascend to the principal buildings by regular flights of smooth or chiselled stone stairs, yet there are several others, even pavilions of elegant architecture, to which the approach is by rugged steps of rock, seemingly rendered rough and difficult by art, in order to imitate the rude simplicity of nature. In such situations the impropriety is glaring and argues a sickly and declining taste meant solely to display vanity and expense.

In Chengde, however, he was greatly impressed by the beauty of the grounds of the Imperial Summer Villa (fig. 1.9), with its lakes, artificial hills and carefully placed architectural features (Staunton, 1797; Barrow,1804; Cranmer-Byng, 1962). After coming to the throne, Qianlong had proceeded to develop the park further and by 1792 had added another 36 scenes to those of his grandfather. To each of these he had given a three-character name, no doubt in deference to Kangxi, who had used four-character names. All this had

Figure 1.9 **View in the park at the Imperial Summer Villa, Chengde.**

ENGRAVING OF A WATERCOLOUR BY WILLIAM ALEXANDER IN BARROW (1804), TAKEN FROM A COPY HELD IN THE RARE BOOK COLLECTION, STATE LIBRARY OF NEW SOUTH WALES.

been achieved by the time Lord Macartney was taken on a tour of the eastern part of the garden on Sunday, 15 September 1793, accompanied by He Shen, Qianlong's chief minister. In his journal for that day he wrote a lengthy description of the park, adding that:

> There is no beauty of distribution and contrast, no feature of amenity, no reach of fancy which embellishes our pleasure grounds in England, that is not to be found here. Had China been accessible to Mr. Brown or to Mr Hamilton I should have sworn they had drawn their happiest ideas from the rich sources I have tasted this day; for in the course of a few hours I have enjoyed such vicissitudes of rural delight, as I did not conceive could be felt out of England, being at different moments enchanted by scenes perfectly similar to those I had known there, to the magnificence of Stowe, the soft beauties of Woburn or the fairy-land of Painshill.

It is interesting to note, as Lord Macartney did, the extraordinary similarity between the Chinese imperial landscape gardens of the 18th century and the landscape gardens created in Britain at the same time. The builders of both took advantage of the topography of their sites, diverted watercourses, formed lakes, built up hills, and placed buildings strategically to provide focal points, to recall famous structures or scenes elsewhere, and to act as sites from which views could be obtained. Yet the cultural backgrounds which gave rise to these gardens could not have been more different and their builders knew nothing of each other. However, in addition to remarking on this resemblance, it appears that Macartney was beset by the feelings many Westerners experience when visiting Chinese gardens for the first time, as he went on to say:

> In many places the lake is overspread with the nenuphar, or lotus (nymphea) resembling our broad-leaved water-lily. This is an accompaniment which, though the Chinese are passionately fond of, cultivating it in all their pieces of water, I confess I don't much admire. Artificial rocks and ponds, with gold and silver fish are perhaps too often introduced, and the monstrous porcelain figures of lions and tigers usually placed before the pavilions, are displeasing to an European eye. But these are trifles of no great moment, and I am astonished that now, after a six hours critical survey of these gardens I can scarcely recollect anything besides to find fault with.

The next day he was taken to see the wilder western section and observed, amongst other things, that:

> It is one of the finest forest scenes in the world, wild, woody, mountainous and rocky, abounding with stags and deer of different species, and most of the other beasts not dangerous to man…. There, at proper distances you find palaces, banqueting houses and monasteries (but without bonzes) adapted to the situation and peculiar circumstances of the place, sometimes with a rivulet on one hand gently stealing through the glade, at others with a cataract tumbling from above, raging with foam, and rebounding with a thousand echoes from below or silently engulfed in a gloomy pool or yawning chasm.

While they were at Chengde sketches of various scenes were made by Lieutenant Henry Parish. These were later used as the basis for the larger watercolour drawings made by William Alexander, the artist attached to the embassy, who also painted scenes in Beijing and various other places visited by the party during their journey. These formed the basis of the folio of illustrations published in 1796 to accompany Sir George Staunton's account of the embassy (Staunton, 1797).

Also included in the group was John Barrow, who seems to have seen more of the Yuanmingyuan than the others and produced his own description (Barrow, 1804). Unlike Attiret, who had been in the country long enough to become attuned

to the niceties of Chinese taste, he was far less enthusiastic. He wrote, for instance, that the

assemblages of buildings, which they dignify with the name of palaces, were more remarkable for their number than for their splendour or magnificence… . In the different courts were several miserable attempts at sculpture, and some bronze figures, but all the objects were fanciful, distorted, and entirely out of nature. The only specimen of workmanship about the palace that would bear close examination, besides the carving of the throne, was a brick wall enclosing the flower garden, which, in no respect is exceeded by anything of the sort in England.

Figure 1.10 **Suzhou Creek, Summer Palace, Beijing**

Amongst his kinder remarks were his statements that intricacy and concealment seemed to be well understood and that 'The trees were placed not only according to their magnitudes, but the tints of their foliage seemed also to have been considered in the composition of the picture'. However his overall impression was that what he had seen fell 'very short of the fanciful and extravagant descriptions that Sir William Chambers has given of Chinese gardening'. Later in his account he commented on various scenes in other parts of the country. Returning to Beijing from the Yuanmingyuan he observed in the main street of Haidian that most of the houses were of two storeys 'before the upper of which was a kind of Véranda full of dwarf trees and flower pots'. Travelling down the Grand Canal near the Yellow River he recorded that 'In the small flower gardens, without which we scarcely observed a single cottage, were balsams, several kinds of beautiful asters, holy-hocks, two species of *Malva*, an *Amaranthus*, and the showy and handsome shrub the *Nerium Oleander*'. At Hangzhou he saw lilacs, *Hibiscus mutabilis* and *H. syriacus* on the shores of the West Lake, recording that its natural and artificial beauties far exceeded anything he had hitherto seen in China. And on the outskirts of Guangzhou he observed the wealth of plants available in the nurseries from which so many previously unknown kinds were subsequently to be introduced to the rest of the world.

In 1794–95 the Dutch East India Company sent a similarly unsuccessful embassy. Its members were received by the emperor at the Yuanmingyuan on at least two occasions and were shown round the garden. André Van Braam, who accompanied the embassy, left us his description of this, taking the by-now familiar line of commenting on its naturalistic appearance (Van Braam, 1798). The party was also taken to the Qingyiyuan (now renamed the Yiheyuan and popularly known as the Summer Palace), where he noted the intriguing street of shops (fig. 1.10)—another version of the scene at the Yuanmingyuan which was amongst those described earlier by Attiret and depicted in one of the paintings of Tang Dai and Shen Yuan.

It was around this time in Britain, and subsequently many parts of the world, that the most popular idea of what a Chinese garden might be like came from the imaginary scene depicted on willow-pattern porcelain. This design was developed by Thomas Turner at Caughley, Shropshire, in 1779 and was taken up with minor variations by many factories. It became what is perhaps the most widespread of domestic designs, remaining popular to this day. Although no more than an example of chinoiserie, it nevertheless depicts the essential features of a Chinese garden—water, rocks, buildings, trellis work and plants of fanciful shape, including what purports to be a weeping willow (fig. 1.11).

Further observations of real plants in China were made when Lord Amherst led another embassy seeking to open up the country to trade in 1816–17. On his arrival at the Yuanmingyuan Lord Amherst, following Macartney's example, refused to agree to prostrate himself before the emperor. Not only this but he refused the emperor's request for an immediate meeting, with the result that the party was sent away in disgrace and nothing was achieved. However, Clark Abel, a botanist accompanying the embassy, was able to

Figure 1.11 **Willow-pattern Plate**

record much information about Chinese garden plants (Abel, 1819). Not long afterwards, John Livingstone (1822; 1824), who was stationed in Macao, produced early accounts of the Chinese method of dwarfing trees and shrubs and of horticultural procedures in general.

Further evidence of the Chinese sensibility concerning the progression of the seasons and its relationship to the flowering of garden plants was given by Robert Morrison (1822), who provided a list of the plants blossoming in each month of the year at Guangzhou. Owing to the exclusion of most foreigners from the rest of the country, little information came from anywhere else in the early part of the 19th century. However, with an actual and very long frontier with China, the Russians seem to have been in a more privileged position than the other foreign powers. They had been allowed to maintain what was called an Ecclesiastical Mission in Beijing, attached to which was Archimandrite Hyacinthe (Bichurin). He translated a Chinese description of Beijing into Russian and published it along with a detailed map of the city showing the locations of the principal monuments, and a French translation of his work appeared in St Petersburg in 1829 (Bredon, 1931; Naquin, 2000). Another to be attached to this mission was the botanist Alexander von Bunge, who spent six months in Beijing in 1830 and was the first to collect a number of the garden plants characteristic of the region (Cox, 1986).

Up till this time almost all the descriptions of Chinese gardens reaching the West had been of the grand imperial gardens of the north. However, from the middle of the 19th century on, detailed information about private gardens began to appear. In 1843 came the publication by Thomas Allom and G.N. Wright of their four-volume *China, in a series of views, displaying the scenery, architecture and social habits of that ancient empire*. Included were pictures and descriptions of the gardens of Chinese merchants in or near Guangzhou and of a pavilion and garden of a mandarin near Beijing. There were also views of Tiger Hill, Suzhou, the gardens of the imperial palace, Beijing, and the so-called Potala at Chengde. The descriptions by the Rev. Wright are flowery and fanciful, and the illustrations owe much to chinoiserie, though it is claimed that they are based on Thomas Allom's original and authentic sketches. According to Wright, Allom had been to China and it may be that some of his drawings were original. Nevertheless it is acknowledged that Sir George Staunton gave permission for the copying of 'several interesting subjects from his beautiful collection of Chinese drawings by native artists'. Others are clearly based on drawings by William Alexander. In the text Wright takes the usual line about pavilions connected by corridors, meandering waterways, bridges, fanciful rocks and grottoes, and lakes with islands, creating an apparent extension of the actual space. For instance, in the text accompanying the illustration of a 'House of a Chinese merchant, near Canton' (fig. 1.12) he expressed the view—no doubt second hand—that in the construction of a Chinese garden the artist must be able to introduce within the villa

an artificial lake, adorn its banks with rock-work and pleasure-grounds, and associate the wildest productions of nature with the most gorgeous creations of art. Bridges, canals, fountains, grottos, rocks worn or wrought into the most extravagant forms, and either insulated in the water or starting from the flower-beds, are the usual objects with which villa pleasure-grounds are decorated; and the fancy that is displayed in their disposition, to foreigners must necessarily appear most admirable, and is amazingly difficult of successful imitation.

While it is not clear whether Allom went to any of the sites described, it is known, however, that in Guangzhou many foreigners visited the gardens of the merchants and also the Fa Tee Gardens, as the nurseries on the outskirts of the city were called. For instance it was in the garden of the merchant Consequa, one of those illustrated by Allom and Wright, that *Wisteria sinensis* first came to the attention of John Reeves, who arranged for it to be propagated (Le Rougetel, 1982). Presumably he was the person responsible for sending it to Britain in 1816.

Meanwhile, in order to redress their trade deficit, the British East India Company had begun bringing opium to China from India. The opium habit was new to China but a ready market developed and before long money was flowing out of the country rather than in. In retrospect, the importation of opium to China and the social and economic havoc which it caused can only be seen as disgraceful. Not only this, but the foreigners failed to understand that the restrictions placed upon them by the Chinese were a result of the vast difference in their cultures. For one thing, the merchant class was ranked at the bottom of the Confucian social order and mercantile activity was seen as morally questionable. And to the Chinese the demands of the foreigners for changes to the manner in which they were treated were incomprehensible.

Such was the extent of the opium problem that the Chinese government became alarmed and banned the smoking and importation of the drug. Since the importers defied this edict, in 1839 the Chinese blockaded the section of Guangzhou where the British and Americans were allowed to operate and forced them to surrender their huge stock, which was then destroyed. The British reacted by declaring war, the so-called First Opium War in which the Chinese imperial forces were defeated in 1842. Under the treaty negotiated at the conclusion of this war the Chinese were obliged to open the additional ports of Xiamen (Amoy), Fuzhou, Ningbo and Shanghai to foreign trade, a huge indemnity was imposed in payment for the destroyed opium, and various other humiliating concessions were extracted.

It was these changes of circumstance that made possible the four journeys made by the plant-collector Robert Fortune between 1842 and 1858. While his writings and collections were devoted principally to plants, many of them garden plants, he also had a little to say about the nurseries, gardens, temples and cemeteries in which he saw them growing. In 1843, for instance, he admired the rockeries in a mandarin's garden in Ningbo and noted that such gardens were 'very limited in extent, but the most is made of it by windings and glimpses through rockwork, and arches in the walls, as well as by hiding the boundary with a mass of shrubs and trees' (Fortune, 1847). Nevertheless he was moved to observe that 'The gardens of the English residents in Shanghae far excel those of the Chinese in the number and species of trees and shrubs they contain, and also in the neat and tasteful manner in which they are laid out and arranged'.

In Guangzhou, as well as giving a detailed description of the Fa Tee Gardens, Fortune also visited the nearby garden of the merchant Howqua. He recorded the existence of walls, ponds, artificial rockwork, a banyan, bamboos, fruit trees, good specimens of southern Chinese ornamentals and 'a multitude of dwarf trees without which no Chinese garden would be complete'. Amongst other things he remarked upon were the 'amusing notices' cautioning visitors against undesirable behaviour. Amongst examples he recorded was one attached to a fruit tree which read: ' Ramblers here *will be*

Figure 1.12 House of a Chinese Merchant, near Canton. FROM ALLOM & WRIGHT (1843).

Figure 1.13

Sign at the

Baiyunguan,

Beijing

excused plucking the fruit'. Similar notices in English can still be seen in Chinese parks and gardens (fig. 1.13). Fortune also mentioned potting sheds, a nursery for raising young plants, and a kitchen garden (Fortune, 1853). With all these features Howqua's garden sounds to have been very similar to the larger private gardens of northern China, although, since he made no mention of them, presumably it had no need for the ingenious greenhouses found in the north.

This garden was also visited by the Rev. W.A.P. Martin, who arrived in China in 1850. He took a rather uncharitable view of its charms and reported (Martin, 1900) that, although extensive, it made

> no attempt at landscape beyond heaps of rockwork, which resembled mountain scenery as much as a brick resembles a house. Rows of evergreens, twisted into the shapes of birds and beasts, gave us the first example of a form of bad taste peculiarly Chinese.

A little more information was provided by the Abbé Huc's *A Journey Through The Chinese Empire* (Huc, 1855). In it he gave descriptions of Chinese agriculture and horticulture but, as far as gardens are concerned, it is chiefly notable for giving a translation of Sima Guang's 11th-century description of his garden in Luoyang. This was one of China's most famous gardens and it included such things as a grotto, 'pointed rocks heaped fancifully together', beds of medicinal herbs, flowers of various kinds, waterways, and pavilions on hills.

In due course it emerged that the concessions extracted at the conclusion of the First Opium War had failed to satisfy the ambitions of the Western powers. As a result, when a British vessel, the *Arrow*, was seized in 1856 by the Guangzhou water police on suspicion of smuggling, Britain, later joined by France, used this as a pretext for declaring war on China once again. This was the Second Opium War and when in 1858 the Anglo-French forces sailed north for Tianjin (Tientsin) and attacked and occupied the Dagu forts

thus opening the way to Beijing, the Chinese capitulated. However, when the British and French came to ratify the Treaty of Tientsin in 1859, instead of proceeding overland to Tianjin as they were told to do by the Chinese, they tried to force their way up the river but were repulsed by the forts at its mouth and experienced considerable losses.

Another Anglo-French expedition was mounted the following year to wipe out this disgrace and to force the Chinese to ratify the treaty, with Lord Elgin and Baron Gros being appointed to head the combined force. During this campaign a party of British and French sent to negotiate a settlement was captured, most were tortured, and less than half of them were returned alive. To avenge this atrocity, Lord Elgin ordered the burning of the Yuanmingyuan and most of the other imperial properties on the outskirts of Beijing, following their looting by the British and French troops.

On the approach of the Anglo-French force in 1860 the emperor Xianfeng fled to Chengde, where he remained until his death the following year. It was left to his brother, Prince Gong (fig. 1.14), to deal with the foreigners and the ratification of the treaty. The consequence of all this was that the Chinese were obliged to concede to the legalisation of the opium trade, freedom of missionary activity, the opening of further ports and the Yangtze River for foreign trade, foreign control of customs, the right of foreigners to reside in Beijing, and a great deal more. As a result foreigners were able to visit and reside in many parts of the country, foreign legations were set up in Beijing for the first time, and a new era of reporting on conditions in China began.

Figure 1.14

Prince Gong.

PHOTOGRAPH BY JOHN THOMSON (1873–74), TAKEN FROM A COPY IN THE RARE BOOK COLLECTION, STATE LIBRARY OF NEW SOUTH WALES.

Figure 1.15 **Entrance to British Legation, Beijing.** FROM BOREL (1912).

In the period leading up to the ratification of the Treaty of Tientsin, not only had the Manchu administration had to endure interference in its affairs by the Western powers, but at the same time it had had to contend with the Taiping Uprising (1850–64). The Taiping leaders had assembled a vast army and, with beliefs based in Christianity, were attempting to set up a 'heavenly kingdom' with equality for everyone. The imperial forces had failed to suppress the Taipings, who had captured many important cities in the southern half of the country and had set up their headquarters in Nanjing. Following its defeat in the Second Opium War, the imperial government appears to have realised that it should adopt Western military techniques in order to suppress the rebels. At the same time the treaty powers had abandoned their neutral stance towards the Taipings who, amongst other things, were determined to ban the opium trade. They then agreed to supply the Manchus with modern arms and equipment, and people to train and lead their forces. However, by the time the Taipings were defeated, many of the cities, temples and gardens south of the Yangtze had been devastated.

In March 1861 the foreign legations began establishing themselves in Beijing. One of the people involved in this was Dr D.F. Rennie, who was attached to the British Legation. He kept a diary of his experiences during the legation's first year there and this included brief descriptions of many of the principal sights of the city (Rennie, 1865). Members of the various legations soon adopted the habit of going for picnics and undertaking excursions into the countryside, as a result of which he was able to provide descriptions of various places of interest in the surrounding area. Amongst those he visited was Badachu, the so-called Eight Great Sites, a series of temples built one above the other on a hillside which was soon to become a favourite summer resort for those attached to the legations. And, amongst other things, he went to a temple fair in the north of the city where plants were offered for sale. Colonel Neale, who accompanied him, bought pomegranates, geraniums, roses and passionflowers there, all in pots. This was probably the Huguosi, a temple where fairs were held which were famous as a source of ornamental plants and later were much patronised by Westerners resident in the city.

The British Legation was set up in Lianggongfu, a mansion and garden originally given by Kangxi to his thirty-third son, whose descendants had the title of Dukes of Liang. The noble family had been unable to maintain it and it was leased to the British. Dr Rennie gave a description of its layout and appearance, remarking that:

> The interior, though out of repair, is still very handsome; the ceilings of the state apartments being beautifully decorated with gold dragons within circles on a blue ground, which again are in the centres of small squares of green, separated by intersecting bars in relief of green and gold… . Moral sentiments, painted in gilt letters on ornamental boards, are placed over the entrances of the various buildings in the different courts.

He went on to say that arrangements had been made with a Chinese builder to put the place in thorough repair, retaining as much as possible its Chinese character.

All this, it seems, had been achieved by the time Robert Fortune arrived in Beijing in September of that year as, in giving his own description of the mansion, he was able to report that the whole place had been put in admirable order and to describe it as 'a most gorgeous place' (Fortune, 1863) (fig. 1.15). Fortune undertook a general tour of the sights of the city, including the Lama Temple, but like everyone else he was not able to enter the Imperial City. However, he admired Coal Hill (Jing Shan), recording that 'very pretty this little hill looked, crowned as it is with temples, summer-houses, and trees'. He was also able to peer into what is now Beihai Park and note that:

> Here also we found the Lama Mosque, surrounded by trees and giving an Indian character to the scenery. Although we could not enter the sacred enclosures, we got glimpses of pretty gardens with rock-work and artistic bridges, which gave us very favourable impressions of its internal beauties and made us long for a nearer view.

He, too, went to Badachu and on the way there he visited a cemetery where he admired the avenues of juniper, cypress and pine shading the tombs. It was near one of these that he first saw and was puzzled by a mature white-barked pine (*Pinus bungeana*), one of the most characteristic trees of northern China. And having been impressed by Chinese cemeteries he was moved to write:

When the nations of Europe were crowding their dead in the dismal churchyards of populous towns, and polluting the air, the Chinese, whom we have been accustomed to look upon as only half-civilized, were forming pleasant cemeteries in country places, and planting them with trees and flowers. They were doing ages ago in China what we have been doing only of late years.

It is because I, too, have enjoyed visiting Chinese cemeteries that I have included examples in this book.

Fortune was disappointed to find that most of the plants in Chinese gardens in the north were the same as those he had seen on his earlier expeditions to areas further south. However, amongst the few plants new to him was the upright form of *Forsythia suspensa* (fig. 1.16), a plant found in almost every garden in northern China (Fortune, 1864).

For the Westerners who began to come to China in increasing numbers at this time the only acceptable accommodation was that provided by the missions, legations and, to a lesser extent, temples, which had traditionally let out rooms to travellers. And, not unexpectedly, they tended to concentrate their sightseeing very much on the gardens, temples and famous scenic areas that had long been the focus of Chinese tourism. Soon printed guides began to be published and in due course—particularly after the building of railways—hotels catering for Western visitors were built in the main centres. The earliest guide I have come across is N.B. Dennys's *Notes for Tourists in the North of China* which was published in 1866. He went on to compile and edit a more comprehensive work, *The Treaty Ports of China and Japan*, which appeared the following year (Mayers et al., 1867). In 1870 further and more detailed information about Beijing and its environs was provided by the Rev. Joseph Edkins (1870). Edkins's description was included in the second volume of the Rev. Alexander Williamson's (1870) *Journeys in North China, Manchuria, and Eastern Mongolia; with Some Account of Corea*. In the 1860s the Rev. Williamson undertook several journeys from Beijing with the purpose of selling Christian tracts,

Figure 1.16 Rustic stairway and forsythia, Xumifushou Temple, Chengde

testaments and bibles which had been translated into local languages. In recounting his experiences on these journeys he has left us early descriptions in English of the sights of many places including Xi'an, Chengde, Qufu, Tai Shan and Nanjing. From this time on, more and more guides appeared, and eventually companies such as Thomas Cook & Son produced guides of their own with descriptions and recommended itineraries.

Presumably accommodation was not a problem for A.B. Freeman-Mitford, who went to Beijing as an attaché to the British Legation in the years 1865–66. In the letters he wrote at the time (Freeman-Mitford, 1900) he had much to say about gardens, and he seems also to have been more receptive of the canons of Chinese taste than most of the earlier British visitors had been. Although his letters were not published until 1900, he has left us a picture of the nature and state of Chinese gardens in the 1860s, drawing attention to those of temples, wealthy private individuals, and peasants, as well as the imperial estates.

On his way to Beijing in 1865 he visited the Guangzhou garden of a merchant he called Po-Ting Qua and reported that:

> Terraces, summer-houses, stairs, drawbridges, carp-ponds, rock-work and flowers are thrown together most fantastically, exactly like the gardens that the ladies and gentlemen on tea-cups and plates walk about in. The doors are cut in the walls in quaint shapes, such as circles, jars, bottles, etc. … Such things as flower beds are unknown here. The plants grow anyhow, without order or arrangement, but they are carefully tended, and indeed the whole place was beautifully kept, and there seemed to be a large staff of gardeners and carpenters, who play a conspicuous part in a Chinese garden.

The members of the various Western legations, missions and businesses which established themselves in Beijing at this time were in the habit of withdrawing to the Western Hills during the hottest months and renting rooms at temples. In July 1865 Freeman-Mitford went to the Biyunsi (Temple of the Azure Clouds) (fig. 1.17) and was able to write:

> Our temple … is set in a nest of rockwork, fountains, woods and gardens… . Our habitation consists of several little houses on one side of the temple, we dine in an

open pavilion, surrounded by a pond and artificial rockery, with ferns and mosses in profusion; high trees shade it from the sun, and close by a cold fountain pours out of the rock into the pond, in which we can ice our wine to perfection. The pond was dried up and the fountain had been turned from its channel, when we arrived; but we got together a few coolies and soon set that right.

While there he was able to visit the adjoining imperial hunting lodge (now the Fragrant Hills Park) and the nearby Wofosi (Temple of the Sleeping Buddha). Although they were 'equally in ruins' his descriptions of them are evocative. On another occasion he visited the ruins of the Summer Palace which, like the imperial hunting lodge at the Fragrant Hills, had been largely destroyed by the French and English troops in 1860. His party breakfasted in a pavilion by the lake and he subsequently wrote:

> It was a lovely spot. The lake is a mass of lotus plants now in full flower, there are quantities of little islands covered with trees and buildings. A number of boats with naked fishermen in them gave a touch of wildness and barbarity to the scene …

After breakfast they explored the ruins on Wanshou Shan (Longevity Hill) where he observed that of the great octagonal three-storeyed palace not one stone lay on another any longer, and a white marble balustrade alone showed where it stood. However it appears that many of the rocks used to ornament the garden had survived as he remarked that:

> Some of the rock-work is very quaint. When the Chinese come upon a quaintly shaped rock they mount it on a pedestal and make an ornament of it. There are many curious specimens at Wan-Shao-Shan.

As far as I am aware Freeman-Mitford is the first European to mention this feature, which is seen mainly in the gardens of the north. He seems to have been the first, too, to have drawn attention to the 'land boats' which are such a feature of Chinese gardens, as during his excursion to the

Figure 1.17 (over page) **Garden at the Temple of the Azure Clouds, Fragrant Hills, Beijing**

Figure 1.18 (left)

Miniature landscape, Jingci Temple, Hangzhou

Figure 1.19 (below left)

Rockery, Dajue Temple, Western Hills, Beijing

Summer Palace he observed a 'sort of jetty …, built of huge blocks of stone in the shape of a junk being launched into the lake, forty-one paces long by nine broad'. This must have been the base of the land boat, the wooden superstructure of which had been destroyed and was eventually replaced with a marble version by the Dowager Empress Cixi.

Later in 1865 he went on an excursion to the Great Wall and the Ming tombs and was able to report that:

> The cottages of the different villages had an air of comfort and tidiness rare in China; almost every one had a little flower garden fenced in by a hedge of millet stalks, trailed over with gourds, convolvulus and vines.

Then in April 1866 he described a visit to a Mandarin's house, saying:

> It is very pretty, with innumerable courtyards round which the dwelling-houses are built. The principal court surrounds a small artificial pond, in the centre of which is a sort of glass summer-house approached by two little miniature bridges with tiny white lions of white marble guarding them at intervals. Rockeries, which are a very favourite garden ornament, caves, grottoes, and turrets with battlements, all on a Liliputian scale, are around wherever there is room, in a most picturesque defiance of order and architecture. The only attempts at flowers and shrubs are a few of the famous dwarfed trees, trained so as to represent with their branches characters of good omen, such as Happiness, Longevity, etc. A broad terrace walk surmounts the whole.

It is hard to be certain exactly what sort of a garden he was describing here. It may even have been one of those curious miniature landscapes which are still occasionally seen standing in the middle of pools in the gardens of temples (fig. 1.18). In more recent times creations of this type have been described by Rolf Stein (1990).

In August 1866 he went to stay at the Dajuesi (Great Awakening Temple) some 40 km from Beijing in the mountains beyond the Fragrant Hills. He found the grounds and buildings to be properly maintained and gave a translation of a description of the temple and its charming grounds by his friend Liu. To this he added his own impressions of the garden, rockery, pool and stream which lay behind his quarters, which were in part of what in Qianlong's time was an imperial short-stay residence (fig. 1.19). Just as Fortune had done after seeing Howqua's garden in Guangzhou a few years earlier, he recorded that:

> All over the garden there are notices to "relations and friends" who may visit the temple to abstain from damaging buildings and trees, plucking flowers or cutting down the bamboos, a notice the spirit of which, as it says, "all respectable persons will observe of their own accord, and those who do not will be fined."

While at the Dajuesi he also rode over to see the Heilongtan (Black Dragon Pool), a shrine built in the Ming, repaired in Kangxi's reign, and to which Qianlong added a Dragon God temple in 1738 (fig. 1.20). It was a site to which people came to pray for rain. It also became a favourite site for excursions by Westerners, one of the first being Dr D.F. Rennie (1865), who went there for a picnic with notables from the French, Russian and Prussian legations in 1861. It came to be regarded as a famous beauty spot by subsequent visitors, including Juliet Bredon (1931) and George Kates (1967).

At this stage it seems worth reflecting on the impressions of Europeans so far. The principal features that have come in for comment are the 'windings' and so on, the curious rocks and rockeries, and the plants. While in the 18th century our informants were at pains to stress the 'naturalness' of Chinese gardens, once we get to the 19th this is rarely mentioned, if at all. A realistic view of Chinese gardens as seen through Western eyes is at last beginning to emerge.

As might have been expected, in the period after 1860 Western knowledge of Chinese plants expanded rapidly. A difficulty involved in this had been the connecting of the names of plants used in the Chinese literature with Western botanical names. Perhaps the greatest achievement in this regard was that of Emil Bretschneider, a physician attached to the Russian Legation in Beijing for most of the period 1866–83. It is to Bretschneider's monumental works (1881; 1883; 1895) that we are principally indebted for bringing

together and clarifying the names of plants mentioned in the classical literature, including the pharmacopoeias. His publications concerning the history of European botanical discoveries in China are also outstanding (Bretschneider, 1880; 1898). As well as all this, he carried out much historical and archaeological research on the region in which he was stationed (Bretschneider, 1879).

From the middle of the 19th century on, an increasing number of snippets of information about Chinese ornamental plants and gardens also began to appear (e.g. Lay, 1846; Doolittle, 1866; Cantoniensis, 1867; Sampson, 1869; André, 1892). Also, further paintings and drawings of gardens reached Europe to reinforce the written impressions, for example the export painting of Pan Khaqua's garden reproduced by Titley and Wood (1991), which shows a large number of potted plants displayed on stone tables and balustrades. But it was with the introduction of the camera that the reality of Chinese gardens was finally able to be transmitted to those in other countries.

The history of photography in China has been outlined by Clark Worswick (Worswick & Spence, 1978), who has pointed out how fortuitous it was that the opening of China occurred at the same time that photography arrived on the scene, and by Régine Thiriez (1998). It seems likely that the earliest photographs depicting gardens are the images taken by Felice Beato in Guangzhou in April 1860 and when he accompanied the British forces to Beijing in October of that year. Many of his photographs were wrongly or inadequately

Figure 1.20
Black Dragon
Pool near
Beijing.
FROM GRAHAM (1938).

labelled but amongst those of Guangzhou were several of the grounds of the Guangxiao Temple and, among those of Beijing—the first known to have been taken in that city—were a panorama of the Forbidden City and Jing Shan (fig. 1.21) and views of the Lama Temple, Huangsi, the Temple of Heaven, and the Summer Palace both before and after the looting and fire. He was followed by John Thomson, who was in China during the period 1868–72, and Emil Rusfeldt, who had a photographic business in Hong Kong from 1872–74. Reproductions of some of their photographs can be seen in Thompson (1873–74, 1898), Worswick and Spence (1978), Crombie (1987), Pearce (1998) and Harris (1999). Gardens also feature in the images of A. Boyarsky, who was the official photographer accompanying a Russian research and trading expedition to China in 1874–75 (Naumkin, 1993). Of note, too, are pictures of the ruins of the European palaces at the Yuanmingyuan taken in the 1870s and reproduced by Gilles Genest (1984) and Régine Thiriez (1998). Other photographs of interest are those taken in the

early part of the 20th century by Donald Mennie (1920, 1920?, 1926) and Heinz von Perckhammer (1928), and the further examples taken between 1906–09 which have been published by Boerschmann (1982). And in the period 1906–25 Daijo Tokiwa and Tadashi Sekino made seven expeditions to China, subsequently publishing a huge collection of photographs of Buddhist temples (Tokiwa & Sekino, 1926). In addition to all of the above, from the late 19th century on, most authors writing about gardens in China have illustrated their commentaries with photographs.

Amongst those providing written information about Chinese gardens in the second half of the 19th century was Constance Gordon Cumming (1890), who travelled widely in the country in the first six months of 1879, getting about in a leisurely fashion in boats and sedan chairs. At the beginning of her tour she visited the garden of a wealthy mandarin in Guangzhou, her description of which was along the now-familiar lines. However, she broke new ground by recording the presence of animals in a private garden of this type. While

Figure 1.21 (left) View of Jing Shan and the Forbidden City from Qionghua Island, Beihai, Beijing, October 1860.

ALBUMEN SILVER PHOTOGRAPH BY FELICE BEATO ENTITLED *VIEW OF PEKIN TAKEN FROM THE HILL IN THE IMPERIAL CITY SHOWING THE WINTER PALACE OF THE EMPEROR, 1860*. NATIONAL GALLERY OF AUSTRALIA, CANBERRA.

Figure 1.22 (right) Watching the fish, Yuyuan, Shanghai

a small deer had been shown in one of the pictures of Consequa's garden by Allom and Wright (1843), they made no mention of it in the text. Miss Gordon Cumming, on the other hand, recorded that:

> A couple of tame deer, which symbolise happiness, and several gorgeous peacocks, which denote exalted rank, enliven the garden. Some geese are also admitted as being emblematic of constancy, for which reason they figure among gifts of a bridegroom to his bride.

During the Ming and Qing many private gardens contained animals, including deer, cranes, peacocks, pheasants, geese, mandarin ducks and ornamental fish. Cats, dogs, rabbits and caged birds—particularly parrots and songbirds—were also popular, as were caged crickets. Deer and cranes were esteemed as symbols of longevity; peacocks, as Miss Gordon Cumming pointed out, denoted wealth and position; pheasants were symbols of good fortune, beauty, dignity,

authority and rank; and mandarin ducks, which like geese were believed to stay with the one mate for life, suggested constancy. Perhaps because immortals were said to fly about on the backs of cranes, these birds have always enjoyed special prestige. In the 17th century, for instance, there was a village near Suzhou which supplied the whole region with these birds (Clunas, 1996).

These days the only animals likely to be seen are goldfish and ornamental carp. The popularity of these relates both to their appearance and to an experience of the famous Daoist philosopher Zhuang Zi (c.369–286 BC), who claimed that by watching the fish swimming in a river he had felt the 'happiness of the fish', a manifestation of the unity of man and nature. The presence of fish in garden ponds affords a reference to this, and special pavilions, bridges and terraces are often provided for watching them (fig. 1.22).

Returning to Miss Gordon Cumming's tour, amongst the numerous sights she took in was the British Legation in Beijing (fig. 1.15). While the restoration of the Lianggongfu sounds to have been largely in authentic style, Miss Gordon Cumming's pen recorded that:

> The whole is considered a good specimen of Chinese official architecture, and it has recently been restored both inside and outside at considerable cost of gaudy paint and gold, in the Chinese style of very intricate lines and patterns of the very crudest and most uncompromising colours—pure scarlet pillars &c., jarring with the brightest emerald green and Albert-blue lavishly laid on. To eyes that have recently rejoiced in the subdued crimsons and green-*ish* and blue-*ish* tones, and soft pearly greys, and delicate touches of gold of harmonious Japanese decorations, there is a fascination of positive pain in these screaming colours.

An idea of this use of colour can be obtained from figures 1.1 and 1.41, and it is certainly something which may not always seem pleasing to the Western eye. However, the colours and colour combinations, being auspicious and imbued with symbolism, have been widely used, particularly in the north for the residences and garden pavilions of members of the imperial family. Since ancient times it has been traditional in imperial buildings for the roofs to be yellow, the columns red, and the roof supports, eaves, brackets and ceilings polychrome—green, blue and gold predominating. In the residences and gardens of relatives of the emperor much the same applied, though they were not allowed the yellow roof tiles. On the other hand the bright colours used in imperial palaces and gardens were generally considered unacceptable for the gardens of the scholars, most of which were in the lower Yangtze region. But in the north, where the winters are cold and gardening is not a year-round activity, garden and residential buildings were often painted —red and green being favoured for the woodwork.

As far as plants were concerned, amongst the consequences of the relative freedom for travel by foreigners which prevailed after 1860 was that missionaries and others were able to begin collecting in the west of the country. However, as a result of the excitement generated by the discovery of the richness of the native flora, information about gardens and garden plants in western China was slow to emerge. Amongst the few early observations made were those of Archibald Little, who travelled up the Yangtze from Shanghai to Chongqing and back in 1883. As a result of his fortnight's stay in Chongqing, he has left us a picture of the city and the surrounding countryside prior to there being any noticeable Western influence apart from that of the missionaries (Little, 1888). As well as giving numerous descriptions of the natural history of the region, he recorded various kinds of garden. For instance, on Sunday, 15 April 1883 he was invited to dinner in a pavilion overlooking an orange garden in what he described as one of

> the numerous public gardens which abound within and without the walls of the pleasure-loving city of Chung-king. These gardens cover two or three acres of ground, and are cut up by rockwork (here natural), trees, and hillocks into park-like grounds. Large and small pavilions are scattered throughout, so arranged as to secure perfect privacy to each party of visitors. For the hot weather caves have been excavated in the soft sandstone rock, which are much affected by the Chinese as being cool and draughtless. These "tang" are mostly owned in shares by a group of friendly families, and form in fact institutions analagous to our clubs; they differ, however, in that families are admitted and that the host brings his own cook and provisions.

As well as visiting this unusual type of garden, he also went to a merchant's country house outside the city and was entertained in a hall which looked out on 'a handsome enclosed courtyard, filled with orange, camellia, and azalea trees growing in large pots placed on stone pedestals' (fig. 1.23). He saw similar orange trees and flowering shrubs in another country house, 'celebrated for its flower-garden', where the proprietress, a widow, let out courtyards for dinner parties in order to make ends meet. On another occasion he called at an 18th-century country house and garden which had been given to the Catholic Mission by the Tung family. While he was not overly keen on the coloured prints in the makeshift chapel 'with Notre Dame au Sacré Coeur in the centre, tearing open her heart with most unpleasant effect', he found the place to be 'the finest example of a Chinese residence I had yet visited'. Here there was a series of courtyards built one above another on a slope within a walled enclosure of a little over four acres. While the buildings were in good condition, the grounds were 'filled with the luxuriant vegetation of the latitude, long untended, and rendering the winding paths almost impassable'. Amongst other features, he recorded that in the lowest courtyard there was 'a deep fishpond, surrounded by a stone quay and crossed by two zigzag bridges of carved stone'. And while riding there he had reflected that:

> The Chinese, in their love of privacy and retirement, never enjoy a view from the windows of their own dwelling, except it be that of the miniature enclosed gardens surrounding them, hence partly the oppressive dulness with which they afflict the foreigner.

Archibald Little's wife first came to China in 1887 and spent some years there as a result of his having become involved in various enterprises. Amongst the places they visited were the Yangtze gorges, Chongqing, Emei Shan, Kangding, Ningbo, Hangzhou, Tianjin and Beijing. Like her husband, Mrs Little wrote of her travels and experiences, illustrating her writing with photographs, mostly her own. Her first description of a private garden was of one in Shanghai (Little, 1901):

> Mr. Tee San's garden is one of the most fascinating spots in China, with the bright autumn sunshine glinting through the pretty bits of trellis-work on to its fantastic rocks, and zigzag bridges, and pretty pavilions, and lighting up the truly exquisite specimens of chrysanthemums sometimes on show there... . But it is not so much worth while to go to this garden in order to see the chrysanthemum, as to admire the infinite variety of Chinese decoration crowded into what is really a very confined space, but which is made to appear a garden large enough to lose oneself in. Rows of bamboo stems of soft blue-green china relieve the monotony of the walls, with their open air-spaces in between, as do also various graceful interlacings of tiles. There are doors of all sorts and sizes, like a horseshoe, like a pentagon, like a leaf cut down the middle by the leaf stem, and with the outer edge fluted like a leaf. There are,

of course, artificial mounds made out of rockwork, and grottoes, and quaint lumps of stone, looking as if they had been masses of molten metal suddenly hardened in their grotesqueness; also, as a matter of course, inside the pavilions there are various specimens of that landscape stone—dear to the heart of the Chinaman, and said to come from Yunnan—framed and hanging on the walls. There used to be also a magnificent peacock; a mandarin duck, with its quaint, bright, decisive colouring; golden pheasants; a scarlet faced monkey, and a pale faced; a little company of white geese, and another of white rabbits. But to enumerate the treasures of the garden gives no idea of the artistic skill with which it has been laid out; so that every one who sits down in it even in the most commonplace manner, and even those most unpicturesque of human beings, Chinese men and women, immediately becomes an integral part of the picture.

Figure 1.23 Azaleas on stone pedestals,
Zhuozhengyuan, Suzhou

She went on to mention a gnarled and knotted root serving as a stand for a flower-pot, a white stork (probably a crane) in the pavement 'all formed of little bits of broken tile', the patterns in the walls and pebble pavements (fig. 1.24), the 'drums of soft blue-green and green-blue for garden seats', the play of light and shade, and much more. While one might be forgiven for wondering just how picturesque Mrs Little appeared in the eyes of the Chinese and whether she, too, really became an integral part of the picture, there can be no doubt concerning her ability to conjure up, in a few words, a realistic depiction of a typical private garden of the region. And although she made no mention of the symbolism which is to be found in every facet of the Chinese garden, she

custodians demanded a second payment to let them out. This was all too much for Mr Little who

> took up a big beam, and smashed open the door. It fell lintel and all, and the latter so nearly killed a child in its fall the crowd was awed. This just gave us time to get on our donkeys … As there are other porcelain arches in Peking, it might be as well for other visitors to avoid the Hall of the Classics altogether, we thought.

Of all the sights on view in Beijing at the time, the finest to Mrs Little's mind was the British Legation. Unlike Miss Gordon Cumming did, she does not seem to have found the

appears to have grasped the basic tenets of its design.

Later, when Mr and Mrs Little first went to Beijing in 1888, very few of its sights were accessible and, of those that were, most were in a poor state. Not only this but visiting them involved much argument about payment and the subsequent inconvenience of being followed about by a crowd of onlookers. Mrs Little (1901) records that they were advised not to go to the famous Lama Temple in the north-east of the city ('such a set of rowdies are the Lamas'), but they settled on a visit to the Confucian Temple nearby and the adjoining porcelain arch and Hall of the Classics. While they were impressed by the old trees, they were surprised that so famous a building as the Hall of the Classics had been allowed to fall into disrepair. Things reached a climax at the end of their visit when the door of the hall was shut in their faces and the

Figure 1.24 (above)
Laying paving in a garden, Yangzhou
Figure 1.25 (right)
The Beitang (North Church), Beijing

colours crude and uncompromising, but perhaps they had faded a little by then.

Towards the end of the 19th century, a group of scholars and officials convinced the young emperor Guangxu that the deplorable state of the country would not improve unless the administration was reformed and the way paved for industrialisation in the manner that it had been in Japan. In 1898 the emperor issued a series of reforming decrees, but this did not suit the beliefs of the Dowager Empress Cixi, who then placed him under what we would call house arrest for the remainder of his life. Those members of the reforming group who had not escaped were arrested and executed, and the old order continued.

At about this time an organisation known as the Boxers—on account of the boxing-like exercises which formed part of their training—sprang up in Shandong. It began as an anti-Manchu society but soon became the focus of rapidly mounting resentment against foreigners as well—missionaries in particular. The unrest and anti-foreign feeling spread to Beijing and, perhaps principally in order to deflect anger from the dynasty and apparently with the encouragement of the Dowager Empress, a joint attack was organised in 1900 against the foreign legations and missions by the Boxers and the imperial army. The legations were besieged and thousands of Catholics took shelter in the grounds of the Beitang (North Church) (fig. 1.25). After 55 days a force organised

by the foreign powers arrived, relieved the situation, and looted and inflicted further damage on the city and its surroundings. The court had fled to Xi'an prior to the arrival of the foreign troops and, as a result of this, it became possible for the first time for outsiders to enter not only the Imperial City, which included the principal imperial gardens, but the Forbidden City itself.

Amongst those making up the French contingent was Pierre Loti, the naval officer and novelist, who stayed for a time in a palace inside the abandoned Imperial City in 1900. In *Les Derniers Jours de Pékin* (1902) he described the dam-

age and gave his impressions of the scene there, including the plantations of sombre conifers, the temples, the moat of the Forbidden City, 90 feet wide and filled with dead and dying rushes, the double ramparts 'd'un rouge de sang', and the fantastic palaces. Of the emperor's apartment he said, in his characteristic style, that the air was full of the scent of tea leaves, dried flowers and old silk. A colossal tomb, he called the place.

Another who was able to explore the abandoned imperial properties was Mrs Little, who returned to Beijing in 1901 after an absence of several years. Although the foreign troops

had inflicted considerable damage, nevertheless she reported that 'Tourists generally are all raving about the Summer Palace, and it is quite a place to spend a happy day in, if it were but for the pure air by the lakeside among the hills' (Little, 1905). She also gave a description of the buildings and gardens of the Forbidden City, noting that while the trees were as they should be, it was evident that the gardeners had fled or were no longer supervised, as the jasmines were out of control and no potted flowers decked the rockwork. She was able, however, to do something not now permitted—to climb the enormous rock mountain in the Imperial Garden and take in the view from its summit (fig.1.26). She was also able to visit the three lakes, Behai (North Sea), Zhonghai (Middle Sea) and Nanhai (South Sea), which lay within the Imperial City to the west of the Forbidden City.

Figure 1.26 Rock Mountain in the Imperial Garden, Forbidden City, Beijing

On this occasion the Littles had gone to stay in 'the largest garden in all Peking', which had earlier belonged to a nephew of the empress. It was in the north-east of the city not far from the scene of their earlier contretemps at the Hall of the Classics. Mrs Little's words and photographs reveal the garden to have been in typical, somewhat severe, northern style, with a rock mountain in the centre, various pavilions, a lake, a watercourse, decorative bridges, walls, variously shaped doorways, trees, and a garden of white lilacs (fig. 1.27). They were there for two months in the summer and, while she lamented the lack of flowers, she felt that the great beauty of the garden was in the 'exquisite effects of light and shade'. These comments would apply equally well to the one or two large gardens which once belonged to the Manchu princes and which are still to be seen in Beijing.

As well as her descriptions of the imperial gardens, Mrs Little left us her own impressions of the Beitang, various temples in the city, the Jade Spring Hill, the ruins of the Yuanmingyuan, the temples in various parts of the Western Hills, the Western Qing Tombs, the Ming Tombs, and the Imperial Hot Springs and their grounds. She also drew attention to the role of temples as guardians of old trees and as places for people to gather, saying:

> **In this most utilitarian country in many parts there is not a tree left but that which shades some ancient temple's walls. The temples are also the great gathering place for the enjoyment of the village, much as the public-house is with us in England. People meet one another there, drink wine, eat hot cakes, send up crackers, play with sham dragons or with lions according to the time of the year, hold their club dinners, settle their clubs and other village affairs.**

Recognising the architectural, horticultural and historical value of temples, she was concerned about what might happen to them 'in the event of the Chinese becoming as a nation Christians'. As it turned out it was not this hoped-for eventuality but a very different set of circumstances that led to the disappearance of most of them. Nevertheless, those which remain continue to provides sites where people can gather and relax.

Others to do the usual rounds of Beijing sights and write descriptions of them at about this time were Lady Susan Townley (1904), A.S. Roe (1910) and Henri Borel (1912), but

Figure 1.27

Mrs Archibald Little's garden in Beijing.

FROM MRS LITTLE (1905).

they added little of note. A.S. Roe, however, visited many other parts of China during her tour of 1907–09, including Chengdu, Nanjing, Hangzhou and Yangzhou. Since, apart from Marco Polo, no Westerner before her seems to have written anything much about Yangzhou, it seems surprising that almost all she had to say was 'Yancheo is one of the largest cities in this part of China, and is a favourite place for retired officials and merchants, who come hither and fritter their substance away in idle pleasures'. She made no mention of the famous Slender West Lake nor any of the gardens belonging to the people of whom she was so censorious. She did, however, include in her book the earliest photograph I have seen of the Five Pavilion Bridge—the focal point of the landscape of the Slender West Lake (fig. 1.28)—although she made no reference to it in the text.

Figure 1.28 **Five Pavilion Bridge, Slender West Lake, Yangzhou.**
FROM ROE (1910).

Another person to provide some incidental information about gardens in Beijing was Princess Der Ling (1911), a Manchu of aristocratic lineage. Her description of the gardens of her own family's enormous mansion suggests that they had come under Western influence as she reported that there were

> many different varieties of flowers in prettily arranged flower beds, running along winding paths, which wound in and out between the lakes. At the time we left for Paris, in the month of June, 1899, the gardens were a solid mass of flowers and foliage, and much admired by all who saw them.

On her return from Paris in 1903 she became First Lady-in-Waiting to the Dowager Empress, a position which she held for two years. This enabled her to record her own observations about the gardens of the Forbidden City, the Sea Palaces—as the residences around the lakes to the west of the Forbidden City were called—and the Summer Palace. She described the holding of festivals in these gardens and the interest and involvement of the Dowager Empress in the cultivation of lotuses, chrysanthemums and bottle gourds (*Lagenaria siceraria*) (fig. 1.29).

As it happens, further details about actual Chinese gardening procedures had become available in the West with the appearance in Paris in 1900 of *Miroir des fleurs: guide pratique du jardinier amateur en Chine au XVIIe siècle*, a translation by J. Halphen of Chen Haozi's *Huajing* (Mirror of

Flowers) of 1688—as far as I know, the first translation of a Chinese gardening book into a European language. In this book Chen described 350 kinds of ornamental plants and set out the tasks to be carried out each month, just as many modern gardening books do.

William Geil's much-quoted *Eighteen Capitals of China* appeared in the same year as Princess Der Ling's memoirs. However, apart from mentioning a variety of garden plants and a lake shore in Qin'an, Gansu, where streams wound about amongst artificial rockwork, with lily beds here and there and arched bridges joining islets, he added little to our knowledge of the gardens of the country (Geil, 1911). The same can be said of Backhouse and Bland (1914) in their now largely discredited *Annals & Memoirs of the Court of Peking*. However, this contains illustrations from a scroll entitled *Scenes of Court Life*, by Chiu Ching (Jiu Jing), a painter of the 15th century. These show courtyards ornamented with trees and rocks, including specimens mounted on marble stands. While by this time there were undoubtedly many paintings of this type in museums and private collections outside China, some of which were described and reproduced in specialist journals (e.g. Lauffer, 1912–13), they do not seem to have attracted the attention of those interested in Chinese gardens. Hence the reproductions in this book would have reached a wider audience.

Meanwhile change had continued to sweep over China. On their return to Beijing in 1902, Cixi and her ministers reluctantly began to introduce reforms, including in 1905 the abolition of the traditional examination system for selecting candidates for positions in the bureaucracy. She died on 15 November 1908, at which time it was announced that the emperor Guangxu had died the previous day—a state of affairs that aroused some conjecture. She had named her two-year-old great nephew, Puyi, as his successor, with the result that the power passed to a group of Manchu princes, with Puyi's father, the second Prince Chun, as regent. The Qing dynasty managed to survive only a little longer, however, until its downfall was achieved by an uprising which established a republic in 1911.

Unfortunately the promises of social change held out by the overthrow of the Qing administration were never realised, and much of the country, including the north, fell into the hands of regional army generals, or 'warlords' as they were called. Then in 1931 the Japanese occupied Manchuria and in 1937 began their conquest of much of the rest of the

Figure 1.29
Bottle gourds
for a sale on
the path to
the summit
of Tai Shan,
Shandong

Figure 1.30 (right) **Nine Dragon Pine (***Pinus bungeana***), Jietai Temple, Western Hills, Beijing**

Figure 1.31 (below right) **Wen Zhengming, 1533—The Clean Retreated Bower, Zhuozhengyuan, Suzhou.**

TAKEN FROM A COPY OF KERBY (1922) HELD IN THE MITCHELL LIBRARY, STATE LIBRARY OF NEW SOUTH WALES.

country. Following their defeat civil war broke out in 1946. The Communist army finally triumphed over the Nationalists and Mao Zedong proclaimed the People's Republic of China in Beijing on 1 October 1949.

In spite of the unstable conditions which prevailed between 1900 and 1937, during this period much written and photographic material about gardens and everything else in China became available in the West. Not perhaps unexpectedly, the plant-hunters such as Ernest Wilson (1913) and Reginald Farrer (1916) provided little information about gardens, and not a great deal more was revealed by F.N. Meyer (1916) and P.H. Dorsett (1928; 1931), who carried out explorations on behalf of the United States Department of Agriculture. Dorsett, however, was one of the many people who drew attention to the famous white-barked pine (*Pinus bungeana*) on the terrace at the Jietaisi near Beijing (fig. 1.30).

Information of a quite different nature was provided by Kate Kerby's *An Old Chinese Garden*, published in Shanghai in 1922. This contained reproductions of Wen Zhengming's paintings and poems of 1533 describing the Zhuozhengyuan in Suzhou, the garden which was later to become known all over the world as the Humble Administrator's Garden. Mrs Kerby thus revealed to readers of English the relatively unpretentious nature of a Chinese garden of the early 16th century (fig. 1.31). In a different vein again were the many books containing observations of a horticultural nature which followed, including *Peking* by Juliet Bredon (1931), the first edition of which was published in 1919. Her descriptions of the numerous gardens and temples of the city and the Western Hills provided a picture of their features and condition at the time, as did *The Temples of the Western Hills visited from*

Figure 1.32 Half-moon shaped pavilion, Qiyefu, Beijing, 1922, with the last emperor's younger brother. FROM OSVALD SIRÉN (1926).

Peking by G.E. Hubbard (1923) and *The Imperial Palaces of Peking* by Osvald Sirén (1926), who had been to Beijing in 1922. The three volumes of Sirén's work consisted largely of magnificent photographs and included depictions of the Imperial Garden in the Forbidden City, the gardens of the three adjoining lakes, the Summer Palace, the Jade Spring Hill, the ruins of the Yuanmingyuan and the Fragrant Hills Park, and the gardens of several of the Manchu princes. These revealed to the outside world the appearance of many gardens in the imperial properties, and they remain an invaluable record (fig. 1.32).

Further details concerning gardens in Beijing were provided by Juliet Bredon and Igor Mitrophanov (1927) in *The Moon Year*. They gave descriptions of the events, ceremonies and festivals which occurred each lunar month. Amongst other things they described the peony viewing held annually by the President of the Republic in the gardens of the Sea Palaces. They recorded that after the formal greetings were over the guests were free to wander in the gardens, where the peonies were set out in rows in terraces faced with yellow-glazed tiles. And the peonies were not the only things to impress them, as their observation which follows shows:

> We pause in open pavilions whose roofs are draped with
> wisteria. Here and there long purple-blue sprays hang as
> a curtain, staining the sunlight as it passes through. A
> mauve carpet of fallen petals covers the marble floor.
> Above our heads, the bees in the blossoms make a sound
> like the drone of the sea in a shell.

They went on to indicate that, pre-eminent amongst the places those not fortunate enough to be invited could view the peonies, was a temple they called 'Tsung Hsiao Ssu' (Zongxiaosi), where the finest plants, many of them more than 200 years old, were surrounded by low walls of open brickwork or tiles. This temple was in the south-west of the city but, as far as I know, no trace of it survives.

In 1929 Ernest Wilson's *China Mother of Gardens* was published. In it he devoted one chapter to gardens and gardening in that country, but even this dealt almost entirely with plants. It is clear, however, that in his travels he had acquired an understanding of garden-making by the Chinese, for he wrote:

> Given a piece of ground, no matter if it be small, and
> devoid of natural beauty, or badly situated, they will
> patiently transform it into a mountain-landscape in
> miniature. With strange-looking, weather-worn rocks,
> dwarfed trees, bamboo, herbs, and water, a piece of wild
> countryside is evolved, replete with mountain and
> stream, forest and field, plateau and lake, grotto and dell.
> A network of narrow winding paths, traverses the garden,
> and rustic bridges in various designs are thrown across
> the infantine streams. The whole effect is encompassed
> within a comparatively few square yards, though the per-
> spective is one of seemingly many miles.

In 1931 Edwin Howard's *Chinese Garden Architecture* appeared. In 1919 he had been to Beijing, Qufu and Tai Shan in Shandong, and Putuo Shan in Zhejiang. Like so many visitors to China he noted that much of the architecture had fallen into decay. Nevertheless his photographs of gardens in the places he visited provided an interesting addition to the record. Likewise Matilda Thurston (1931), who went to live in Nanjing in 1915 and stayed several years, described gardens in that city and, like Ernest Wilson, pointed out how the Chinese were able to get the experience of wild mountainous scenes from a landscape of very small area. She was unusually perceptive, too, about the role of buildings in gardens, writing that:

> Buildings belong in gardens as they belong in the land-
> scape of the country itself—the pleasure pavilion
> fronting the lake or smaller body of water, the hexagonal
> *ting* perched high on the miniature mountain, the quiet

Figure 1.33 Ginkgo known as 'The Emperor's Wife', Tanzhe Temple, Western Hills, Beijing

little room for meditation and writing, the boat pavilion sometimes built on a stone base in the water, as at the Summer Palace in Peiping, sometimes set in a grove of bamboo as in the Djang Garden. The Chinese enjoy their gardens sitting down and have pavilions conveniently placed where the view is good or where one may want to stop and drink tea.

Matilda Thurston also reproduced a photograph of a diminutive mountain landscape of the type mentioned earlier in this chapter, made of rocks and complete with miniature steps, pavilions and bridges, but gave no location for it.

In 1932 Ann Bridge conjured up in words further images of the gardens of temples in the Western Hills in her novel *Peking Picnic* (1932), drawing attention to the white-barked pines at Jietaisi and the famous ginkgos at Tanzhesi (fig. 1.33). In the same year there appeared descriptions and photographs of the temples at Chengde by Sven Hedin, who went there in 1930. He commented on the then ruinous state of these temples and of the gardens of the Imperial Summer Villa, about which little had been heard since Qianlong's time. Further photographs and descriptions of these came from Tadashi Sekino (1935), who went to Chengde in 1933–34 after the Japanese had invaded the district and added it to their state of Manchukuo. Chengde was also visited about this time by Peter Fleming (1934), who left us another description of the town and its decaying monuments.

About the same time Carroll Brown Malone's (1934) *History of the Peking Summer Palaces under the Ch'ing Dynasty* was published—the first lengthy study of Chinese

Figure 1.34

Prince Puru, the last descendant of Prince Gong to live at Gongwangfu.

FROM SIRÉN (1949).

gardens by a Westerner. In this he went into considerable detail about the construction and subsequent history of the imperial gardens to the north-west of the city during the Qing. While something had survived of several of these at the time he wrote, he observed that it was only the Summer Palace which remained to represent the magnificence of the departed empire.

In 1935 there appeared *In Search of Old Peking*—a comprehensive description of the sights of the city and its environs. The authors, Arlington and Lewisohn, not only drew attention to a large number of palaces, mansions, temples and gardens, but provided information about their history and, in some cases, maps and plans. Of particular interest were the details provided of Nanhai and Zhonghai, access to which had rarely been available to the public. At the same time they bemoaned the decay and destruction of the quiet beauty and wonderful tradition of the city. Historic buildings and monuments had been razed, sometimes on official orders, temples had been left to go to wrack and ruin, famous beauty spots had become a wilderness of weeds, and wonderful groves of ancient trees had been cut down and sold for timber.

Even so, Osbert Sitwell, who visited Beijing in 1934, gave effusive descriptions of the gardens there in several of the books which he wrote subsequently (Sitwell, 1935; 1939; 1974). Like most European visitors he found the rockeries puzzling but admired the forsythias, wisterias and other seasonal flowers. In April he was invited to Gongwangfu, perhaps the only princely mansion which was still occupied at that time by a member of the family. This was Prince Puru (fig. 1.34), a grandson of Prince Gong. Prince Puru was in the habit of holding a party each year at the family mansion when the crabapples were in bloom. The trees were able to be viewed at eye level from the tops of the rockeries, and Sitwell recorded that the old Manchus present remained there admiring the blossom for a full hour—a charming glimpse of a vanished world. Then, in early May, he went to a garden party given at the Summer Palace by the mayor of Beijing and was greatly impressed by the tree peonies and yellow roses (probably *Rosa xanthina*).

George Kates (1952), in his *The Years That Were Fat: the last of old China*, was another author to provide information about various gardens in and around Beijing in the 1930s. Particularly evocative was his description of the courtyards of his own house there. He also had some comments to make on the Chinese tendency to allow things to run down. He saw it as a paradox that a nation which so enjoyed the possession of physical property should take so little care of it.

A further insight into the use and significance of plants in relation to the seasons became available to those unable to read Chinese when in 1936 there was published *Annual Customs and Festivals in Peking*, an English translation by Derk Bodde of Tun Li-ch'en's *Yen-ching Sui-shih-chi* (Tun, 1965). Tun was a Manchu who wrote this work at the very end of the 19th century and it is a fascinating record of a world long gone.

At this stage it is interesting to note that, apart from a few observations made in Guangzhou and the area around Shanghai, European descriptions of Chinese gardens up till the early 1930s were almost entirely concerned with those of the north. The gardens of the lower Yangtze region, the subject of so much attention nowadays, had gone largely unnoticed. Even Mrs Little (1901; 1902), in describing her visits to Hangzhou and Suzhou, had nothing to say about their gardens other than that the Board of Foreign Affairs in Hangzhou was 'situated in a most fantastic garden, full of rocks and with a fine wistaria hanging its tresses of fragrant, lilac flowers over a corridor, made like the bridges in the Shanghai city tea garden in a variety of different slants'. Otherwise in these cities she seems to have devoted all her energy to giving anti-footbinding lectures to the Chinese.

Perhaps the first mentions of these gardens to become available in English were those provided by Shen Fu's *Six Records of a Floating Life*, a translation of his autobiographical memoir originally written in 1809. This was serialised in *Hsi Feng* and the *T'ien Hsia Monthly* in 1935 and subsequently published in various editions. Shen was a native of Suzhou, a keen gardener, and a minor official whose duties obliged him to work in other parts of the country from time to time. As well as giving an insight into Chinese horticulture, he commented on gardens in Suzhou and elsewhere, including those around the Slender West Lake in Yangzhou, which had long been highly regarded in China but about which little or nothing was known in the West.

Further details about Suzhou gardens became available in 1936 when the first English guidebook to the city, F.R. Nance's *Suzhou, The Garden City*, was published in Shanghai (Clunas, 1996). More importantly, in same the year in the *T'ien Hsia Monthly*, also published in Shanghai, there was a lengthy illustrated article in English by Chuin Tung entitled

'Chinese Gardens, especially in Kiangsu and Chekiang'. Beginning in 1931 the author had been to see as many gardens as he could find in the lower Yangtze region. In his article, after remarking that 'Whatever gardens we see are but remnants of a bygone glory' and bemoaning the introduction of glass and concrete, he went on to record more than 10 gardens in or near Suzhou, and others in Yangzhou, Changshu, Nanxun, Jiaxing, Shanghai, Nanxiang, Hangzhou, Wuxi, Taicang, Jiading and Nanjing, in many cases giving details of their history and commenting on their condition. He also compared Chinese and Western gardens, discussed the design of Chinese gardens and the various features of which they are composed, and outlined their history from ancient times to the present. In this article he set the pattern for most of the books and articles about Chinese gardens which have appeared at intervals right up to the present day.

Chuin Tung, incidentally, seems to be the first person writing in English to draw attention to Ji Cheng's *Yuanye*, an English translation of which has been made by Alison Hardie under the title *The Craft of Gardens* (Ji, 1988). It was written between 1631 and 1634 and is the first known manual devoted entirely to garden design and construction in China. Ji Cheng was originally a painter and, rather than giving step-by-step instructions, his words were more in the nature of general advice about the selection and development of a site to take advantage of its natural features. He also cautioned against what he considered to be bad taste, particularly in his remarks about the selection of rocks and the construction of rock mountains. As well as this he gave patterns of architectural details and designs for pebble paving (fig. 1.35). By

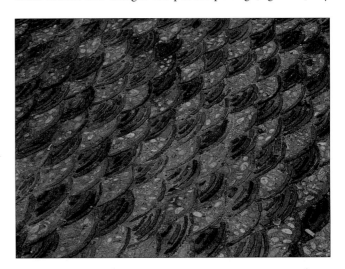

Figure 1.35 **Wave-pattern paving, Heyuan, Yangzhou. This design was one of those included in Ji Cheng's *Yuanye*.**

Figure 1.36 Retired abbot in his garden, Wenshu Monastery, Chengdu. FROM PRIP-MOLLER (1937).

seen in the early part of the 20th century. Like Tung (1936), she dealt with the history and design of these gardens, along with descriptions of imperial, private and temple gardens she had seen in Beijing, Hangzhou and Suzhou. She also mentioned gardens in Shanghai, Yangzhou, Nanjing and Guangzhou. Like Mrs Little and Osvald Sirén before her, she was in Beijing at a time when it was possible to visit the lakes in the Imperial City, and her descriptions and photographs of these revealed something of their character to the outside world. She also visited the Summer Palace, surviving gardens of the princes, and the temples of the Western Hills.

As well as providing descriptions, she drew attention to the symbolism of various garden features, the unity of house and garden, the role of ideographic inscriptions, and the reverence accorded ancient trees. She pointed out, too, that the Chinese sought tranquillity in their gardens, where they 'became absorbed in the subtleties of music, painting, calligraphy and conversation'. She is the first Western writer I have come across to mention that the garden of the scholar was not only a refuge but an intellectual exercise—an aspect of the Chinese garden which has come in for much comment by later writers.

In the course of several sojourns in Beijing Dorothy Graham had a number of gardens there, including one which was part of a property belonging to a Manchu who had been an official at court. These gardens gave her the opportunity to enter into the garden culture of the city and to describe, like Cibot (1778) and Bredon (1931), the ingenious Chinese greenhouses in which plants were kept over winter or forced into bloom at appropriate times. And no doubt it was her Western upbringing which led her to be expansive about the plants and the way the changing of the seasons was emphasised by the various kinds which could be bought from the hawkers who regularly brought them round. She commented on the symbolism of these plants and noted, too, that the Chinese nurserymen had taken over the sorts introduced by the foreigners—pansies, daisies, carnations, salvia, snapdragons and many more—plants which today are prominent everywhere in China in displays of potted plants (fig. 1.37).

To my knowledge Dorothy Graham was also the first of the long series of writers about Chinese gardens to mention Cao Xueqin's late 18th century novel *Hongloumeng*—English translations of which exist under the titles *Dream of the Red Chamber*, *A Dream of Red Mansions* and *The Story of the Stone*. In the novel the Jia family build a garden, the Daguan

pointing out the dangers of garden-making by those who lacked the correct degree of taste, he emphasised the wisdom of employing a 'master of the craft' to undertake the direction of workmen in the practical tasks. He also stressed the importance of bearing in mind the seasons and of arranging the siting of buildings to take advantage of views, even when this was contrary to the advice of the geomancers who, one assumes, were invariably consulted. In recent years Ji Cheng's book has been the subject of an astonishing amount of analysis and interpretation by scholars, both Chinese and Western.

The gardens of temples came in for attention once more with the publication in 1937 of J. Prip-Moller's *Chinese Buddhist Monasteries*. In this he included photographs of the interesting courtyard gardens of the Wenshu and Baoguang Monasteries in Chengdu (fig. 1.36), so providing an early record of temple gardens in western China.

This was followed in 1938 by Dorothy Graham's *Chinese Gardens*. She was the first Westerner to attempt a comprehensive account of the subject, based largely on what she had

Yuan, adjacent to their mansion in Beijing. The description of its design and construction, the process of appending names and inscriptions to its various features, and its subsequent use and decline, gives the reader an understanding, not only of what the garden of an aristocratic family of the time must have been like, but also of the part it played in their lives (Cao, 1973–86).

Although it is far less comprehensive than Dorothy Graham's book, a well-informed general article about Chinese gardens by Florence B. Robinson appeared in *Country Life* (N.Y.) in April 1939. In it she described succinctly the nature of these gardens and, amongst other things, expressed the very sensible view that:

> They express an attitude towards life quite opposed to that of the Occident and so they may not be copied successfully in the West. Nevertheless they expound many lessons and the West can learn much of value from them.

Publications by various foreigners who had been in China in the 1920s and 30s continued to appear during and after the Sino-Japanese War. Amongst the most significant was the

study of Prince Gong's mansion in Beijing by Ch'ên and Kates (1940), in which they described the history, structure and significance of both the mansion and its remarkable garden. Also in 1940 *Chinese Houses and Gardens* by Henry Inn was published. This is a collection of photographs taken principally in Shanghai, Suzhou and Hangzhou in 1936, and is accompanied by several articles in English by Chinese authors, contrasting Chinese and Western gardens, drawing attention to features of the design of Chinese gardens, pointing out their significance in philosophical terms, and stressing the importance of symbolism.

Another significant step towards the understanding of the Chinese garden was made by Florence Lee Powell. She had photographed the Liuyuan and Shizilin in Suzhou in the spring of 1926 and used the photographs as the basis of her book *In the Chinese Garden* (Powell, 1943). These illustrations are arranged to show various scenes in each garden in the order in which they are encountered by the visitor. It appears that she was the first person to depict a complete Chinese garden in a connected series of photographs, including those of interiors, window grilles, paving and architectural details. The text that relates to them touches on

Figure 1.37 Display of pot plants, Tianyige, Ningbo

symbolism and other matters, and her book is a valuable record of the Liuyuan and Shizilin as they were at the time of her visits (fig. 1.38).

Further attention was focussed on the importance of architectural elements in the Chinese garden by Osvald Sirén (1948), who had visited the country in 1922, 1929 and 1935 and who summed the situation up when he wrote:

> There is undoubtedly some truth in the assertion that even if there were no flowers or trees in a Chinese garden it would nevertheless give the impression of a garden, because of its winding paths and canals, its fantastic hollowed rocks and the glassy stillness of its ponds, and especially because of the architectural elements that are rarely absent. The most significant of these elements are the surrounding walls, with their decorative doors and windows, and the multitude of pavilions, kiosks, bridges and galleries, which, owing to their interplay of light and shade and their rhythmically balanced lines, blend harmoniously with the other elements of the composition.

The following year (1949) Sirén's *Gardens of China* appeared—by far the most important publication relating to this period. Illustrated with his own beautiful photographs and reproductions of works of art, this book remains the classic reference on the topic. It brought together all aspects of the subject, including the Chinese literature. His photographs of gardens in Beijing and Suzhou constitute, like those of Florence Lee Powell, an invaluable record of these places at the time he saw them. Fortunately the

Figure 1.38 Stone bed for tree peonies, Liuyuan, Suzhou, 1926.
FROM POWELL (1943).

majority of these gardens have survived, so it is possible to compare their present appearance with that depicted in Sirén's images (figs 1.39, 1.40).

Next came Hope Danby's *The Garden of Perfect Brightness*, which appeared in 1950. In it she gave much fascinating detail concerning the history of the Yuanmingyuan and the emperors who lived there. She recorded, for instance, that the buildings were designed by members of the Lei family, who had been hereditary palace architects since the time of the Ming emperor Yongle (reigned 1403–24). Their work had been handed down from father to son for six generations, and was to continue for at least another two centuries. It is from their designs, bills and papers that we know exactly what the buildings in the Yuanmingyuan were like.

In 1959 J.L. Van Hecken and W.A. Grootaers published a description of a celebrated small garden in Beijing, the Banmuyuan (Half-acre Garden), complete with plans and photographs. Osvald Sirén (1949) had earlier drawn attention to this garden which lay close to the north-eastern corner of the Imperial City and was renowned in the Ming for its collection of rocks. It is said to have been created by Li Yu (1611–80?), a dramatist, poet and essayist, whose Jieziyuan (Mustard Seed Garden) in Nanjing had achieved fame throughout the empire . By the 19th century the Banmuyuan had fallen on hard times but was acquired in 1841 by Lin Qing, who had occupied various official positions which took him to many parts of China and enabled him to visit numerous famous gardens, particularly during the period when he was Director General of River Conservancy (1833–42). He was deprived of his ranks and titles when a dike along the Yellow River collapsed in 1842, and in 1843 he returned to Beijing and restored the Banmuyuan. It was amongst the gardens described in *Hongxue yinyuan tuqi* (Tracks of a Wild Swan in the Snow), his illustrated autobiographical memoir (Lin, 1847–50). In 1947 his descendants sold the garden to the Scheut Missionary Society and it was restored yet again. However the missionaries, including Van Hecken and Grootaers, were expelled in 1952 and I have not succeeded in obtaining any further news of it.

Despite the ending of World War II, the circumstances following the declaration of the People's Republic in 1949 did not favour the accumulation of further information about Chinese gardens by foreigners. Nevertheless, many public parks were built, botanical gardens were established, and many famous gardens were restored and opened to the

Figure 1.39 (right) **Terrace for Watching the Fish, Gongwangfu, Beijing.** FROM SIRÉN (1949).

Figure 1.40 (above) **Terrace for Watching the Fish, Gongwangfu, Beijing, 1995**

public, having been recognised as important cultural relics and sources of income from tourism. Brief descriptions in English of gardens and temple grounds in Beijing at this time appeared in *Peking—A Tourist Guide*, which was published there by the Foreign Languages Press in 1960. A few years later Stephen Markbreiter (1969) wrote an article in which he discussed Chinese gardens in the light of *The Story of the Stone* and his own experiences, illustrating it with his photographs of gardens in Suzhou. And, although it did not appear until 1978, Maggie Keswick's *The Chinese Garden* has

its origin in this period, as she was one of the few foreigners to visit Chinese gardens in the 1960s. Her achievement was to have built, as it were, on the work of Chuin Tung, Dorothy Graham and Osvald Sirén, making available a wealth of information about all aspects of the topic. Like Dorothy Graham, she was one of the few people writing in English to pay any

Figure 1.41 Inscriptions on and beside a pavilion, Baotuquan, Ji'nan

particular attention to the significance of the presence of name boards and inscriptions in gardens (fig. 1.41).

Since these name boards and inscriptions are, like the abundance of rock, amongst the features of Chinese gardens that the unprepared Western visitor is likely to find difficult to appreciate, it seems appropriate to include a few words about them here. They serve the same function as the long-established practice of giving poetic names to the principal scenes ('jing') in large gardens and natural scenic areas. Garden buildings usually have names inscribed on boards hung above the doorway, and it is also common to see stone or grey terracotta name plaques over the entrances to court-yards. Very often there are also couplets written vertically on either side of doorways or hung on the pillars of open pavil-ions. As well, there are sometimes inscriptions written on rocks and/or on tablets of slate mounted on walls.

Choosing these names and composing inscriptions became an essential part of making a garden, setting the mood for each particular site. The Jia family's garden in *The Story of the Stone*, for instance, was not considered complete until all the structures within it were named and embellished with poetic couplets (Cao, 1973–86). Perhaps equally impor-

tantly, this practice gave the owner of a garden and his liter-ary colleagues an opportunity to show off their knowledge and their skills in calligraphy and the composition of poems. References to Daoist philosophy, Confucian ideals, literature, and famous places and people were all used to bring a high moral and cultural tone to a garden. It was an advantage, too, if someone important gave a name which could be inscribed in their own calligraphy over the door of the relevant build-ing. This brought honour to the proprietor in the same way as did the writing of poems and prose about the garden, and similar prestige accrued if it became the subject of paintings. According to Clunas (1996), these activities also played an important part in the establishment of ties of patronage, clientage and alliance among members of the elite.

Maggie Keswick and subsequent authors have also drawn attention to the analogy between the use of calligraphic inscriptions in gardens and the custom of writing colophons on paintings. In China calligraphy by the artist, his contem-poraries, and later figures is regarded as an integral part of a painting. The same applies to gardens, even though the garden owner had to engage in the extra step of having the cal-ligraphy engraved on plaques, tablets and rocks. This practice ensured that gardens, like paintings, acquired an extra dimension over time through the accumulation of inscriptions recording the poetic thoughts of those who had visited them.

In the time following Maggie Keswick's visit to China, much good work was undone and much of China's heritage destroyed during the so-called Cultural Revolution of 1966–76. In their determination to wipe out all remaining traces of traditional Chinese culture, the Red Guards repeated many aspects of the behaviour of the Taipings on a nationwide scale. Temples were desecrated or destroyed, botanic gardens ploughed up and put to productive use, and other gardens neglected or razed. Fortunately, however, many famous sites were spared by being occupied by government departments or by officials of the Communist Party. Others were protected by the intervention of concerned officials, including Deng Xiaoping.

After Mao died in 1976, things gradually improved, restoration work recommenced, and the outside world began to hear about Chinese gardens once more. At the same time Chinese landscape architects and scholars began to take an interest in gardens again. A detailed survey of the gardens of Suzhou, *Suzhou gudian yuanlin* (The Traditional Gardens of Suzhou) by Liu Dunzhen, was published in Beijing in 1979. In it Liu described 15 gardens and gave plans of each. An abridged translation by Frances Wood appeared in 1982 (Liu, D., 1982) and a full translation by Chen Lixian in 1993 (Liu, 1993). Then in 1983 Chen Congzhou produced *Yangzhou yuanlin* (The Gardens of Yangzhou). As far as I know this has not been translated into any other language, but in it he described the gardens in the park surrounding the Narrow West Lake and 16 others, giving plans of each. In addition to these works an updated survey in English of the gardens of the lower Yangtze region has been published by Tung (1997).

In the West another significant general work to appear was *The Gardens of China: History, Art, and Meanings* by E.T. Morris (1983), and from the 1980s on there has been a flood of publications by Chinese and Western scholars about every aspect of the Chinese garden. In view of this there seems little point in my repeating at length the information they provide concerning the structure and meaning of Chinese gardens. This is readily available elsewhere, and anyone wishing to become acquainted with such material is referred to the Bibliography and References. However, the general picture that has emerged is that in the more sophisticated gardens the arrangement of scenes, the siting of hills and lakes, the disposition of trees and other plants, and the placement of various types of building required the same type of planning as a landscape painting. Also, the manner in which mountains, rocks and trees were depicted in landscape paintings was imitated in gardens. This was so whatever the scale, at the smaller end of which rocks, bamboos and other plants were arranged against whitewashed walls, which became the equivalent of the paper or silk used by artists. And the whole composition was arranged, as many authors have noted, so the visitors moving through it were made to feel as if they were strolling through a three-dimensional painting.

But while these gardens were arranged to express a profound view of the world and man's place in it, at the same time they were designed to be lived in and enjoyed. Hence there were places for receiving guests, viewing the moon, playing music, painting, writing poems, practising calligraphy, putting on plays, holding ceremonies, viewing seasonal flowers, relaxing, eating out of doors and so on. Not only this but, as Clunas (1996) has pointed out, the garden had also become a way of proclaiming its owner's wealth and taste to a wide audience. Gardens had long been open, or at least visitable by request, and by the end of the 16th century access was even freer, many even being listed in guidebooks.

Most of the gardens we see today are modern restorations of Qing originals. However, this state of affairs should be viewed in the light of the fact that gardens everywhere tend not to be long lasting or at least tend to undergo major changes. And in China there seems always to have been an acceptance of cycles of renewal and decay. For example, as those who have stayed in Chinese hotels will be aware, the Chinese appear never to have embraced the concept of maintenance with any enthusiasm, as both Philip Elwood (1930) and George Kates (1967) noted. Perhaps this has resulted from the dangers and uncertainties with which they have long had to contend. There are, for example, many instances where famous buildings have repeatedly been allowed to fall into ruin before being restored or rebuilt, very often under the patronage of a member of the imperial family. Also, since wood is used as the principal structural element of traditional Chinese buildings, destruction by fire has always been a common occurrence. Not only this, but roof tiles have traditionally been laid in mud over boards so, when seeds lodge in the crevices, before long vegetation takes hold and damage ensues. No doubt it was this general state of affairs which, after 50 years' experience of the country, led L.C. Arlington

Figure 1.45 (previous pages) **Formal garden at the Beijing Botanical Garden (North Garden)**

Figure 1.42 (right) **Reconstruction in progress in 1995, Shizilin, Imperial Summer Villa, Chengde**

Figure 1.43 (below) **Shizilin, Imperial Summer Villa, Chengde, after restoration was completed**

Figure 1.44 (bottom) **Cultivar of *Camellia reticulata* in the camellia garden at the Kunming Horticultural Landscape Botanical Garden**

(1931) to say 'Throughout the length and breadth of China there is scarcely a single building, save a few pagodas, which by any stretch of the imagination can be called old'. While this view is perhaps a little extreme, much the same can be said of the gardens.

Nevertheless, in spite of everything that has happened, a surprising number have survived and been restored. Fortunately much of this work has been done using traditional techniques and materials (figs. 1.42, 1.43), with the result that it is hard to tell what is original and what is not. In some cases, however, when concrete has been employed instead of the original timber, brick and stone, the results are

Figure 1.46 **Garden ornaments at the flower and plant market near the Temple of Heaven, Beijing**

less felicitous. It is quite clear, however, that most of these places are in a far better state now than they have been for at least 100 or 150 years, and restoration is continuing.

While almost all the gardens surviving from the past are now in the hands of public bodies, the recent return to private ownership of houses means that there are once more privately owned gardens, albeit small, and no doubt larger ones will follow. And a seemingly unlikely development is the building of impressive new temples. An interesting example, which I have not seen, is the Huangdaxian Temple, a Daoist establishment near Jinhua in Zhejiang, around which 10 000 camellias have been planted (Shao, 2000).

It was not until the original Republican period that the first botanical gardens were established and the number has increased dramatically since 1949. Likewise there are now public parks in almost all major cities and towns. And display gardens devoted to particular kinds of plants are beginning to appear—for instance the International Camellia Species Garden in Jinhua, Zhejiang, the camellia garden in the Kunming Horticultural Landscape Botanical Garden at Kunming (fig. 1.44), and the tree peony gardens at Luoyang and Heze.

Although some Chinese landscape architects are designing modern gardens by building on the traditions of the past, Western influences are being felt more and more in the world of Chinese gardening. Not surprisingly both the botanical gardens and many of the parks are based on Western models. Here and there, too, gardens have been built in a formal European style (fig. 1.45), and Western classical urns, fountains and garden statuary are appearing all over the place (fig. 1.46). In similar fashion the international repertoire of garden and indoor plants is gaining a foothold. Fortunately, however, the renowned traditional private and imperial gardens have remained largely unaffected by these manifestations of the globalisation which involves us all.

In the light of all of the above, it has been my intention in the remainder of this book to build on the observations of those who have gone before me by describing Chinese gardens, both old and new, as seen through my Western eyes in the closing years of the 20th century. I have also included such additional historical and background material as seemed to me appropriate.

CHAPTER 2

The Centre

In this chapter 'The Centre' are included the provinces of Shaanxi, Henan and Shandong, which embrace that portion of the Yellow River valley and its tributaries where Chinese civilisation is believed to have evolved. It was here, chiefly in present-day Shaanxi and Henan, that for 900 years the imperial dynasties from the Qin (221–207 BC) to the Northern Song (960–1126) established their capitals. This is the region where Chinese garden-building had its origins and underwent much of its development. It was here, too, that the Tang poets extolled the beauty of nature and came to have considerable influence on garden-making, both here and elsewhere in the country. However, as a result of the upheavals taking place with the falls of successive dynasties and the destruction caused by the repeated disastrous flooding of the Yellow River, little trace remains of the early gardens of this region. Nevertheless, there are still many sites of both horticultural and historical interest.

Figure 2.1 **Han tombs near Xi'an, Shaanxi**

The earliest spaces recorded in China which might be called gardens were the hunting parks of the semi-mythological rulers of the Xia, Shang and Zhou 'dynasties' (c.2000–221 BC). These parks, known as 'you', were said to have contained ponds and menageries, as well as terraces and buildings for holding entertainments and ceremonies. The oblong hall facing south, the cornerstone of Chinese architecture, made its appearance before the middle of the 2nd millennium BC and ordered groups of buildings arranged as symmetrical courtyards followed suit. Chinese buildings developed their characteristic appearance in the 1st millennium BC, when a bracketing system was introduced which enabled heavy tiled roofs with upturned eaves to be supported (Cheng, 1998).

The Chinese empire, as traditionally recognised, was established when the ruler of the state of Qin, having eliminated all opposition and unified the country, declared himself emperor Shihuangdi in 221 BC and established his capital near present-day Xi'an. He laid out a park, the Shanglin, on an unprecedented scale near the city. It was not destroyed when the short-lived Qin dynasty was succeeded by the Han (206 BC–AD 220) and the Han emperors continued its development. Since almost nothing remains other than the site, our knowledge of it comes from records and literary descriptions. From these, as was noted by Cibot (1782), it appears to have reached its greatest splendour during the reign of the Han emperor Wudi (141–87 BC) and to have been one of the most magnificent imperial gardens in the history of China. Although primarily still a hunting park, it included palaces, pavilions, farms, orchards, individual gardens, collections of plants and animals from all over the country, and lakes, the most famous of which were Kunming Lake and Taiye Lake.

The imperial gardens of this era incorporated many of the features which, one way or another, have been reproduced in Chinese gardens ever since. And these gardens confirmed and assured, by microcosmic imitation, the hold of the emperor on his domain. So, even in this early period, gardens had come to be much more than pleasant landscapes. And, according to Wang Juyuan (Qiao, 1982), it is recorded in the *Hanzhi kao* (Treatise on Systems of the Han) that it was at this time that the 'you' came to be called 'yuan', the name that has been applied to Chinese gardens ever since.

Private gardens seem to have emerged a little later than the imperial parks, but it is known that the nobility and high-ranking officials began to have gardens laid out during the Han and the practice continued thereafter. Although there had been an attempt to suppress Confucianism during the Qin, in the Han the teachings of Confucius were adopted as the state orthodoxy, and appointments to the civil service were awarded only to those who were successful in stringent examinations on the Confucian classics. From that time on such appointments became the only socially acceptable route to success in China for almost 2000 years. So it was that, even as early as this, gardens were increasingly likely to be made not by hereditary aristocrats, but by the new elite of Confucian scholars appointed to run the civil service. Since Confucian ethics also included an ideal of 'recreation through the arts', as time went by gardens also came to be seen as places for self-cultivation.

It was in this period, too, that the design of gardens came to be greatly influenced by Daoism, a philosophical system which stressed the harmony of man and the universe and which had also absorbed many folk beliefs. For instance, the early Chinese believed there were beings known as the Immortals, who flew about on the backs of cranes. Amongst the places where they were believed to dwell were three islands, Penglai, Fangzhang and Yingzhou, floating in the Eastern Sea off the coast of Shandong. On learning of this, the Qin emperor Shihuangdi sent an expedition to find these islands in the hope of learning from the Immortals the recipe for their success. And during the Han a Daoist sect developed a series of practices including breathing exercises, sexual techniques, diet, and the ingestion of potions in this search for everlasting life.

Another manifestation of this search for immortality was the building of 'replicas' of the three mystical islands in the Taiye Lake of the Shanglin in the hope of luring one or more of the Immortals to land there and divulge their secret. Which emperor it was who built these islands is unclear. Some authors say it was Shihuangdi (Tsu, 1988; Cheng, 1998), others say it was Gaozu (also known as Gaodi), the first Han emperor, (Qiao, 1982; Wang, J.C., 1998) or Wudi, the sixth Han emperor (Keswick, 1978; Titley & Wood, 1991). Anyway, whoever it was, this action established the 'lake with three islands' as a feature which has been reproduced ever since in Chinese gardens (fig. 2.2).

The mystical islands of the east were matched in the west by the Kunlun Mountains, the legendary home of Xiwangmu, the Queen Mother of the West, whose fabulous peach orchard produced fruits which bestowed immortality on those who

Figure 2.2 Island in the West Lake, Hangzhou

ate them. Before moving on, then, it seems appropriate to say something about mountains, artificial versions of which are also such a feature of Chinese gardens. In China animistic beliefs had invested mountains with magical powers in early times. Climbing them was the closest one could get to the heavens. They were the favoured resorts of hermits and, like the mystical isles, they were said to be the haunts of the Immortals.

Since many Chinese mountains have become landscapes altered by the presence of stairways, pavilions and temples, it seems pertinent here to mention the most famous. There are five mountains of particular significance to the Daoists—Song Shan in Henan (the Central Mountain) (fig. 2.3), Heng Shan in Shanxi the Northern Mountain), another Heng Shan in Hunan (the Southern Mountain), Hua Shan in Shaanxi (the Western Mountain), and Tai Shan in Shandong (the Eastern Mountain). These mountains were seen as standing at each corner and at the centre of the Chinese world. Emperors made pilgrimages to them and offered sacrifices, confirming the 'mandate of heaven' which had been conferred on them.

After the introduction of Buddhism to China, Chinese mountains also took on resonances with the Buddhist cosmic mountain, Mount Sumeru, and Mount Potalaka, the home of Guanyin. Thus famous Daoist mountains came to be shared with the Buddhists, who also established four sacred mountains of their own—Emei Shan in Sichuan, Wutai Shan in Shanxi, Jiuhua Shan in Anwhei, and Putuo Shan in Zhejiang. While few if any Chinese can have set foot

on all nine of these holy mountains, this feat was achieved in the years 1935–36 by Mary Mullikin and Anna Hotchkis, whose description of their travels makes interesting reading (Mullikin & Hotchkis, 1973).

As well as the nine famous mountains mentioned so far, there are numerous others scattered throughout the country which are less well known but are of similar significance. And, apart from the famous Buddhist and Daoist mountains, the Chinese have long admired the fantastic peaks of the Huang Shan, the countryside around Guilin, and the Stone Forest in Yunnan. It seems certain that these extraordinary landscapes have influenced the depiction of mountains in painting, poetry, prose and gardens.

Following the fall of the Han there was a period of disunity between the 3rd and 6th centuries, but the rulers of the various states continued to build luxurious gardens in their capitals. Men of letters, on the other hand, took to withdrawing from society in such times of upheaval in order to retain their integrity, often retiring to caves or huts in the mountains where they could behave as they wished and where contact with nature gave satisfaction and inspiration for their literary and artistic endeavours.

The archetype of this course of action was the famous scholar Tao Yuanming (365–427), who first gave poetic form to the ideal of a cultivated scholar's retreat. By nature he thought little of rank and was not prepared to be subservient to high officials. According to accounts in the Chinese literature, he gave up his position as a magistrate at Pengze in Jiangxi and retired to his farm near Lu Shan, where he grew

chrysanthemums in his simple garden (Davis, 1983). This type of eremitism, along with the rise of landscape poetry and painting, was amongst the influences which lay behind an increasing naturalism in garden design at this time. And it was Tao Yuanming's horticultural endeavour which, more than any other factor, popularised the cultivation of the chrysanthemum and established it as a symbol of moral integrity and the ability to survive adversity—the qualities of the ideal Confucian gentleman.

Tao Yuanming also achieved fame through his recounting of the story of the Peach Blossom Spring. According to this tale, a fisherman found a spring emerging from a cave behind a grove of blossoming peach trees on the bank of a river. Walking through the cave he perceived a faint light at the far end and emerged into a utopian world. As is usual in such stories, he was unable to find his way there again, but his adventure typifies the appealing idea of passing through space and time from one realm of existence to another, towards enlightenment, happiness, renewal and immortality. This story stimulated poets, painters and garden designers to create their ideal worlds. It is not surprising, then, that caves are often to be found in the artificial mountains in Chinese gardens and that in some cases it is possible to pass through them.

Quite apart from this, caves, grottoes and springs have taken on significance in China for other reasons. Certain Immortals were believed to live in caves, Buddhist monks practising austerities withdrew there, and hermits took shelter in them. Springs and pools, too, were seen as having mystical properties. Dragons were believed to dwell there and, as well as this, many of them ultimately achieved fame as sources of water of the highest quality for brewing tea.

Amongst the people from this period who have had a lasting influence on gardens, it would be remiss to omit mention of Wang Xizhi. He was a retired scholar of the landed gentry class who held a gathering of scholar friends at the Lanting (Orchid Pavilion) near Shaoxing, Zhejiang, in 353. At this gathering cups of wine were floated on a winding stream and the person in front of whom a cup stopped had to drink the wine and compose a poem. In later centuries men of letters constructed garden pavilions with channels cut in the floor so they could continue this tradition (fig. 2.4).

The trend towards more naturalistic and refined gardens continued during the short-lived Sui dynasty (581–618), when the country became unified once more. The emperor Yangdi (reigned 604–17) rebuilt the city of Luoyang and constructed an extravagant pleasure park, the Xiyuan (West Garden), on a scale comparable to that of the Shanglin of the Qin and Han. In this park a stream flowed south through 16 small gardens before joining a lake about 5 km in circumference in which there were the now-traditional three islands. The overall layout of the gardens, palaces and pavilions was said to be in harmony with the surrounding landscape. In winter, when the branches were bare, artificial flowers were tied to them, as has been mentioned in the previous chapter. This practice has continued here and there in China to this day, although it may not appeal to all Western eyes.

The succeeding Tang dynasty (618–907) was a period of peace and prosperity in which the arts reached new heights and several sizeable imperial parks were established in and

Figure 2.3 (left) Songyue Pagoda, Song Shan, Henan
Figure 2.4 (right) Floating cup stream in the Pavilion of the Ceremony of Purification, Palace of Tranquil Longevity, Forbidden City, Beijing

a collection of rare and beautiful rocks. In one of his poems he wrote, 'Why should I turn to famous mountains? All beautiful peaks are here' (Cheng, 1999). Also the first-known illustrations of dwarfed trees are in tomb paintings of this period, so it seems likely that the Chinese art of dwarfing trees and creating miniature landscapes in containers arose about this time. These dwarfed trees and miniature landscapes are called 'penjing', a word which means 'potted scenery', though such things are usually known in English by the Japanese name of 'bonsai' (fig. 2.5).

around the capital Chang'an (present-day Xi'an). According to Schafer (1968), the Tang royal parks were not as extravagant as those of the Han but they contained wheat fields, orchards, flower gardens, mews, kennels and even tiger pens. The period was also notable in that the empress Wu Zetian (reigned 690–705) appears to have been the first ruler to have established a 'summer palace' in the hills, to which she removed the entire court to avoid the heat of the plains. A thousand years later several such summer palaces were to be built by the Qing emperors, who also moved the court each summer. Also, according to J.C. Wang (1998), the most famous of the Tang imperial parks, the Furongyuan (Hibiscus Garden), was opened to the public on holidays, setting a precedent for imperially owned public parks.

During the Tang, Chang'an, which lay at the eastern end of the Silk Road, became a cosmopolitan city with many foreign traders and artisans. As a result it was a time when China came under outside influences, and when many exotic plants, animals and birds were introduced. It was also the golden age of Chinese poetry. Its poets not only wrote poems about beautiful landscapes but also built gardens in the countryside. For example, Wang Wei (699–759) immortalised his retreat, the Wangchuan Villa, in both a much-copied hand scroll and in poems, imbuing it with a feeling of tranquillity and spirituality. This, together with the character of the man who made it, has ensured its lasting influence on gardens in China.

It seems to have been in the Tang that the fashion arose for displaying rocks in gardens. Yet another poet, Li Deyu (787–849)—who, incidentally, was one of the first people to record the growing of azaleas—ornamented his garden with

The vogue for ornamenting gardens with interestingly shaped rocks reached new heights during the Northern Song in the extraordinary garden of the emperor Huizong (reigned 1101–1125) at his capital Kaifeng (known then as Bianjing). This was the Genyue (Longevity Mountain), a garden consisting mainly of a rock-studded landscape representing mountains, rivers and gorges. A special bureau—the Huashigang (Flower and Rock Network)—was set up in Suzhou to search for trees, flowers and rocks which were sent to Kaifeng in barges towed along rivers and canals. Apparently Huizong had thousands of rocks brought from Suzhou and Huzhou to be used in the construction of his garden. There were pavilions built on the peaks, mansions on the level ground, orchards of apricots and plums, and even a farm. Rare plants were collected from all over the empire and there were birds and animals as well. There were miniature replicas of many of the most admired landscapes in the realm and, together with the plants and animals, it could be seen to represent not only the empire but also, perhaps, the universe (Hargett, 1988–89). While not on as grand a scale as the Shanglin, this garden was considered to surpass all previous imperial gardens in its aesthetic effect. Unfortunately it was destroyed soon after its completion when the city was captured by the Jurchen invaders. After the fall of Kaifeng the administrative centre of China was never to return to the Yellow River valley. The court fled south and established the Southern Song dynasty (1127–1279) with Hangzhou (then known as Li'nan) as its capital.

During the Northern Song there were also many private gardens in Kaifeng and Luoyang. In fact the period has been seen by some authors as the golden age of Chinese gardening. Scholar-officials began building retreats in the cities, finding that they could reproduce nature and create an illusion of escape without having to move off to the mountains. And since the population of the cities was growing and land was becoming expensive, gardens were built on a small scale but with many different types of scenery arranged within them. These gardens have survived only as literary descriptions, as for example in Li Gefei's *Luoyang mingyuan ji* (Notes on the Famous Gardens of Luoyang), and it seems that, as in other eras, not all of them were free from extravagance and ostentation.

One of the most famous of the Luoyang gardens was that of Fu Bie, which had a lake, bridge, roofed walkway, halls, pavilions on hilltops, bamboos, trees, flowers and a view of the whole garden from the top of a rockery (Cheng, 1999). In sharp contrast to this was the Duleyuan (Garden of Solitary Enjoyment) of Sima Guang (1020–86), a composition of great simplicity which has already been mentioned in the previous chapter. In it there was an extensive collection of medicinal plants but very few flowers. Also Sima Guang had planted bamboos in a circle and tied their tops together to make a rustic pavilion. Although this garden appears to have been the least pretentious of those in Luoyang at the time, it was much visited on account of Sima Guang's reputation. While its nature may perhaps have resulted from a degree of snobbishness on the part of its creator, Sima Guang's descriptions of his garden and his life in it, like those of Wang Wei in the Tang, have made it one of the most influential historical gardens in China.

Although I am conscious that the introduction to this chapter may already have outlived its welcome, in order to prepare the reader for what follows I have thought it prudent, in conclusion, to say something about the gardens of temples. Taking a broad view, I have included in this book not only Daoist and Buddhist temples and monasteries, but memorial temples and shrines, mosques, and even a Christian church. As far as layout is concerned, they all resemble the traditional Chinese house, with a series of courtyards arranged along one or more axes, usually running south-north (fig. 2.6). However, the courtyards tend to be larger and, although symmetrically arranged, very often

Figure 2.6 The library, Xiangguo Temple, Kaifeng

contain a greater array of plants and features. Like some of the larger houses, temples may also have a separate area developed as a garden or as an enclosure for penjing. And in some there are the remains of the 'travelling palaces' of the Qing emperors.

The location of so many famous Daoist temples in mountain environments has its origin in the ancient worship of nature. These temples and their gardens are often reached by a long and arduous ascent, symbolic of the effort required to communicate with the Immortals. And it would appear that in building their temples the Buddhists followed suit when choosing sites. Respect for nature has also meant that the grounds belonging to and surrounding temples have often been left as natural forest, and thus they have played an important conservation role—as noted by Rebecca Cotton (1999). In some places a natural spring was incorporated in the grounds and used to feed a small stream which ran through the enclosure. Such temples have long attracted visitors not only on account of their religious significance but also because of the natural beauty of their sites—a combination of plants, water, mountains and views. In cities, on the other hand, temple gardens were often the only areas of green

space available to many people until the appearance of public parks in the 20th century. Their trees and flowers continue to be greatly appreciated by visitors and certain temples have become renowned for particular plants.

The gardens of temples and monasteries are also of significance in that preserved there, as Mrs Little (1905) and many others have noted, are trees that have survived to a remarkable age—something impossible almost everywhere else in a country starved of fuel and building materials. Just as articles tempered by time were considered more pleasing to the eyes of Chinese men of taste than new ones, the most valued of all plants in Chinese gardens are old trees (fig. 2.7). These have been admired, and even worshipped, since ancient times. Venerable trees clinging to mountainsides are seen as symbols of longevity and the ability to endure hardship. They are a common feature in landscape paintings and trees of this type are treasured in gardens, even when they begin to die back. They are often retained after they have died completely, and are used as supports for wisterias and other vines. The respect for old trees is such that in gardens and parks all over China trees believed to be 100 years old or more are recorded and have labels affixed to their trunks.

Figure 2.7 **Thuja (*Platycladus orientalis*) reputed to be over 2000 years old, Songyang Academy, Song Shan, Henan**

In temple gardens not only are there specimens of trees traditionally planted there—pines, thujas, junipers, ginkgos and Chinese horse chestnuts, for example—but other plants which it would appear monks have brought into cultivation. Daoist monks, for instance, began cultivating many plants used for preparing what they believed to be life-prolonging potions. As well as this, it seems that many garden plants were first cultivated by monks and that gardening monks were responsible for moving them around the country. It is believed, too, that Buddhist monks were responsible for the introduction of many Chinese garden plants to Japan.

It is interesting that in Cao Xueqin's novel, *The Story of the Stone*, Grandmother Jia, when visiting the nun Adamantina in her Green Bower Hermitage, is moved to remark 'Monks and nuns always have the best-kept gardens. They have nothing else to do with their time.' This suggests that it was generally held that monks and nuns were good gardeners. Apparently some of them were garden designers too, as it is recorded, for instance, that the gardens of several Buddhist institutions were remodelled during the late Ming by the monk Shilian (Clunas, 1996).

After 1949 religion was frowned upon by the Communist authorities. Temples were closed, their property confiscated, and their occupants dispersed. Many were pulled down and others converted to alternative uses. Attacks on temples were especially fierce during the Cultural Revolution, but after Mao's death these policies were gradually relaxed. Surviving temples have been restored as tourist attractions and many have become active once more.

Shaanxi

Shaanxi was the scene of much of China's early history, particularly in the valley of the Wei, a major tributary of the Yellow River. It is not surprising, then, that it was in the area around Xi'an that imperial hunting parks, palaces, lakes and gardens were built from at least as early as the Zhou until the fall of the Tang. However, little remains of all this other than a few minor relics, a lake or two, and a great many tombs. It seems to have been here that the pattern for the layout of tombs of members of imperial families began to be established. These days, by far the best known of these imperial tombs is the first—that of the Qin emperor Shihuangdi, with its buried army of terracotta warriors arranged to the east of the burial mound. This site is east of the city, south of the

Figure 2.8 Pomegranate at the Huaqing Hot Springs, Xi'an, said to have been painted by Yang Guifei in the 8th century

Wei River at the foot of Li Shan. To the north of the river are many Han and Tang tombs. These were originally surrounded by walls and the enclosed areas included buildings, statues, trees and plants. Thus these spaces could be regarded as gardens.

It was under the Han that early contacts were made with central Asia. The first introduction of exotic plants to China of which there is a known record is the bringing of lucerne (alfalfa) and grapes from that region in 126 BC. The establishment of the Silk Road—the caravan route which connected Chang'an with the Mediterranean—was undoubtedly responsible for the movement of plants in both directions. Pomegranates (fig. 2.8) are first recorded in China in the late 3rd century, and walnuts and many other plants followed soon after. Thus Chang'an became an important point of entry for exotic plants.

Today in the countryside around Xi'an wheat is the principal cereal crop, and apples, pears, peaches, apricots, persimmons, Chinese dates, walnuts, grapes, occasional plantations of Chinese gooseberries, and a small amount of rape are all to be seen. Of particular note, in view of the region's history, is the presence of numerous pomegranate orchards. These are conspicuous, for instance, along the road leading from the city to the army of terracotta warriors. There are said to be two main kinds, sweet and sour, one used for eating, the other, which is the higher priced, for medicinal purposes. Paulownias are grown, too, but not in the immense numbers seen in Henan, and white cedars (*Melia azedarach*) are planted here and there.

In Shaanxi there must still be gardens other than those described below, particularly in the grounds of temples. It would be interesting, for instance, to go to Hua Shan, the western sacred Daoist mountain 120 km east of X'ian. It has five peaks, the highest being 2200 m, and it can now be ascended by cable car. It was amongst the sites visited by the Rev. Alexander Williamson (1870) in the 1860s while on one of his tract and bible-selling expeditions. At that time its temples had been largely destroyed by the Mohammedans, whose mosques he saw in Xi'an and which he stated to be the oldest in China.

Xi'an and Environs

Xi'an today spreads far beyond the Ming walls enclosing the centre of the city. The principal street trees are sophoras, planes, poplars and, not surprisingly, pomegranates, which have become the floral emblem of the city. Many cultivars are grown for ornament, including singles and doubles, both red and white, and a double with variegated flowers which appears to be the same as that known in the West as 'Legrelliae' (fig. 2.14). The dwarf kind is also grown.

As mentioned above, there were many imperial and private gardens in and around Chang'an in earlier periods, but little remains of any of this. Nor for that matter is there now any evidence of the beautiful private parks and mansions with ancient trees in their courtyards of a century ago mentioned by William Geil (1911). There are only a few gardens in Xi'an today and, of these, by far the most interesting is that of the Great Mosque in the centre of the walled city. There are also two small parks within the walled area, and outside the south-western corner of the walls a much larger park, the Xingqing Palace Park. A short distance from the South Gate is the Small Goose Pagoda, and about 3 km further south is the Big Goose Pagoda, both of which stand in extensive

grounds. Further south still is the Xi'an Botanical Garden.

Other than visits to the tomb of Shihuangdi and the terracotta army, excursions to the east of the city include those to the Banpo Museum and the Huaqing Hot Springs, while to the north-west, on the other side of the Wei River, are the impressive Han and Tang tombs.

DA QINGZHENSI (GREAT MOSQUE)

There are said to be at least 30 000 Moslems in Xi'an, and hence this is a very active mosque. It was founded in 742, during the Tang when the city was full of foreign Moslems. Although it has been repeatedly restored, the layout, on an east-west axis, is believed to be Ming, dating from 1392. The buildings in Chinese style are arranged along the central axis and lateral boundaries, and appear to be much the same as those shown in the photograph taken at the beginning of the 20th century and included in Boerschmann's *Old China in Historic Photographs* (1982). Most of the area, however, is taken up with symmetrically arranged gardens in the four courtyards which the buildings surround. There are huge old gleditsias and ailanthuses, as well as wintersweets, jujubes, modern roses, and waterlilies in large basins of stone and iron. An old wooden archway stands in the first courtyard and beyond it is a five-roomed hall. In the middle of the second courtyard there is an elaborate stone gateway built in the Ming (1368–1644). The minaret, in the form of a three-storeyed pagoda, stands in the centre of the third courtyard and immediately to the west of this is the hexagonal Phoenix Pavilion. On either side of the pavilion, flights of steps lead up through a pair of stone pailous to the fourth courtyard, a large stone terrace on which stands the prayer hall, which only Moslems may enter. This terrace is ornamented with stone basins and potted plants, including a pair of ginkgos which have had their branches intertwined lattice-fashion to create vase shapes (fig. 2.9). On a lower level on either side are wooden frames over which honeysuckle (*Lonicera japonica*) is growing. With its history, interesting buildings and planting, and Chinese Moslems in white gowns and caps walking to and from prayers, this garden has a presence all its own.

XINGQING GONGYUAN (XINGQING PARK)

This large park just outside the south-eastern corner of the city wall is the site of the Xingqing Palace of the Tang emperor Xuanzong (reigned 712–56). It consists principally of a large lake around which there are modern buildings in

Figure 2.9 (right) Terrace in front of the prayer hall, Great Mosque, Xi'an, with a vase-shaped ginkgo in the foreground

Figure 2.10 (below)

Xingqing Park, Xi'an

Figure 2.11 (below) Big Goose Pagoda, Xi'an

classical style (fig. 2.10). It has been planted with trees and shrubs, chiefly robinias, junipers, *Acer truncatum*, *Cercis chinensis*, and flowering peaches, including a group of a purple-leaved cultivar. The lake is edged with weeping willows and, although the standard of maintenance is not high, the park, with its historic associations, has a peaceful atmosphere.

DAYANTA (BIG GOOSE PAGODA)

It is not clear how or when this square brick pagoda was given its unusual name. It is all that remains of a temple built here in 647 by the emperor Gaozong in honour of his mother prior to his accession. The seven-storey pagoda is 64 m tall and was built soon after the founding of the temple as a fireproof store in which to house sutras brought back by a monk who had travelled to India (fig. 2.11). Like all old buildings in China it has had its ups and downs, but it is now in a much better state than that shown in a photograph taken almost a century ago (Boerschmann, 1982).

The Ci'en Temple, of which it forms part, was originally large with many buildings and courtyards, but most of the site is now open space treated as a garden in contemporary style. Amongst the plants

Figure 2.12 Small Goose Pagoda, Xi'an

with paulownias, persimmons, walnuts, thujas, junipers, pomegranates, and tall privets (*Ligustrum lucidum*). As the grounds have not been spruced up to attract tourists in the way they have at the Big Goose Pagoda, it is a much quieter and more appealing place

XI'AN ZHIWUYUAN (XI'AN BOTANICAL GARDEN)

This garden of about 20 hectares was founded in 1959 and is not far south of the Big Goose Pagoda. Although like almost all Chinese botanical gardens it does not have the funds to allow it to be maintained to quite the standard of most botanical gardens elsewhere, it has some excellent collections. There are medicinal plants, a lotus pond, wisteria pergolas, cultivars of *Prunus mume*, tree and herbaceous peonies, Chinese rose species—including both the single and double forms of *Rosa roxburghii*—and a large area devoted to gymnosperms, trees, and shrubs, mostly of Chinese origin. At the time of my visit, in late May, *Syringa reticulata*, *Philadelphus pekinensis* (fig. 2.13), and pomegranates were in bloom in this section. The pomegranates included a plant with red flowers, each with many more petals than the double red cultivar usually seen.

BANPO BOWUGUAN (BANPO MUSEUM)

This museum incorporates the site of the Banpo Neolithic Village, which was discovered in 1953 and dates back to about 4500 BC. It may seem odd that I have included it here, but I have done so for two reasons. Firstly, the roofed-over excavated area is approached through a large courtyard with single-storey museum buildings along its left and right sides. This courtyard is arranged as a modern formal garden, largely planted with a collection of pomegranate cultivars (fig. 2.14). It is well cared for and at flowering time it is worth visiting for these alone. Secondly, the entrance to the 'Matriarchal Clan Village' on the terrace overlooking the garden at its far end is a fascinating example of modern Chinese taste (fig. 2.15). I am sorry I was not brave enough to enter, as *China*, the Lonely Planet guide (Storey et al.,1998), tells me that it is staffed by 'matriarchs in Neolithic garb, high heels and reinforced stockings'.

are persimmons, double pink oleanders, modern roses, a soap-pod tree (*Gleditsia sinensis*), a large paulownia, and, in front of the principal hall at the rear of the compound, two potted ginkgos trained into vase shapes like the ones at the mosque.

XIAOYANTA (SMALL GOOSE PAGODA)

The Small Goose Pagoda stands in the grounds of the Jianfu Temple which was founded in 684, also by Gaozong. The pagoda is square, built of brick, and was originally 15 storeys high, but earthquake damage has left only 13. At about 45 m it is not as tall as the Big Goose Pagoda but is a more elegant structure (fig. 2.12). Again it is not clear how it received its name but perhaps it was just by association with its larger neighbour. It dates from 707 and also was built as a fireproof store in which to house sutras brought from India.

Again relatively few temple buildings remain, although there is a large bronze bell cast in 1192. Most of the area is a garden in which there are many more large trees than at the Big Goose Pagoda. There are several ancient sophoras, along

Figure 2.13 (right)

Philadelphus
pekinensis, Xi'an
Botanical Garden

Figure 2.14 (far right)

Pomegranate
'Legrelliae', Banpo
Museum near Xi'an

Figure 2.15 (below)

Entrance to the
Matriarchal Clan
Village, Banpo
Museum

77

HUAQINGCHI (HUAQING POOL)

This site, popularly known as the Huaqing Hot Springs, is at the foot of Li Shan, not far from the terracotta army. Water from the hot springs here has been channelled into baths from early times. The first villa was built here during the Zhou, Shihuangdi had a residence here, and so did the Han emperor Wudi. However, nowadays the place is chiefly associated with Xuanzong. He enlarged the palace originally built here by his great grandfather, Taizong, the first Tang emperor. Xuanzong spent the winters here with his favourite concubine, Yang Guifei, whose adopted son led an uprising against him. As a result he was eventually obliged to order her execution. This, together with his subsequent decline and death, became a favourite subject of Chinese romantic poetry and painting.

What remains of this historic site has now become a park, restored and opened to the public in 1956. Near the entrance is a large pool planted with waterlilies and with an octagonal pavilion on the terrace above it on the far side (fig. 2.16). This scene has not, I fear, been improved by the modern marble boat on the right-hand side and a white statue of Yang Guifei, rising from the water and far less plump than tradition would have her. Further on are other spaces, in one of which a pavilion, now a tea house, sits picturesquely in the middle of a pool. Overhanging the pool is a pomegranate said to have been painted by Yang Guifei—one of several in the grounds claimed to have been planted during the Tang (fig. 2.8). Beyond this again are buildings housing two ancient marble bathing pools which have been excavated. That the larger rectangular one was used by Xuanzong and the smaller, in the shape of a begonia blossom, by Yang Guifei is a claim about

Figure 2.16 Main pond at the Huaqing Hot Springs

Figure 2.17 (right) View of garden at the tomb of Huo Qubing near Xi'an

which the visitor is entitled to make up his or her own mind. Nearby is a small building containing the bedroom where Chiang Kai-shek stayed in 1936 while in Xi'an to direct an offensive against the Communists.

There are various other spaces and courtyards which on the whole have been planted in modern style with both red and white pomegranates, *Viburnum odoratissimum*, purple bougainvillea in pots, modern roses, and hedges of *Euonymus japonicus*.

MAOLING AND THE TOMB OF GENERAL HUO QUBING

To include these places in a book about gardens may seem an indulgence. However, although all their buildings, walls and plants have long since gone, it was from the imperial tombs of the Han and Tang that the design of the tombs of the imperial families of later dynasties evolved, as has been mentioned above. Many of these can certainly be classified as gardens. Also the construction of artificial mountains over the graves may possibly have been to suggest the home of the Immortals.

There are nine Han tombs near Xi'an, none of which has been excavated. All that remains in each case is a mound. Of these Maoling, the tomb of the emperor Wudi (died 87 BC) is the one usually visited. It is a large trapezoid mound 40 km north-west of the city. Until recently it was bare, but it has now been densely planted with young thujas—the tree traditionally planted on the grave mounds of emperors. Nearby is the tomb of one of his generals, Huo Qubing (died 117 BC). Although not excavated, the site has been developed as a modern garden, overlooked by a pavilion which has been built on top of the grave mound (fig. 2.17). From this pavilion there is also a view of Han grave mounds in the neighbouring countryside.

The garden itself is perfectly symmetrical and seems French or Italian in its inspiration. I was struck by the resemblance of the layout to that of the Villa Garzoni in Tuscany,

though this must surely be accidental. Inside the gate there is a large circular basin with an arrangement of rocks at its centre. On either side of this and the central axis are matching flower beds, pavilions, and clipped shrubs, some in the form of animals. The flower beds are edged with neat hedges and contain herbaceous peonies, modern roses, and other plants. And on the path up to the top of the mound there are roses with small leaves and pale yellow, double flowers, rather like *Rosa xanthina* but flowering later. However, the most remarkable features of this extraordinary garden are the roofed walkways on either side of the mound in which huge stone statues of animals and human figures found at the site are displayed (fig. 2.18). These are the forerunners of those used

Figure 2.18 Stone animals, tomb of Huo Qubing

to line the 'spirit roads' of later tombs—a feature which developed during the Tang and reached its greatest expression in the Ming tombs of Nanjing and Beijing.

QIANLING

This is the tomb built for the Tang emperor Gaozong (died 683) and his empress Wu Zetian (died 705). It is 85 km northwest of Xi'an and was built on a natural hill. It is approached by a straight road 3 km long which rises up between two artificial mounds on which towers were constructed, one of which has recently been rebuilt. At this point two obelisks mark the beginning of the spirit road, a succession of stone animals and human figures lining the approach to the tomb mound (fig. 2.19). Notable amongst these are the pair of winged horses at the beginning and the two curious ostrich-like birds which follow. These are thought to represent the 'vermilion bird', symbol of the south. On the left in front of the mound is a stele inscribed with a eulogy of Gaozong and, on the right, the stele known as the 'stele with no inscription' was intended to have one for Wu Zetian. Beyond these are the remains of two more towers and beyond them two groups of now-headless statues representing the foreign delegates who attended Gaozong's funeral. Beyond these again, in front of the enormous tomb mound, are two huge stone lions, a stele erected by the Qing emperor Qianlong, and the remains of the Hall of Offerings.

Originally this whole enormous complex was surrounded by a double wall many kilometres long. With its buildings and trees intact it must have been an astonishing composition. Other Tang tombs were even larger. For instance Zhaoling, the tomb of the second Tang emperor, Taizong (died 649), was surrounded by a wall approximately 60 km long. These amazing creations were systematically destroyed when the Tang fell. However, a certain amount of restoration work has taken place and a visit to Qianling and to the nearby tomb of Princess Yongtai (died 701), which has been excavated revealing wonderful murals, conjures up a vision of their original magnificence.

Henan

With the recent separation of Chongqing from Sichuan, Henan, with close to 100 million people, is now China's most populous province. Archaeological evidence indicates that it was here that the Shang dynasty arose from an earlier neolithic culture. Following the fall of the Shang, later dynasties continued to establish their capitals in Henan or near Xi'an in neighbouring Shaanxi. As far as gardens are concerned, Henan's periods of greatest significance were undoubtedly during the Tang—when Luoyang was the secondary capital—and the Northern Song—when the capital was at Kaifeng and Luoyang continued to flourish. Also the slopes and surrounds

Figure 2.19 Qianling, tomb of Gaozong and Wu Zetian

of Song Shan, which lies between Zhengzhou and Luoyang, have been home to important Daoist and Buddhist temples for more than 2000 years.

As in Shaanxi, wheat is the principal crop in Henan in the cooler part of the year, followed by maize, soybeans, sweet potatoes and cotton in summer. Apple, pear, peach and apricot orchards are common, there are occasional vineyards, and Chinese dates (*Ziziphus jujuba*) are grown extensively around the capital Zhengzhou. Paulownias (*P. elongata*) are widely planted in the countryside and, at the time of my visit, occasional plots of the tree peony cultivar 'White Phoenix' were in bloom amongst the wheat fields. Presumably they were being grown for danpi, the root bark which is used in Chinese traditional medicine. And in various places I saw flooded fields in which lotuses were being grown to produce the leaves, seeds and roots used so widely in Chinese cookery.

Luoyang

Luoyang is in north-western Henan on the banks of the Luo, a tributary of the Yellow River. It was the capital of nine dynasties, beginning in 770 BC when the Zhou built a walled city there, remains of which have been found beneath the present Wangcheng Park. It flourished under the Northern Wei (one of the Six Dynasties), when they made it their capital (494–534), and it later became the capital of the Sui. After the fall of the Sui it became the secondary capital of the Tang, and eventually the principal capital during the last years of the dynasty. It was near Luoyang in the 9th century that the poet Li Deyu built his garden ornamented with unusual rocks.

Luoyang remained a city of importance during the Northern Song, when the capital was transferred to Kaifeng. It was during this period that it became renowned for its gardens, many of which are described in Li Gefei's *Luoyang mingyuan ji* (Notes on the Famous Gardens of Luoyang). These have all gone and the city's fame these days rests chiefly on the Buddhist sculptures of the Northern Wei, Sui, and Tang, carved from the cliffs lining the Yi River at nearby Longmen, and on its reputation as a centre of tree peony culture.

The Tang empress Wu Zetian (reigned 690–705), who built a palace here, is credited with introducing the tree peonies, which had already become fashionable in the capital, Chang'an. Their introduction to Luoyang became the basis of a tradition that the empress had banished them to Luoyang because, in Chang'an, they had refused to obey her command to bloom in early spring at the same time as the

Figure 2.20 'Yao Huang', a tree peony known in the 11th century

wintersweet. Anyway, whatever the reason, Luoyang became the main centre of tree peony culture in the 10th and 11th centuries. Our chief source of knowledge about this lies in various books written at the time about the flowers and plants of Luoyang, in particular Ouyang Xiu's *Luoyang mudan ji* (Account of the Tree Peonies of Luoyang) written in 1034. In this book he described, amongst other things, how flowers of the finest varieties—'Yao Huang' ('Yao's Yellow') and 'Wei Hua' ('Wei's Flower'), a soft pink—were sent to the Song emperor at Kaifeng, packed in bamboo cages filled with cabbage leaves (Needham, 1986). These two varieties are still grown today (fig. 2.20). The tree peony is regarded as the 'king of flowers', a symbol of riches, aristocracy and the yang principle, and in 1994 was chosen to be the national flower.

As a result of its tree peony heritage and with the aim of improving the prosperity of the city, the local authorities in recent years have set about making Luoyang once more a centre of tree peony culture. A tree peony festival is held annually from 15 to 25 April each year, and this attracts thousands of visitors. Tree peonies are planted along Zhongzhou Lu, the main thoroughfare, and planes, deodars, paulownias and sophoras are used as street trees throughout the city. The principal gardens open to the public are Wangcheng Park, the tree peony gardens in the northern suburbs, and the garden of the Baima Temple east of the city.

WANGCHENG GONGYUAN (ROYAL CITY PARK)

This park is situated on Zhongzhou Lu to the west of the city centre and is the city's chief recreational space as well as being the focus of the Tree Peony Festival (figs 1.2, 2.21). It is a large, well-worn park through which the Jian River, a tributary of the Luo, winds. Also in this park are a children's playground, a small zoo, an aquarium and other 'attractions'. There are said to be more than 20 000 peony plants in over 300 varieties. These are planted in beds on both sides of the Jian River, which can be crossed by a bridge or by chairlift—an invention which seems to have captured the Chinese imagination.

Apart from the tree peonies, there is an array of Chinese and introduced plants, including crepe myrtles, flowering peaches, forsythias, wintersweets, flowering quinces, magnolias, maples, *Viburnum odoratissimum*, *Hibiscus syriacus*, *Spiraea cantoniensis*, *Photinia serrulata*, and both the single and double forms of *Rosa xanthina*.

GUOSE MUDANYUAN
(BEAUTY OF THE EMPIRE TREE PEONY GARDEN)

This garden is in the northern suburbs of the city at a slightly higher altitude than the city centre, hence the tree peonies here bloom a little later (fig. 2.22). It covers a large area and is divided into three separate sections in which there is an enormous number of plants in about 400 varieties, all labelled. In the area furthest from the entrance there is a large block of 'White Phoenix', the variety principally grown to produce the danpi mentioned above. This peony probably should not have a cultivar name since the plants are grown from seed and are variable. It is now considered to be a distinct species, *Paeonia ostii*. There are also many herbaceous peonies, which flower a little later and so extend the period of the display. Additional features are an artificial hill with a pavilion on top and a wisteria pergola which leads to another pavilion.

LUOYANG MUDANYUAN
(LUOYANG TREE PEONY GARDEN)

Within walking distance of the Beauty of the Empire Tree Peony Garden and on the same road, this garden appears to have been planted recently. As its centrepiece it has a large white statue of the Mother of the Peonies (fig. 2.23). Here again there is a vast number of different varieties, including some I did not see elsewhere. The plots are separated by fences on which grape vines are growing, and there are also herbaceous peonies, flowering peaches and both weeping and contorted willows.

Figure 2.21 (above left) **Entrance to Wangcheng Park, Luoyang, at the time of the tree peony festival**
Figure 2.22 (left) **Beauty of the Empire Tree Peony Garden, Luoyang**
Figure 2.23 (right) **Mother of the Peonies, Luoyang Tree Peony Garden**

Figure 2.24 (above) **Uppermost terrace, Baima Temple, Luoyang, showing a wintersweet and an old juniper supporting a trumpet vine (*Campsis grandiflora*)**

Figure 2.25 (left) **Scene on the main axis of the Baima Temple, Luoyang**

BAIMASI (WHITE HORSE TEMPLE)

The Baimasi was established by the Han emperor Mingdi (reigned 57–75) a few kilometres east of the present city and, although Buddhism is believed to have been introduced a couple of centuries earlier, it is the oldest known Buddhist foundation in China. It is said that the emperor dreamt of a foreign god and sent envoys to the Western Regions in search of him. They returned to Luoyang on white horses, bringing with them Buddhist sutras and images (Yang, 1984). The temple was built to house the sutras and two Indian monks who had been brought back with them. These monks were accommodated on a terrace, where they translated the sutras.

The temple grounds are large and the principal buildings are laid out as usual along a north-south axis. Outside the gate are two stone horses, possibly Song in date. Inside, in the

south-eastern and south-western corners of the grounds, are two tombs, said to be those of the Indian monks. In the Hall of Celestial Guardians and the Great Hall, the principal statues stand beneath fine Ming carved and gilded canopies and in the hall behind are 18 exceptionally beautiful lohans, believed to be Yuan. The lohans were the followers of the Buddha who were entrusted with remaining in the world to sustain the teaching. Steps behind this lead up to a terrace, claimed to be the one where the monks translated the sutras. On this terrace are a pair of wintersweets and two ancient junipers, up one of which climbs a trumpet creeper (*Campsis grandiflora*), which also appears to be very old (fig. 2.24).

Elsewhere in the courtyards along the main axis there are ginkgos, bamboos, chrysanthemums, pomegranates, thujas, deodars, Japanese cherries and tree peonies (fig. 2.25). On either side of the main axis are two large rectangular gardens planted with tree and herbaceous peonies and modern roses. Each of these gardens is divided into four by paths at the intersection of which is a double-roofed, octagonal pavilion. At the southern end of the garden on the eastern side there is a mulberry said to be more than 400 years old.

Song Shan

Song Shan is near Dengfeng, about 70 km south-east of Luoyang. At 1440 m it is not a high mountain and is almost totally devoid of tree cover. However it is the central mountain of the five Daoist sacred mountains to which the emperors of the past made ceremonial visits. Amongst those to go to Song Shan were the Han emperor Wudi in 110 BC and the Tang empress Wu Zetian, who made several visits. The mountain also attracted Buddhists and, according to Wood (1992), Wu Zetian frequently stayed at the Songyue Temple when she went there. This was built during the Northern Wei period as an imperial residence, later becoming a Buddhist temple. All that remains now of the original temple is the brick pagoda built in 523. This is possibly the oldest surviving pagoda in China and is picturesquely situated at the head of a valley with the mountain rising behind (fig. 2.3). These days, as far as gardens are concerned, the mountain's principal attractions are the Zhongyue Temple, the Shaolin Temple, and the Songyang Academy.

ZHONGYUEMIAO (TEMPLE OF THE CENTRAL MOUNTAIN)

This Daoist temple was established under the Qin, though the present buildings date from the late 18th century. Although it is the largest temple in Henan, it is visited mainly by people who still have Daoist beliefs. This, together with the fact that the buildings are slightly run down and it is avoided by most foreign tour groups, gives it a certain genuineness and quiet charm.

Outside the gate is the usual array of stalls selling everything from incense sticks to brassieres and, inside to the right, are four iron statues of guardian figures, accurate

representations of 11th-century soldiers, cast in 1064 (Wood, 1992). It is said that touching them makes you strong, pressing a defective body part against them will result in a cure, and that if you walk towards one of them with your eyes shut and manage to touch it you will have good luck. Consequently this part of the temple grounds presents a lively sight.

The large enclosures which surround the principal buildings are thickly planted with thujas, many of which are said to date from the Tang and Song. They are certainly old and several of them have marvellously contorted trunks (fig. 2.26). As a result of the Chinese penchant for seeing resemblances, some of them have been labelled with names such

Figure 2.26 **Old thuja, Zhongyue Temple, Song Shan**

as 'The Monkey' and 'A Sheep Asleep in a Cave'. As well as the old thujas there are also junipers and wutongs (*Firmiana simplex*). All this, together with the temple buildings, their contents, the devout visitors and glimpses of the mountain rising behind, creates a picturesque scene.

SONGYANGJIAN (SONGYANG ACADEMY)

This is one of China's most famous academies. It was established in the early Song and housed in a temple founded in 484. One of its courtyards is notable for two ancient thujas, which it is claimed were seen by the emperor Wudi when he came to Song Shan in 110 BC, though how they came to be incorporated in the grounds of a temple founded six centuries later is not clear. Apparently there were originally three, to each of which he gave the title of General. Those surviving are the first and second generals. The first general is leaning at a precarious angle but looks reasonably healthy. The second is much larger and, although hollow and split, shows no signs of dying (fig. 2.7). Whatever the truth of all this, they are probably amongst the oldest surviving cultivated trees in China.

Osmanthuses, tree peonies and *Cercis chinensis* are conspicuous amongst the plants in other courtyards. And, again, the famous mountain rising behind provides an imposing backdrop.

SHAOLINSI (SHAOLIN TEMPLE)

The Shaolin Temple was founded in 495 and in 527 an Indian monk, Bodhidharma—founder of the Chan (Zen) school of Buddhism—is supposed to have come here after crossing the Yellow River on a single reed and to have spent nine years sitting facing a wall. Nowadays the temple is chiefly famous for the martial arts practised by the monks, supposedly to help their concentration while meditating. As a result the Shaolin Temple has become a major tourist attraction and a small town has sprung up around it. There are martial arts academies and monks give demonstrations to tour groups.

The temple buildings were restored in the 18th century and the name board over the gate is in the emperor Kangxi's calligraphy. In 1928 most of the buildings were burned down by the warlord Shi Yousan and presumably the restorations did not escape the attention of the Red Guards in the early 1970s. However, amongst the present buildings, the Thousand Buddha Hall at the rear of the complex is said to

be Ming and has interesting frescoes depicting, on one side, 500 lohans paying homage to Vairocana and, on the other, 13 martial monks rescuing a Tang emperor. The smaller building in front of this hall appears also to have escaped destruction. It is claimed to be Qing, and has a name board in Qianlong's calligraphy.

In the entrance courtyard, with drum and bell towers rising above it on either side, a collection of old stone steles is arranged amongst thujas and ginkgos, the largest of which is said to be 1400 years old (fig. 2.27). The trees in other courtyards include wutongs, walnuts, sophoras, *Cercis chinensis*, and a specimen of the Chinese quince (*Pseudocydonia sinensis*), the bark of which is handsomely mottled with orange and grey.

Up the road a little is the temple's graveyard, known as the Talin (Forest of Stupas), where there are more than 200 brick stupas in various styles containing the remains of notable monks and dating from the Tang to the present. These are in a garden setting and are an interesting sight (fig. 2.28).

Figure 2.27 (below) Ginkgo said to be 1400 years old, Shaolin Temple, Song Shan

Figure 2.28 (right) Forest of Stupas, Shaolin Temple

Kaifeng

Kaifeng, which lies just south of the Yellow River about 200 km east of Luoyang, is the site of the capitals of several early kingdoms. It reached its greatest importance as the capital of the Northern Song dynasty from 960 until 1126, when it was captured by the invading Jurchen and the court was forced to flee south to Hangzhou. Kaifeng has also been a source of fascination to Westerners on account of its historic Jewish community. It is not clear when they arrived and, like the Moslem Chinese in China proper, they are of Han Chinese appearance.

As well as the destruction brought about by the Jurchen, Kaifeng has more than once been devastated by the flooding of the Yellow River. Most of the buildings were destroyed when the dikes were deliberately breached in 1642, either by the rebel forces opposing the Ming or by the defenders of the city. It was flooded again in 1855 when the river changed course and, as a result of these catastrophes, little remains of its former magnificence. However, records, literary accounts and paintings, such as a wonderful hand scroll by Zhang Zeduan now in the Palace Museum in Beijing, provide much evidence of its grandeur during the Northern Song. The Imperial Way which ran from north to south through the city was described as being 300 m wide with covered arcades where merchants traded on each side. Painted barriers partitioned off a central route which was reserved for the emperor and confined traffic to the arcades. Two narrow canals filled with lotuses ran beside the arcades and flowering plums, apricots and peaches were planted alongside, so that in spring the scene was said to resemble a piece of brilliantly coloured embroidery (Wood, 1992).

It was in Kaifeng that the Song emperor Huizong built his famous garden, the Genyue, using rocks brought from Lake

Figure 2.29 (above) Dragon Pavilion, Kaifeng

Figure 2.31 (right) Topiary Garden, Dragon Pavilion Park

Tai and plants sent from far and wide. This and other gardens there did not survive the fall of the city in 1126. The lakes within the walled portion of the city perhaps date back to this time, for example those in Longting Park, which occupies the site of an imperial garden and leading to which the Imperial Way has recently been recreated as a tourist attraction. Regrettably, however, the lotus-filled canals and flowering plums, peaches and apricots have not reappeared, with the result that the scene shows little resemblance to any piece of embroidery.

LONGTING GONGYUAN (DRAGON PAVILION PARK)

This park occupies the north-western corner of the old city and incorporates several lakes which probably date from the Song. The area was later the site of a Ming palace but the only part of the park not to have been submerged in the flood of 1642 was the eminence on which the Dragon Pavilion now stands (fig. 2.29). In 1692 a pavilion was built here where officials came to offer their respects on the emperor's birthdays and in 1696 it was given the name Dragon Pavilion. What this was like I do not know, as the present substantial structure on the site is of relatively recent date.

From the south gate of the park, which is at the end of the restored Imperial Way, a long causeway leads to the Dragon Pavilion between the Yangjia Lake on the west and the Panjia lake on the east. About halfway along a subsidiary causeway leads to a small island. The main causeway is planted with willows and there are beds of seasonal flowers such as cockscombs and chrysanthemums. White clover and *Oxalis articulata* (fig. 2.30) are used as ground covers—as they are in many parts of China nowadays—and in various parts of the park there is the usual array of traditional trees and flow-

Figure 2.32 **Iron Pagoda Park, Kaifeng**

ering shrubs. These include the yuccas which have become a frequently encountered part of the repertoire everywhere in the country.

The Dragon Pavilion itself stands at the northern end of a courtyard planted with koelreuterias and from it there is an expansive view over the lakes, around which bridges and buildings in traditional style

Figure 2.30 *Oxalis articulata*, **Dragon Pavilion Park, Kaifeng**

TIETA GONGYUAN (IRON PAGODA PARK)

The octagonal Iron Pagoda is all that remains of the Youguosi (Protect the Country Temple). The most conspicuous landmark of Kaifeng, the pagoda was built in the first half of the 11th century, has 13 storeys and is almost 55 m tall. It is not made of iron but is so-called because of the colour of the tiles which cover its sur-

are to be seen. To the north of the pavilion is an area densely planted with thujas surrounding small pavilions aligned with the axis of the Dragon Pavilion, and beyond that again is an eccentric topiary garden in semi-Western style (fig. 2.31).

face. The site, which lies just inside the north-east corner of the city walls, has been developed as a modern park (fig. 2.32). Here there is a reconstructed temple hall outside which there is a topiary elephant and a large garden in which, once

Figure 2.33

White clover

used as a ground

cover, Iron

Pagoda Park

again, white clover is used as a ground cover (fig. 2.33). Apart from the views of the pagoda the most attractive parts of the park are a large lotus pond and the old lake, bounded on its northern and eastern sides by the city wall. Pavilions have been built out into this lake and along its shores to take advantage of the views. As at the Dragon Pavilion Park, the grounds have been planted with a range of traditional Chinese garden plants, including Marvel of Peru (*Mirabilis jalapa*) which, like the yuccas, has become a favourite exotic plant with Chinese gardeners.

XIANGGUOSI (XIANGGUO TEMPLE)

This Buddhist temple was founded in 555 on the site of an earlier palace. Its name was given to it by a Tang emperor in the early 8th century to commemorate one of his pre-imperial titles (Wood, 1992). The buildings were swept away by the flood of 1642 and the present structures, dating from 1766, have been restored in recent times.

The temple is entered through a stone pailou and in the first courtyard there are the usual bell tower on the right and drum tower on the left. Here too there are various ornamental plants in pots and a pergola supporting a grape vine. In the second courtyard there is a rectangular pool crossed by a stone bridge and in the centre of the third is a raised platform with a collection of penjing in enclosures on either side. This leads to an octagonal building with upswept eaves in the centre of which is a pavilion housing a statue of Guanyin, said to have been carved from a single piece of ginkgo wood. This statue depicts her manifestation with 1000 arms and eyes, symbolising her ability to see all dangers and assist all those in need. The statue actually has only 42 arms, which has become the conventional way of representing the 1000. Beyond this is another

Figure 2.34 *Luffa acutangula* on a juniper, Xiangguo Temple, Kaifeng

Figure 2.36 **Main courtyard, Baogong Memorial Temple**

courtyard on the far side of which is a library for the sutras. Leading to this is a short avenue of *Juniperus chinensis* 'Kaizuka' with penjing arranged in front behind a low border of clipped shrubs (fig. 2.6). Amongst other plants I noticed in various courtyards were wisterias, dwarf pomegranates, balsams and a brilliant red cultivar *of Amaranthus tricolor*. However, the most conspicuous plants at the time of my visit were the loofahs (*Luffa acutangula*), which had been planted to grow over the junipers in various parts of the grounds and which had totally enveloped their supports in a mantle of leaves, flowers and developing fruits (fig. 2.34). As the young fruits of this plant are esteemed as a vegetable, I assume that the monks at this establishment are keen on them.

BAOGONGMIAO (MEMORIAL TEMPLE TO LORD BAO)

Lord Bao was a wise and trusted judge during the Song. This temple dedicated to his memory is a modern construction on the shore of Baoqogong Hu (Lord Bao's Lake), which is in the south-western corner of the walled city. The entrance opens onto a large courtyard fronting the lake, with a rock mountain on the right and a wall of *Juniperus chinensis*

'Kaizuka' on the left. Behind this is a row of an unusual pomegranate with yellow fruits (fig. 2.35). The principal courtyard is laid out in traditional style with the main hall devoted to an exhibition relating to Lord Bao's life and famous judgements. The plants here and throughout the temple are almost all those traditionally used in Chinese gardens (fig. 2.36).

Figure 2.35

Yellow-fruited

pomegranate,

Baogong

Memorial

Temple, Kaifeng

Shandong

With close to 90 million people, Shandong is now China's second most populous province. It is here that the Yellow River, fed by tributaries in distant Qinghai, turns north-west and empties into the Bohai Sea. Here, too, Tai Shan, the eastern and most revered of the five sacred Daoist mountains, continues to attract pilgrims, as does Qufu, the birthplace of Confucius in the south of the province.

As in Henan, droughts, floods and the changes of course of the Yellow River have repeatedly brought death, destruction and starvation to this province. On top of this it has been subjected to a great deal of interference by the foreign powers. Qingdao was used by the Russian fleet as a winter anchorage in 1895 and in 1897 was seized by the Germans. They laid out a new foreign quarter and extended their influence inland by building a railway linking it to the provincial capital, Ji'nan. No doubt Western interference in this region did much to stimulate xenophobia, and it was in Shandong at the end of the 19th century that the Boxers arose and began their campaign to rid the country of foreigners. Then in 1914 the Japanese, anxious to obtain a foothold in China, took advantage of the outbreak of World War I and declared war on Germany, capturing Qingdao in November of that year. They took over the old German concessions and were not ousted until the end of World War II. As a result of these happenings, however, Shandong was one of the first provinces to experience industrialisation, and German and Japanese architectural remains are still a feature of the region.

The principal crops grown in Shandong are the same as those of neighbouring Henan. At the time of my visit in late September the harvesting of maize, cotton, peanuts, soybeans, apples and pears was in full swing, along with small amounts of foxtail millet and red sorghum—the cereal which gave its name to a famous Chinese film. These two grains were once the principal summer crops in northern China but have now largely been replaced by maize. Also conspicuous at this time of year are fields of sweet potatoes. Interesting, too, are the vineyards, particularly around Qufu and Yantai, where there are joint ventures with foreign wine-producing companies. The silk industry, which was once of major significance, is now of only minor importance. The popular rough-textured fabric known throughout the world as shantung used to be woven in the province, but now the raw silk produced here is usually sent elsewhere for processing.

As it happens, Shandong is rarely remarked upon for its gardens, other than for the tree peony fields at Heze in the far south-western corner of the province. I have not visited this town but there is now a huge industry there raising new varieties and producing plants which are sent to many parts of China and exported to over 20 countries. More than 600 varieties are grown and the peony fields occupy over 3000 hectares. Beginning in 1992 a peony festival has been held there each April and, like the one in Luoyang, this attracts a huge number of visitors to the principal display areas. There are five gardens of this type in and around Heze (Wang et al., 1998). Apart from these, however, there are many sites in the province which qualify as gardens, particularly at and near Ji'nan, Qufu, Tai'an and Qingdao. There is also a famous garden at Weifang, the Shihuyuan (Ten Tablets Garden), which I have not visited. It was completed in 1885 (Johnston, 1991).

Ji'nan and Environs

Ji'nan, the capital of Shandong, is situated more or less in the centre of the province a few kilometres south of the Yellow River. It is now a large and prosperous modern city, almost unrecognisable to anyone who saw it 20 years ago. It is also high on the list of Chinese cities affected by atmospheric pollution. It has long been famous for its springs, which were first recorded in the 7th century BC. There are said to be 72 of these in the city but as a result of the increased use of water and the falling of the water table most of them are now dry or almost so. The most famous are the Heihuquan (Black Tiger Spring), which emerges from a cave; the Wulongtan (Five Dragon Pool), which is fed by five springs; the Zhenzuquan (Pearl Spring), where the water was said to bubble up like pearls; and the Baotuquan (Fountain Spring or Spring with the Vertical Jet). The most attractive at the present time is the last mentioned, as it is situated in a large and interesting park. Also worthy of comment are the Daming Hu (Lake of Great Brightness), the Ji'nan Botanical Garden, Thousand Buddha Mountain, and the Shentong Temple, some distance southeast of the city. And amongst the narrow lanes of the remaining part of the old city, immediately to the south of Daming Lake, there remains a glimpse of the Chinese enthusiasm for ornamental plants even where there is no obvious room for them. My eye was caught there by the plum-purple flowers of a cultivar of *Hibiscus syriacus* peeping over a wall and, in a corner, a clump of *Mirabilis jalapa* with *Ipomoea quamoclit*, yet another favourite exotic, climbing over it.

Figure 2.37 **Preparing to plant a butterfly, Baotuquan Park, Ji'nan**

Figure 2.37 **Preparing to plant a butterfly, Baotuquan Park, Ji'nan**

BAOTUQUAN GONGYUAN (SPRING WITH THE VERTICAL JET PARK)

The park is so-called because of the three springs which arise there in a pool. This spring, which was mentioned in the Spring and Autumn Annals concerning a meeting of nobles which took place here in 694 BC, was regarded by Shen Fu (1809) as 'the crowning glory' of Ji'nan's 72 springs. Originally the water emerged from the springs here with considerable force, forming jets which rose above the surface of the pool. Now, however, it is mirror calm. On the northern side a large pavilion has been built out over the water and in the south-western corner there is a smaller one, the Guanlianting (Pavilion for Viewing the Waves), on the front pillars of which a couplet is hung. Standing in the water on either side are two stone tablets inscribed respectively with the words 'Diyiquan' (First Spring) and 'Baotuquan' (fig. 1.41).

The general areas of the park are planted with the usual range of Chinese trees and shrubs, including the edible hawthorn (*Crataegus pinnatifida*), along with displays of bedding plants. At the time of my visit the gardeners were busy plastering mud onto a large wood-framed butterfly prior to planting it up with bedding plants to create a celebratory feature for the national day (fig. 2.37). This sort of thing appears to be a tradition in China, where dragons, peacocks, phoenixes and multicoloured spheres are also regularly created using the same technique. Elsewhere in the park there are the Kanyuan, with a collection of penjing, and the Hall to Commemorate Li Qingzhao (1084–1151), one of China's most famous women poets who was born in Ji'nan. While this was first built only in 1956 and restored as recently as 1980, the plants in its courtyards have grown sufficiently to endow it with considerable charm. In the central space there are crabapples, bananas and nandinas, all underplanted with liriopes.

By far the most interesting garden in the park, however, is the Wanzhuyuan (Ten Thousand Bamboo Garden). This was originally built in the Yuan (1279–1368) and was famous for its bamboos. Later it became the residence of Wang Ping (1661–1720) and after the fall of the Qing it was 'bought' by the local warlord, Zhang Huaizhi, who lived there from 1912–27 and enlarged it. The property was eventually restored and opened to the public in 1986 as a memorial to Li Kuchan, a modern painter famous for his depictions of hawks. What one sees there now is an excellent example of a large courtyard house in northern style. Two of the courtyards are occupied by pools, presumably once spring fed but now, alas, dry. These are crossed by causeways and in the centre of one there is a hexagonal pavilion. Almost all of the remaining courtyards have been planted symmetrically with four trees, all of one kind in each. These courtyards are named after the trees they contain, which include crabapples (*Malus spectabilis*), magnolias (*Magnolia denudata*),

Chinese quinces (*Pseudocydonia sinensis*) (fig. 2.38) and pomegranates. The Apricot Courtyard, which is one of the largest, differs in having bananas and other traditional plants as well as the apricots which give it its name (fig. 2.39). A few other plants are to be seen on the secondary axes of the enclosure, including a single form of *Rosa chinensis*.

Figure 2.38 (left) Quince Courtyard, Wanzhuyuan, Ji'nan

Figure 2.39 (below) Apricot Courtyard, Wanzhuyuan

DAMING HU (LAKE OF GREAT BRIGHTNESS)

According to Wood (1992) this name was originally that of another lake further to the north.
When this became covered by streets the name
was transferred during the Jin—a dynasty
which controlled much of the north from
1115–1234. The present Daming Hu lies just
inside the line of the now-demolished northern wall of the city and, following traditional
practice, there were originally 10 scenes with
poetic names. There are six small islands, on
the largest of which is a famous pavilion ornamented with a couplet by the Tang poet Du
Fu, who is said to have visited it. Around the
willow-lined shores of the lake there are small
gardens, various memorial halls and a display
of penjing. Parts of the
lake are filled with lotuses,
as is a rectangular pond
in the Tiegong Memorial
Hall (fig. 2.40). Elsewhere
sophoras, koelreuterias,
crepe myrtles, paulown-
ias, privets, osmanthuses,
roses and various other
traditional trees and
shrubs have been planted
and there are the usual
displays of bedding plants (fig. 2.41).

The Daming Hu is one of the places
visited by Shen Fu (1809). Although he
was there in the winter and saw only
bare willows and mists rising from
the expanse of water, he admired the
pavilion in the centre of the lake and
surmised that it must have been lovely
there in the summer drifting in a boat
with some wine amongst the lotuses.

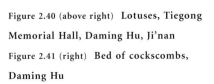

Figure 2.40 (above right) **Lotuses, Tiegong
Memorial Hall, Daming Hu, Ji'nan**
Figure 2.41 (right) **Bed of cockscombs,
Daming Hu**

Figure 2.44 (left)

Lotus Pond, Ji'nan

Botanical Garden

Figure 2.43 (right)

Sophora in fruit,

Thousand Buddha

Mountain Park,

Ji'nan

QIANFO SHAN (THOUSAND BUDDHA MOUNTAIN)

The Thousand Buddha Mountain is on the southern outskirts of the city at the northern extremity of the Taishan Range and is good example of a modified landscape. The mythical pre-dynastic emperor Shun, who is supposed to have reigned from 2317–2208 BC, is said to have ploughed the soil here, and it is famous for the Sui carvings in the grounds of the Xingguosi (Temple of the Flourishing State) on the upper slopes. On the rare clear days the views from the pavilions on various high points are said to encompass the Daming Lake and the Yellow River. The large park through which the mountain is approached is unusual in containing a Japanese garden, the Yingfangyuan (fig. 2.42). Otherwise it is of no particular distinction, although at the time of my visit the sophoras in fruit were looking most attractive (fig. 2.43).

JI'NAN ZHIWUYUAN (JI'NAN BOTANICAL GARDEN)

Founded in 1986, this botanical garden is unusual in that admission is free, it is in the centre of the city and is well maintained. Amongst the attractions are a conifer collection and a large area devoted to flowering peaches, apricots and forms of *Prunus triloba* and *P. davidiana*. Elsewhere there are collections of magnolias and roses, along with many crabapples, pears, wintersweets, wisterias and forsythias. There are also an impressive lotus pond (fig. 2.44) and a huge display greenhouse, which is especially popular in winter.

Figure 2.42 (below) Japanese garden, Thousand Buddha Mountain Park, Ji'nan

Figure 2.45 Grounds of the Shentong Temple, Qinglong Shan, with the mountains rising behind

Figure 2.46 (above) Simenta and old thuja, Shentong Temple

Figure 2.47 (left) Forest of Stupas, Shentong Temple

SHENTONGSI (COMMUNICATE WITH THE SPIRIT TEMPLE)

The temple bearing this name is 33 km south-east of Ji'nan, on the lower slopes of Qinglong Shan (Green Dragon Mountain) (fig. 2.45). It is famous for the Simenta (Four Door Pagoda), probably built in 611 and believed to be the oldest surviving stone pagoda in China. It stands in front of a much revered tree said to have been planted in the Han (fig. 2.46). According to the accompanying tablet it is the Nine-trunked Pine, even though it is a thuja, as are all the trees said to date from the Han which I have seen. Compared with the others—which not surprisingly are looking a bit the worse for wear—this one is in excellent health with scarcely a dead twig to be seen.

The pagoda stands on one side of a wooded valley and forms part of an interesting landscape. Carved on the cliff on the opposite side there are many Buddhist sculptures, most of which are thought to date from the Tang. And on the valley floor is the burial ground of the monks, another example of a 'forest of stupas' (fig. 2.47). The most impressive of the memorials is the Longhuta (Dragon and Tiger Pagoda), the burial monument to a monk who is thought to have lived between the 10th and 14th centuries. Also of interest are the stones placed in the angles of the branches of the thujas—a practice which is still widely held to increase the likelihood of giving birth to a son.

The Shentong Temple is believed to have been the earliest Buddhist temple in Shandong, although, other than those mentioned above, the original temple buildings disappeared long ago. However, the whole area is now being restored and the temple itself has recently been rebuilt at the mouth of the valley. This appears to have been carried out using traditional techniques and materials and to be Tang in style. When I saw it in September 2000, with the timber still unpainted, it looked wonderful with the wooded hills rising on either side and the mountains behind.

Qufu and Environs

Qufu, about 170 km south of Ji'nan, is where Confucius, who is believed to have lived from 551–479 BC, was born. A collection of his statements, based on the moral precepts of his time, were gathered together by his disciples and have become known in the West as the Analects. Confucius also became associated with a group of texts known as the Five Classics. Although it seems that his teachings were largely ignored in his own time, they have had a monumental effect on Chinese culture for more than 2000 years. Because of this Qufu has an importance to the Chinese quite out of proportion to its size. The name Confucius, incidentally, is a latinised version of Kongfuzi (Master Kong) and 77 generations of the Kong family have lived in Qufu.

Since much of the town was destroyed by an earthquake during the reign of Kangxi (1661–1722), most of the present buildings date from after that time. As was to be expected, many of these were badly damaged during the rampages of the Cultural Revolution. However, much restoration has been carried out since and Qufu remains one of the most interesting places in China. One of the earliest Western visitors was the Rev. Alexander Williamson (1870) who visited it twice in the 1860s and subsequently wrote brief descriptions of the principal sights.

For better or worse, the sights of Qufu are now managed by the Chinese Confucian International Tourism Company Limited, a joint venture between the local government and several other enterprises, which was established to encourage tourism. This company has recently come under fire for condoning methods of cleaning which have seriously damaged parts of the Confucian Temple. Presumably it is also responsible for the recent construction of The Analects Garden of Confucius about 300 m south of the old town. According to the tourist literature, this incorporates buildings and courtyards in traditional style, pools, a lake with islands, and 500 stone tablets inscribed with sayings attributed to the sage. As I have not seen this *pièce de résistance*, I am unable to include a description of it below.

KONGMIAO (CONFUCIAN TEMPLE)

A temple was first constructed here as a memorial to Confucius in 478 BC. In the light of its historical and architectural significance, the Confucian Temple at Qufu was listed as a World Heritage Site in 1994. Along with the Forbidden City in Beijing and the Imperial Summer Villa at Chengde, it is one of the three main classical architectural complexes in China. At various times it has undergone enlargements and reconstructions and now consists of three parallel axes running north-south, along each of which there are gates, courtyards and halls. In its present manifestation it covers 22 hectares and stretches for approximately a kilometre from south to north.

The first gate, which is exactly opposite the south gate of the town, leads to a bridge over a stream and on to a second gate in a wall, beyond which is a courtyard with two further pailou-type gates. Beyond this is a grassy courtyard in which a stream is crossed by three marble bridges, and this is followed by another unpaved courtyard in which there is nothing but trees—mostly junipers and thujas. The next courtyard is paved and is notable for the three-storeyed Kuiwen Pavilion on its northern side, which was used to house books presented by the emperors. It was first built in the Northern Song, rebuilt in 1191 and enlarged in 1504. It survived the earthquake and is one of the most famous wooden buildings in China. Behind this is a courtyard in which there are 13 stele pavilions and in the north-east corner of which there is an ancient sophora. In the north wall of this space there are five gates, and here the compound becomes divided into three axes which are separated from one another.

Next on the central axis is the principal courtyard. Just inside the main gate is an old juniper with a marble surround. This is said either to have been planted by Confucius or to be an ancient replacement for it. This courtyard is paved and planted with nine rows of trees, again mostly thujas and junipers. An unusual feature of the most easterly row is that

at its southern end there is an old Chinese chestnut (*Castanea mollisssima*), a tree rarely seen planted anywhere in China other than in chestnut orchards. Centrally placed in this space is the Apricot Altar, a pavilion marking the spot where Confucius is supposed to have propounded his views beneath an apricot tree. The present building dates from 1596 and has apricots, crabapples and junipers planted beside it (fig. 2.48).

On a raised platform beyond the Apricot Altar is the chief building in the complex, the Hall of Great Achievement. The first hall was built here in 1018 but the present structure, according to the notice in front of it, was completed in 1730. This building, like most of the larger halls of the temple, is roofed with yellow tiles and rivals in grandeur the principal halls in the Forbidden City. Across its front the lower roof is supported by 10 stone columns each carved from a single block of stone with bas-reliefs of dragons, clouds and pearls. It is said that when Qianlong visited the temple these columns were wrapped in red silk so that he would not see them, as there was nothing so elaborate in the Forbidden City. At the sides and rear the remainder of the lower roof is supported by 18 octagonal columns. Each of these, too,

Figure 2.48 Apricot Altar, Confucian Temple, Qufu

Figure 2.49 (right) **Song ginkgo and Tang sophora, Hall of Poetry and Rites, Confucian Temple**
Figure 2.50 (below right) **Well said to have been used by Confucius and the Wall of Lu, Confucian Temple**

is carved from a single block of stone and its surface engraved with 72 dragons— a number said to be that of Confucius's original disciples. Thus the total number of these dragons is 1296, which is claimed by some to be the number of stars recognised in ancient Chinese cosmology, and the total of 28 columns is the same as the number of sections into which the heavens were divided.

Behind the Hall of Great Achievement, on an extension of its platform, is the Hall of Sleep dedicated to Confucius' wife, Qi Guan. This, too, dates from 1730, although it was also first built in 1018. The lower roof here is supported by 22 octagonal stone columns etched with designs of flowers. Behind this again is the final courtyard of the central axis, which is densely planted with old thujas, junipers and sophoras. On the northern side is a comparatively modest building, the Hall of the Relics of the Sage, containing carved stone plaques made in the late 16th century from Song paintings depicting events in the life of Confucius.

The western axis, where there are halls dedicated to Confucius' parents, was inaccessible at the time I was there, but the eastern one could be visited through a separate entrance on payment of an additional admission charge. In the first courtyard is the Hall of Poetry and Rites, built in 1504, in front of which are two ginkgos said to date from the Song and a sophora claimed to have been planted during the Tang (fig. 2.49). In the courtyard behind, shaded by old junipers and sophoras, is a well said to have been used by Confucius and a small structure known as The Wall of Lu (fig. 2.50). A ninth-generation descendant is said to have concealed copies of the Confucian classics in a wall when the Qin emperor Shihuangdi (reigned 221–210 BC), who was anti-Confucian, ordered a 'burning of the books'. The concealed

copies were not rediscovered until 154 BC, when part of Confucius' original home was being demolished to make way for extensions to the palace of Prince Gong of Lu, a son of the Han emperor Jingdi. The Wall of Lu was built later to commemorate this episode. The remainder of this axis is now used for staging musical entertainments for tourists.

Amongst plants in the courtyards there are pomegranates, nandinas, junipers, flowering quinces, Banksian roses and weeping sophoras. There are also ornamental rocks on carved stands (fig. 2.51). However, not surprisingly, it is the main garden which is of greatest interest. In both its position and in being more or less symmetrically arranged, it has much in common with the Imperial Garden in the Forbidden City. It was originally built in 1503 and reconstructed when one of Qianlong's daughters, known as Madam Yu, was married to the 72nd Duke in 1772. It has

Figure 2.51 (above) **Rocks on stands, Confucian Mansion, Qufu**

Figure 2.52 (right) **Pool, rockery, and pavilion in the garden of the Confucian Mansion**

KONGFU (CONFUCIAN MANSION)

This lies immediately to the east of the Confucian Temple. The present mansion was constructed here for the Kong family in the early Ming and renovated and enlarged in the Qing. It covers 16 hectares and consists of many courtyards and buildings arranged along three axes and, at the northern end, there is a separate large garden. The main inhabitant was always the Yansheng Duke, the oldest male direct descendant. The last to live here was the 77th Duke, who left in 1940 for Chongqing to escape the Japanese and later went to Taiwan. Other than in recent times, the only Western visitor I have come across to have recorded a visit to this mansion was the Rev. Williamson (1870) who, on sending his card, was invited to call by the then holder of the title.

also been affected by Western influences in more recent times, which is not surprising since the mansion remained inhabited by the family until 1940. Nevertheless, while it may not appeal to everyone's taste, this garden is remarkable as a rare example of an actively managed private Qing garden of northern type which has survived into the 21st century.

Just before the entrance to the garden there is a stand on which a collection of penjing is displayed, and opposite this is a large service area where potted plants of various types are produced for decorating the mansion and the garden. At the time of my visit chrysanthemums were very much to the fore.

To the right as one enters the garden proper there is a rock mountain with a pool, bridge and pavilion at its base (fig. 2.52). On the approach to this part of the garden is a clump of what I took to be *Clerodendrum bungei*, though the corollas each had only four petals and were much paler than the form usually seen outside China. Nearby is a lotus pond, an enormous trumpet vine (*Campsis grandiflora*) climbing the wall, a wisteria pergola and collections of potted osmanthuses, cycads and oleanders. Against the centre of the north wall there is a large pavilion and, here and there, ornamental rocks are displayed on pedestals.

The garden is remarkable for its wealth of traditional Chinese garden plants. In addition to those already mentioned there are grapes, *Jasminum mesnyi*, wintersweets, lilacs, yuccas, junipers, *Trachycarpus fortunei*, pistacias, *Hibiscus syriacus*, forsythias, crepe myrtles, aspidistras, liriopes, redbuds, bamboos, morning glories, loquats, crabapples (*Malus spectabilis*), apricots, peaches, and the Chinese matrimony vine (*Lycium chinense*) amongst others. And in the north-western corner there is a large bed of tree peonies.

Much of the rest of the garden consists of rectangular enclosures surrounded by hedges of *Euonymus japonicus* or iron fences—no doubt installed to keep tourists at bay. The enclosure immediately to the west of the central axis contains a collection of herbaceous peonies and, on its southern side, a border of *Begonia grandis* subsp. *evansiana* and a stand on which a collection of cymbidiums (mostly *C. goeringii* and *C. ensifolium*) is displayed (fig. 2.53). Along with the plum, pine, bamboo and chrysanthemum, the plants most intimately associated with art, literature and everyday life in China, are these cymbidiums. Although they produce inconspicuous flowers they make their presence felt very discreetly by means of their delicious and pervasive scent. This

Figure 2.53 **Cymbidiums and begonias in the garden of the Confucian Mansion**

characteristic is said to have been admired by Confucius himself, who noted also that they did not withhold their fragrance for lack of appreciation. Thus the orchid, too, became a symbol of the superior way of life of those adhering to Confucian principles.

As in the gardens and nurseries of Beijing and its environs, there are also many plants which are not able to endure winters out of doors. These are grown in pots and include *Jasminum sambac*, large-flowered gardenias, figs and a wonderful collection of citrus varieties. Amongst these are two kinds of pomelo, ordinary citrons, fingered citrons, and several kinds of orange, including one with small, rough-skinned fruits. In winter these plants are removed to large greenhouses in the north-western corner of the garden which, apart from having their south-facing walls glazed rather than covered with paper, are exactly like those described in Beijing in the 18th century by Cibot (1778).

Figure 2.54 A traditional Chinese greenhouse, Confucian Mansion

They have the same sunken interiors with benches for accommodating the plants. They are the only surviving examples of this type of greenhouse which I have seen (fig. 2.54).

KONGLIN (CONFUCIAN FOREST)

A straight road leads north from the centre of Qufu to the Konglin, a little more than a kilometre away. This is the Confucian burial ground which, along with the Confucian Temple, is one of the sights described and illustrated by Lin Qing (1847–50). It was also described by the Rev. Williamson (1870) who went there in the 1860s. It occupies about 200 hectares and is surrounded by a wall 7 km long. The enclosure is entered through an elaborate gate from which a path lined with old thujas and stalls selling souvenirs runs between two red walls to the actual burial ground. Close to the

entrance is an artificial stream crossed by a stone bridge. Legend has it that the first emperor, Shihuangdi, tried to destroy the fengshui of Confucius' tomb by having this river dug where there was none before. But, since according to fengshui beliefs a tomb should have a hill behind and flowing water in front, he actually improved it.

There are said to be 100 000 graves and 100 000 trees in the enclosure. Whatever the actual figures may be there are certainly a lot of both, as members of the Kong family have been buried here since the Han. The trees are supposed to have been planted by disciples and family members and no doubt some of them have been. However, since most of them are native oaks, it could be that these are largely self-sown and part of the natural flora of the area. Other trees present are pistacias, sophoras, thujas, junipers and an occasional koelreuteria and albizia. Between them are innumerable mounds, tablets and more elaborate monuments (fig. 2.55). Nowadays annual flowers are planted along the sides of the paths running through the forest and, at the time of my visit in September 2000, there were African marigolds, four o'clocks, China asters,

Figure 2.55 (left)

Stele pavilion, Confucian Forest, Qufu

Figure 2.57 (right)

Tomb of Madam Yu, Confucian Forest

dwarf dahlias and chrysanthemums, around which hordes of striking swallowtail butterflies were hovering. Other insects were chirruping in the trees and it was fascinating to stroll through this wooded landscape which has been evolving for more than 2000 years.

The principal feature, of course, is the tomb of Confucius. This lies north of the bridge and is approached through an avenue of carved stone animals and guardian figures at the end of which is a Hall of Sacrifices (fig. 2.56). Behind this is a rectangular enclosure in which there are two stele pavilions, one of which contains a stele engraved with Qianlong's calligraphy. The mound which is supposed to be the tomb of Confucius is at the northern end of the enclosure, and

a few metres to its south-east is the tomb mound of his son, Kong Li. Also buried here is his grandson, Kong Ji, whose tomb mound is a few paces to the south-west of that of his grandfather.

Of interest elsewhere are the Ming tombs in the western part of the forest, the tomb of Qianlong's daughter, Madam Yu (fig. 2.57), which is to the north of the tomb of Confucius, and that of the 76th Duke, who died in 1919, which is in the eastern area. Both these are approached along short avenues of stone animals and figures.

Figure 2.56 (over page) **Sacrificial hall, Tomb of Confucius**

Figure 2.58 (left) **Stele pavilions, Yanmiao, Qufu**

Figure 2.59 (above) **Main hall, Yanmiao**

YANMIAO (TEMPLE OF YAN HUI)

This temple lies inside the old town on the eastern side of the road leading to the Confucian Forest. Yan Hui was Confucius' favourite disciple and came to be worshipped along with his teacher. The Yanmiao is said to have been built on the site of his house in Humble Alley by the first Han emperor and it has

been restored in the Yuan, Ming and Qing. Unlike the Confucian Temple which it resembles, it receives few visitors and its wooded courtyards, with doves cooing, have a charming and peaceful atmosphere. The Rev. Williamson reported the enclosure to be full of cypresses and tablets, and his description still holds today, even though the 'cypresses' are actually thujas and junipers. There are also a few koelreuterias and paulownias, but I could not find the 'fine white pine, so rare in Shantung' which had impressed him.

Proceeding along the central axis, the first courtyard contains a well, said to have been used by Yan Hui. This is covered by a pavilion which also shelters a stele inscribed with 'The Well of Humble Alley' in Kangxi's calligraphy. Amongst the trees on the opposite side of the central path there is an ornamental limestone rock of the type dredged up from Tai Hu (Lake Tai) in Jiangxi and known generally as Taihu rocks. In the second courtyard there are two stele pavilions (fig. 2.58) and in the third there is a small central pavilion beyond which stands the main hall. This is on a raised stone platform and the lower roof is supported by 22 stone columns (fig. 2.59). Four of those at the front are carved with bas-reliefs of dragons and the remainder are octagonal. Two of these are engraved with a pattern of dragons and the remainder with flowers (fig. 2.60). Behind this hall there is a smaller one devoted to the worship of Yan's wife, and on the western axis there are halls dedicated to his father and mother.

ZHOUGONGMIAO (TEMPLE OF THE DUKE OF ZHOU)

Amongst other things, Confucius stressed the duty of rulers to set an ethical example and wished for a return to what he regarded as the golden age of the Duke of Zhou. The Duke of Zhou is a semi-historical figure of the Zhou dynasty, who assisted in the suppression of the preceding Shang dynasty and, in a series of expeditions eastward into what is now Shandong, brought the whole Yellow River plain under Zhou control. He is also credited with establishing the regulations by which the Zhou ruled.

The Zhougongmiao is just outside the north-east corner of the moat and occupies the site of a temple said to have been built by the duke's son in the late 11th century BC. As usual, it has been repeatedly restored in the centuries that have followed. It is a smaller and simpler temple than the Yanmiao and has only one axis. It is equally tranquil, is filled with trees of the same type, as the Rev. Williamson recorded, and receives few visitors. It is entered through an imposing wooden gate with a grey-tiled roof, above which rise four wooden columns, each capped with glazed figures of

Figure 2.60 **Detail of pomegranate pattern on one of the columns of the main hall, Yanmiao**

heavenly warriors seated on drums (fig. 2.61). Inside there are three courtyards. The first contains little other than trees; in the second there is a single stele pavilion ornamented with wooden panels carved with dragons; and in the third there is a relatively modest main hall—the Hall of the First Sage— with inscriptions by Qianlong. In the subsidiary buildings on either side there are exhibits relating to the Duke of Zhou.

As happened everywhere in Qufu, this temple sustained much damage during the Cultural Revolution. However the broken steles have been reassembled and, accompanied by the sound of birds and insects, the views of the faded buildings amongst the old trees conjure up a vision of a bygone age.

SHAOHAOLING (TOMB OF SHAOHAO)

Supposedly Shaohao was the son of Huangdi, the Yellow Emperor, considered to be the first of the five legendary pre-dynastic rulers. Huangdi is said to have lived in the 3rd millennium BC, to have invented the bow and arrow, boats, carts, ceramics, writing and silk, and to have fought a battle against alien tribes, thus securing the Yellow River plain for his people (Ebrey, 1996). He also came to be considered the first ancestor of the Chinese (Han) race.

This myth is believed to have developed during the late Zhou and early Han and to have provided a model of perfect

Figure 2.62 *Ipomoea nil* at the Tomb of Shaohao, Qufu

Figure 2.61 Entrance to the Zhougongmiao, Qufu

Figure 2.63 (right) **Entrance to the Tomb of Shaohao**

Figure 2.64 (below right) **Second court-yard, Tomb of Shaohao, with the pyramidal mound in the background**

rulership which played a role in transforming China into a unified nation. The Confucianists saw the Yellow Emperor as a culture hero who brought civilisation to humankind by defeating chaos and establishing social institutions that would allow humanity to prosper in harmony (Yeung, 1998).

Who it is, if anybody, that is buried in Shaohao's tomb is hard to imagine, but perhaps it was given this designation to add credence to the myth. It lies about 4 km east of Qufu and is approached through an enclosure which is the site of a memorial to the Yellow Emperor built in 1012. All that remains of this is a lake on either side of which is an enormous stone tablet. It was originally intended that these tablets be carved on site but the Song court was driven south before this was done. They lay on the ground for centuries but have recently been erected on raised stone platforms. At the time I was there self-sown morning glories (*Ipomoea nil*) added colour to the scene (fig. 2.62).

From this enclosure a straight road runs a few hundred metres through fields to the actual tomb at the north-east corner of Jiuxian village. A short avenue of old thujas lines the approach to a carved stone pailou of 1739 (fig. 2.63), behind which a gate leads to a courtyard in which there is a small Hall of Sacrifices with an inscription by Qianlong, who visited the tomb in 1748. The tomb mound lies in a second courtyard and is unusual in that it is in the form of a shallow pyramid which was covered with slabs of stone by the emperor Huizong in 1111 (fig. 2.64). There is a small pavilion on top, as noted by the Rev. Williamson (1870), but no sign remains of the old tree which he saw growing out of the middle of it. Immediately north of the pyramid is an earth mound of approximately the same size, but whether this is another ancient tomb or was erected for geomantic reasons I do not know. In a small hall on the eastern side of the enclosure there is an exhibit featuring Shaohao and his father.

The charm of this place depends very much on its rural setting and, once again, on the trees and tranquil atmosphere. When Qianlong visited it he ordered the planting of 421 thujas and four junipers in the courtyards. According to the people manning the gate at the time I went there, 391 of these survive.

Figure 2.65 Old thuja in front of the Hall of Great Achievement, Nishan Fuzimiao

NISHAN FUZIMIAO (NISHAN CONFUCIAN TEMPLE)

This temple stands on the thuja-clad eastern slopes of Ni Shan, about 30 km south-east of Qufu. It is said to have been founded in the 10th century close to the spot where Confucius is supposed to have been abandoned by his father at birth because he was such an ugly baby. It seems a tigress took him to the grotto which lies behind the temple and cared for him, while an eagle fanned him with its wings to keep him cool. This unexpected turn of events apparently convinced his parents to reclaim him and rear him themselves after all.

The temple is arranged on the usual three axes. In the principal courtyard a pathway leads between thujas and steles to the Hall of Great Achievement (fig. 2.65). The roof of this is supported by octagonal stone columns engraved with dragons like those at the Confucian Temple in Qufu (fig. 2.66). On the axis to the right there is a lecture hall in front of which are two old apricot trees, and on the axis to the left are halls dedicated to members of Confucius' family. This is yet another peaceful place with interesting old trees and few visitors.

Tai'an and Environs

Tai'an is the gateway to Tai Shan, the most famous of the five Daoist holy mountains, the religious significance of which goes back to even earlier cults. Hence it has been important for well over 2000 years. The city lies at the southern foot of the highest point of the Taishan Range, which rises here to 1545 m. Apart from the Daimiao, it has little to offer the tourist, but there are sites of horticultural interest on its northern outskirts and along the climb to the mountaintop. The Arboretum of the Shandong College of Forestry is also near Tai'an. I have not seen it but I understand it has collections of ornamental and economic plants. The Rev. Williamson (1870) was an early Western visitor to this town, where he attended a fair at the Daimiao and ascended the mountain, subsequently writing short descriptions of both.

DAIMIAO (TAISHAN TEMPLE)

The temple was built for the use of emperors coming to worship and make sacrifices to the god of the mountain, an old name for which was Dai Shan. It is said to date back to the Han and has been rebuilt repeatedly in succeeding dynasties. In the 20th century it suffered much interference and damage, including being used for offices and shops during the 1920s. It has now been restored and, although it once had many more buildings, it remains one of the largest temples in China. It was visited by an endless succession of emperors, including the indefatigable Qianlong.

The halls are arranged, as usual, along three north-south axes, and the southernmost portion, consisting of a series of pailous and gates, is separated from the main enclosure by a

Figure 2.67 Stone bixi supporting a stele, Daimiao, Tai'an

road from which the first courtyard is entered. This now contains a large garden showing Western influences. Beds edged with clipped thujas contain tree and herbaceous peonies, roses, crepe myrtles, magnolias and many other traditional plants. In a courtyard to the west of this is the remains of a Han sophora which died in 1951 but in the centre of the rotting trunk of which another has been planted.

A pair of Ming bronze lions flank the gate leading to the second courtyard where there is a bed of dwarfed pines along with numerous old thujas, junipers and commemorative steles. These steles stand on the backs of stone bixis, as they do almost everywhere in China (fig. 2.67). The tortoise-like bixi is a mythical animal said to be the first of the nine sons of the dragon and to possess enormous strength.

To one side of the second courtyard, on the eastern axis, there is a group of buildings which was a Qing travelling palace. In a courtyard here is a stele which was carved in 209 BC to record the visit of the second emperor of the Qin and which was originally on the summit of the mountain.

To the north of the travelling palace and also to the east of the main axis is the Courtyard of the Han Cypresses. As is usual these 'cypresses' turn out to be thujas—the Chinese name for which is 'cebai' (sideways cypress), an allusion to the flat branchlets. These trees

are supposed to have been planted by the Han emperor Wudi when he visited the temple in the 2nd century BC. If this is so they presumably are younger than those mentioned earlier in this chapter which he admired in 110 BC at the Songyang Academy near Song Shan in Henan. There were originally five at the Daimiao but only three of these, looking a trifle world-weary, are still alive at the time of writing. Goodness knows how old they really are.

Figure 2.66 Detail of dragon pattern on the columns of the Hall of Great Achievement, Nishan Fuzimiao

Next on the principal axis is the main courtyard. In the centre, amongst more old trees and steles, is a marble platform decorated with Taihu rocks (fig. 2.68). And beyond this another Taihu rock, the Fusang Stone, which is the focus of one of those odd games of chance which seem to be played at temples all over the country. If one is blindfolded, goes round the rock three times anticlockwise, then three times clockwise, before walking north and touching the fissure on the south side of an ancient thuja, good fortune, it seems, is sure to ensue. Repeated attempts to achieve this feat were carried out while I was there but none was successful. The thuja, by the way, has an interesting history. Apparently an official of the Tang dynasty brought a lawsuit before the God of Mount Tai against the empress Wu Zetian because, according to Chinese tradition, a woman could not ascend the throne. Whatever the rights and wrongs of this situation may have been, the official did not succeed and, upon committing suicide, turned into this tree.

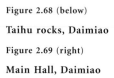

Figure 2.68 (below)

Taihu rocks, Daimiao

Figure 2.69 (right)

Main Hall, Daimiao

The principal hall, the Tiankuangdian (Hall of Heavenly Blessing), stands on a marble platform on the north side of this courtyard with hexagonal stele pavilions on either side (fig. 2.69). A wooden building 22 m tall with double eaves and yellow tiles, it is one of the three great halls of this type in China—the others being the Hall of Supreme Harmony in the Forbidden City and the Hall of Great Achievement at the Confucian Temple in Qufu. It is dedicated to the God of the Mountain and was originally constructed by the Song emperor Zhenzong (reigned 998–1022). It was restored in 1956 and the interior is decorated with a mural said to date from the Song but which has been much retouched.

Behind the Tiankuangdian is the Houqingong (Rear Palace), dedicated to the mountain god's wife. On either side of this are ginkgos 29 m tall planted in 1669—a male on the western side and a female on the eastern. There are also crabapples and junipers.

Behind the Houqingong on the eastern side is a courtyard in which there is a hexagonal iron pagoda. It was cast in 1533 and originally had 13 storeys, only three of which have survived. It was brought from elsewhere as was the bronze pavilion which is in a matching courtyard on the eastern side. This

originally stood on the summit of Mount Tai and was cast in 1615 to house a figure of Bixia Yuanjun (Goddess of the Azure Clouds), as the goddess of the mountain is called. The courtyard which the bronze pavilion now overlooks houses a large collection of penjing (fig. 2.5). Most of these are pines of various sorts, including *Pinus bungeana*. There is also a large wisteria pergola in this area.

I was hoping to find the enormous wisteria which had been photographed in the temple grounds in 1907 by F.N. Meyer. He labelled his photograph 'One of the largest Wisterias in the world, growing in the courtyard of the Ta

Miais (big temple). This specimen is several centuries old.' In the photograph it appears to be growing over a dead tree, probably a juniper or thuja. I could find no trace of it, though in the first courtyard of the temple, there was a similar but smaller specimen growing over a dead thuja.

TAI SHAN

One of the earliest examples of Chinese travel writing is that of Ma Dibo, who accompanied the emperor Guang Wudi to Tai Shan in AD 56 and left an account of the journey (Strassberg, 1994). There have been numerous descriptions

Figure 2.70 The 'mother and daughter sophora', Daomugong, Tai Shan

since and many of the features mentioned are still to be seen. The northern gate of the Daimiao marks the beginning of the traditional route up the southern side of the mountain. The road from here leads north under two pailous, on the second of which there is a wisteria. The climb proper begins at the Hongmenguan (Hall of the Red Gate), beyond which the stepped path makes its way through a forest of thujas. A kilometre or so along is the Daomugong (Grandmother Temple), so named because the Goddess of the Mountain, Bixia Yuanjun, is frequently referred to as 'grandmother' and has been regarded throughout China as being responsive to requests for sons. It is a small temple in the first courtyard of which are two ginkgos and a round pond, into which people throw coins and which is surrounded by small trees of *Buxus microphylla* var. *sinica*. On the far side is the 'mother and daughter sophora', a tree with an old decaying main trunk from the base of which a vigorous young branch has developed. This tree is much revered and has written supplications

tied to it (fig. 2.70). In other courtyards there are pines, bamboos, lilacs, an old apricot and a tall *Euonymus japonicus*.

On the roof of a shop a little lower down than this temple there was, at the time of my visit, a vigorous bottle gourd (*Lagenaria siceraria*) bearing a crop of its characteristic fruits (fig. 1.29). Amongst other things these are a symbol of longevity and are for sale at various points along the route. Also on the balcony of a restaurant on the opposite side of the path there was, at the time of my passing, a display of pot plants which included hydrangeas, *Rohdea japonica*, and a small-leaved hosta. Otherwise there is little of horticultural interest along the track. After a time the thujas give way to pines and there are many crabapples which appear to have been planted. The temples on the summit likewise have little to offer those interested in gardens. Much of the summit area is now occupied by souvenir shops, restaurants and hotels. While this is not quite what I expected, I suppose things are not really all that different from the way they were hundreds of years ago. As a contrast to all of this, the cable car which runs down the far side of the mountain provides an interesting view of the unspoiled native vegetation which cloaks the precipitous northern slopes. When I visited in late September, a species of *Sorbus* with orange foliage and large bunches of red fruit was conspicuous at the upper levels.

PUZHAOSI (TEMPLE OF UNIVERSAL ILLUMINATION)

This Buddhist temple is built against the base of the mountain a little to the west of the start of the main path to the summit. It is said to have been founded during the Six Dynasties period (265–589) and has been expanded and restored on subsequent occasions. Although many of its old features remain, it is now a museum devoted to the Christian warlord Feng Yuxiang, who stayed here at various times from 1932–35. Tablets inscribed with his poems have been placed in the grounds.

In front of the temple wall there is now a modern garden with an array of traditional trees, shrubs, perennials and annuals. At the time of my visit cockscombs, balsams and China asters were in full bloom (fig. 2.71). As well as these there were African marigolds, red salvias, four o'clocks, *Ipomoea quamoclit* and *Yucca gloriosa*—all American plants which became popular in China long ago. Above this in the

Figure 2.71 (right) China asters, Puzhao Temple, Tai'an

first courtyard of the temple there are old thujas, and in front of the small main hall in the second courtyard are two tall ginkgos and two pines (*Pinus tabuliformis*) said to date from the Ming. Behind this is a library in front of which is a Song (some say Six Dynasties) pine (fig. 2.72). Amongst the trees in an adjoining courtyard on the western side is another pine planted during the reign of Guangxu (1875–1908) and which is exceptionally low growing and flat topped, conforming perfectly to the specific epithet *tabuliformis* (table-shaped). There are also bamboos and many other trees and shrubs in recent extensions to the temple gardens.

LINGYANSI (TEMPLE OF THE DIVINE ROCK)

This lovely old temple, beautifully situated against the western side of the Taishan Range, 20 km north of Tai'an, also has a long history. It was founded at least as far back as the Tang and, in its heyday, there were many more buildings than at present and some 500 monks lived there. On entering, there are the usual bell and drum towers in a courtyard filled with old trees, including junipers, thujas, sophoras, koelreuterias, paulownias and persimmons. On the far side of this space stands the main hall in front of which are three ancient ginkgos and a tall *Malus spectabilis*. To the left of the hall there is

Figure 2.72 **Song pine, Puzhao Temple**

Figure 2.75 (over page) **Tomb Pagoda Forest, Lingyan Temple**

Figure 2.73 (below) **Persimmon and juniper, Lingyan Temple, north of Tai'an**

Figure 2.74 (bottom) **Stones in the angles of the branches of a thuja, Lingyan Temple**

a square enclosure in which there is an old juniper (yuanbai) with persimmons (shi) planted beside it (fig. 2.73). This pairing suggests the auspicious saying 'Baishi ruyi', which translates roughly as 'May your affairs be 100 times what you wish them to be'.

Behind the main hall is the Thousand Buddha Hall which contains three Ming bronze Buddha images and, around the walls, 40 life-size painted clay lohans modelled and posed to appear to be discussing the sutras. These are thought to have been made in the Song and are amongst the finest Buddhist statues in China. They survived destruction by the Red Guards as a result of the proximity of an army camp where the officers ensured their protection.

On a raised terrace to the west of the Thousand Buddha Hall there is a nine-storeyed brick pagoda built in 753. A path leads west from here past an old persimmon and lilac and through a plantation of thujas to the Huichong Pagoda. Many of the thujas have stones in the angles of their branches as described above at the Shentongsi south of Ji'nan (fig. 2.74). The Huichong Pagoda, which is the tomb of a monk who died in the 8th century, is an imposing square stone structure with four openings, very similar in appearance to the Square Pagoda at the Shentongsi. It sits on a terrace above the general burial ground of other important monks, known as the Mutalin (Tomb Pagoda Forest). Here there are 167 stone pagodas or stupas, no two the same, grouped amongst the thujas (fig. 2.75). Like the lohans in the Thousand Buddha Hall, these monuments were not damaged during the Cultural Revolution.

Qingdao

The recent history of this city has been outlined in the introduction to this section about Shandong. It is named Qingdao (Green Island) after the small island at the western end of its principal bay, Qingdao Bay. Until the German occupation it was little more than a fishing village but now even the old German town, dominated by the governor's enormous mansion perched on a hilltop, is relatively inconspicuous amongst the forest of skyscrapers and other developments which have appeared. Not only is it now one of China's chief ports, but the beaches along many kilometres of the southern coast of the peninsula on which it is situated have been developed with hotels, villas and apartment blocks in a manner which rivals Waikiki, Miami and Queensland's Gold Coast. And I suppose I should mention the Tsingtao Brewery, established here in the early 20th century by the Germans. This event undoubtedly led to the present popularity of beer throughout the country.

From a garden point of view the city is worth visiting in order to go to the Taiqinggong, a Daoist temple on the coast to the east. Otherwise, apart from Zhongshan Park and the Qingdao Botanical Garden, there is little of interest to the gardener in the city itself, although tourists are often taken to the seaside suburb of Badaguan (Eight Great Passes). Here there are eight streets each named after a famous pass and lined with a different species of tree. The three I saw had deodars, ginkgos and *Acer truncatum*, respectively. Also, an unusual feature of the city is the abundance of Japanese cherries—no doubt a relic of the prolonged Japanese presence in the area. There is even a cherry blossom festival here each spring.

ZHONGSHAN GONGYUAN (ZHONGSHAN PARK)

It seems that almost every city in China has a Zhongshan Park. Qingdao's is in the eastern part of the city on the lower slopes of a conspicuous hill, Taiping Shan, which is crowned with a television tower which can be ascended for the views it affords. It is a large park, covering about 80 hectares, and includes a children's playground and other features. There are avenues of cherries and a wide variety of other trees and shrubs, amongst which I noticed *Zelkova schneideriana*. To the right of the main entrance there is an enclosed garden on the site of Huiqian Village, which was swept away by the Germans in 1904 and replaced with an experiment farm. An old sophora remains from the time and the ground around a lake has been planted with willows, ginkgos, *Prunus triloba*, azaleas, pyracanthas, cotoneasters and bamboos. In addition to these it is ornamented in the summer months with pots of frost-tender plants, including *Michelia champaca* and cultivars of *Hibiscus rosa-sinensis* (fig. 2.76).

Figure 2.76 Cultivar of *Hibiscus rosa-sinensis*, Zhongshan Park, Qingdao

Figure 2.77 *Camellia japonica* 'Jiangxue' said to be 700 years old, Taiqinggong, Lao Shan

QINGDAO ZHIWUYUAN (QINGDAO BOTANICAL GARDEN)

Although not that remarkable, I have included this garden simply because it is there, not far from the city centre on the slopes of Taiping Shan, to the north-east of Zhongshan Park. It was founded in 1976 and has collections of cherries, camellias and conifers, along with specimens of *Cornus kousa*, *Pyracantha crenulata*, and *Albizia julibrissin*, amongst others. From the pavilions on top of the ridge there are good views over the city.

TAIQINGGONG (TEMPLE OF SUPREME PURITY)

Also known as the Xiagong (Lower Temple), the Taiqinggong is situated 25 km east of Qingdao beside the sea at the foot of Lao Shan, the highest peak of which reaches a mere 1133 m. However, rising above the eastern sea in which the fabled Islands of the Immortals were thought to float, it attracted the attention of Daoists long ago. It was believed that magic herbs grew on the mountain which would cure all known diseases and which could make humans immortal. It appears that it was for this reason that the Qin emperors Shihuangdi and Wudi visited the mountain and that in the 8th century the Tang emperor Xuanzong sent officials there to search for the coveted herbs. From the 10th century on many Daoist monasteries were established here but only a few survive, the best known and most frequently visited being the Taiqinggong. It was founded during the Song but the present buildings date from the time of the Ming emperor Wanli (reigned 1573–1620).

From the gardener's point of view the temple's chief attraction is its collection of enormous old trees, the size and vigour of which would appear to have been favoured by the gentle maritime climate. For a start, near the entrance there are two ginkgos claimed to be 1000 years old. Then in the principal courtyard there are two old plants of *Camellia japonica*, one of which, 'Jiangxue' ('Red Snow'), is said to have been planted 700 years ago. Presumably it is the oldest known example of this species in cultivation (fig. 2.77). Nearby is a wonderful specimen of *Catalpa bungei*, 150 years old according to its plaque.

Figure 2.78 *Campsis grandiflora* on a juniper, Taiqinggong

Immediately to the west of this courtyard is a large space in which there are no longer any buildings but which is shaded by further enormous trees including elms (*Ulmus pumila*), one of which has grown in a reclining position and is known as the Dragon's Head Elm. Also here are an immense, straight-trunked tallow tree (*Sapium sebiferum*), 200 years old and the tallest I have seen anywhere, further towering catalpas and, on the raised surrounds, an old crepe myrtle, pomegranate and yellow osmanthus. Above this area is another interesting courtyard, where in the Sanhuangdian (Three Emperors Hall) there are inscriptions by Khubilai Khan and Genghis Khan. Amongst the plants here are tree peonies, camellias, *Hibiscus syriacus* and an ancient juniper to the top of which an old trumpet vine (*Campsis grandiflora*) has climbed (fig. 2.78).

Below the western part of the Taiqinggong there is a flat area where there was once a Buddhist temple. This is now occupied by a small tea plantation, on the northern side of which there is a handsome specimen of *Kalopanax septemlobus*, a large-leaved deciduous tree native to the region. Along the eastern side there is an old sophora and a border of bamboo, and on the southern side what is probably the largest ginkgo I have seen.

Outside the temple I was interested to see numerous stalls selling peaches, long associated by the Daoists with longevity and immortality. I was told they are grown in the district and there were two kinds, large round ones and the curious

Figure 2.79 Flat peaches bought outside the Taiqinggong

Chinese flat peaches. The latter were the more expensive of the two, no doubt because they are the ones traditionally considered to be able to confer longevity or perhaps even immortality. I bought a few to photograph (fig. 2.79) and subsequently ate them. I am now waiting to see what happens.

Unfortunately I did not have time to visit other temples on and around Lao Shan. The Shanggong (Upper Temple), which is some distance above the Taiqinggong, the Taipinggong (Temple of Supreme Peace) on the northern slopes, and the Huayansi (Magnificent Rock Temple), a Buddhist temple on the eastern slopes, would no doubt be worth visiting.

CHAPTER 3

The North

Included in this chapter are the provinces of Hebei and Liaoning, together with the cities of Beijing and Tianjin and their surrounds, which are now separate administrative areas. This region is traversed by the Great Wall, which was originally built to keep out the non-Han peoples to its north. Much of the history of this part of China relates to the occasions when these people from north of the wall established themselves to its south.

After the fall of the Tang, the Khitan, a Mongolian-speaking tribe from the area around Chengde, moved south, establishing the southern capital of their Liao kingdom on the site of present-day Beijing in 936. They in turn were driven out in 1125 by another of the northern tribes, the Jurchen, rulers of Manchuria at that time, who continued south into Henan, capturing the Song capital, Kaifeng, in 1126. They occupied territory as far south as the Huai River, established a new capital on the Liao site, and assumed the dynastic title, Jin.

Figure 3.1 **Mountains in northern Hebei**

Then in 1210, the Mongols, under Genghis Khan, invaded the Jin kingdom, capturing their capital in 1215, and finally defeating them in 1234.

Although from that time on the Mongols controlled the north, it was not until Genghis' grandson, Khubilai, drove south that their conquest of the rest of the country began. Khubilai declared himself 'Great Khan' in 1260 and, in 1271, moved his capital from Karakorum south to Beijing, taking the title 'Emperor of China' under the dynastic name, Yuan, even though the Southern Song were not finally defeated until 1279.

The native Ming dynasty regained control of the region in 1368, establishing Beijing as their capital in 1420. However, after a period of considerable success, from the late 16th century on the power of the dynasty began to decline. The last four emperors were ineffectual and, following a severe famine in 1628, the people rose against the regime. In 1644 the rebel leader, Li Zicheng, swept unopposed into Beijing, and the emperor Chongzhen committed suicide, it is said, by hanging himself from a tree in what is now Jingshan Park. The triumph of Li Zicheng and his peasant army was short-lived, as soon afterwards the Manchus moved south, occupying the city and establishing Shunzhi, the six-year-old grandson of Nurhachi, who had brought the tribes of the north under his control, as the first Qing emperor of China. Over the next few decades the Manchus brought the whole country under their administration and, although they remained a tiny minority, they managed to maintain control for well over 250 years. Building on the foundations laid by the preceding rulers, it is these people who are responsible for most of the gardens still existing in the north today.

During the successive reigns of Kangxi (1661–1722), Yongzheng (1723–35) and Qianlong (1736–95) China prospered and expanded. From a garden point of view—in fact, from almost all points of view—the most important of these three were Kangxi and his grandson Qianlong. The enormous imperial gardens built by these emperors were astonishing achievements, with their southern influences, picturesque placement of buildings, and incorporation of natural features and views beyond their boundaries. Since much remains of their efforts in renovating, expanding and building gardens, it seems appropriate here to say something more about them.

Kangxi (1654–1722) was the third son of the first Qing emperor, Shunzhi, whom he succeeded in 1661. He led military expeditions to consolidate Qing rule, made six tours of inspection to the lower Yangtze region between 1684 and 1707, and engaged Jesuit missionaries to assist with scientific, architectural and artistic endeavours. One of the results of his, and subsequently his grandson's, journeys to the south was that they built in their gardens copies of famous sights and gardens they had seen there (fig. 3.2). This seems also to have had an influence on the design of private gardens in the north during the Qing.

Amongst Kangxi's enterprises was the construction or renovation of various large gardens on the outskirts of Beijing, including the Changchunyuan, the Yuanmingyuan and the Jingmingyuan. He was also responsible for the construction of the Bishu Shanzhuang (Mountain Villa Where You Can Escape the Heat) at Chengde, some 250 km northeast of the capital, thus reviving the practice of removing the court each year to a 'summer palace'. The Changchunyuan (Garden of Exuberant Spring) was the first Qing 'imperial short-stay villa' type of garden. It was built in the 1680s on the ruined site of the Qinghuayuan, a Ming garden near the present Beijing University. After it was complete, Kangxi spent most of his time there, and Qianlong lived and studied there till he came to the throne.

Kangxi's own account of the construction work shows his regard for the virtues of frugality. There was no luxurious ornamentation or elaborate carving and, wherever possible, advantage was taken of the previous condition of the ground (Malone, 1934). As mentioned in Chapter 1, Matteo Ripa (1844) saw it in the early years of the 18th century, as did John Bell (1763).

Some idea of how imperial gardens were constructed can be gleaned from the material available about the building of imperial gardens from the late 17th century on. For instance, when Kangxi built the Changchunyuan, it was designed and supervised by Ye Tao, an artist born south of the Yangtze who specialised in landscape painting, and the rockeries were executed by Zhang Ran, the best-known rock master of the time who worked in the service of the court for more than 30 years. Zhang Ran was the son of Zhang Lian, a famous garden designer in the Yangtze delta region (Jellicoe et al., 1986).

Qianlong (1711–99) came to the throne in 1736, eventually abdicating in 1795 in order to avoid ruling for more than 60 years—the length of the reign of his illustrious grandfather. Like Kangxi, he was highly versed in China's traditional culture and he, too, made use of the talents of the Jesuit missionaries. His reign is famous for his conquests along

Figure 3.2 Misty Rain Pavilion, Imperial Summer Villa, Chengde

China's western and southern frontiers, as a result of which the country expanded to its greatest extent ever, incorporating Xinjiang, Tibet, Outer Mongolia and parts of Russia.

As his grandfather had done, he undertook six tours of inspection to the south, the first in 1751 and the last in 1784, and became involved in further expenditure on gardens. He carried out alterations to the imperial gardens in Beijing and initiated further work at the Yuanmingyuan, the park at the Fragrant Hills and the Bishu Shanzhuang at Chengde. As well as all this he built the Qingyiyuan (later renamed Yiheyuan, generally known in English as the Summer Palace) and arranged for the renovation or rebuilding of many famous temples. The scope and nature of his achievements in these fields, however, indicates that he was less constrained by notions of frugality and restraint than his grandfather had been.

In spite of the success of Qianlong's reign, the great costs of his military campaigns and extravagant lifestyle had seriously depleted the government reserves, leaving the country unable to withstand foreign encroachments in the succeeding century. Also, the impending problems in this regard were not helped by his refusal to grant concessions to the embassy of Lord Macartney, which had been sent to seek the opening

of China to British trade. As well as all this, by the end of his reign corruption was rising unchecked, and the traditional cycle of peasant uprisings and general unrest which herald the end of a dynasty had begun.

As outlined in Chapter 1, for most of the ensuing two centuries conditions can hardly be said to have been favourable for either the preservation or construction of gardens anywhere in China. Nevertheless, even after 1860 a surprising number of gardens were built or restored. There were even plans to rebuild the Yuanmingyuan. After the destruction of 1860 the hereditary palace architects, the Leis, and their contractors, the Jins, were called in to examine the state of the property. They prepared plans for the restoration and it began in the last days of 1873 but, in view of the projected expense, the work ceased a few months later (Danby, 1950). While these plans never came to fruition, the Dowager Empress Cixi eventually managed to have the Summer Palace restored in 1888, from which time it became her favourite residence. It was restored again after the damage which had been inflicted by the Allied Forces in 1900. In spite of everything that has happened, it is in the north that we can still find one of the greatest concentrations of gardens in the country.

Figure 3.3 *Xanthoceras sorbifolium*, Palace of Tranquil Longevity, Forbidden City, Beijing

Beijing and Environs

Like almost everywhere in China, Beijing has had a long history and various names. This history has been well documented by authors such as Bretschneider (1879), Favier (1902) and Bouillard (1929). A major settlement was established here at some time during the Zhou period (c.1050–221 BC) and, as outlined above, the northern Liao and Jin empires built their capitals there in the 10th and 11th centuries. The Liao built a city the design of which was influenced by Chinese city planning. It was surrounded by a square wall almost 22 km in circumference and had an imperial palace in the centre. After its capture and destruction by the Jin in 1125, it was made their capital in 1153 and rebuilt on a larger and grander scale. The Jin ruler, who came to the throne in 1161, was responsible for the construction of palaces, gardens, temples and country resorts. The Daning Palace (Palace of Great Peace), built in 1179 in the north of the city, was the predecessor of Beihai Park and was modelled on the Song emperor Huizong's Genyue at Kaifeng. A lake, named the Taiye Lake after the famous lake in the Shanglin of Qin and Han times, was dug and earth piled up to make an island, Qionghua Dao (Splendid Jade Island), on which Taihu rocks from the Genyue were placed. A palace was built on top of this island, where the white dagoba now stands. The Jin also had country resorts or 'travelling palaces' at Yuquan Shan (Jade Spring Hill) and at Xiang Shan (Fragrant Hills). A little over 30 years later, however, the Daning Palace was ruined when the Mongols captured the city (Cheng, 1998).

When Khubilai Khan made the city his capital in 1271 he gave it the Chinese name Dadu (Great Capital). With the fall of the Southern Song dynasty in 1279, it became the capital of the whole country for the first time. During Khubilai's reign a large area was enclosed within walls to form a new city, the checkerboard arrangement of the streets was established, palaces were built, the Taiye Lake was developed further,

On the whole, the northern gardens are in a more stiff and formal style than those of areas to the south, and it is often said that they are not imbued with the refined taste of the scholar gardens of the Yangtze delta region. However I prefer rather to think of them as being different. They have a style and charm of their own, no doubt a reflection of both the harsher climate and the taste of their creators. Many of the plants they contain are the same as those seen in gardens elsewhere in the country, even though some of them have to be protected during winter. At the same time, northern Chinese plants, not or only rarely seen elsewhere, are also grown. Notable amongst these are *Prunus davidiana*, *P. triloba*, *Forsythia suspensa*, *Malus spectabilis*, *Syringa oblata*, *S. laciniata*, *S* × *persica*, *S. reticulata*, *Rosa xanthina*, *Xanthoceras sorbifolium* (fig. 3.3) and *Iris lactea*. Along with the northern style of architecture, the presence of these plants adds greatly to the distinctive character of the gardens of this region. Not surprisingly, most of these are to be found in the Beijing administrative area, though there are also a few in the province of Hebei, which surrounds it, and in Liaoning.

Beijing Shi

Beijing Shi is an independent administrative area now separated from the province of Hebei which surrounds it. As well as the city of Beijing such things as the Ming Tombs, part of the Great Wall, and several famous country temples are included within its boundaries.

and a canal was constructed to connect the city to the Grand Canal. Khubilai took the site of the Daning Palace as the centre of the new capital, which consisted of three cities, basically square and one inside the other—the Outer City, the Imperial City and the Palace City. The Taiye Lake in the centre of the Imperial City and the Imperial Garden in the north of the Palace City, which lay to the east of the lake, were the two main palace gardens. The lake had two islands—the small Yingzhou Island (now the Round City), connected by a marble bridge to the larger Qionghua Island of the Jin to its north. Like that of the Jin imperial garden, the layout was a continuation of the Qin and Han tradition of 'Islands of the Immortals' and the names given to the buildings also suggested immortality.

To the west of the Taiye Lake there was another imperial garden, symmetrically arranged like the present Imperial Garden in the Forbidden City. The Yuan emperors also continued to use the Jin resort at Yuquan Shan, and a canal, the Jade River, was constructed to connect it to the capital so that they could go there by water.

At the beginning of the succeeding Ming dynasty, the first Ming emperor, Hongwu, made Yingtianfu (present-day Nanjing) his capital, renaming the Mongol capital Beiping (Northern Peace) and placing it under the rule of his fourth son. After his father's death this son, Yongle, usurped the throne from the rightful heir in 1403, renaming the city Beijing (Northern Capital) and changing the name of Yingtianfu to Nanjing (Southern Capital). In 1420 Beijing was officially made the capital of the Ming empire.

During the Ming dynasty the old city of Dadu was largely demolished and new walls, palaces, temples and gardens were constructed on an even grander scale a little further south. The design followed the ancient pattern of a square oriented to the points of the compass with the emperor's palace in the centre. The walled enclosure in the centre of the city was known as the Imperial City, within which lay the Forbidden City and the imperial gardens. Within the Imperial City the hill to the north of the Forbidden City was made with the soil extracted during the excavation of the palace moat. The Taiye Lake, to the west, was rearranged as three 'seas'—Beihai (North Sea), Zhonghai (Middle Sea), and Nanhai (South Sea)—with three islands—Qionghua Dao, Yantai Dao (Circular Terrace Island, now the Round City), and Nantai Dao (South Terrace Island). This region was known generally as the Xiyuan (West Garden) and the beauty of its lakes, hills,

gardens and pavilions, along with its association with the throne, ensured its wide fame.

While no new imperial gardens were constructed on a grand scale during the Ming, smaller gardens were built or rejuvenated in the environs of the city, particularly in the Haidian district to the north-west and in the vicinity of Yuquan Shan. Also a huge area of pasture land south of the city was walled and developed as a hunting park.

And while, as has been made clear earlier in this chapter, there can be no doubt that the gardens of the north were influenced in the 18th century by those of the lower Yangtze region, it has been suggested that in the 15th century the reverse may have been true (Clunas, 1995; Naquin, 2000). Officials from Suzhou and elsewhere were entertained in the imperial gardens when they visited Beijing and no doubt visited other gardens as well. Descriptions of such visits are to be found in the writings of 15th-century officials and were the models for the numerous 'garden records' composed in the 16th century by Suzhou writers (Clunas, 1995).

When Beijing fell to the Manchus in 1644, they immediately took over the palaces and gardens of the Ming and, as mentioned earlier, built or redeveloped others, particularly in the region to the north-west of the city. In the Haidian district, for instance, there were several large gardens belonging to Manchu princes and high officials and, in the city itself, there were others. Also the Qing emperors, Qianlong in particular, were great builders of temples, both within the imperial domain and elsewhere. A substantial proportion of these were staffed by lamas, as not only had the emperors become personally involved in Tibetan Buddhist beliefs but it accorded with their vision of an empire which they had expanded to take in huge areas where such beliefs were dominant.

With the fall of the Qing dynasty in 1911, Beijing remained, nominally at least, the seat of government, as has been mentioned in Chapter 1. But in 1927 Chiang Kai-shek, leader of the Nationalist Party, declared Nanjing to be the capital of his Republic of China and in 1928 Beijing was renamed Beiping once more. It was occupied by the Japanese from 1937–45, who revived Beijing as its name, and in 1949 it was chosen as the capital of the People's Republic of China. Thus, apart from relatively short breaks, Beijing has been the capital of China for more than 700 years.

The old Ming and Qing city has undergone changes since 1949 that have made it almost unrecognisable. The city walls have been demolished, the Tiananmen (Gate of Heavenly Peace) has been rebuilt and the great square opened up in front of it for parades and ceremonies. At the same time a major east-west road, Changan Avenue, has been built traversing its northern end, greatly diminishing the effect of the north-south alignment of the old city. Most of the temples have gone and few of the tracts of single-storeyed, grey-roofed houses, with their tree-filled courtyards, remain, having been replaced by concrete apartment blocks and administrative and commercial buildings. Nevertheless, in spite of this, the ravages of the Red Guards, and the other upheavals of the past century or so, a surprising amount remains in and around the city to attract those interested in gardens. No doubt there are still gardens in the old part of the city about which I do not know but which have survived as a result of being occupied by government departments or retired officials. Examples which I have come upon are the Keyuan and the Liu Yong Yuan. Although permission to visit these is not easy to obtain I have included them below as they are rare examples of small Qing urban gardens. I have also included brief mention of the Ming Tombs, which are situated in the northern part of the Beijing administrative area.

While those so inclined will find horticultural interest in Beijing's public parks, for reasons of space I have not included all of them here. Likewise I have omitted the Beijing Medicinal Botanical Garden in the Haidian district and the Beijing Educational Botanical Garden in the south-west of the city, as I have not visited them. Also there are places frequently mentioned in the older literature which may still exist but which I have not managed to find. It would be interesting, for instance, to know whether the impressive avenue of old white-barked pines (*Pinus bungeana*) still survives at the Longmensi (Dragon Gate Temple) in the hills west of the city. It was described by Hubbard (1923), who said that the temple had gone but that a Ming tomb to which the avenue led remained. The few inquiries I made about this were met with blank looks. Another famous sight was the Heilongtan (Black Dragon Pool), which lay on the road from Beijing to the Dajuesi and which has been mentioned in Chapter 1. From the early 20th century there are lyrical descriptions by Western visitors of the pool overhung by wisteria in which, apparently, Europeans were allowed to swim, as Juliet Bredon (1931) did. George Kates (1967) was another to record doing so in the 1930s while the lavender blossoms dropped onto the water. Dorothy Graham (1938) photographed it around

this time (fig. 1.20), and it was also visited by Osbert Sitwell (1939), who recorded that, like most places he saw, it was rotting away and that soon little would be left. It may well be that his prediction has come true as, even though the district where it was situated is now called Heilongtan, when I attempted to find it no one I encountered there had heard of it or the temple with which it was associated.

A conspicuous feature of the gardens and parks of Beijing in spring is the carpet of self-sown *Orychophragmus violaceus* (fig. 3.4), the mauve flowers of which are similar to those of honesty (*Lunaria annua*). It is said that the Manchus brought this plant from the north and, according to Dorothy Graham (1938), it evokes, as it sways in the wind, the plains extending to the horizon. It should also be noted that, whereas in the Forbidden City and in many of the older gardens in and around Beijing the rockeries are made of Taihu rocks brought from the south, the large and elaborate rockeries, which are such a feature of later Beijing gardens, are usually made of rock from the Western Hills. Presumably at that time Taihu rocks had become too expensive, if not impossible, to procure for most such compositions.

GUGONG (IMPERIAL PALACE)

The Imperial Palace is usually known in the West as the Forbidden City and, although most of the buildings have been repeatedly rebuilt or restored, it retains its Ming layout. The philosophy underlying the design and use of the various parts of the enclosure are explained well by Ru and Peng (1998) and will not be gone into here. It was officially opened to the public in 1925 and its principal gardens are the Imperial Garden, the garden of the Palace of Tranquil Longevity, and the garden of the Palace of Compassion and Tranquillity.

The Imperial Garden (Yuhuayuan) lies at the rear of the complex and on its central axis. Measuring only 80 × 140 m, it retains what is believed to be its original symmetrical Ming design. On a terrace on the central axis is the principal building, the Hall of Imperial Tranquillity, to which the emperor came on New Year's Day to worship a Daoist water god charged with protecting the palace from fire (Béguin & Morel, 1997). On the western side of this is a double-roofed

Figure 3.4 (opposite page) *Orychophragmus violaceus* beneath the thujas, Temple of Heaven, Beijing

pavilion, the Pavilion of a Thousand Autumns (fig. 3.5), and on the eastern side is its partner, the Pavilion of Ten Thousand Springs. The upper roof of each is circular, alluding to heaven, and the lower square, alluding to earth, an arrangement symbolising the harmony of the universe. Behind these pavilions is a pair of pools and against the rear wall on the eastern side an immense rock pile, the Hill of Accumulated Refinement, topped by the Pavilion of the Imperial Prospect (fig. 1.26). This is sufficiently tall to allow a view over the wall, though it is not now accessible to the public. It was ascended by the imperial family on festivals, such as the Double Ninth (the ninth day of the ninth lunar month), when it was the traditional practice to ascend hills.

It must have been the only place from which the women of the court could obtain a glimpse of the outside world. It was from here, too, that Mrs Little (1901) was able to survey the scene after the court had fled to Xi'an. And on 23 October 1924 the deposed emperor Puyi, who after 1911 had been allowed to continue living in the northern part of the Forbidden City, climbed this eminence in the company of his tutor, Reginald Johnston, to observe the troops who had occupied Coal Hill during the *coup d'état* which a few days later was to result in his expulsion.

The Imperial Garden contains many old trees and shrubs, including pines, junipers and catalpas (fig. 3.6). There are also beds of tree and herbaceous peonies, *Parthenocissus*

Figure 3.5 (above) **Pavilion of a Thousand Autumns, Imperial Garden, Forbidden City,**

Figure 3.6 (left) ***Catalpa bungei*, Imperial Garden, Forbidden City**

Figure 3.7 (right) **Rock mountain seen from the Hall of Ancient Flowers in the garden of the Palace of Tranquil Longevity, Forbidden City**

tricuspidata trained over rocks, an old wisteria climbing a dead tree trunk, a fine specimen of the 'Dragon's Claw' Chinese date (*Ziziphus jujuba* 'Tortuosa') and many other traditional garden plants. As well as these there are pieces of petrified wood arranged amongst bamboos as 'stone bamboo shoots', together with fantastic rocks, pieces of coral, and fossils displayed on elaborate marble pedestals. In fact so much has been placed in this small area that it presents a somewhat confused aspect, particularly when crowded with visitors. However it is a garden of great historical interest and was much frequented by members of the imperial families and their attendants, both for pleasure and for carrying out ceremonies associated with the seasons.

The garden of the Palace of Tranquil Longevity was built in the eastern part of the compound in 1771, the 36th year of Qianlong's reign. With its rockeries, grottoes and pavilions, it conjures up the atmosphere of gardens he had seen in the south. It is only about half the size of the Imperial Garden but seems smaller even than that, as it is divided into five courtyards. Entering from the south, the first is the most impressive of these, with the Hall of Ancient Flowers situated centrally on the northern side and the Pavilion of the Ceremony of Purification (fig. 2.4), which has a cup-floating stream cut into its floor, on the western side. On the eastern side there is a rock hill with a cave in its base and a terrace, the Terrace for Receiving Dew, on its summit (fig. 3.7).

Figure 3.8 A courtyard behind the Palace of Tranquil Longevity, Forbidden City

To the south of this are two small courtyards with trees and rockwork, and to the north of the Hall of Ancient Flowers there is a larger courtyard. The garden is shaded by trees and various features have been given names suggesting the peaceful retirement which Qianlong anticipated. It remains peaceful today, as few of the tourists who throng the Forbidden City find their way there.

To the north of the garden of the Palace of Tranquil Longevity there are further small garden courtyards (fig. 3.8), in the northernmost of which is a well with a stone cover. This is the Zhenfeijing (Well of the Pearl Concubine), in which Guangxu's favourite concubine, Zhenfei, is supposed to have been drowned on Cixi's orders in 1900 for attempting to persuade him to stay in Beijing and face the consequences of the defeat of the Boxers.

On the opposite side of the palace enclosure is the garden of the Palace of Compassion and Tranquillity. Like the Imperial Garden, it occupies a rectangular space, is symmet-

rically arranged, and is not broken up into courtyards. There are several buildings of which the most notable is the Brookside Pavilion, centrally placed towards the southern end. This spans an oblong pond and has doors and windows on all four sides from which views of the garden are obtained. As this garden has not been open at the times of my visits, I am relying here on the description and photograph of Ru and Peng (1998). However, there are said to be trees of various kinds and beds of tree and herbaceous peonies. The garden, including the Brookside Pavilion, was first built in the Ming and renovated in the Qing during the reign of Qianlong, when new buildings were added.

Also not accessible at the time of writing is the small garden beside the Wenyuange (Pavilion of Literary Depth), built in the years 1774–76 by Qianlong and recently restored (fig. 3.9). It was constructed to house the first copy to be completed of the *Siku quanshu* (Complete Collection of the Four Treasuries), a collection of 36 000 manuscript volumes compiled on Qianlong's orders, ostensibly with the intention of preserving rare works from oblivion. However, it involved a literary inquisition on a scale, as Wood (1992) points out, not to be repeated until the Cultural Revolution of the 1960s. Works submitted for inclusion were scrutinised for anti-Manchu sentiments, hundreds of volumes were destroyed, and authors and their families were killed or subjected to posthumous disgrace. Several copies of the collection were made and housed in various parts of the country in specially constructed buildings, the design of which was based on that of the Tianyige, a famous library in Ningbo, and its adjoining garden. The Wenyuange is one of these and has a roof of black tiles with a border of green ones. Black being the colour associated with water, it was regarded as giving protection against fire.

LAODONG RENMIN WENHUAGONG (WORKERS' CULTURAL PALACE)

This park to the right of the entrance to the Forbidden City is the site of the Taimiao (Imperial Ancestral Temple), established by the Ming emperor Yongle in 1420. The most sacred place in Beijing after the Temple of Heaven, it was rebuilt in 1544 and consists of three imposing halls arranged along a central axis. It was renamed the Workers' Cultural Palace in 1950.

The park surrounding the walled enclosure in which the temple buildings are placed is thickly planted with thujas, most of which are ancient. There are also junipers, walnuts and a few specimens of *Rosa xanthina*. As

well as these, to the west of the temple buildings a collection of tree peonies has been planted beneath the thujas (fig. 3.10).

ZHONGSHAN GONGYUAN (SUN YAT-SEN PARK)

This park is on the left of the entrance to the Forbidden City and, like the Workers' Cultural Palace, contains old thujas and much else of interest. According to *Peking: A Tourist Guide* (1960), it occupies the site of a temple dating back to the Liao and Jin and some of the thujas date from this time. Not far from the entrance an avenue of ginkgos leads to the Shijitan (Altar of the Land and Grain), originally built in 1421, where the emperors came in spring and autumn to make sacrifices and pray for and give thanks for the harvest. This is a square

Figure 3.9 (above right)
Wenyuange, Forbidden City

Figure 3.10 (right)
Tree peonies, Workers' Cultural Palace, Beijing

marble terrace on which are spread coloured earths representing the five directions—north, south, east, west and the centre—and symbolising imperial control of the various regions of the country (fig. 3.11). Juliet Bredon (1931) recorded that in the early days of the Republic this ancient platform was used for fireworks displays and boxing bouts. Now, thank goodness, its dignity has been restored, and its present appearance is much the same as when Miss Gordon Cumming (1890) saw it in 1879.

North of the altar is the Hall of Prayer, later dedicated to Sun Yat-sen, where the sacrificial implements were kept. Also dating from 1421, it is said to be the oldest well-preserved

Figure 3.11 (below)
Altar of the Land and
Grain with Hall of Prayer
behind, Zhongshan Park,
Beijing

Figure 3.12 (bottom)
Conservatory, Zhongshan
Park, Beijing

Figure 3.13 (above)
Tulips, Zhongshan Park, Beijing

wooden building in Beijing. Also of interest near the western edge of the park is the Lanting Beiting (Pavilion of the Orchid Pavilion Steles), a pavilion housing steles salvaged from the Lanting Bazhu (Eight Pillars of the Orchid Pavilion) at the Yuanmingyuan. Elsewhere there are extensive roofed walkways and a conservatory in late Qing style in which displays of potted plants are mounted (fig. 3.12). There is also a rock and earth mountain with a pavilion on top and, in the southwestern corner, a winding lake with extensive rocky surrounds which, like the avenues of ancient thujas, appears to have survived unaltered from the era before the park was

opened to the public in 1914. At this time it was called Zhongyang Gongyuan (Central Park) but in 1928 it was renamed Zhongshan Gongyuan in memory of Sun Yat-sen—Zhongshan being the Pinyin transliteration of a surname he later adopted.

There are also seasonal displays of bedding plants, particularly near the entrance. At present tulips (fig. 3.13), which have become popular all over the country, occupy much space in spring. Elsewhere there is much that is Chinese. For instance, in the northern part of the garden there is a large tree peony garden amongst the thujas, and elsewhere there

Figure 3.14 (left) *Syringa × persica* **and** *S. laciniata*, **Zhongshan Park, Beijing**

Figure 3.15 (below left) *Viburnum sargentii*, **Huifangyuan, Zhongshan Park, Beijing**

bamboo grove to an open area planted with Chinese trees and shrubs, including *Pinus bungeana*, *P. tabuliformis*, *Magnolia denudata*, *Chimonanthus praecox*, *Poncirus trifoliata*, *Prunus mume*, *Viburnum sargentii* (fig. 3.15), *Cotoneaster multiflorus*, *Campsis grandiflora*, *Juniperus chinensis* 'Kaizuka', *Firmiana simplex* and *Ulmus pumila* 'Pendula'. Beyond this area is a courtyard formed by four buildings of traditional design which are used for exhibitions of orchids and other seasonal flowers.

JINGSHAN GONGYUAN (JINGSHAN PARK)

Jing Shan (Mountain with a Beautiful View) is the name given in the Qing to the hill built up on the site of an earlier Yuan imperial garden with earth excavated during the construction of the moat of the Forbidden City. It was created for geomantic reasons to protect the palaces against evil influences coming from the north (Arlington & Lewisohn, 1935). The hill was formerly known by Westerners as Coal Hill, as it was said, probably erroneously, that coal was stored at its foot during the Ming. It consists of five eminences, the tallest in the centre, on each of which a pavilion was built during the reign of Qianlong. It was from the Pavilion of Everlasting Spring at the highest point that Felice Beato was able to photograph the view over Beihai in 1860.

are wisterias, lilacs (*Syringa oblata*, *S. laciniata*, and *S. × persica*) (fig. 3.14), flowering peaches, smoke bushes, *Rosa xanthina* and other Chinese trees and shrubs.

A little to the west of the Altar of the Land and Grain there is a separate modern garden, the Huifangyuan (Garden of Assembled Perfumes), for which there is an additional admission charge. From the entrance a path leads through a

The hill was originally included in the Imperial City to which, in normal times, visitors had no access, but was opened to the public in 1928, since when the whole area has been developed as a garden. As well as a wide variety of trees and shrubs, there are plantings of daylilies, *Hosta plantaginea*, *H. ventricosa*, tree and herbaceous peonies and many other ornamental plants. While there are now tree peonies in many parts of the park, perhaps the most interesting area is the original tree peony garden at the eastern end. Bordered by rows of *Sophora japonica* 'Pendula' (fig. 3.16), it contains magnificent old peony plants, some about 2 m tall, and is a splendid sight in May (fig. 3.17).

BEIHAI GONGYUAN (BEIHAI PARK)

This park includes the northernmost of the three lakes which occupy that part of the imperial enclosure which in the late Qing came to be known to Westerners as the Winter Palace. Felice Beato's photographs of 1860 show Beihai to have been drained and Qionghua Island to be looking a little the worse for wear (Harris, 1999), so there can be no doubt that things have looked up since then. When the original republic was established the Winter Palace was taken over by the new government but, after the Provisional Chief Executive moved out in 1925, all three lakes and their surrounds were opened as public parks (Bredon, 1931). Beihai now forms the focus of a site where there was originally a secondary palace of the

Figure 3.16 (right) *Sophora japonica* 'Pendula', **Jingshan Park, Beijing**

Figure 3.17 (below) **Tree peonies, Jingshan Park**

Liao rulers, though the lake was not dug until the Jin took over. The park includes the peninsula known as the Round Town, Qionghua Island, and a number of temples and gardens on the northern and eastern shores which were built during the reign of Qianlong. Since it is now much frequented and much changed, a visit can certainly be enhanced if one listens to what Osvald Sirén (1926), when writing of it, described as 'the whispering of bygone ages'.

Entering at the southern end, one comes immediately to the Round Town, the site chosen by Khubilai Khan for his palace. It is a raised circular enclosure surrounded by a castellated wall and contains several interesting trees, including white-barked pines said to date from the Jin or possibly even the Liao (fig. 3.18). In the centre of the enclosure is a small blue-tiled pavilion built in 1745 to house an enormous carved jade bowl. This is claimed have been presented to Khubilai Khan in 1265 but to have become lost at the end of the Yuan and not rediscovered until the early Qing, when it was found in a small temple where it had been used for pickling vegetables. Although Beihai had become a public park, even in Sirén's (1926) time the Round Town was inaccessible to visitors except by special permission, as it was occupied by

Figure 3.18 (left)
Pear and white-barked pine in the Round City, Beihai Park, Beijing

Figure 3.19 (above)
View of Qionghua Island and Jing Shan from the lake, Beihai Park

Figure 3.20 (below) **Statue of an Immortal holding a dish for receiving the 'heavenly nectar', Beihai Park**

the families of high officials. Eventually, however, it was opened to the public though there is now a separate admission charge.

A handsome marble bridge connects the Round City to Qionghua Island which lies immediately to its north. This island, often referred to as Hortensia Island, is dominated by the white dagoba erected on its summit in 1651. It was built as part of a Lamaist temple constructed to celebrate the first visit by a Dalai Lama to Beijing. Many of the Ming buildings on the island were demolished during the early Qing and most of the structures we see today date from the time of Qianlong, who rearranged things to resemble the famous Jinshan Island on the Yangtze near Zhenjiang (fig. 3.19).

Amongst objects dating from earlier times are the Taihu rocks—presumably those brought here from the Genyue at Kaifeng by the Jin—and, on the eastern side, a stele inscribed Qiongdao chunyin (Qionghua Island in Spring) which was moved to this position by Qianlong—a poem by whom is inscribed in his calligraphy on the back. Also of note, on the northern slope, is a bronze statue of an Immortal standing on a marble column and holding a dish above his head for receiving the 'heavenly nectar' (fig. 3.20). This statue was supposedly cast for the Han emperor Wudi, who was advised by Daoists that drinking dew mixed with powdered jade would bring him immortality. It is said to have been brought here from Shaanxi by Khubilai Khan in the late 13th century. In striking contrast to all these things is the Kentucky Fried Chicken outlet which has been set up on the southern shore. I am told, however, that efforts are now being made to have this removed. On the other hand, I hope there are no moves to get rid of the small business on the western shore of the island which rents battery-operated boats, as hiring one of these and gently sailing around the lake admiring the scenery is an adventure worth undertaking.

As well as the buildings and rockeries, there are many plants to admire on the island. In addition to numerous old catalpas (*C. bungei*), there are flowering peaches, crabapples (*Malus halliana*), wisterias (fig. 3.21), and lilacs (*Syringa oblata* and an occasional plant of *S. meyeri*), along with specimens of *Rosa xanthina*, *Xanthoceras sorbifolium* and other trees and shrubs typical of northern gardens. In addition to these, the lake beside the bridge leading from the Round City is planted with lotuses and is a magnificent sight in summer.

The northern shore of the lake is lined with weeping willows. It can be reached from Qionghua Island by returning to the mainland by the bridge on its eastern side and walking north or, less strenuously, by taking the ferry across from the northern side. The most conspicuous feature here is the group of pavilions known as the Five Dragon Pavilions, dating from 1602. These are built out over the water and the middle one, which has a circular roof sitting above a square one, is said to have been used by the emperors for fishing. Set back from the water behind these is a series of buildings dating from the Qianlong era, most of which were originally temples. In the grounds of and around these are bamboos and a variety of trees and shrubs, including crabapples (*Malus spectabilis*), flowering peaches and ginkgos.

In the north-western corner of the park is an enclosure formerly known as the Daxitian (Large Western Heaven), the grounds of which have been redeveloped as a small botanical garden. One can still see here several plants which are now otherwise rare in Chinese gardens—for example *Solanum aculeatissimum*, *Aquilegia flabellata* and *Sedum erythrostictum*—and in autumn the buildings and grounds are usually occupied by a chrysanthemum display.

Immediately to the east and directly behind the Five Dragon Pavilions is the Chanfusi (Temple of Happy Meditation), beyond which are buildings now used as a restaurant. Set back to the east of these is the Nine Dragon Screen. This is a screen wall covered with glazed-tile dragons which was built in 1417 in front of a temple which no longer exists. To the east of this again is the recently restored Xiaoxitian (Small Western Heaven) or Tianwangdian (Temple of the Heavenly King). It has interesting drum and bell towers and a fine Ming principal hall in which three splendid Buddha statues have been placed. As well, nine unusually refined statues of lohans have been arranged along each of the east and west walls.

Next door is the Jingxinzhai (Studio of the Pure Heart), a fine surviving example of a small northern garden (fig. 3.22), and it looks almost exactly the same today as it did in the photographs which Osvald Sirén (1926) took in 1922. Although it was originally built in the Ming, in its present form the Jingxinzhai dates from the reign of Qianlong, who had it rebuilt as a study for the princes. In the late 19th century it was a favourite retreat of Cixi. Rising along its northern side is a large rock mountain, up over which runs a roofed walkway. On a smaller eminence there is an octagonal pavilion which overlooks a rectangular one built out over a pond, which is surrounded by rocks over which *Parthenocissus tricuspidata* is growing. Of particular note amongst the trees in the garden is David's peach (*Prunus davidiana*).

Returning south along the eastern bank of the main

Figure 3.21 (left) **Wisteria pergola, Qionghua Island, Beihai Park**

Figure 3.22 (opposite page) **Jingxinzhai, Beihai Park**

Figure 3.23 (left) Crabapple at Huafangzhai, Beihai Park

Figure 3.24 (below) Haopujian, Beihai Park

lake through an avenue of tall poplars (*Populus × tomentosa*), one passes a children's playground which occupies the site of the former Altar of the Silkworms and Hall of Imperial Silkworms. Beyond this is a group of buildings arranged around a rectangular pond. This is the Huafangzhai (Painted Boat Studio), beside the entrance to which is a white crabapple (fig. 3.23). A path which winds south from here through a ravine of artificially arranged rocks leads to an irregularly shaped pond crossed by a long marble bridge, on the far side of which is the Haopujian (Hao Riverside Study) (fig. 3.24). Its name refers to the Hao River, which was where Zhuang Zi observed the fish and felt their happiness. Both these gardens date from the Qianlong period. Further on still, on the shore of the main lake, is the Imperial Boathouse. From here a path takes the visitor back past Qionghua Island to the southern entrance of the park.

ZHONGNANHAI (MIDDLE AND SOUTH LAKES)

Zhongnanhai is the name given nowadays to the walled enclosure in which Zhonghai and Nanhai lie. After the fall of the Qing in 1911, the Presidents of the Republic made it their home and foreigners were not usually admitted except for receptions and garden parties until 1925. Likewise, following the establishment of the People's Republic, the highest government officials have set themselves up in this part of the former domain of the imperial family. It is guarded around the clock by the military and remains inaccessible to the public. As Storey et al. (1998) have observed, it is China's new Forbidden City.

An idea of what it contains or contained can be obtained from the photographs of Donald Mennie (1920) and Osvald Sirén (1926, 1949), the plans and descriptions of Arlington and Lewisohn (1935), and Dorothy Graham's (1938) descriptions and photographs. These make it clear that there are or

Figure 3.25 View into Zhonghai with the Water Cloud Kiosk on the right

were many charming gardens and pavilions. Some of the latter have subsequently been removed to Beijing parks (Hu, 1991). In Sirén's time there was a high wall along the southern side of the public bridge which separates Zhonghai from Beihai so that it was impossible to see in at all. The bridge was rebuilt and widened in 1956 and no longer has this feature, so a general view of Zhonghai is available to all (fig. 3.25). The only discernible features of interest, however, are the roof of the Hall of Ten Thousand Virtues and the nearby Water Cloud Kiosk, now sadly run down, of which Sirén took such beautiful photographs (fig. 3.26). However, although you can gaze at it from the bridge, if you get out a camera and attempt to photograph it, armed soldiers rush out, gesticulating wildly, and forbid it. On the other hand, no one takes the slightest notice if you photograph it from the battlements of the Round City a few metres to the north.

In the late 19th century Zhonghai became the home of the Dowager Empress Cixi, who went to live on its western shore. European-style buildings were constructed there at this time and, judging by what can be seen from the bridge, there are probably now many more. Fortunately the light railway which Cixi had built to carry her from Zhonghai to Jingxinzhai on the northern shore of Beihai has disappeared.

Nanhai is separated from Zhonghai by a strip of land penetrated only by a canal spanned by bridges. Its chief feature is the Yingtai (Ocean Terrace), the name of which refers to Yingzhou, one of the three Islands of the Immortals. The island underwent renovation early in the Qing dynasty and, after the failure of the Reform Movement of 1898, Cixi had the emperor Guangxu, who supported the movement, imprisoned here and at the Summer Palace until his death in 1908. While Nanhai cannot be seen at all from outside, judging from the aerial photograph of the three lakes published by Hu (1991), it appears that, while there are now many modern buildings, Yingtai has been left undisturbed.

As well as the information provided by Mennie, Sirén, Arlington and Lewisohn, and Dorothy Graham, there is an earlier description of Yingtai by Mrs Little (1905), who was able to go there in 1901 after the court had fled to Xi'an. She wrote:

> The most beautiful spot in Peking, if among so many picturesque retreats there be one more enticing than the others, is the island on the lake where the Emperor for the last two years before his flight was confined as in a gilded prison. It is covered with yellow-tiled pavilions, each more picturesque than the other, with summer-houses, boat house, rockery, petrified trees, fantastic little Chinese gardens, and is connected with the mainland with a wooden drawbridge which was withdrawn when Kwangshu lived there ...

Figure 3.26 Water Cloud Kiosk, Zhonghai, in 1922.

FROM SIRÉN (1926).

BEITANG (NORTH CHURCH)

This church is situated a short distance west of the bridge which separates Beihai and Zhonghai. It is the only church mentioned in this book but I have included it on account of the small garden which lies in front of it. The Beitang is the third church of that name built in Beijing, the first being completed in 1703 a little to the east of the present building on land given to the French Jesuits by Kangxi. However, as a result of the suppression of the order in 1773, the land was sold in 1827 and the building demolished. Then, following the treaty signed in 1860 which stipulated that the land be returned, a new church was built on the site in 1867. This did not last long either, as when Cixi came to live on the shore of Zhonghai in 1885 she objected to its presence nearby. Arrangements were then made for a new building, which opened in 1888, to be erected further to the west. Its predecessor, which was not demolished until 1911, was used as a storehouse by Cixi. Some of the worst fighting of the Boxer Rebellion took place when the Beitang was besieged in 1900. More than 4000 Chinese Christians had sought refuge here under the care of Bishop Favier and some hundreds were killed while assisting with its defence. It fell on hard times

Figure 3.28 Grotto at the Beitang

again during the Cultural Revolution when it was vandalised before being used as a school. Eventually it was restored to the Beijing Catholic Patriotic Association and reopened in 1985.

The church is of Gothic design and the interior, with its soaring columns painted in traditional Chinese green and red, is both unusual and impressive. The facade is painted grey and white and in front, on either side, is a pair of Chinese-style pavilions (fig. 1.25). A double white multiflora rose is planted against the marble steps leading up into the pavilion on the west side (fig. 3.27) and a double pink, which looks to be a multiflora hybrid, is next to the steps of the eastern one. Elsewhere in the garden there are China roses, a single white crabapple, a walnut and other plants. The most conspicuous feature, however, is a grotto with a statue of the Virgin. While the statue is in the taste in which she is frequently represented all over the world, the grotto is notable as an unusual example of the Chinese art of piling rocks (fig. 3.28).

GONGWANGFU (PRINCE GONG'S MANSION)

Immediately to the north of Beihai and Jing Shan is a part of old Beijing which so far has escaped demolition. This area lies around the so-called Back Lakes, which are part of the system of lakes and canals which bring waters from the Jade Spring to the Forbidden City, Beihai and Zhongnanhai. Here there is still a maze of narrow streets known as hutongs, lined with traditional single-storeyed courtyard houses, amongst which remain a few of

Figure 3.27 White multiflora rose, Beitang, Beijing

the mansions of the Manchu princes. These are known in Chinese as 'fu', and by the end of the 19th century there were more than 50 of these in Beijing. The families of the sons of emperors were allowed to enjoy possession of a fu for three generations, after which it reverted to the emperor, who granted it to a son of his own or a daughter on her marriage (Edkins, 1870). The most impressive of the survivors is Gongwangfu, the mansion and garden of Prince Gong, which has come through the vicissitudes of the last century or so more or less intact.

A detailed history and description of this estate is given by Ch'ên and Kates (1940). In the late 18th century the emperor Qianlong gave it to his controversial favourite, He Shen, who built an extravagant mansion and garden. Then,

when Qianlong died in 1799, He Shen was disgraced and forced to commit suicide by Qianlong's successor, Jiaqing. The bulk of the property was confiscated and conferred upon Prince Qing, Qianlong's 17th and youngest son, who lived there with his sister. When he died in 1820 there followed a complex series of inheritances until 1851, when it passed to Prince Gong (fig. 1.14), the 6th son of the emperor Daoguang, who took up residence there the following year.

As mentioned earlier, Prince Gong came to notice in 1860 when, after the emperor had fled to Chengde, he was left to deal with the English and French following their campaign of 1860. Subsequently he was placed in charge of China's foreign affairs and managed with great skill to steer the country on a safe course from 1861 until 1884, when he fell from

Figure 3.29 (left) Entrance courtyard,
Gongwangfu, Beijing

Figure 3.30 (below) Building with pillars
painted to resemble bamboo, Gongwangfu

Figure 3.31 (opposite page) Cup-floating
pavilion, Gongwangfu

favour and was displaced. He was reinstated in 1894 but China's position had deteriorated in the meantime and he declined to accept full responsibility again, spending most of his last days at his country garden, a little to the north of what is now Beijing University in Haidian, and at the Jietaisi in the Western Hills.

Following his death in 1898, his grandson, Puwei, inherited the title and the property, and when he died it passed to his younger brother, Prince Puru, the last of the family to live there (fig. 1.34). In the late 1930s it was acquired by the Catholic University of Peking and eventually passed into public ownership. The mansion itself is enormous, consisting of three parallel axial arrangements of buildings and courtyards running north-south. Anyone wishing to read about it is referred to the paper of Ch'ên and Kates, which details, amongst other things, how Prince Gong had his studies decorated with excerpts from Tang verses and pots of chrysanthemums, as many as a hundred in one room. At the time of writing the mansion is used as a music school and residences. The garden lies to the north of this, separated from it by a two-storey building which runs east-west across the full width of the property. The garden is surrounded by artificial hills, so that even its own walls are not visible and the outside world is excluded.

It is clear that Prince Gong was responsible for the construction of this garden, which according to Ch'ên and Kates (1940) he named Langrunyuan, which they translate as the Garden of Moonlit Fertility, and which was also the name of his garden at Haidian, which was also still in existence in the 1930s. However, according to Chen (1999), the name of the garden at Gongwangfu is now Cuijinyuan (Garden Gathering All Splendours). In the opinion of Ch'ên and Kates, it is the finest city garden in northern China.

It was arranged as 20 scenes or views, in the manner frequently encountered in Chinese descriptions of famous places, each with a name which gives some idea of the manner in which it was enjoyed. Like the mansion, it is constructed on three north-south axes. The principal entrance, in semi-foreign style, leads into the central axis through an elaborate rockery of Western Hills rock and past a tall Taihu stone into a large courtyard. This space has buildings and covered walkways on its northern, eastern and western sides, a pool in the centre, and is planted with white-barked pines, sophoras and other trees and flowering plants (fig. 3.29). Beyond this is another pool in front of a grotto at the base of a tall rock mountain made, in this instance, of Taihu rock. This is the highest such structure in the garden and is crowned with a pavilion in front of which is a terrace for viewing the moon. On either side of the pavilion sloping walkways lead down to ground level and on the far side of it, at the end of a steep path through a rockery of Western Hills stone, is a handsome building the pillars of which are painted to resemble bamboo (fig. 3.30).

The eastern axis is more in the nature of a residential section, with buildings and walkways surrounding small courtyards. On its southern side there is a small vegetable garden and nursery area, at the western end of which is an octagonal pavilion with a cup-floating channel in the floor, looking exactly as it did in Sirén's photograph (fig. 3.31). The principal courtyard of the building complex is intersected at right angles by two paths and the four beds so created are planted with tree and herbaceous peonies and roses. Over the door at the northern end there is a wooden portico on which wisteria is trained. The principal building in this section is an elaborately decorated theatre where Prince Gong enjoyed entertaining friends. At the time of my last visit it was being used to stage entertainments for tourists. To the rear of this building there are further small courtyards, one planted with bananas, which lead back to the environs of the rock mountain.

The western section of the garden provides a complete contrast. Much of its area is made up of a rectangular pond in the centre of which is a pavilion—the Terrace for Watching the Fish (figs 1.39, 1.40). Running along the eastern side of the pond is a long covered walkway, and to the north there was a planting of crabapples (*Malus spectabilis*)—one of the 20 scenes. It was here when they were in bloom each year that Prince Puru entertained Chinese and foreign guests. When Osbert Sitwell (1935; 1974) went to one of these parties in April 1934 he recorded that the ponds were dry and, as mentioned in Chapter 1, he enjoyed looking down on the blossoms from the tops of flights of stone steps. Dorothy Graham (1938) described how these trees had been pruned so that

Figure 3.32 Great Wall and Pavilion of Admirable Fragrance, Gongwangfu

they had multiple trunks. When I first went to this garden in 1994 no crabapples remained, but on returning in 1996 I found that they had been replanted, and in 2000 were growing well.

At the southern end of the pond is a pavilion which looks out over the scene to its north, and to its east there is an unusual two-storeyed structure, the Miaoxiangting (Pavilion of Admirable Fragrance), ascribed to the years just before 1890 (fig. 1.1). Old photographs show there to have been crabapples in this vicinity too. Close behind is the garden's most eccentric feature, a small-scale replica of part of the Great Wall, on top of which one can walk for some distance (fig. 3.32). It is called Elm Pass, an alternative name for Shanhaiguan, the place where the Great Wall meets the sea.

In the north-western corner of the garden there is an area which is no longer accessible. This was the original service area where there were as many as four 'huadong' (flower caves)—traditional Chinese greenhouses of the type described by Cibot (1778). These houses would have been used for protecting frost-tender plants and for forcing flowers in the traditional manner in the winter months. There is a record from as late as 1906 relating how one of these used to be cleared out in autumn and furnished with tables and couches as a warm retreat for Prince Gong's second son, Zaiying, the father of Puwei and Puru, who returned to live there in 1902, having been deprived of all his ranks in 1900 because of his pro-Boxer activities (Ch'ên & Kates, 1940; Hummel, 1943).

The garden now looks much as it does in Osvald Sirén's (1949) photographs, although at the time he took them the pond was empty and there were weeds growing between the stones of its base. Since it is not amongst the princely mansions he described after his visit to Beijing in 1922 (Sirén, 1926), presumably he saw it during his visits of 1929 and/or 1935. It is also clear that it has undergone much restoration since the time of Ch'ên and Kates, whose mentioning of the past presence in it of deer, dogs, cranes, hawks, falcons and caged birds does much to conjure up a picture of it in its heyday.

It is sometimes claimed that Gongwangfu provided the inspiration for the garden in Cao Xueqin's *The Story of the Stone*. However, since the novel was published in the late 18th century and Prince Gong's garden was built at least 60 years later, this cannot be so. There remains, of course, the possibility that He Shen had a garden of this type on the site in

Figure 3.33 Roofed walkway, Former Residence of Soong Qing Ling, Beijing

the 18th century, but even this would have been very new at the time Cao Xueqin was writing.

SONG QINGLING GUJU
(FORMER RESIDENCE OF SOONG QING LING)

Situated not far from Gongwangfu, on the northern side of the Back Lakes, this was the home of Soong Qing Ling (Madam Sun Yat-sen) from 1963 until her death in1981. Also known in English as the Soong Qing Ling Memorial Residence, this property is of interest because her house was built in the garden of Qiyefu (Mansion of the Seventh Prince), which originally belonged to Yihui (1799–1838), a great grandson of Qianlong. In 1859 it was given to Yihuan (1840–91), a half brother of Prince Gong who became the first Prince Chun. His fifth son, Zaifeng, inherited the property and the princedom in 1891. In 1906 his son, Puyi, who became the last emperor in 1908, was born here. Prince Chun, who acted as regent for his infant son and was thus the actual ruler of China, failed to abide by the ancient custom whereby the home of a prince who had ascended the throne could not continue to be inhabited by his relatives. According to Arlington and Lewisohn (1935), Puyi's subse-

quent misfortune has been attributed to this state of affairs. In fact Prince Chun and the ex-emperor's younger brother were still living at Qiyefu when the garden was visited and photographed by Osvald Sirén in 1922. And, before fleeing to the Japanese Legation in Tianjin, Puyi returned here briefly in 1924, when he was obliged to leave the Forbidden City (Johnston, 1934).

Dorothy Graham (1938) was another to see this garden, which she described as 'static twilight', mentioning an oval pool and a pavilion on a hillock. These are still there and, although Soong Qing Ling's house was built in this garden, much of it has survived. Along the northern side of the entrance drive there is a rocky ravine beyond which is an elaborate roofed walkway (fig. 3.33) which runs along the southern edge of the lake. This lake is bordered with rockwork and overhung by tall sophoras and other deciduous trees. It is the centrepiece of the garden and presents a placid scene of great charm (fig. 3.34).

Figure 3.34 (over page) The lake, Former Residence of Soong Qing Ling

Beside the walkway, on an artificial hill, is a fan-shaped pavilion in the same late Qing style as the half-moon shaped one depicted in Osvald Sirén's (1926) photograph, which may well have been in the same position (fig. 1.32). And the roofed walkway at the southern end of the lake, though clearly also a restoration, appears identical to the one shown in another of Sirén's photographs taken in this garden. Both these photographs also show Puyi's younger brother.

As well as the features mentioned above, there are others of interest in the garden, including a selection of traditional flowering plants and a bridge across the far end of the lake. North of this is a second artificial hill, crowned in this instance with a double-roofed circular pavilion which looks out on a modern rockery (fig. 3.35).

MEI LANFANG GUJU (FORMER RESIDENCE OF MEI LANFANG)

This house is in Huguosi Jie, a little to the west of Gongwangfu. The street gets its name from the Huguo Temple which used to be famous for the plant market that was held there at regular intervals, and which supplied many

Figure 3.35 Rockery, Former Residence of Soong Qing Ling

of the potted plants used to ornament the houses and gardens of Beijing.

I have included Mei Lanfang's house as it is both open to the public and a good example of an old-style courtyard house. For fengshui reasons the gate on the street is in the south-east corner of the property. Inside is a narrow space with a high wall on its northern side in the centre of which there is an entrance to the principal courtyard. Outside this entrance there are mature specimens of *Catalpa ovata* on one side and *Toona sinensis* on the other. Immediately inside is a spirit screen, beyond which two persimmons and two crab-apples (*Malus spectabilis*) are symmetrically placed (fig. 3.36). The principal hall on the northern side is on a raised platform, and on either side of it is a small square courtyard containing a lilac (*Syringa oblata*). From each of these spaces a moon gate opens into a passage which leads to subsidiary buildings.

Mei Lanfang (1894–1961) was a famous interpreter of female roles in the Beijing Opera. Several of the rooms of his former house have been arranged as a museum relating to his career. They contain costumes, mementoes, photographs, and an explanation of the meaning of a wide range of operatic gestures. Amongst the photographs are several of Mei Lanfang in the courtyard with foreign celebrities, including the Italian soprano Amelita Galli-Curci, who paid him a visit in 1929.

KEYUAN (SUFFICIENCY GARDEN)

Like Gongwangfu and Soong Qing Ling's residence, this is another late Qing garden which has survived, albeit in a state of romantic decay. It is in Maoer Hutong to the east of Gongwangfu and was established during the reign of Xianfeng (1851–61) by Rong Yuan, a Qing official (Zhou, 1995). The property has now been divided up for various purposes and, at the time of my visit in 1995, the garden, which is east of the original living quarters, was occupied by a retired official and was not open to the public. However, after knocking on the door, my companions and I were graciously admitted and were told we were the first foreigners who had been allowed to visit the garden for several decades. It is quite small, consisting only of two courtyards surrounded by buildings and covered walkways. The columns supporting the roofs of these walkways and buildings are linked beneath the eaves with intricately carved panels with patterns of pine, bamboo and plum blossom.

Figure 3.36 (above) **Principal courtyard, Former Residence of Mei Lanfang, Beijing**

Figure 3.37 (right) **Three stones arranged on a pedestal, Keyuan, Beijing**

The first courtyard is the larger of the two and contains at its southern end an elaborate rockery surmounted by a small hexagonal pavilion. This rockery acts as a screen for the southern entrance. Beyond this is a pond, dry and decayed at the time of my visit, which is crossed by two small bridges. Beyond that again, in front of the middle hall, is a space shaded by junipers, persimmons, walnuts and other trees, and ornamented with a traditional stone sundial, a large Taihu stone mounted on a plinth, and a grouping of three upright stones, representing the Islands of the Immortals and the character for mountain, 'shan' 山 (fig. 3.37).

The second courtyard is only about half as big and has the main hall at its northern end. There are further rockeries here and, as in the first courtyard, the ground was covered at the time with self-sown *Orychophragmus violaceus*.

LIU YONG YUAN (LIU-YONG'S GARDEN)

Liu Yong's garden is in Lishi Hutong in the same area as the Keyuan. Liu Yong was a high official during the Qianlong period, at which time, according to Qiao (1982), he lived here and built the garden. This lies beyond a series of halls and courtyards (fig. 3.38) in the north-western corner of the property. It covers an area of only about 1400 square metres and along its northern boundary is an earth mound studded

Figure 3.38 Courtyard, Liu Yong Yuan, Beijing

Little were advised to avoid the temple altogether. Lady Susan Townley (1904) reported that the lamas were 'a set of the most villainous-looking rascals one would be likely to meet anywhere in China' but that after 1900 their behaviour improved and the temple became safe to visit. Apparently this must have been so, as by the time of the Littles' second sojourn in Beijing in 1901 Mrs Little (1905) recorded that she found it a favourite place to wander in. Nowadays the foreigners cer-

with rocks representing a mountain range which rises behind a small pool. Amongst the plants in the garden are various trees, including a catalpa said to be 300 years old, along with tree peonies and other flowers.

The whole property appears to have undergone renovation and modernisation in recent times, so how closely it resembles Liu Yong's original house and garden is hard to judge. At the time of my visit it was occupied by a film company.

YONGHEGONG (PALACE OF HARMONY)

Better known to Westerners as the Lama Temple, this is in the north-eastern corner of the old city. An outline of its history and a description of its buildings have been given by Bouillard (1931a). Established in 1694, it was originally the home of Kangxi's son who, after his father's death, became the emperor Yongzheng. Following the custom that the residences of those who became emperor could not continue to be inhabited by members of the family, it was made into a temple. In 1744 this became a lamasery with a large number of lamas in residence. Visiting it in the latter part of the 19th century was apparently a dangerous excursion for foreigners, as has been mentioned earlier, since there are reports of their being attacked or otherwise harassed by the lamas. Nevertheless curiosity drew many Europeans there and their writings suggest that they found the lamas more interesting than the temple itself and few omitted to remark on their failings. Miss Gordon Cumming (1890), however, seemed unconcerned when she went there in 1879, though she described the monks as 'insolent people'. As has been noted in Chapter 1, when they first went to Beijing Mr and Mrs

tainly have nothing to fear other than an excessive admission charge, as there are few lamas and, beginning in 1979, the temple has been restored as a major tourist attraction (fig. 3.39). Like the Forbidden City and the Temple of Heaven, it is included in most itineraries, no doubt on account of its size and elaborately decorated exteriors and interiors. It is for this reason that I have included it here, even though it is of only modest interest from a garden point of view. The buildings appear exactly as they did when photographed by Felice Beato in 1860.

A long approach through garden beds leads to a series of five halls and courtyards, around which there are numerous subsidiary buildings. In addition to the garden beds lining the approach, amongst the colourful and elaborately decorated buildings there are bamboos, pines, persimmons, catalpas and junipers.

Figure 3.39 Lama Temple, Beijing

The other famous lama temple in Beijing, the Huangsi (Yellow Temple), lies about 3 km north-west of the Yonghegong. Unfortunately at the times I have been in Beijing it has not been open to visitors. In the 17th century the eastern part of the site was prepared as a residence for the Dalai Lama when he came to Beijing and in 1720 the whole temple was restored by Kangxi for Mongolian and Tibetan lamas (Bouillard, 1931a). The 6th Panchen Lama died here of smallpox following his return from Chengde where he had been to pay his respects on the occasion of Qianlong's 70th birthday in 1780. Qianlong subsequently had a white marble stupa constructed there in his memory. A visit to see this monument seems to have been an essential part of the Beijing itinerary for early Western visitors, many of whom described

and photographed it. However the temple is now a training college for lamas, and all I was able to see was the gate and a distant glimpse of the tops of the five marble towers of the memorial stupa.

KONGMIAO (CONFUCIAN TEMPLE)

The Confucian Temple, a short walk west along the tree-lined Guozijian Jie from the Lama Temple, is a tranquil site that, like the Imperial College next door, was regarded more favourably by the early foreign visitors. It was founded in 1302 and has been frequently restored. For example, in Qianlong's time most of the halls were retiled in yellow. It is the largest Confucian Temple in the country after the one at Qufu, Confucius' birthplace. Unlike the Lama Temple, this

temple and the neighbouring Imperial College seem not to be on many itineraries these days, with the result that visiting them is a far more pleasant excursion.

On either side of the main gate of the Confucian Temple are some old boulders, commonly called 'stone drums', which were found in Shanxi in the Tang and bear almost illegible inscriptions which are believed to describe a hunting expedition. They have a complex history of being moved from place to place and are said to date from the Zhou but may be replicas of the originals. Miss Gordon Cumming (1890) saw them in 1879 and gave a history of their travels, saying that 'To avoid all danger of their ever being lost a set of exact copies have been made by Imperial command'.

The Littles went there some years later, prior to going on to the Imperial College, and Mrs Little (1901) recorded that 'The vast courts with their old, old fir trees, gave me far more pleasure even than the marble balustrades, or the ancient granite so-called drums we had gone to see'. Things there are much the same today and my visits have left me with a similar opinion. According to Mrs Little (1905) some of the 'old, old firs' were planted in the Song but since the temple was not founded until the Yuan this seems unlikely. And, as so often turns out to be the case, they are actually junipers and thujas. Some of these have wisterias climbing on them and others have hostas planted around their bases. Under the trees in the first courtyard are a large number of steles engraved with the names of more than 50 000 candidates successful at the highest level in the imperial examinations from

the early Ming to the late Qing. The Rev. W.A.P. Martin (1900), another to visit this place in the second half of the 19th century, felt that the steles overshadowed by the venerable trees presented the appearance of a graveyard, as did Pierre Loti (1902) who saw them in 1900. I suppose in a way they do (fig. 3.40). Further on, in the main courtyard, the huge main hall stands on a white marble platform. The subsidiary buildings now house the Beijing City Museum.

GUOZIJIAN (IMPERIAL COLLEGE)

The Imperial College, immediately west of the Confucian Temple, was founded about the same time and from then on it was the most prestigious college in the country. Miss Gordon Cumming came on here from the Confucian Temple to see the famous Hall of the Classics and recorded that:

> **The approach to this hall is by a triple gateway of peculiar pai-low form, most beautifully decorated with green and yellow porcelain tiles, so that the whole appears to be made of China. A very ornamental pavilion, decorated with gold dragons on a green ground, stands in the centre of an ornamental tank, and is approached by several beautiful marble bridges.**

A few years earlier John Thomson (1873–74) had photographed the Hall of the Classics framed by the central gateway of the arch, just as I did 130 years later (fig. 3.41).

As Miss Gordon Cumming had done, the redoubtable Littles also came on from the Confucian Temple on their ill-fated visit to see the arch and the centrally placed hall, as has already been recounted in Chapter 1. Late in 1900 it was also visited by Pierre Loti, another to describe the arch and the hall standing in the pool.

Figure 3.40 (left) **Steles at the Confucian Temple, Beijing**

Figure 3.41 (opposite page) **Hall of the Classics viewed through the central opening of the Porcelain Arch, Imperial College, Beijing**

Figure 3.42 Wisteria on old thuja, Imperial College

The arch is still as much as all these people described it and as it appears in John Thomson's photograph and, although not open to the public at the times I have visited it, the Hall of the Classics, or Biyonggong (Hall of Sovereign Harmony) as it is properly called, is now in much better condition than it was at the time Mr Little was driven to attack one of its doors. It was completed in 1784 and the emperors used to come here in the second month of every year and expound on the Confucian classics. It is a square double-roofed building standing in the middle of a pool crossed by four marble bridges and surrounded by old sophoras. There are also many ancient thujas here, claimed to be at least 300 years old, perhaps dating even to the Yuan. Although some of

these have died, they have been retained and wisterias planted to grow over them (fig. 3.42). There are also junipers, poplars and walnuts in the enclosure. The college now houses the Capital Library.

TIANTAN (TEMPLE OF HEAVEN)

The Temple of Heaven, where the Ming and Qing emperors used to perform the most important ceremonial rites of the year, is in the south of the old Chinese part of the city. The enclosure containing the temple buildings was first built in 1420 and is surrounded by a park of more than 270 hectares. Felice Beato photographed it in 1860 and, while his pictures show the buildings to be in tolerable condition, the paving, stairways and, in some places, even the roofs are supporting an abundant growth of weeds (Harris, 1999). Numerous visitors have described it subsequently, including Miss Gordon Cumming, who came here in 1879 when there were still 'pleasant pastures wherein the bullocks, sheep, and other animals destined for sacrifice graze till their last hour draws near, without a thought of the slaughter-house which lies hidden in a grove in the north-east corner'.

All this, of course, is long gone, but a large grassy park remains on either side of the axis along which the temple buildings are arranged. Much of this park is filled with old thujas planted in rows and the ground under these is a sea of mauve in spring when self-sown *Orychophragmus violaceus* is in bloom (fig. 3.4). There are also persimmons and, in the south-western corner of the enclosure, a large orchard of fruit trees. As far as the temple buildings and their immediate surrounds are concerned, while weeds are not entirely absent, things have improved a great deal since 1860. And from the vicinity of the temple's most imposing building, the Hall of Prayer for Good Harvests, an avenue of ginkgos now leads west to a nursery area and rose garden. While by Western standards the rose garden is unremarkable, it contains an interesting collection of Chinese and overseas varieties. The nursery area nearby is used from time to time for displays of roses and chrysanthemums. As well as all this, here and there in the park are ornamental buildings transferred from Zhongnanhai.

BEIJING HUASHI (BEIJING FLOWER AND PLANT MARKET)

Close to the Temple of Heaven is the principal flower and plant market of central Beijing. A visit to this provides an insight into present-day gardening in the city. Here one can buy a wide range of flowers and plants, both real and artificial, together with pots, potting mixes, the equipment needed for penjing, and so on. At the time of my visit in early November there were modern indoor plants, ornamental citrus trees, chrysanthemums (fig. 3.43) and huge heaps of narcissus bulbs (*N. tazetta*), much in demand for bringing into bloom for the Chinese New Year. But most impressive of all was the section devoted to garden statuary. Not only were there Chinese lions in various sizes, but white marble reproductions of such things as the Venus de Milo and Antonio Canova's Cupid and Psyche—the same curious mixture that one sees in such places in the West (fig. 1.46).

FAYUANSI (TEMPLE OF THE SOURCE OF THE LAW)

The Fayuansi is in the southern part of the city not far from the well-known Cow Street Mosque. Although most of the present buildings are relatively modern, historically it is the oldest temple in Beijing, having been founded in 645. The northern Song emperor Huizong was imprisoned here after his capture by the Jin in the 12th century and, in 1734 it became a Buddhist college and was given its present name. It is now a Buddhist college once more and the activity associated with this adds interest to a visit (fig. 3.44).

The temple consists of the usual drum and bell towers and a series of halls and associated buildings. There are

Figure 3.43 (above right)

Chrysanthemums for sale at a

plant and flower market, Beijing

Figure 3.44 (right) **Entrance to**

the Fayuan Temple, Beijing

Ming bronzes of good quality, Ming and Qing steles on which are inscribed the history of the temple, and old incense burners. Amongst the plants are the usual junipers, ginkgos and sophoras, some said to date from the Tang and Song, as well as other trees, such as *Sophora japonica* 'Pendula', *Aesculus chinensis* and *Malus spectabilis*. But the chief horticultural feature is the large number of lilacs (*Syringa oblata*) planted in the courtyards (fig. 3.45). These are a wonderful sight from

Figure 3.45 Lilacs, Fayuan Temple

Figure 3.46 The lake, Daguanyuan, Beijing

early to mid-April and have been the subject of much favourable comment over the years. To visit the temple at this time is a great delight, as it is a sea of mauve and white bloom and the scent wafts through the courtyards and halls.

DAGUANYUAN (GRAND VIEW GARDEN)

I have already drawn attention to the Daguanyuan, the fictional garden in Cao Xueqin's 18th-century novel *The Story of the Stone*. In the 1980s the Chinese authorities built a garden with this name in the south-western corner of the old Chinese city, basing its design on the description given in the novel.

It is arranged around a lake (fig. 3.46), and includes a series of rockeries (fig. 3.47), walled enclosures (fig. 3.48) and prospects, each named as in the novel. While it is relatively new, still a little bare and subject to the problems associated with a large number of visitors, it could be argued that it is as good a place as any to become acquainted with the philosophy on which the Chinese garden is based.

It has been laid out and built in accordance with traditional principles and techniques, and the plants are all Chinese garden plants. There are flowering peaches, *Prunus triloba*, magnolias, Chinese roses (fig. 3.49), lilacs, wisterias, *Philadelphus pekinensis*, *Iris lactea*, *Sorbaria sorbifolia*, fine

Figure 3.47 (left) **Wisteria and** *Parthenocissus tricuspidata* **on a rockery, Daguanyuan**
Figure 3.48 (above) *Campsis grandiflora* **and** *Hosta plantaginea* **in autumn, Daguanyuan**

the Cultural Revolution. It was restored again in 1981 and is now home once more to Daoist monks and novices. The temple is large with many courtyards ornamented with trees, potted plants, stonework and roofed walkways (fig. 3.51). Enormous old ginkgos and sophoras have survived

Figure 3.49 (left) **Roses growing over rocks, Daguanyuan**

Figure 3.50 (below left) **Cultivar of *Paeonia lactiflora*, Daguanyuan**

Figure 3.51 (below) **A courtyard at the Baiyunguan, Beijing**

collections of tree and herbaceous peonies (fig. 3.50), and much more. Of course familiarity with the novel greatly enhances the enjoyment of a visit, but there is much to appreciate anyway.

BAIYUNGUAN (WHITE CLOUDS TEMPLE)

The Baiyunguan in the east of the city is the chief Daoist temple in Beijing. It is said to have been founded in the 8th century and to have acquired its present name in 1394. It has undergone various restorations and alterations and, like other religious institutions in China, it was hard hit during

Figure 3.52 (right) A waterway, Beijing Zoo
Figure 3.53 (below right) Tree peony garden,
Beijing Zoo

Figure 3.52 (right) A waterway, Beijing Zoo

Figure 3.53 (below right) Tree peony garden,
Beijing Zoo

the disturbances of the last century or so,
and running alongside one of the walkways is a row of walnuts. In one of the rear
courtyards there is an ordination platform
and in another a stage.

BEIJING DONGWUYUAN (BEIJING ZOO)

The Beijing Zoo occupies the site of a
Qing imperial park on the banks of the
canal bringing water to Beijing from the
Jade Spring. It was originally the property
of one of the sons of the first Qing emper-
or, Shunzhi. It became ruined but was
refurbished in the mid-18th century by
Qianlong in honour of his mother's 60th
birthday. It subsequently declined but was
redeveloped by Cixi on her return from
Xi'an in 1902, when it was used to house
a collection of animals from Germany
with which she had been presented. It was
opened to the public in 1908 but fell into
disrepair and after a long period of neglect
was revived and reopened in 1950.

The itinerary of most visitors to
Beijing includes a visit to this zoo, usually
to see no more than the giant pandas
imprisoned in a depressing enclosure near
the entrance. However, those who venture
beyond the pandas will find some interesting relics of the earlier garden. There is
a lake, now the home of a collection of
water birds, winding waterways edged
with rocks (fig. 3.52), and pavilions in
various styles. A few rocky hills survive
and there are many traditional trees,
shrubs and flowering plants. I was particularly taken with the tree peony garden,
which is circular and completely surrounded by a roofed walkway in late Qing
style (fig. 3.53).

ZIZHUYUAN GONGYUAN (PURPLE BAMBOO GARDEN PARK)

The Purple Bamboo Garden Park is immediately west of the zoo. According to Wood (1992), it was the site of lakes and a canal built during the Yuan in order to regulate the flow of water from the Jade Spring and the Bai River into the city. Travelling palaces were built here during the Qing so that members of the imperial family going to and from the Summer Palace by boat could stop and rest. The lakes remain, bordered with rocks and willows, but little else has survived from earlier times (fig. 3.54). The area has now been developed as a public park with a children's playground, a tea house and ornamental planting.

WUTASI (FIVE PAGODA TEMPLE)

This temple is directly north of the zoo on the opposite side of the canal. During the reign of Yongle (1403–24), five golden Buddha images and a model of the Diamond Temple at Bodhgaya were presented to the emperor by an Indian monk. A temple, originally called Zhenjuesi, was then built here to house these objects. Later a building topped with five pagodas modelled on the Diamond Temple was constructed in the centre of the compound (fig. 3.55). It was completed in 1473. The temple was restored by Qianlong in honour of his mother's 70th birthday in 1761, but unfortunately it was ransacked by foreign troops in both 1860 and 1900. Little now remains of the original other than the platforms on which buildings stood, the stone centrepiece with its five pagodas, and two enormous old ginkgos which stand in front of it. They are said to be at least 1000 years old, although it seems unlikely to me that they predate the temple by more than 400 years. Nevertheless they provide a wonderful frame for the view of the old stone building with its five pagodas. Mrs Little (1905),

who went there shortly after the Boxer Rebellion, admired these trees but was fearful that they might complete the destruction already wrought by the foreign troops. A century on there is no evidence for the justification of her fears.

The temple compound is approached from the canal along a path lined with stone animals, and the area in front of the remaining building has been developed as a modern formal garden. Although bare in photographs from the early part of the 20th century, the grounds on either side are now planted with persimmon trees, amongst which is displayed a large and interesting collection of ancient steles and sculptures gathered together from the city and its surrounds.

WANSHOUSI (TEN THOUSAND LONGEVITIES TEMPLE)

The Wanshousi is outside the north-western corner of the Purple Bamboo Garden Park, a little further west along the northern bank of the canal which runs past the Wutasi. Said to have been founded in 1577, it was rebuilt by Qianlong in 1761 and its present appearance dates from this time. After a period of neglect it has been restored once more as the Beijing Art Museum and the buildings on either side of the main axis are used to house a collection of paintings and sculpture.

Outside the entrance there are some old sophoras and, in the first courtyard, there is an enormous example, along with a catalpa and two junipers—one of which has died and has wisteria growing over it. The next courtyard has been arranged as a modern formal garden which does not sit happily with the buildings surrounding it. The rear courtyard, however, appears to have been left alone. In the centre of this is a large rock and earth mountain on which old elms (*Ulmus pumila*), junipers, ailanthuses and ginkgos are growing. There is a pavilion on the top where Cixi rested on her way to the Summer Palace and surveyed the scenery. Behind the rock mountain there is an octagonal pavilion containing a stele on which there are inscriptions in Chinese, Manchu, Mongolian and Tibetan commemorating the rebuilding of the temple (fig. 3.56). Beyond this again, but not open to the public, is a two-storey building in semi-European style built at the same time.

Figure 3.54 Rockwork, Purple Bamboo Garden Park, Beijing

Figure 3.55 (above)
Wuta Temple, Beijing,
framed by old ginkgos

Figure 3.56 (right)
Stele pavilion and
rock mountain,
Wanshou Temple,
Beijing

BEIJING DAXUE (BEIJING UNIVERSITY)

I have included Beijing University because it occupies the grounds of two former mansions. One of these was the Shaoyuan (Ladle Garden), which was built in the late 16th or early 17th century by the painter Mi Wanzong. The other was the 18th-century garden of He Shen, who at the time also owned what subsequently became known as Gongwangfu. It was here in 1792 that he received Lord Macartney when he was on his ill-fated embassy to the court of Qianlong. Much later, in 1922, Yenching University, founded by American Methodist missionaries, established itself on the site of these two gardens. Although this was subsequently developed further when it became Beijing University and little remains of any 18th-century building, some of the garden of He Shen's villa has survived. This includes a tree-covered hill and a large lake with the stone base of a land boat against the rock-lined shore (fig. 3.57). Dorothy Graham (1938) mentioned this and that the lotus pool and winding stream of the Ladle Garden could still be seen in the grounds, but whether these are still there I could not determine.

Land boats, by the way, are a common feature of Chinese gardens, recalling not only the pleasures of travelling by water but ancient sayings such as 'floating like an untied boat', an expression suggesting the ability of the mind to travel at will regardless of other restrictions (Hu, 1991). In many gardens, in fact, such structures are referred to as 'untied boats'.

QINGHUA DAXUE (QINGHUA UNIVERSITY)

Like Beijing University, which is nearby, Qinghua University occupies a site which was a garden. It began life in 1911 as the Imperial Qinghua College in the grounds of the former country seat of one of the Manchu princes (Malone, 1934). In 1928 the college, which was originally set up to prepare Chinese students who were intending to go to America, formally became a university. A lake and island still exist here and presumably were part of the original layout (fig. 3.58). According to Malone, this garden was called Qinghuayuan (Clear and Beautiful Garden), although it did not occupy the same site as the garden originally given that name. This was the garden of Li Wei, father-in-law of the Ming emperor Wanli (reigned 1573–1620), who was the first to build a villa and garden in the Haidian district north-west of the city. The original Qinghuayuan had the reputation of being the most beautiful garden north of the Yangtze. The Qing emperor Kangxi later built his Changchunyuan (Garden of Exuberant Spring) on the site.

YUANMINGYUAN (GARDEN OF PERFECT BRIGHTNESS)

Adjacent to Beijing and Qinghua Universities is what remains of the Yuanmingyuan. This name is nowadays applied to the site of three adjoining gardens—the Yuanmingyuan, Changchunyuan and Wanchunyuan. Of these the Yuanmingyuan was the first to be built and the others were

Figure 3.57 **Remnants of the garden of He Shen's villa, Beijing University**

Figure 3.58 View in the grounds of Qinghua University, Beijing

added later. As mentioned in Chapter 1, it was begun by Kangxi in 1709 for his fourth son, who later succeeded him as the emperor Yongzheng. Although in 1731 much of the garden was destroyed by an earthquake, it was restored, enlarged and developed further by Qianlong, with the result that by 1744 there were 40 named scenes. It was this garden that was described by Jean-Denis Attiret in his famous letter written in 1743. Notable, too, is Che Bing Chiu's (2000) recent comprehensive and scholarly account of the appearance, history and significance of this remarkable creation.

Following the completion of the Yuanmingyuan, Qianlong ordered the construction of the Changchunyuan (Garden of Everlasting Spring) on its eastern boundary. This was built on a different site from that of Kangxi's Changchunyuan (Garden of the Exuberant Spring—the character 'chang' in this name is different from that in Qianlong's garden). It was on a narrow strip of land in the northern part of his Changchunyuan that Qianlong had European-style buildings and fountains constructed with the aid of the Jesuit priests Giuseppe Castiglione and Jean-Denis Attiret, who provided the designs; Michel Benoist, who directed the the hydraulic works; and Pierre d'Incarville, who was in charge of the gardens (Cranmer-Byng, 1962). These buildings had no place in the Chinese tradition apart from emphasising the grandeur of the emperor but, as Titley and Wood (1991) have noted, they represent the reverse of the fashion for chinoiserie which

was all the rage in Europe at much the same time. A detailed description of these palaces, their fountains and gardens has been given by Loehr (1940), along with reproductions of the engravings of them commissioned by Qianlong. These illustrations show formal gardens in European style, with flower beds, clipped shrubs and even a maze.

Qianlong also arranged for the Wanchunyuan (Garden of Ten Thousand Springs) to be built on the southern boundary of the original Yuanmingyuan. When completed the whole complex covered an area of 350 hectares and contained more than 3000 different buildings. Unlike the Summer Palace and the Imperial Summer Villa at Chengde, it was not a sweeping composition exploiting its natural site and taking advantage of borrowed views. It was built on flat ground on which lakes, watercourses and artificial mountains were constructed, and consisted of many separate 'scenes', each with its own buildings and features. Nevertheless, it was one of the most remarkable gardens ever created. All the more unfortunate, then, that it was amongst the imperial estates devastated by British and French troops in 1860. Although, as mentioned earlier, proposals were subsequently put forward for its rebuilding, they were never acted upon. Even now it is suggested from time to time that the whole garden might be restored.

Today the only features that remain of this remarkable creation are the lakes and waterways, mounds of earth, a few

rial to the humiliation of the Chinese people by the foreign powers (fig. 3.60).

The whole site of the Yuanmingyuan is now much used by the residents of Beijing for excursions, picnics and fishing. The two principal lakes in the Yuanmingyuan proper, Houhu (Back Lake) and Fuhai (Sea of Happiness), are still there. The island in the centre of the latter, where once there was an elaborate palace, is connected to the shore by a new bridge and at the time of my last visit you could take speedboat rides.

Figure 3.59 (left)
Ruins of a garden,
Yuanmingyuan,
Beijing

Figure 3.60 (right)
Ruins of the Great
Fountain,
European Palaces,
Yuanmingyuan

foundations and fragments of stone (fig. 3.59), and the ruins of the European buildings. Photographs taken in the 1870s show the shells of these buildings to have been more or less intact and to have been surrounded by trees and shrubs, while others taken in the early part of the 20th century reveal much less to have survived of either buildings or vegetation (Sirén, 1949; Genest, 1984; Thiriez, 1998). When these ruins were visited by Mrs Little (1905) there was still here and there 'a hanging cluster of plaster flowers, coloured blue and red, yellow and violet', and there was apparently much more remaining than there is at present. But, while there are no longer any coloured plaster flowers to be seen, the surviving ruins have been tidied up and are now a popular attraction as a memo-

YIHEYUAN (GARDEN OF THE PRESERVATION OF HARMONY)

Known generally to foreigners as the Summer Palace, this garden is situated in an area which attracted interest when a travelling palace was built there by the Jin in 1153. At this time water from the Jade Spring was conducted to the foot of what was then known as Jin Shan (Golden Hill) to form a lake. During the Yuan the hill was known as Weng Shan (Jar Hill), and in the Ming it became a favoured destination for excursions. Early in the 16th century the Ming emperor Zhengde had a travelling palace there and a temple was built on top of the hill. In 1750, in order to celebrate the 60th birthday of his mother in 1751, Qianlong began rearranging the whole area. The lake was dredged and enlarged, the hill reshaped, and numerous buildings constructed. He gave many of these buildings names associated with his mother's long life and renamed the garden Qingyiyuan (Garden of Clear Ripples), the hill Wanshou Shan (Longevity Hill), and the lake Kunming Hu (Vast Bright Lake)—a reference to the Kunming Lake created in the Shanglin near Xian some 1900 years earlier (Cheng, 1998). This lake occupies three-quar-

ters of the 300 hectares of the garden. It was divided into three parts by causeways, in a manner reminiscent of the West Lake at Hangzhou, each part with an island—an arrangement suggesting the three Islands of the Immortals. Amongst numerous features of note were the Xiequyuan (Garden of Harmonious Interest) and the Back Lake, which runs around behind Wanshou Shan. In 1794 make-believe shops were built along the narrow middle part of this in imitation of a canal in Suzhou.

Felice Beato photographed individual buildings here in October 1860 before the site was looted and burned, erroneously calling it the Yuanmingyuan—as did most of the early visitors. He also took a panoramic view of Wanshou

Shan shortly after the destruction (fig. 3.61). Dr D.F. Rennie (1865) went there in 1861 and produced a written description of the charred buildings and various features which had survived, including the Bronze Ox, the Seventeen Arch Bridge, the Jade Belt Bridge and the willow-lined causeways. Likewise, Freeman-Mitford (1900), who visited it in 1865, noted that, in most areas, '… there is not a stone that has not been split by the action of the fire'. The Rev. Edkins (1870) also went there and described the burnt buildings and the features that had survived, including the marble boat 'rudely shaped and placed there as a monstrous curiosity'. In the 1870s others to see the ruined garden were John Thomson (1873–74) and A. Boyarsky (Naumkin, 1993)—both of whom photographed it—and Miss Gordon Cumming (1890). Although Miss Gordon Cumming admired the lake and the Seventeen Arch Bridge she was moved to remark that 'truly it is sickening, even now, to look on such a scene of devastation'. While at this time it was impossible to visit most other imperial properties, including the remains of the Yuanmingyuan, according to Dennys (1866), 'Admittance to Wan-shou-shan is obtained by civility and bribes, as is usual in most parts of China …'.

This procedure was brought to an end when Cixi, with funds apparently diverted from having been allocated to the establishment of a national navy, had it partly rebuilt in 1888 and gave it its present name, Yiheyuan. According to a newspaper of the time quoted by Mrs Little (1901), she went for a trip on the Kunming Lake in a steam launch shortly before the completion of the work. Mrs Little also provided some information, gleaned from an official report, concerning the manner in which the enterprise was achieved. It seems that 20 large firms were contracted to undertake the work and that more than 10 000 workmen were engaged in order to hasten its completion. Of these, some 3000 were carvers who, knowing the date for completion was at hand, struck for a wage rise of 300 per cent, a demand in which they were joined by the carpenters. When their employers refused to comply with this exorbitant request, thousands of workmen, carvers, carpenters and masons began a violent demonstration. The officials on guard, finding the police unable to cope, especially as the carpenters were armed with axes, called on the rifle brigade, imperial guards and cavalry for assistance. They were quickly on the scene and surrounded the demonstrators. Negotiations then began and it seems that all parties

Figure 3.61 Longevity Hill, Summer Palace, Beijing, after the burning, October 1860.

ALBUMEN SILVER PHOTOGRAPH BY FELICE BEATO ENTITLED
VIEW OF THE IMPERIAL SUMMER PALACE, YUEN MING YUAN,
AFTER THE BURNING, TAKEN FROM THE LAKE, OCTOBER 18TH, 1860.
NATIONAL GALLERY OF AUSTRALIA, CANBERRA.

were satisfied with a rise of 100 per cent.

Following its completion the Summer Palace became a favourite retreat of Cixi's, and much has been written about the days when she resided there. In 1900 it was damaged again by foreign troops and in 1901 Mrs Little (1905) was able to 'wander through it at one's own sweet will' after the dowager empress had fled to Xi'an. She felt that Cixi's restoration had been poorly carried out and that it was 'a sort of glorified Rosherville [an amusement park of the time in Kent, with a zoo and theatrical entertainments], though rendered very charming by its situation and the art with which the Chinese adapt buildings to their positions'. Cixi had it restored again after her return in 1902 but, after her death in 1908 it was closed down by Guangxu's widow. Then following the revolution of 1911 the Articles of Favourable Treatment agreed to by the new republic stipulated that the Yiheyuan still belonged to the imperial family and was to serve as a residence for Puyi. In fact, as has been mentioned earlier, he was allowed to stay in the rear of the Forbidden City until 1924. In 1914 the Summer Palace was opened by the imperial family for an entrance fee and in 1924, after Puyi had fled from Beijing, it became a public park. After a period of neglect it was refurbished in 1961, and in recent years there has been further rebuilding, particularly on the northern side of Longevity Hill where there had been no restoration in Cixi's time.

Echoing Mrs Little, Sirén (1926) felt that its character depended, generally speaking, much more on its situation and the way nature had been remodelled than on its architectural monuments. I cannot help but agree with both of them. For my taste its beauty relates primarily to its scale and setting, particularly when viewed from the lake and its eastern shore. The view across the water to the willow-lined principal causeway with its pavilions and bridges, the Yuquan Shan with its two pagodas rising behind, and the Western

Hills beyond, is deservedly famous (see Contents pages). And with the recent restorations on the northern slope of Longevity Hill the garden must now look much as it did when it was remodelled by Qianlong.

However, these days most visitors are given little chance of fully appreciating the scene. They arrive at the principal eastern gate, proceed through the residential apartments, and then battle with the throngs along the 700 m roofed walkway which runs along the shore of the lake as far as the Marble Boat, before leaving by the gate in the north-west corner. Others do the same in reverse.

A far better course of action is to enter by the south-eastern gate close to the Bronze Ox. In 1755 Qianlong had the Bronze Ox cast and inscribed to record the completion of his work on the lake, following the example of the legendary Great Yu, who is supposed to have recorded his work to mitigate flooding on an iron ox. A little to the south of the ox is an unusually large octagonal pavilion with a double roof, in front of which is the Seventeen Arch Bridge which leads to Penglai, the island on which there is the Temple of the Dragon King. There are splendid views from here across to Yuquan Shan, the causeway, the elegant Jade Belt Bridge, and back to Wanshou Shan.

From the island there is a regular ferry service across to the Marble Boat which, before its destruction was a wooden structure built in 1750 on a stone base. There is an interesting photograph of this base taken in 1874 by A. Boyarski (Naumkin, 1993) and it was on this that Cixi had built a marble replica of a paddle steamer—a lasting monument to her taste. From here a stroll east along the roofed walkway provides further views across the lake and brings one to the residential section. On the western approaches to this, a little up the slope, is a charming fan-shaped pavilion and, amongst the buildings which follow, the Lodge of the Propriety of Weeding should claim the attention of gardeners. Nearby there is an interesting rockery in the courtyard of the Hall of Jade Ripples. It was in this building that Cixi, when she was in residence at the Summer Palace, kept the emperor Guangxu imprisoned.

In the far north-eastern corner of the palace grounds is the Xiequyuan (Garden of Harmonious Interest). This was originally built by Qianlong as a copy of the Jichangyuan at Wuxi. This copy was called the Huishanyuan, named after the hill at the foot of which the Jichangyuan is situated. It was seriously damaged in 1860 and was renamed Xiequyuan after its restoration in 1893 (fig. 3.62). Largely untouched by the tourist hordes, it consists, like the garden upon which it was modelled, of a series of buildings and walkways around a lotus pool, which is fed with water led to it through a narrow rocky gorge. At one point the water is crossed by the Fish-knowing Bridge—yet another reference to Zhuang Zi's allusion in the 4th century BC to the unity of nature and humankind.

A path from the Garden of Harmonious Interest leads west along the shore of the Back Lake through a little-visited wooded area to Suzhou Creek, where the shops have now been reconstructed on the stone bases of the originals (fig. 1.10). This intriguing scene was noted by Van Braam (1798), when he and other members of the Dutch East India Company's embassy were shown round the garden in

YUQUAN SHAN (JADE SPRING HILL)

This hill and the famed spring, the First Spring Under Heaven, have attracted attention since the Jin and Yuan. Tradition has it that it was the foremost of the 'Eight Famous Sights of Beijing' in Jin times. According to Hu (1991) a country palace was first built here during the Jin dynasty by Emperor Zhangzong (reigned 1190–1209), and in subsequent times it became a favoured site for excursions and for the building of gardens, temples and pagodas. In 1680 Kangxi had 65 hectares on the southern slope of the hill enclosed for the construction of a travelling resort and garden. Zhan Ran, who had executed the rockeries at his Changchunyuan, also worked here. Kangxi first called this garden Chengxinyuan (Garden of a Limpid Heart) but renamed it Jingmingyuan (Garden of Tranquillity and

February 1795. Above this, on the northern slope of Wanshou Shan, there are further interesting buildings, including a porcelain pagoda and a Tibetan-style temple. At the western entrance to the Back Lake the imperial boathouses create a picturesque scene (fig. 3.63), and throughout the garden there is a great array of traditional trees, shrubs and flowering plants. The causeways are planted with willows and peaches (fig. 3.64) and the lotuses in the lake at the foot of Wanshou Shan are a famous sight in summer.

Figure 3.62 (above) **Garden of Harmonious Interest, Summer Palace, Beijing**
Figure 3.63 (right) **Imperial boathouses, Summer Palace**

Figure 3.64 Peaches and willows on a causeway, Summer Palace

Brightness) in 1692. On top of the main peak, which was included in the garden, a Buddhist temple was built, modelled on that on Jinshan Island in the Yangtze at Zhenjiang (Cheng, 1998). In the centre of the temple was the seven-storey octagonal pagoda which is now the focal point of the famous view from the Summer Palace. A smaller but more fanciful pagoda was built on the lesser peak.

The Qing emperors could reach the base of this garden by taking a boat under the Jade Belt Bridge and up the Jade River. It was visited, enjoyed and cared for by Qianlong, who wrote poems on its 16 famous scenes. According to Malone (1934), he was employing 100 gardeners there by 1747. It was severely damaged by the French and British in 1860 but, while photographs taken of the hill by A. Boyarsky in 1874 show it to be treeless, the pagodas and adjacent buildings appear still to have been in good condition (Naumkin, 1993). It was partly reconstructed during the reign of Guangxu and, when Mrs Little (1905) managed to talk her way in one October, she said there were 'beautiful trees inside and a lake, and many relics of the grand days of old, when the Palaces were built'. She went on to mention the spring and caves, above which were temples and 'the most exquisitely beautiful pagoda I have ever seen'. Below and to the west of this was a palace enclosure in which there was another pagoda which she greatly admired. And, although she felt that the pagoda crowning the hill was 'not remarkable', she was impressed by the view from there over the Summer Palace and the surrounding countryside.

Almost a quarter of a century later, Sirén (1926) described the ruins shaded by magnificent trees as 'uncommonly picturesque' and his photographs give us a glimpse of it in decay. Whether anything other than the pagodas now remains I do not know, as at the time of writing the whole hill is occupied by the army and surrounded by a high wall. Although little evidence of anything other than the tree-covered hill and the pagodas can be seen from outside (fig. 3.65), when I got out my camera to photograph the general scene from a couple of hundred metres away a soldier came running in a great state of alarm. It seems that the view here is guarded against would-be photographers as zealously as that into Zhonghai. I felt a bit like Mrs Little (1905) who, on her way here, had been warded off at the Summer Palace by the guards 'springing forward waving their swords directly they caught sight of us'.

BEIJING ZHIWUYUAN (NANYUAN)
(BEIJING BOTANICAL GARDEN, SOUTH GARDEN)

This garden was established in 1955, west of the Summer Palace and 18 km north-west of the city on the southern side of the main road to the Fragrant Hills. It is affiliated with the Institute of Botany of the Chinese Academy of Sciences and is a centre for botanical and horticultural research. It was here in March 1960 that the last emperor, Puyi, was assigned to work as part of his 'rehabilitation'. As did most botanical gardens, it suffered badly during the Cultural Revolution when most of its collections were destroyed and it was used as a pig farm. However, it soon revived and now has collections of many different groups of plants including lilacs, peonies, *Malus* species (fig. 3.66) and cotoneasters. Also, an impressive new conservatory has recently been completed.

Figure 3.65 Jade Spring Hill

BEIJING ZHIWUYUAN (BEIYUAN) (BEIJING BOTANICAL GARDEN, NORTH GARDEN) AND WOFOSI (TEMPLE OF THE SLEEPING BUDDHA)

A little to the west of the above, on the north side of the same road, this garden is affiliated with the Parks and Landscape Bureau of Beijing. It is principally a recreational area with collections of many different ornamental plants, such as tree peonies, lilacs, flowering peaches and other *Prunus* species, bamboos, forsythias, conifers and crepe myrtles. Amongst other plants to attract my attention was a group of *Rhodotypos scandens* (fig. 3.67). There are also areas laid out as formal gardens in Western style (fig. 1.45), and in spring large crowds are attracted by displays of daffodils, tulips and hyacinths.

Aside from all of this, the chief claim to fame of this garden is that it has been established around the Wofosi, an interesting old temple founded in the Tang and expanded during the Yuan. As a result of its proximity to imperial resorts and gardens, it was later visited and supported by various Ming and Qing emperors, for whom accommodation was built here. A.B. Freeman-Mitford (1900) went there in 1865 and perceptively recorded that:

> The shrine is held in great reverence, and is decorated with an inscription by Chien Lung [Qianlong] himself, who seems never to have lost an opportunity of writing and building; of both these favourite pastimes of his, Wo-Fo-Ssu bears examples, for leading out of one of the courts of the temple is a most beautiful little Imperial abode, now falling into decay, like everything else here, but which once must have been perfectly lovely.

After the usual ups and downs, including having accommodated the YMCA's out-of-town headquarters, the temple is now restored. The compound is approached through an avenue of ancient thujas (fig. 3.68) which, along with the temple, was photographed and described by Mrs Little (1905), amongst others. In the various courtyards there are many handsome old trees, including *Sophora japonica*,

Figure 3.66 (right) Crabapple, Beijing Botanical Garden, South Garden

Figure 3.67 (far right) *Rhodotypos scandens*, Beijing Botanical Garden, North Garden

BIYUNSI (TEMPLE OF THE AZURE CLOUDS)

This temple, which is adjacent to the Fragrant Hills Park a short distance from the Temple of the Sleeping Buddha, is believed to date from the Yuan. However, the most important of the present buildings, the Diamond Throne Pagoda and the Luohan Hall, were built in 1748. It early became a favourite destination for excursions by Westerners. Dr D.F. Rennie (1865), for instance, mentioned going there for a picnic in 1861. It is picturesquely sited against the hills and the entrance, guarded by two Ming stone lions, is reached across a bridge over a ravine, with tall junipers rising on either side. In the first courtyard there are handsome stone bell and drum towers amongst pines, apricots and persimmons (fig. 3.70). In the second courtyard there is a pool and on the south side of the third is the Lohan Hall containing 500 lacquered wooden figures. Behind a Chinese horse chestnut to the rear of this courtyard is the hall where Sun Yat-sen's body lay from 1925–29 before it was removed to his mausoleum in Nanjing. Beyond this is a narrow space planted with *Forsythia suspensa*, a white form of *Syringa oblata*, and tall poplars. Above this, surrounded by pines, is the imposing Diamond Throne Pagoda, a white marble version of the five-pagoda building at Wutasi.

Along a secondary axis to the east there is a series of courtyards developed as gardens, in the first of which there are forsythias, lilacs and other ornamental shrubs. From here a moon gate leads to another enclosure with long beds of

Ailanthus altissima, *Koelreuteria paniculata* and *Ginkgo biloba* (fig. 3.69). Also here is an old wisteria growing over a dead juniper. Of note, too, are specimens of *Aesculus chinensis*, a tree frequently planted in Buddhist temples in China. Since *Shorea robusta*, the tree under which Buddha was both born and died, is not hardy in much of the country, *A. chinensis* has been adopted as a substitute, even though it bears little resemblance. To the west of the principal axis of the temple there is a large courtyard almost filled by a waterlily pool, and beyond this a path leads into a semi-wild area known as the Cherry Valley Nature Reserve, where there was once a Daoist hermitage.

daylilies and *Hosta plantaginea*. At the northern end of this axis there is an elaborate rockery crowned with a pavilion in amongst tall pines (*Pinus tabuliformis* and *P. bungeana*), beyond which is a pool, once fed by a rocky cascade which is now dry (fig. 1.17). It was this garden about which Freeman-Mitford (1900) wrote in 1865, as noted in Chapter 1. Many years later Dorothy Graham (1938) also wrote about it, mentioning its pool, rocks, stream and twisted trees. It still remains much as she and Freeman-Mitford described it, although it would be nice if the stream could be made to run again. And, alas, no trace remains of the splendid grove of *Pinus bungeana* which the temple once overlooked and which was photographed by Mrs Little (1905) during her visit.

XIANGSHAN GONGYUAN (FRAGRANT HILLS PARK)

The Fragrant Hills Park was used as a hunting ground by the emperors, beginning in the 12th century when a travelling palace was built here by the Jin. Buddhist temples were established here as early as the Ming (Cheng, 1998) and at this time it became, like Yuquan Shan and Weng Shan, a favourite destination for outings. Later Kangxi had a hunting lodge built in the park and Qianlong first visited it in 1743 and instigated further development. By 1745 an extensive area on the east-facing slope had been walled and arranged as an elaborate garden, Jingyiyuan (Garden of Tranquillity and Pleasure). There were 28 named scenes, about each of which the emperor composed poems in 1745 (Malone, 1934). In 1780 he also built there the Zhaomiao (Luminous Temple) to commemorate the visit of the Panchen Lama and his own 70th birthday. It is in Tibetan style, reminiscent of the Xumifushou Temple, which he had built at Chengde at the same time and which has a similar pagoda. Later still, the emperor Jiaqing (reigned 1796–1820) restored and enlarged a small garden originally built during the reign of the Ming emperor Jiajing (1522–67). This is called the Jianxinzhai (Studio of Introspection), an elegant courtyard residence overlooking a pool. Surrounded by a circular walkway and with its pavilions built out into the water, it is an imaginative composition which was restored in 1958 (fig. 3.71).

In 1860 and again in 1900 the Fragrant Hills Park suffered the same fate as the other imperial country resorts. According to Sirén (1926), there was further devastation at the time of the revolution in 1911. After that parts of the park were put to

Figure 3.71 Jianxinzhai, Fragrant Hills Park

various uses including a girls' school. Apart from the
Luminous Temple and the Studio of Introspection little else
exists of the original garden. There was once amongst the features here a street of make-believe shops, like those at the
Yuanmingyuan and the Summer Palace, the remains of which
were noted by Freeman-Mitford in 1865. The whole site has
now been converted into a public park ornamented with the
usual trees, shrubs and flowers (fig. 3.72). Amongst these
there are some fine forms of *Weigela florida* (fig. 3.73) and a
group of *Tilia mandshurica*. The latter is of interest as it used
to be grown in Buddhist temples in northern China where it
is too cold for the bodhi tree (*Ficus religiosa*)—the tree under
which Buddha is said to have received enlightenment. It
seems probable that this linden was chosen as a substitute on
account of its similarly shaped leaves.

Figure 3.72 (top) **Lake in the Fragrant Hills Park**

Figure 3.73 (above) ***Weigela florida*, Fragrant Hills Park**

There is a chairlift to Xianghu Feng (Incense Burner Peak), the highest point in the park, from which there is a view back to the city on the rare days when it is clear. The interesting vegetation of the slopes above the developed area has been described by Roy Lancaster (1989). Here the autumn colour of the smoke bushes (*Cotinus coggygria*) attracts crowds of visitors, as does that of *Acer truncatum*.

Just outside the eastern wall of the park is the Xiangshan Hotel designed by I.M. Pei in 1982. Although inconveniently situated and fading fast, it is worth visiting for its architecture and for its garden—a modern interpretation of traditional themes. It is build round a large pond in the centre of which is a white marble platform carved with a cup-floating channel and connected to the shore by zigzag bridges (fig. 3.74). According to Morris (1983), Pei followed the Chinese tradition of saving many of the old trees on the site, some of the ginkgos there being as much as 800 years old.

DAJUESI (GREAT AWAKENING TEMPLE)

The Great Awakening Temple is on the slopes of Yangtai Shan, a few kilometres to the north of the Fragrant Hills. A temple was built here during the Liao and it is said that during the Jin it was considered to be one of the eight great gardens of the Western Hills. It was re-established with palace funds in 1428 at request of the Empress Dowager Zhang, the mother of the Ming emperor Xuande, and renamed Dajuesi. In the 1470s another dowager empress paid for major renovation, helping it to become one of the great monasteries of the Western Hills (Naquin, 2000). Subsequently it was expanded further and refurbished in the Qing during the reigns of Yongzheng and Qianlong. What remain today are two series of east-facing buildings built along east-west axes, an orientation believed to reflect the custom of the Liao people. Along the principal axis there are three large halls with old pines, junipers, catalpas, persimmons and sophoras growing around them. Behind the principal hall is a ginkgo, the survivor of a pair shown on Hildebrand's (1897) plan of the temple, said to be 1000 years old. Higher up the slope is a neglected garden shaded by old trees under which there is a dagoba built in Qianlong's time (fig. 3.75). Higher still there is a rectangular pool into which water pours from a dragon's head spout (fig. 3.76), above which is a pavilion surrounded by rockeries which overlooks the whole garden. Originally there were small streams flowing beside the steps which lead up both sides of the hill, but these were dry in 1996 when I visited the temple.

Next to this part of the garden is a huge rockery which lies behind the second axis, along which are the buildings

Figure 3.74 (opposite page) Garden of the Xiangshan Hotel

Figure 3.75 (far left) Dagoba, Dajue Temple, Western Hills, Beijing

Figure 3.76 (left) Pool at the Dajue Temple

once used as a travelling palace by the imperial family. The principal courtyard of this section has been replanted and contains, amongst other things, young magnolias, *Philadelphus pekinensis* and beds of lycoris.

An evocative description of this temple and its garden has been left to us by Freeman-Mitford (1900), who rented the Pavilion of the Reposing Clouds, one of the buildings on the residential axis, as a summer retreat in 1866. 'It is too far from Peking to be very convenient,' he wrote, 'but it is well worth the extra ride, and the advantage of being fifteen miles from the other temples inhabited by Europeans is incalculable …'. It appears to have been spared any serious attention from the Red Guards and, while the magnolias, tree peonies and streams of water which Freeman-Mitford described have gone and the 'most beautiful rockwork, all covered with tufts of feathery grass, mosses, ferns, and lycopods' is now bare (fig. 1.19), the place retains much of its atmosphere. Juliet Bredon (1931) records that, at the time of her visit, the two main halls were in good condition having been repaired a few years earlier by rich Chinese bankers but, by the time I went there, the main halls, though structurally sound, had lost their paint and the statues inside them were peeling and draped in faded yellow—all quite lovely. But already the restorers were at work on the entrance, and no doubt by now the whole temple is gleaming and brightly coloured once more.

BADACHU (EIGHT GREAT SITES)
This is the name now applied to an area in the southern part of the Western Hills where a group of temples was built in the middle of the 15th century on sites where religious establishments had been founded at various times beginning in the 7th century. Dr D.F. Rennie (1865) visited Badachu in 1861 and described the various temples and the magnificent view. Robert Fortune (1863) went there the same year and some of his description has already been given in Chapter 1. As mentioned there, the temples are arranged successively up a steep slope and from the 1860s on they were used as summer retreats by many of the foreigners living in Beijing. The Rev. W.A.P. Martin (1900), for instance, records that the uppermost of the temples 'sheltered me and mine for fifteen summers'. Presumably it was from the company of people such as these that Freeman-Mitford (1900) took such care to distance himself.

Mrs Little (1905) visited it not long after the Boxer Rebellion and said that it would be hard to say which of the temples was the most fascinating. She felt the most immediately appealing at first sight was that known to her as the Lion's Nest, which commanded a splendid view over the plain and had gardens and terraces laid out in the style of the Summer Palace, with a long gallery running from the residential section to a seat from which the best view was obtained. Various other people have left records of their visits, including Juliet Bredon (1931).

By 1949 little remained, though some restoration was carried out after this time. However, until recently the site was occupied by the military and closed to the public. Now, however, the temples have been restored, for the most part in unfortunate taste, there is a chairlift to take you almost to the top and, if you are so inclined, you can descend in record time by using an alarming roller-toboggan course on which speeds of 80 km per hour can be achieved. All that aside, it is worth walking either up or down, as there are old pines, ginkgos, catalpas (*C. bungei*), bamboos and other plants of interest in the precincts of the temples. Also the higher levels are clothed with semi-natural vegetation in which, as at the Fragrant Hills, smoke bushes predominate, so this area is colourful in autumn.

When the second of the temples on the ascent, the Lingguangsi (Temple of the Divine Light), was destroyed in 1900, only the base of a pagoda dating back to the Liao was left. In this base was found a sandalwood box bearing an inscription from 963 saying that it contained a tooth of the Buddha. A new pagoda was built to house it in 1959 (fig. 3.77). It was at this temple that Robert Fortune (1863) stayed in 1861 and where he saw some fine old ginkgos, one of which had *Wisteria sinensis* climbing over it. He also recorded that 'Amongst the plants cultivated by the priests for their flowers, I observed oleanders, moutans, pomegranates, and such things as I had already noticed in the gardens of Peking'.

The uppermost temple, the Zhengguosi (Temple of Buddhahood), traditionally believed to have been built where a Tang hermit had lived in a cave, was also amongst those destroyed in 1900. Fortune admired the view from here and wrote 'Looking to the eastward I could see the walls and watchtowers of Peking, and the roofs of its yellow palaces'. Both Fortune (1863) and Rennie (1865) mention looking down from here on the Yuanmingyuan, but it must have been what is now known as the Summer Palace that they observed. Nowadays, when it is clear, there is a distant panoramic view of modern Beijing.

Figure 3.77 Lingguang Temple, Badachu, Western Hills, Beijing

JIETAISI (TEMPLE OF THE ORDINATION PLATFORM)

The Jietaisi, which was founded in 622, is in the southern part of the Western Hills about 35 km south-west of Beijing, most beautifully set against a densely wooded hillside where the predominant tree is *Quercus dentata*. The marble ordination platform for which it is renowned was originally constructed during the Liao (907–1125), though most of the surviving buildings are Qing. It was visited in 1861 by Messrs Wyndham and Douglas of the British Legation, who admired the view over the plain and said that the trees were very fine. They were shown one specimen said to be 1000 years old (Rennie, 1865). Presumably this was the Nine Dragon Pine mentioned below.

Susan Naquin (2000) has drawn attention to the fact that, perhaps because of its role as a place where monks and nuns were ordained, the temple also had a reputation for decadence. Apparently in spring temporary stalls were set up not only for wine and tea but also for prostitutes. As Susan Naquin puts it, this was not only 'allegedly a last chance for the monks-to-be but very convenient for dalliance by visitors'.

These days not even the wine or tea are to be seen, nor were any of these excitements mentioned by Mrs Little (1905), who was amongst the many tourists to have admired the view from the terrace, some 120 m long and 6 or 7 m wide, which runs along the front of the temple. This in many ways is its most interesting feature, as growing on it are two very famous pines. The Nine Dragon Pine, a nine-trunked specimen of *Pinus bungeana*, is said to be more than 900 years old and was given its name by Qianlong (fig. 1.30). Many visitors have commented on it since, as they have on the nearby

Sleeping Dragon Pine, an old specimen of *P. tabuliformis* which leans out, dragon-like, almost horizontally from the terrace. There are further examples of both species in other parts of the temple along with lilacs, *Acer mono*, *Weigela florida* and other traditional garden plants (fig. 3.78). Below the terrace there is a garden of tree peonies and a separate garden in which stands a group of funerary stupas in stone and brick dating from the Liao, Yuan and Ming.

As well as admiring the old pines on the terrace, Dorothy Graham (1938) noted that the most beautiful garden within the temple's walls was that built by Prince Gong, who retired here in the late 19th century when he withdrew from political life. As far as I could determine, little of this remains.

Figure 3.78 *Syringa oblata* and pines, Jietai Temple, Western Hills, Beijing

TANZHESI (TEMPLE OF THE POOL AND ZHE TREE)

The Tanzhesi is situated a few kilometres on from the Jietaisi, at a slightly higher altitude and similarly beautifully sited on a steep slope. As far as its buildings, layout and magnificent old trees are concerned, its appearance now is little different from that shown in Donald Mennie's (1920) photograph taken in the early years of the 20th century. Like the Jietaisi, it has attracted visitors at least since the late Ming. It dates back to the Western Jin dynasty (265–317), though the present buildings are Ming and Qing. On the main axis, the first courtyard contains old pines and through a moon gate to its east there is a small orchard of flowering peaches. On the north side of the first courtyard is the main hall, which is tiled with imperial yellow tiles as the temple enjoyed imperial favour under Khubilai Khan—whose daughter was a Buddhist nun and is buried here—and also under Qianlong, who built a travelling palace on the eastern axis.

Stairs behind the main hall lead up to the largest courtyard in the complex. It is dominated by four enormous trees—two Chinese horse chestnuts, the significance of which I have explained above under Wofosi, and two ginkgos. These ginkgos have been mentioned by numerous Western visitors. The one on the right is said to date from the Liao and is known as the King of Trees, a title conferred on it by Qianlong. That on the left, known as the Emperor's Wife, was supposed to have put forth a new trunk every time a new emperor was born (figs 1.33, 3.79). Beneath these, on either side of the central path, there are two large beds of tree peonies, and beside the steps leading up from here to the Vairocana Hall there are two beds of the herbaceous kind (fig. 3.80). Elsewhere there are lilacs and crabapples.

Figure 3.79 **View over the rooftops, Tanzhe Temple, Western Hills, Beijing. The two famous ginkgos can be seen coming into leaf in the background.**

188

Figure 3.80 Herbaceous peony, Tanzhe Temple

The Tanzhesi gets its name from the pool and zhe trees which were once features for which it was famous. The zhe tree (*Maclura tricuspidata*) is a relative of the mulberry and its leaves can be used for feeding silkworms. Also its bark is believed to cure women of sterility. Both the pool and the trees were gone by 1900 according to Tun (1965), but Juliet Bredon (1931) recorded that a few stumps remained in the early part of the 20th century. A group of young zhe trees has recently been planted outside the entrance.

The Tanzhesi and the Jietaisi served as the setting for Ann Bridge's novel *Peking Picnic* (1932), which makes interesting reading for anyone who has visited these splendid temples and who is interested in the times with which it deals.

On the eastern axis of the temple is the travelling palace, in the courtyards of which there are beds of daylilies, bamboos and tree peonies. Of interest among the buildings here is an open-sided square pavilion with a cup-floating channel cut into the stone floor (fig. 3.81). This feature appears in the wood-block print of this garden in Lin Qing's *Hongxue yinyuan tuji* of 1847–50. On the western axis there is a small ordination platform and, at the highest point, the Guanyin Hall, from which there are splendid views over the trees and roofs of the rest of the temple. And on the hillside below there is a collection of funerary stupas dating from the Jin to the Qing. This is an exceptionally picturesque area as the stupas vary much in size and design and are shaded by huge sophoras and horse chestnuts (fig. 3.82).

Figure 3.81 Cup-floating pavilion, Tanzhe Temple

Figure 3.82 **Funerary stupas, Tanzhe Temple**

statues, known in English as a 'spirit road' or 'spirit way'. Individually positioned tombs usually have their own spirit roads, whereas in the case of grouped tombs one road may serve the whole group. Each of the tombs consists of two walled enclosures which are linked. The first, often called the 'square city', is square in plan (representing the earth) and contains buildings for the carrying out of rituals. Behind this is the tomb mound (usually circular, representing heaven) enclosed within battlemented walls. Behind the principal building in the first courtyard is a stone altar on which stand five marble versions of ritual bronze vessels and, beyond this again, a stele tower in the style of a city gate. This rises above the walls surrounding the tomb mound, which traditionally is planted with thujas (*Platycladus orientalis*). This tree is exceptionally long-lived and is a symbol of longevity and immortality. Pines and junipers, which have similar associations, are often grown in and around tomb enclosures as well, and the square courtyard is often planted with a variety of plants in a manner resembling that of the principal courtyards of temples. Not only do the grounds of many imperial tombs show similarities to those of temples, but the careful siting of groups of tombs in the landscape by geomancers has created some impressive large-

MING SHISANLING (THE THIRTEEN MING TOMBS)

The most impressive of Chinese burial grounds are the imperial tombs, the design of which has its beginnings in the tombs of the Qin and Han. They are arranged in the same axial fashion as traditional houses, palaces and temples, and the design of the buildings is based on palace architecture. In typical examples there is a straight approach lined with stone

scale compositions. The best surviving examples are the Ming and Qing tombs outside Beijing, a history, description and plans of which have been provided by Bouillard (1931b).

When the Ming emperor Yongle made Beijing his capital in 1421, he engaged geomancers to choose a suitable site for the imperial tombs. They selected a valley bounded to its north by a semicircle of hills about 50 km north-west of the city. Yongle's own tomb, Changling, was the first to be built there. It was completely restored in the 1950s and is open to the public, as is Zhaoling, the tomb of Longqing who died in 1572. Also open is the first of the tombs to have been excavated, Dingling, the tomb of Wanli who died in 1620.

After 1860 the Ming Tombs soon became one of the principal sights to attract Western visitors. Mr Wyndham of the British Legation visited the area in 1861 and remarked on the avenue of stone animals and figures. He noted that there were 13 tombs and that Yongle's appeared to be the largest (Rennie, 1865). John Thompson (1873–74) went there c.1870 and photographed the spirit way with its stone animals standing in a treeless landscape. He also photographed the main hall of Yongle's tomb, where at the time weeds were growing prolifically in its courtyard and on its steps and roof, and recorded that the burial mound was planted with 'cypresses and oaks'. Many years later Mrs Little (1905) wrote of her excursion to the site, describing its natural beauty and grandeur, and the lengthy approach before:

> **Clumps of foliage then become visible in the distance, enclosing the golden-roofed buildings clustered round the different tombs, some at three, some at four miles' distance, but all alike beautifully enshrined in the bosom of the hills, at the upper end of the long wide valley.**

She photographed the spirit way, still in a treeless landscape (fig. 3.83), and went on to report that many of the marble bridges and architectural ornaments had been destroyed and that the way to Yongle's tomb could only be found with difficulty through millet fields and persimmon orchards. Lady Susan Townley (1904) and, later, Juliet Bredon (1931) described the site in somewhat similar terms.

The road to the Ming Tombs now passes through a district of hawthorn orchards before arriving at a stone pailou, a gate and a double-roofed stele pavilion containing a giant stele carved with the names of the emperors buried here. Beyond this is the spirit road lined with carved stone figures, now backed by an avenue of trees (fig. 3.84), and some kilometres beyond this is the Changling. This follows the pattern of a large courtyard in which the principal hall stands. This is very grand, only slightly smaller than the Hall of Supreme

Figure 3.83 (above right)
Mrs Little's photograph of the approach to the Ming Tombs, 1901. FROM MRS LITTLE (1905).

Figure 3.84 (right)
The approach to the Ming Tombs today. PHOTOGRAPH: R. CLOUGH.

Harmony in the Forbidden City. Beyond this is the marble table bearing five marble versions of ritual vessels, and beyond that the stele tower, rising above the battlemented circular wall that surrounds the tomb mound, which is planted with thujas and oaks. All in all, though it has been greatly spruced up, it remains much as Mrs Little described it. The other tombs, varying in size and states of decay, are similar. Detailed descriptions of all the tombs are given by Bouillard (1931b) and Paludan (1981).

As mentioned above, early photographs show the tombs in more or less barren surroundings. It seems that most of the planting here is modern and the site is best appreciated as a landscape based on fengshui principles. Enjoyment of this, however, is challenged by the fact that it is now one of China's chief tourist drawcards, usually visited in combination with tour of the Great Wall at Badaling, a few kilometres to the north-west. Amongst the 'attractions' built in the environs of the tombs are a golf course, a museum, a hotel, a fountain, an amusement park, a swimming pool, shops, restaurants and much more.

Hebei

Hebei is both culturally and economically the most advanced province in northern China. Its history is, in effect, that outlined for the region at the beginning of this chapter. While most of the garden sites are now within the separate Beijing administrative area, the Eastern and Western Qing Tombs remain in this province, as does the town of Chengde, where the Imperial Summer Villa and the Eight Outer Temples are found.

The countryside of Hebei is full of interest, both on the North China Plain and in the mountains to its north and west. Although the original eastern section of the Great Wall lay further north, the present wall, dating from its reconstruction and expansion during the Ming, passes through the northern part of the province and reaches the sea at Shanhaiguan on the border with Liaoning. Much of the arable land of Hebei is devoted to crops of wheat and maize, and there are orchards of apples, pears, peaches, persimmons and walnuts. Apricots are grown, too, both for the fruits and for the kernels, which traditionally have taken the place of almonds in China. In the north, particularly, there are also orchards of *Crataegus pinnatifida*, the bright red fruits of which are popular candied. Vegetables are grown in vast quantities as well, cabbages and turnips being staples in the region. Hazelnuts (*Corylus heterophylla* and *C. sieboldiana* var. *mandschurica*) are commonly seen in markets in the mountainous regions, but whether they come from cultivated plants or are collected in the wild I do not know.

QING DONGLING (EASTERN QING TOMBS)

The Qing Tombs are in two groups on opposite sides of the city of Beijing. The Eastern Qing Tombs were the first to be established and are in Xunhua county about 125 km to the east of the city in a beautifully sited and geomantically auspicious area of about 48 square km encircled by hills. Lady Susan Townley (1904) considered them to be finer than either the western group or the Ming Tombs, and visitors today may well come to the same conclusion. Five emperors are buried here along with various empresses and concubines. The tombs of Qianlong, the Dowager Empress Cian (fig. 3.85) and the Dowager Empress Cixi were plundered and damaged in the 1920s but have been restored and are open to the public. The main spirit road leads to the Xiaoling, the tomb of Shunzhi, the first Qing emperor. To the left of this spirit way a subsidiary road leads to Qianlong's tomb, Yuling, and further on to the tombs of Cian and Cixi. Descriptions of all the tombs are given by Bouillard (1931b).

The Qing Tombs are similar in layout to the Ming Tombs, but each is usually preceded by a short spirit road of its own. Qianlong's grave mound is covered with grass but in many of the later tombs the mounds have been asphalted over, an unattractive state of affairs. The courtyards and the areas surrounding the tombs are planted with trees, principally pines and thujas, which create a pleasant ambience.

QING XILING (WESTERN QING TOMBS)

The Western Qing Tombs are near the town of Yixian, approximately 125 km to the south-west of Beijing. They were established when the emperor Qianlong decided that sons should not be buried in the same area as their fathers—though this procedure was never strictly followed. The tombs of the emperors, their consorts and concubines are scattered over an area of approximately 100 square km at the foot of the Yongning Mountains. An interesting feature of the Western Qing Tombs is the interment there in 1995 of the ashes of the last emperor, Puyi, who died in 1967. Belatedly he has become the fifth emperor to be buried there. However, the site of these tombs is less picturesque than that of its east-

Figure 3.86 Tailing, tomb of the emperor Yongsheng, Western Qing Tombs

ern counterpart, as the area is larger, there are fewer tombs, it is less densely planted and the hills are further away. As with the eastern group, descriptions of all the tombs can be found in Bouillard (1931b). Contrary to my view, he found the western ensemble no less attractive than the eastern, saying that it was particularly beautiful at sunset when the surrounding hills became tinted with purple-violet.

The first, most important, and most frequently visited tomb here is that of Yongzheng, who died in 1735. This is called Tailing and is a good example of the Qing style of tomb (fig. 3.86). The courtyards are thickly planted with pines and the grave mound, unlike those of most of the Eastern Qing Tombs, is covered with thujas. Lady Susan Townley (1904) noted that, unlike the Ming Tombs, those here were in good repair. She gave a description of the Tailing, as did Mrs Little (1905). Unlike visitors today, she was able to observe, in the halls where the sacrifices were prepared, 'two sheep still whole, many other carcases cut up, one large vessel full of livers and internal organs of various kinds'. And driving down the

valley she saw 'the Imperial herds and flocks kept for the purpose, black oxen and white sheep'.

Visitors also often go to Chongling, the tomb of Guangxu, who died in mysterious circumstances in 1908 at the age of 38. He and his empress were buried here in 1915, four years after the overthrow of the dynasty. It is unimpressive, as it has no spirit way and is in poor repair. However it was robbed and then excavated, so you can go down under the mound, which is bare, and see the coffins of the emperor and empress lying side by side. To one side of this enclosure is the green-tiled tomb of Guangxu's concubine, Zhenfei, the one who is said to have been drowned in a well in the Forbidden City in 1900.

Figure 3.85 (over page) Tomb of the Dowager Empress Cian,

Eastern Qing Tombs. PHOTOGRAPH: R. CLOUGH.

Chengde

When the Qing dynasty was established it was held that the annual custom of the imperial family engaging in hunting and military exercises in the north was necessary in order to retain their fighting ability. In 1681 Kangxi had an area of 9000 square km set aside for these activities at the junction of the highlands of Hebei and Inner Mongolia, some 300 km north of the capital. The imperial entourage would set forth, camping along the route, and would be away for up to three months. A description of these trips has been left to us by Jean-Francois Gerbillon, a Jesuit who accompanied Kangxi in 1691, 1696, and 1697 (Moyriac de Mailla, 1780). Eventually a series of travelling palaces was built to accommodate the party on its journeys to and fro. Lord Macartney described those where he stayed on his way from Beijing to Chengde in 1793, saying that they were 'all constructed upon nearly the same plan and in the same taste' and that they were 'enclosed by high walls and laid out in parks and pleasure grounds with every possible attention to picturesque beauty' (Cranmer-Byng, 1962).

Chengde, where Kangxi had one of his travelling palaces, used to be known as Rehe (Warm River) on account of the hot springs which feed into the Wulie River and prevent it freezing in winter. This name was translated by Western visitors as 'Jehol'. It is about 250 km north-east of Beijing and was little more than a village until 1703 when Kangxi began to build there the Bishu Shanzhuang (Mountain Villa Where You Can Escape the Heat). Aside from the hunting and other outdoor activities, his travels to the north and the building of the Imperial Summer Villa were political in nature, being used to establish stable relationships with the Mongolian, Uighur and Tibetan peoples north of the Wall and to secure the northern frontier against foreign invasion. The villa became an important political centre outside the capital to which the whole court removed itself in summer. According to Liu Junwen (1982), Kangxi's successor, Yongzheng, did not go there but Qianlong, who became emperor in 1735, reinstated the annual visits. And, as well as developing the Imperial Summer Villa, Kangxi and Qianlong built a series of temples to the east and north of the estate.

When Qianlong abdicated in 1795 he was succeeded by his fifth son who became the emperor Jiaqing. When Jiaqing died at Chengde in 1820 this was seen as a bad omen and the annual visits were discontinued by his successor, Daoguang.

It appears not to have been visited again by the imperial family until the emperor Xianfeng fled there in 1860, leaving Prince Gong to deal with the imminent arrival of the French and British troops. After peace was restored Xianfeng refused to return from Chengde, dying there in 1861, after which imperial visits to the Summer Villa ceased. Nevertheless, according to Sekino (1935), it continued to be maintained until the fall of the dynasty and photographs taken there in 1909 indicate that this was so.

The only European known to me to have recorded a visit to Chengde in the second half of the 19th century is the Rev. Alexander Williamson (1870), who went there in 1864. Although he was unable to gain admission to the Imperial Summer Villa, he managed to obtain a view of the trees and grounds by ascending an eminence which overlooked the walls, but the only building he was able to see was a nine-storeyed pagoda. However he was able to visit some of the temples. 'The magnificence of the temples quite took me by surprise;' he wrote, 'I have never witnessed anything like them, and believe they are quite unique'. As well as being impressed, he was clearly pleased to record that he had managed to sell a bible to the chief lama of one of the temples and had distributed tracts to the monks.

Whether Westerners other than missionaries went to Chengde in the years that followed is unclear. However, the fact that Emil Fischer (1924) included it in his *Guide to Peking and its Environs Near and Far*, saying that it took about a week riding on good ponies to get there, suggests that they did. But whether they were able to visit the Imperial Summer Villa I do not know. Anyway it is clear that after the fall of the dynasty in 1911 its fortunes declined. Boerschmann (1982) reported that dozens of beautiful structures were dismantled in the 1920s by the warlord stationed there, whose unruly troops pulled down the pillars with teams of horses. Presumably this was the military governor of the Chengde region, General Tang Yulin, who was living in the Summer Villa when Sven Hedin (1932) went there in 1930 to arrange for a replica of the Golden Pavilion in the Putuozongcheng Zhi Miao (see below) to be made and sent to Chicago for erection at the World Fair of 1933. Hedin and his party went to dinner with the general, who offered them bird's nest soup, shark fins, cognac, beer and much else. At this time the pavilions on the hilltops were almost completely ruined but Hedin reported that the view over the park and out to the temples remained impressive.

In 1933 the Japanese, who had occupied Manchuria in 1931 and named it Manchukuo, invaded the Chengde region, where General Tang Yulin offered no resistance. They added it to their territory and, as Sekino (1935) put it, no doubt quite realistically, restored order and security. Sekino visited Chengde twice during 1933–34, spending three weeks there. He reported that thousands of trees had been cut down, buildings had been demolished for their materials, and valuable artefacts removed. Nevertheless he felt that, with the Imperial Summer Villa and the magnificent temple buildings, there was nothing lacking to make Chengde one of the most beautiful places in the world, to be 'looked upon in much the same way as Nikko of Japan, Agra of India, and Allhambra of Spain'.

Another to go to Chengde at this time was Peter Fleming (1934), who noted that '… the first civilians to enter Jehol on the heels of the Japanese army were twenty lorry-loads of Korean girls'. He went on to record that the Japanese military had set up their headquarters in Imperial Summer Villa, where 'Japanese soldiers, their short legs dangling from the formal lovely bridges, fished unfruitfully in the lily ponds'. During his short stay he also visited the temples and came to the conclusion that the few remaining monks could 'less justly be called caretakers than the impotent spectators of decay'.

No doubt it was as a result of Tadashi Sekino's enthusiasm for the beauty and cultural significance of the Summer Villa and the adjoining temples that the Manchukuo government established an office in Chengde and set aside five million yen for repair work due to be commenced in the spring of 1935. If any of the projected work took place, it seems that there was little evidence of it by the end of World War II, when the park remained largely denuded of trees and most of the buildings were in ruins. It may well be, however, that little would have survived at all had not the region been occupied by the Japanese from 1933–45. Eventually, under the People's Republic, the Imperial Summer Villa and four of the surrounding temples were designated

national treasures in 1961 and much restoration work has been being carried out subsequently.

Chengde is now a large country town subsisting on mining, light industry, and the tourism generated by the presence of the Imperial Summer Villa and the Eight Outer Temples. It is connected with Beijing by rail and the line passes through a picturesque mountainous area. About halfway there is a glimpse of the Great Wall snaking its way over the hilltops and, adding to the interest of the journey, there are wheat fields in the valleys and orchards of pears, apricots, peaches, apples and hawthorns on the slopes. In the town itself the road along the river bank is planted with an interesting selection of trees and shrubs, including *Prunus triloba, P. davidiana, Weigela florida, Rosa xanthina, Syringa oblata, S. pubescens* and *Ulmus pumila* 'Pendula'. Also, on the approaches to the Summer Villa there are street vendors selling every imaginable thing, including goldfish, ornamental rocks (fig. 3.87), dried fungi, apricot kernels, hazelnuts and fresh pork.

Figure 3.87 **Ornamental rocks being manufactured for sale, Chengde**

**BISHU SHANZHUANG (MOUNTAIN VILLA
WHERE YOU CAN ESCAPE THE HEAT)**

Known generally in English as the Imperial Summer Villa or Imperial Summer Resort, the Bishu Shanzhuang lies on the northern edge of the town on the west bank of the Wulie River. Sheltered to its north and west by hills, it covers 564 hectares and is enclosed by a 10 km wall. Four fifths of the area is mountainous and the remainder is flat land and lakes. As mentioned above, the work was begun in 1703 by Kangxi and continued throughout his reign and that of his successors, Yongzheng and Qianlong, spanning a period of more than 80 years. As they had done in and around Beijing, Kangxi and Qianlong built features here recalling famous sites that they had seen on their journeys south. By 1711 Kangxi had constructed a modest palace and had given four-character names to 36 scenes (fig. 1.4).

From 1741 on Qianlong developed the resort further and, by 1792, had added another 36 scenes to those of his grandfather, all with three-character names. All this had been achieved by the time Lord Macartney made his tour of the garden in 1793, accompanied by, amongst others, He Shen, Qianlong's chief minister and the original owner of Gongwangfu in Beijing. While his embassy to Qianlong was a failure, he and his party were fortunate to have seen the Imperial Summer Villa at the time of its greatest perfection.

Although the walled gardens and most of the buildings which were scattered throughout the mountainous area have not survived, a few hill-top pavilions have now been rebuilt and on the flat land much has been done to return the estate to its original appearance. The principal buildings of the residential section are in good condition, trees have been planted, the lakes are full, there are well-maintained buildings on the islands, and the vistas within the garden and out to the surrounding mountains must look much as they did when seen by Matteo Ripa, Mr de Lange and Lord Macartney.

The main entrance gate, the Lizhengmen (Gate of Beauty and Uprightness) is in the south and its name is inscribed on it in Manchu, Mongolian, Tibetan, Chinese and Uighur—a gesture of politeness to the representatives of the border areas who were entertained here. Beyond this is a second gate inside which is a name board inscribed with the characters 'Bi shu shan zhuang' in Kangxi's calligraphy (fig. 3.88). Beyond this another gate leads into the main palace. There were originally three palaces built along adjacent parallel axes. The easternmost has disappeared and the central one, which lies immediately to the east of the main palace, has not been accessible at the times of my visits. It was built in 1749 for Qianlong's mother and concubines.

The main palace consists of a series of courtyards in which the buildings, many of which are connected by roofed walkways, are single storeyed (fig. 3.89). Little of the woodwork is

Figure 3.88 (above left) 'Bi shu shan zhuang' in Kangxi's calligraphy, Imperial Summer Villa

Figure 3.89 (left) The Danbo Jubeng Hall, Imperial Summer Villa

Figure 3.90 (right) **Aerial view of the Imperial Summer Villa c.1933, looking west.**
FROM SEKINO (1935).

Figure 3.91 (above) **The shore of Ruyi Islet, Imperial Summer Villa, with the pavilion at the embarkation point on the right**

painted and the roofs are of grey tiles. This presumably reflects Kangxi's taste for frugality and avoidance of decoration, and is in contrast to the highly coloured and decorated palaces in Beijing. The only two-storeyed building in the complex is that on the far side of the final courtyard. The upper storey of this is reached by climbing a rockery built against the south-eastern corner. The courtyards of the palace are planted with pines (*Pinus tabuliformis*) and there are few other plants apart from those in pots and occasional forsythias and cultivars of *Prunus triloba*.

A path from the northern gate of the main palace leads down to the lake, which is divided into sections of different sizes by causeways, bridges and islands in a manner similar to the Kunming Lake at the Summer Palace (fig. 3.90). Following the traditional pattern, there are three main islands—Huanbi (Surrounding Green) in the south-west, Yuese Jiangsheng (Moonlight and Sound of the River) in the south-east, and Ruyi Zhou (As You Wish Islet) in the north. The buildings on these islands are single-storeyed and in relatively quiet taste. At the northern end of Huanbi and the southern of Ruyi Zhou there are small pavilions and jetties where the ladies of the court embarked when they went on excursions to collect water caltrops (fig. 3.91). Amongst the features of interest on Ruyi Zhou, the largest island, is a small enclosed garden with an open pavilion which looks out onto a pool on the far side of which is a rockery and cascade (fig. 0.3).

Connected to the northern side of Ruyi Zhou by a bridge is a small island on which is one of the few two-storeyed buildings in the park, the Yanyulou (Misty Rain Pavilion), built by Qianlong in 1780–81 (fig. 3.2). It is modelled on the famous building of the same name at Jiaxing, halfway between Shanghai and Hangzhou (see Chapter 5). It is surrounded by a garden and is the principal feature of the northern part of the lake.

To the east of Ruyi Zhou and against the eastern shore is another small island, Jinshan (Golden Mountain) Island, on which there are temple-like buildings and a three-storey pagoda. This appears in Matteo Ripa's engravings and was built by Kangxi in imitation of the famous Jin Shan in the Yangtze, which he had visited on his tours to the south. On each storey of the pagoda there is a tablet inscribed with Kangxi's calligraphy. Like the Misty Rain Pavilion, the Golden Mountain is one of the most conspicuous features of the park (figs 3.92, 3.93, 3.94).

In the north-east corner of the main lake there is a hot spring where the water is said not to freeze in winter, though while I was there I could not detect any perceptible warmth in the water. Far to the south of this, in the south-east corner of the lake, is another of the famous sights of the park, a causeway on which are three double-roofed pavilions, the Mid-lake Pavilions, built by Qianlong (fig. 3.95). And to the east of this across another sheet of water is the recently rebuilt Shizilin (Lion Grove), a small garden with an elaborate rockery modelled on the garden of the same name which he had seen in Suzhou (figs 1.42, 1.43).

From the north-west corner of the lake a canal, lined with

Figure 3.92 (far left)

The Golden Mountain, Imperial Summer Villa, Chengde.

TAKEN FROM A COPY OF THE KANGXI EMPEROR'S POEMS DESCRIBING THE SUMMER RESORT, AN ILLUSTRATED COPPER ENGRAVED EDITION BY MATTEO RIPA, POSTFACE DATED 1712. THE BRITISH LIBRARY [19957 C.4].

Figure 3.93 (above left)

The Golden Mountain, Imperial Summer Villa, 1933.

FROM SEKINO (1935).

Figure 3.94 (left)

The Golden Mountain, 1996

Figure 3.95 (above) **The Mid-lake Pavilions**

Figure 3.96 (right) **The Wenjinge and its garden**

elms, poplars and sophoras and ending at an elaborate rockery, runs north to the Wenjinge (Pavilion of Literary Delights), a library built by Qianlong in 1785 to house the fourth copy to be completed of the *Siku quanshu* (fig. 3.96). Like the Wenyuange in the Forbidden City and the Wensuge at Shenyang, which he built for the same purpose, it is copied from the Tianyige in Ningbo. Though it is in a heavier style than its prototype, it has been placed in a similar setting for fire protection. It faces a pool beyond which there is a large rock mountain through the interior of which there is a passage. The Wenjinge was once surrounded by other buildings the foundations of which can still be seen. One of these, a square, double-roofed pavilion on the approaches, has been rebuilt. It stands above a floor made of rough-hewn blocks of stone with channels between them in which perhaps there was once water.

From outside the Wenjinge appears to consist of two storeys but inside there are three. Originally, like the Wenyuange in Beijing, it was roofed with black tiles, but these were replaced with grey ones when the building was restored. These days visitors seem to take little interest in its

Figure 3.97 Père David's deer at the Imperial Summer Villa

architecture, garden and history, preferring to clamber over the rockery and photograph each other before standing at a marked spot in front of the building where, according to a notice at the entrance, there is 'A wonderful view that you can see the sun and the moon at the same time'. This comes about as from this spot there is a reflection in the pool of a crescent-moon shaped opening in the rockery and, if you care to risk damage to your eyes, you can look up and see the sun. However, perhaps its reflection can also be seen close to that of

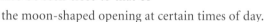

the moon-shaped opening at certain times of day.

To the east of the Wenjinge and north of the lake there is a large flat area at the foot of the hills which was used for archery, exhibitions of horsemanship and suchlike. Also, on part of this area yurts were set up, the largest of which was for the use of the emperors, who received the political and religious leaders of the border areas here. It was here, too, that Qianlong received Lord Macartney.

In the north-eastern corner of this flat area, close to the park wall, are the remains of the Yongyousi (Temple of Perpetual Blessing) built in 1751. The most conspicuous feature here is the Liuheta (Pagoda of the Six Harmonies), named after a famous pagoda in Hangzhou. It is in this area, also, that from time to time a herd of Père David's deer (*Elaphurus davidianus*) are brought from their enclosure behind the Wenjinge and allowed to graze (fig. 3.97). This animal was described by Armand David, a French Lazarist missionary who was in China from 1862–73 and saw a herd in the imperial hunting park south of Beijing. Some years later Mrs Little (1901) quoted an official report of 1891 which recorded that no hunt had been organised there for the

previous 20 years, the deer had bred up, and there was much poaching—the venison being marketed in Beijing as donkey meat or beef in order to evade inquiries of the part of the police. Although an effort was made to stamp out the practice, eventually all the animals were killed and eaten. There was another herd at Chengde which must have suffered the same fate. As a result the animal became extinct in China. Fortunately, as a result of the interest generated by Armand David's discovery, several pairs from the imperial herd were sent to Europe in the latter part of the 19th century and the animal became established there. Then, some years ago, the Duke of Bedford presented the Chinese government with animals from his herd at Woburn and these were used to re-establish the species at Chengde and elsewhere. When the deer disappeared from the park there is unclear, as Sekino (1935) said that there were hundreds of deer roaming there at the time of his visits in 1933–34, but what they were he did not say. These deer were also seen by Fleming (1934).

As well as willows, pines, elms, poplars and other trees, there are now many flowering plants which add interest to the park. Lotuses are once more planted in the lake and, on

Figure 3.98 **View of Club Peak from the causeway leading to Yuese Jiangsheng Island, Imperial Summer Villa**

the islands, causeways and lake margins, there are apricots, *Prunus davidiana*, cultivars of *P. triloba*, forsythias, lilacs (*Syringa oblata*, *S. reticulata*, and *S. × persica*), crabapples (*Malus baccata*) and other shrubs. In the northern area, towards the pagoda, there is a large courtyard planted with tree peonies, and beyond this there are more lilacs and a collection of herbaceous peonies. Also, to the west of the approaches to the Wenjinge there is a large nursery area from which plants are drawn for the continuing restoration of the park.

In spite of the vicissitudes of the past 200 years, the Imperial Summer Villa remains one of the great achievements of Chinese garden design. It is the country's largest surviving imperial park and, as at the Summer Palace outside Beijing, the views to the temples and mountains beyond its walls form an integral part of the composition. Dominating the skyline to the east is the extraordinary Bangchui Shan (Wooden Club Mountain), narrower at the base than the top and resembling a wooden club used to beat washing (fig. 3.98). Matteo Ripa, who saw it in 1711, thought it resembled 'the fabulous club of Hercules' (Ripa, 1844). It is the most prominent natural landmark in Chengde, and

Phillipe Forêt (1995), in his analysis of the design of the park, goes so far as to suggest that the alignment of this peak with the replica of Jin Shan inside the walls, and the Pule Temple, which is outside, is of cosmological and geomantic significance. Be this as it may, it is not likely to affect the appreciation of the scene by most Western visitors. Nevertheless, it is worth taking the chairlift to the mountaintop on which this enormous club-shaped rock stands, as there is a panoramic view from here of the park and the outer temples. And in mid-May, when I visited it, masses of *Spiraea trilobata* and *Deutzia grandiflora* were flowering near the summit, and here and there were the purple blooms of *Pulsatilla chinensis*.

WAIBAMIAO (THE EIGHT OUTER TEMPLES)

There were originally 12 temples built outside the wall of the Imperial Summer Villa, to eight of which the imperial court assigned Lamaists to handle the religious affairs. It was to these that the name Waibamiao referred. They were built between 1713 and 1779 and, as Wood (1992) puts it, 'their religious significance, as noted, was subordinate to their political usefulness in wooing the adherents of Lamaist Buddhism in the border regions of Mongolia and Tibet'. Situated to the north and north-east of the villa, undoubtedly they would also have been considered to have had a geomantic effect in countering the unfavourable influences which were believed to flow from that direction.

Only seven of the original 12 temples now survive, all of them numbered amongst the Waibamiao. The first to be constructed was the southernmost, the Purensi (Temple of Universal Love), built in 1713 on the eastern bank of the Wulie River. It is said to have been constructed for the Mongol princes so that they could continue their Lamaist devotions while in Chengde attending Kangxi's 60th birthday celebrations. It has been closed at the time of my visits so I have seen it only from the outside. It is a modest temple with pines in its courtyards and I doubt that it is of much interest from a garden point of view. It is the only temple surviving from Kangxi's time.

A short distance to the north-east, on the lower slopes of the mountains which rise up to Club Peak, is the Pulesi (Temple of Universal Joy) (fig. 3.99). It was built in 1766–67 for the western Mongols who came each year to pay respect to the emperor. It faces west, which is unusual, and its axis is aligned with Club Peak. On either side of the entrance are tall poles from which banners are flown and which are a feature

of Lamaist architecture. The most interesting part of the temple is the third courtyard in which there is a magnificent round pavilion with a double roof of glazed yellow tiles. Standing on a raised platform, it is reminiscent of the Hall of Prayer for Good Harvests at the Temple of Heaven in Beijing. So far this temple seems to receive few visitors and strolling through its courtyards amongst the old pines is a pleasant experience.

To the north of this, on another ridge, is the Anyuanmiao (Temple of Distant Peace). This was constructed by Qianlong in 1764 for the tens of thousands of western Mongols brought to Chengde as part of manoeuvres to control the desert area of Xinjiang (Wood, 1992). Its design is based on that of a temple in Xinjiang, it faces south-west, which again is unusual, and it consists of two large courtyards. The first has been planted with pines but most of the buildings have disappeared. The main hall in the second courtyard is a towering structure roofed with black and yellow tiles.

Further north again on the other side of the river is the Puningsi (Temple of Universal Peace), the first temple to be built at Chengde by Qianlong. It was constructed in 1755 to commemorate the pacification of what is now northern Xinjiang. In the main courtyard there is an impressive hall in Chinese style, in front of which there are cycads and other plants in pots. This hall backs onto a steep hillside which has been terraced. On the first level, in a commanding position, there is the towering Mahayana Hall. In Tibetan style and five storeys high, it contains a wooden multi-armed statue of Guanyin more than 20 m tall. Higher still there are further Tibetan-style buildings surrounded by extensive rockeries shaded by old pines (fig. 3.100).

The remaining three temples are to the west of Puningsi and face south towards the northern wall of the Imperial Summer Villa. Going west the first

Figure 3.99 (left) **Pule Temple**

Figure 3.100 (opposite page)

Upper garden, Puning Temple

Figure 3.101 Xumifushou Temple

of these is the Xumifushou Zhi Miao (Temple of Happiness and Longevity at Mount Sumeru), which was built for the sixth Panchen Lama when he came to visit Qianlong on the occasion of his 70th birthday in 1780 (fig. 3.101). The design is based on that of the Panchen Lama's residence at Xigaze, Tibet. The sloping forecourt contains various small buildings and is planted with forsythias, flowering apricots and other trees (fig. 3.102). Behind this there is a huge square building, three storeys

high, painted red, and with its outer walls pierced with Tibetan-style windows. Inside is a courtyard which is almost filled by a square hall 17 m high. This is remarkable for its gilded copper roof with dragons on each of its four ridges. To the north-west of this is the three-storey building on a raised platform where the Panchen Lama stayed. It is approached up steps of uneven, rough-hewn rock, so it is assumed that the Panchen Lama was steady on his feet. This area is ornamented with more rocks and there are old pines on either side of the entrance. Above this again is a steep garden area largely covered with rocks and planted with pines and forsythias (fig. 1.16). There are other Tibetan-style buildings here and at the highest point an octagonal glazed-tile pagoda dominates the scene.

Next is the Putuozongcheng Zhi Miao (Temple of the Potaraka Doctrine), which is often called the Potala Temple on account of its resemblance to the Potala—the Dalai Lama's palace in Lhasa (fig. 3.103). It covers the largest area of the Eight Outer Temples and was built between 1767 and 1771 for western Mongols who came to pay respects to Qianlong on his 60th birthday (1770) and the Dowager Empress on her 80th (1771). The temple was also used to celebrate the return in 1770 of the Mongolian Turgut tribe who had migrated as far as the Volga and had undertaken the 5000 km trek back to escape Russian oppression. In front of the Potala-like building which rises high up at the rear of the site is a large open area dotted with Tibetan-style buildings. Many of these are solid and unusable, presumably having been built for effect rather than any particular purpose. This space is planted with pines, an occasional elm and thuja, and numerous lilacs, forsythias and other shrubs (fig. 3.104). The main building, like that at the Xumifushou Temple, surrounds a

Figure 3.102 (left)

Apricot blossom,

Xumifushou Temple

Figure 3.103 (far left)

Putuozongcheng

Temple

Figure 3.104 (below)

Forsythias,

Putuozongcheng

Temple

Figure 3.105 Main hall and ruined upper garden, Shuxiang Temple

stands, surrounded by old pines, and behind it an abandoned rockery leads up to the highest point in the grounds (fig. 3.105). Little restored and rarely visited, for me this temple evokes its past more eloquently than its revamped and more grandiose neighbours.

Liaoning

Liaoning is the southernmost of the three north-eastern Chinese

courtyard in which there is a magnificent, square Chinese-style hall—the Golden Pavilion. This is the building which Sven Hedin (1932) came in the 1930s to have copied for the World's Fair in Chicago. His photographs show it to have been surrounded by collapsed balconies and other signs of ruin, but the whole building has now been restored.

After touring the outer temples, Lord Macartney thought the Potala, where at the time there were 800 lamas, to be 'infinitely superior to the rest in magnitude, splendour and celebrity' (Cranmer-Byng, 1962). He was greatly impressed by the square central hall—the 'Golden Chapel' as he called it—saying that it contained three colossal statues, 'all of solid gold'. Whatever they may really have been made of, these are no longer there, but there are still wonderful views from the roof of the main building, where he was able to view the roof of the 'Golden Chapel' and record that, 'as our conductors assured us in the most solemn manner, it was covered with plates of solid gold'. Almost certainly, however, they were merely gilded copper, as they are now.

The seventh of the temples, the Shuxiangsi (Temple of the Statue of Manjusri), was built between 1774 and 1776. Manjusri was the Boddhisattva favoured by Lamaist Buddhists and hence it was deemed appropriate to build a temple dedicated to him at Chengde. It is in a purely Chinese style based on the ancient temple of the same name at Wutai Shan in Shanxi. Old trees and stone lions stand outside the gate but most of the buildings inside the compound have now disappeared. However, the double-roofed main hall still

provinces that make up what used to be known as Manchuria. The most important part of Liaoning is the plain through which flows the Liao River, which gives the province its name. More than 2000 years ago the Chinese began settling in this part of southern Manchuria, which fell within the boundary established by the first Great Wall built in the 3rd century BC. The Sui and the Tang dynasties continued to exert limited control over the area, but the tables were subsequently turned when powerful kingdoms sprang up in the Manchurian region. In the 10th century the Liao moved south and captured Beijing, as has been mentioned earlier, to be followed by the Jin, the Mongols and, eventually, the Manchus.

After the overthrow of the Mongols in 1368, the Ming dynasty re-established control over southern Manchuria. They attempted to retain control of this region by trying to keep the tribes divided into as many subdivisions as possible and so prevent them from uniting into a power which might challenge their authority. They were ultimately thwarted in this by a leader called Nurhachi, who had brought the tribes together and in 1616 was proclaimed emperor of a new Jin dynasty in the north. In 1621 he captured the Ming cities of Shenyang and Liaoyang and, after his death, his son Abahai, who succeeded him, made further territorial gains. The success of this regime was very much the result of the breaking down of the tribal divisions and the formation of 'The Eight Banners'—army divisions each with a distinctive banner and uniform. All the people were registered under their local banner and taxed and organised according to the needs of the state. As well as this, captured Chinese civil servants were used to help set up the bureaucracy in Shenyang, the capital of the kingdom.

Abahai adopted the name Manchu for his people and changed the name of the dynasty from Jin to Qing. By the time of his death in 1643 the Manchus had expanded west into Inner Mongolia, north into the Amur and Ussuri valleys, east into Korea, and south as far as the Great Wall. Then in 1644, a month after the Ming dynasty was overthrown by a peasant uprising, they occupied Beijing and north China unopposed and gradually obtained control of the rest of the country. Abahai's ninth son, Fulin, became the first Qing emperor of China with the reign name of Shunzhi, as has been mentioned at the beginning of this chapter.

With the weakening of the Qing dynasty in the 19th century, Manchuria became the scene of opposing Chinese, Japanese and Russian ambitions. In 1931 the Japanese succeeded in taking control of the region and set up the puppet state of Manchukuo, bringing the last Qing emperor, Puyi, to be its nominal head of state, eventually enthroning him as Emperor of Manchukuo in 1934. They then set about transforming the region, already well supplied with railways built by the Russians, into an industrial and war base for expansion into Asia.

In 1945, shortly before the end of World War II, Russia declared war on Japan, occupying Manchuria and capturing Puyi. Then, delayed by the Russians and harassed by the Communists, the Nationalist government had difficulty in gaining control of the region, which finally fell to the Communists in 1948 and eventually became fully integrated with the People's Republic. No doubt on account of its history, Liaoning remains one of the most industrialised provinces in the country. It received its present boundaries in 1956 when part of the former province of Jehol was added to it.

The central plain of Liaoning, where the principal cities occur and where most of its agriculture and industries are based, is very flat and there are few trees. Owing to the severity of the winters it remains free of crops until the end of April, and so the countryside is brown and bare for almost six months of the year. The summers, however, are hot, and this allows the cultivation of maize, cotton and other field crops. There are also a few orchards, and large areas are devoted to Chinese cabbages which are stored for use during winter.

Shenyang

Shenyang, earlier known as Mukden, is the provincial capital. From a historical, architectural and garden point of view, the chief places of interest in this city today are the monuments relating to the time when it was the capital of Nurhachi and Abahai. There are also the Arboretum of the Shenyang Institute of Applied Ecology, founded in 1955, the Shenyang Botanical Garden, founded in 1959, and the Shenyang Arboretum, founded in 1963, but I have not visited them. According to Yu (1983), the Shenyang Arboretum has a collection of plants native to Liaoning, such as *Magnolia sieboldii, Syringa wolfii, Rhododendron mucronulatum* and *R. schlippenbachii*. There are also some pleasant modern parks and the street trees are of interest. Amongst those most frequently planted are both upright and weeping willows, poplars, robinias, flowering apricots, pines, ginkgos, ashes (*Fraxinus mandshurica*), and the weeping form of the Siberian elm (*Ulmus pumila*). Also to be seen along the streets are lilacs (*Syringa oblata*), forsythias and various cultivars of *Prunus triloba*. Of particular interest to me was the widespread use of David's peach (*Prunus davidiana*), which becomes surprisingly tall. The trunks of young trees and the major branches of older ones have shiny reddish-brown bark, and it blooms earlier than the forsythias or any other species

of *Prunus* that I saw there—a real harbinger of spring, as the cliché goes. The almost sessile flowers, 4–5 cm across, are white, sometimes slightly tinged with pink (fig. 3.106).

Figure 3.106 ***Prunus davidiana*, Shenyang**

GUGONG (IMPERIAL PALACE)

This palace stands in the centre of the old city of Shenyang, around which the modern metropolis has developed. Originally known as the Palace of the Prosperous Capital, it was renamed the Travelling Palace of Upholding Heaven when the Manchu capital was moved to Beijing. It consists of a walled enclosure within which the buildings and courtyards are arranged along three axes. Construction was begun by Nurhachi when he made Shenyang his capital in 1625, and continued by his son, Abahai. The central and eastern axes date from this time, but were renovated in 1745 by Qianlong, who also added new buildings. Then in 1748 he commenced construction of the western axis.

The eastern axis is dominated by the octagonal, double-roofed Dazhengdian (Hall of Great Government), in the centre of which is a throne on a dais, surrounded by the ring of pillars which support a canopy. This interior is the most striking in the whole complex, and is decorated in dull green and gold. In front of this building is a long courtyard on either side of which is a row of five regularly spaced pavilions—one for the Right Wing Prince, one for the Left Wing Prince and one for each of The Eight Banners. There is nothing in this part of the palace, however, which could be described as a garden.

Facing the gate in the first courtyard of the central axis is the Chongzhengdian (Hall of Supreme Government) built in 1632 (fig. 3.107). It was here that the name of the Qing dynasty was proclaimed in 1636. In front of this, on the eastern and western sides respectively, are the Flying Dragon Pavilion and the Flying Phoenix Pavilion. The courtyard is planted with pines and in front of the Flying Dragon Pavilion there is a large *Syringa reticulata*. In the next courtyard there are more pines and lilacs, both *S. oblata* and *S. reticulata*, along with *Weigela florida* clipped into hemispherical shapes. On the northern side a flight of steps leads up to the Phoenix Tower. On either side of the steps are beds of tree peonies, each surrounded by a stone balustrade. Openings in the north-eastern and north-western corners of the courtyard lead to small subsidiary courtyards in which there are arrangements of Taihu rocks, *Prunus triloba*, *Rosa xanthina* and clipped weigelas.

The three-storey Phoenix Tower acts as a gate leading to another courtyard where the emperor and his family had their apartments. Behind this again, at the northern end of

Figure 3.107 Chongzheng Hall, Imperial Palace, Shenyang

Figure 3.108 (right)

Imperial Garden, Imperial
Palace, Shenyang

Figure 3.109 (below right)

The Wensuge, Imperial Palace,
Shenyang

the axis, is the Imperial Garden, a narrow rectangular space occupying a position similar to that of the Imperial Garden in the Forbidden City in Beijing. It consists of little more than an oblong pond spanned by a bridge, two rock mountains, and some weeping willows and weeping sophoras (fig. 3.108).

The most significant building on the western axis is the Wensuge (Pavilion of Literary Reminiscence), which was built by Qianlong to house the second copy to be completed of the *Siku quanshu*. It is modelled, like the similar buildings in the Forbidden City and in the grounds of the Imperial Summer Villa at Chengde, on the Tianyige at Ningbo. Like its counterpart in Beijing, it is

roofed with black and green tiles. However, unlike the prototype and the other copies, the Wensuge has no garden and stands in a courtyard which is bare except for a single weeping willow (fig. 3.109). According to the plan of the palace, in the courtyard to the north of this there is a garden of herbaceous peonies. At the time of my visit, entry to this area was not permitted, so I was unable to confirm its existence.

ZHONGSHAN GONGYUAN (ZHONGSHAN PARK)

This modern park is in Nanjing Jie near the centre of the downtown area of modern Shenyang. It consists largely of planting, though there are the usual children's playground, a hill with a pavilion on top, and a large paved area used for tai chi and the outdoor ballroom dancing that seems so

popular first thing in the morning everywhere in China. The nice thing about this park is that, while there are a few displays of annual bedding plants, all the trees, shrubs and perennials are northern Chinese plants. In early spring it is particularly attractive when the pears, *Prunus davidiana*, single and double cultivars of *P. triloba*, apricots and forsythias are in bloom (fig. 3.110). The lilacs follow, and the grassed areas are studded with hundreds of plants of *Iris lactea*, the blue flowers of which appear a little later, at the same time as *Rosa xanthina* produces its yellow ones.

Figure 3.110 (overpage) Apricot, *Prunus triloba* and *Forsythia suspensa*, Zhongshan Park, Shenyang

Figure 3.111 (above) **Huang Temple,
Shenyang**

Figure 3.112 (far right) **Entrance to the
East Tomb, Shenyang**

Figure 3.113 (right) **Stone camel amongst
the pines, East Tomb**

HUANGSI (IMPERIAL TEMPLE)

Built in 1638, this Lamaist temple is
also near the city centre. It has clearly
had its ups and downs but appears to
have been restored recently. At present
it consists of little more than a couple of modest halls separated by courtyards in which the usual range of northern
Chinese garden plants has been established (fig. 3.111). It is
once again an active temple, at the time of my visit seemingly in the hands of boy lamas. The appearance of these youths
gave a strong indication that the renovation of the temple
had not yet included the provision of bathing facilities.

DONGLING (EAST TOMB)

Also known as Fuling (Fortunate Tomb), this tomb, about 11
km north-east of Shenyang, is that of Nurhachi, who died in
1626. Construction took from 1629 to 1651 and there were
further embellishments in the 18th century. Detailed descriptions and plans of this tomb and the Beiling (described

below) can be found in Bouillard (1931b). With its architecture, history, native plants and ancient trees, the extensive
enclosure has considerable charm, as was noted by John Birch
(1902), who went there in 1899. Two huge old Siberian elms
stand on either side of the gate (fig. 3.112), inside which,
amongst tall old pines (*Pinus tabuliformis*), is a short avenue
of stone animals (fig. 3.113) mounted on carved pedestals—
two lions, two horses, two camels, two elephants and two
qilin, an imaginary animal made up of the parts of various
others. At the end of this avenue is a flight of more than 100
stone steps which lead up to the gate of the walled 'square
city'. This gate is surmounted by a three-storey tower and
there are two-storey towers at each corner. Outside the
entrance there are some more ancient elms and a few old

apricots. Inside towards the rear is a large hall, but there is little planting apart from a few pines and one or two plants of *Prunus triloba*. Behind the hall is the marble table on which the five marble versions of bronze ritual vessels are arranged (fig. 3.114). A tunnel beneath the stele tower leads from here to the semi-circular enclosure of the tomb mound, beneath which the emperor, empresses and concubines are buried. The mound is treeless but not macadamised.

Figure 3.114 **Marble ritual vessels, East Tomb**

Figure 3.115 (right)

Pear blossom, East Tomb

Figure 3.116 (below right)

Viola mandshurica, **East Tomb**

A walk around the castellated walls of the tomb provides a close-up view of the vegetation of the surrounding park. Here are more pines, *Malus baccata*, pears (fig. 3.115), *Prunus davidiana*, wild white forms of *P. triloba*, elders (possibly *Sambucus sieboldiana*), wild apricots and many other trees and shrubs. On the ground beneath, *Viola mandshurica* (fig. 3.116) is common and the bases of many of the old pines and elms are surrounded by stone edging, within which the ground is thickly planted with hostas. Although not in bloom, they appeared to me to be *Hosta ventricosa* or something similar.

BEILING (NORTH TOMB)

This is the tomb of Abahai and his wife. It is also known as Zhaoling (Clear Tomb), and lies on top of a small hill in the northern suburbs of Shenyang. It is approached through a large park and a horseshoe-shaped waterway lies in front of it in conformity with fengshui beliefs. This is crossed by a stone bridge from which a paved path and flight of steps lead up to the entrance. Inside the layout is identical with that of the Dongling, with an avenue of stone animals leading to the 'square city'. The animals are the same as at the Dongling except that there is an extra pair of qilin and the horses are said to be modelled on Abahai's favourite steeds. Behind the 'square city' is the semi-circular enclosure of the tomb mound, the surface of which in this case is macadamised. A single deciduous tree grows on the top but, as it was still leaf-

less at the time of my visit and far out of reach, I was unable to identify it.

As a result of its proximity to the city, this tomb is frequented by many more tourists than the Dongling. Also it lacks its huge old trees, forested surrounds and romantic atmosphere. Nevertheless pines, apricots, forsythias, *Prunus triloba*, willows and other plants, together with the old buildings, create a picturesque scene (fig. 3.117).

Figure 3.117 (opposite page) **Apricot in bloom beside the entrance to the 'square city', North Tomb**

CHAPTER 4

The South

While it was possible in ancient times to travel south via various lakes and waterways from the Yellow River valley to the Yangtze and beyond, it became necessary, in what is now southern Hunan, to traverse a mountain pass to reach the independent kingdom of Nanyue (modern Guangdong, Guangxi and North Vietnam), which was inhabited by non-Han people. In the 3rd century BC an alternative route was established when a canal was constructed to connect the headwaters of two rivers in north-eastern Guangxi, one flowing south, the other north. This was done primarily to facilitate the movement of troops and supplies needed to establish and maintain control over this region by the government in the north.

Throughout most periods since then, the central government has maintained varying levels of control over the region often referred to in the past as Lingnan (South of the Mountain Range). Viewed from the north, particularly during the Tang, it appeared a

Figure 4.1 **View from the Dragon Bridge, Baisha, Guangxi**

strange and wonderful land, a source of pearls, coral, cassia bark, bananas, lychees, oranges, tropical flowers and exotic birds. Red is the colour associated with the south, the home of the mythical 'vermilion bird' and the scarlet azalea (*Rhododendron simsii*), which seemed to people of the Tang a perfect floral symbol of the region (Schafer, 1967). Even to this day, the south remains in a sense a different country, with its own spoken language and cultural characteristics.

For the purposes of this book, then, I have taken this region to consist of Guangxi, Guangdong, Hong Kong and Macao. As might be expected, the gardens here differ somewhat from those of the north, not only as a result of cultural differences, but because of the tropical and subtropical climates in which frost-tender plants can be grown out of doors. On the other hand, plants which require cold winters in order to grow satisfactorily are either not grown or, like tree peonies, brought down annually from the north and discarded after flowering.

Apart from the observations of foreigners from the 17th century on, there seem to be few surviving records of gardens and gardening in this region. However one of the most notable of all Chinese publications concerning plants, Ji Han's *Nanfang caomu zhuang* (Account of the Plants and Trees of the Southern Regions), which has been translated by

Li (1979), originated in this area. This is traditionally dated at AD 304 and is believed to be the oldest known work on tropical and subtropical botany. It includes descriptions of 80 plants including vegetables, fruits, timber trees and ornamentals (fig. 4.2), as well as comments on the use of ants to suppress citrus pests—the earliest record of an attempt at biological control.

Guangdong

Guangdong is the southernmost of the Chinese provinces and the one with the longest coastline. As well as its physical separation from the early centres of Chinese civilisation, its early exposure to Arab and Western influences has done much to mould its character and course of development.

The gardens described in this province are all in Guangzhou. There are, however, others in the surrounding region which I have not visited. Qiao (1982), Johnston (1991) and Cheng (1999), for example, give descriptions, plans and illustrations of several restored private gardens dating from the second half of the 19th century, including the Qinghuiyuan at Shunde, the Keyuan at Dongguan, the Yuyin Shanzhuang at Nancun, and the Qunxing Caotang at Foshan. However, while such gardens are interesting in exhibiting a total integration of house and garden, according to Johnston (1991) they cannot be compared with their counterparts in Suzhou in terms of aesthetic attainment. Judging by the photographs, a characteristic feature of these gardens is the display of large numbers of orchids and other potted plants on stands, terraces and balustrades—a state of affairs favoured by the climate. This extensive use of plants in pots presumably has a long history, having been noted by early Western visitors to the region, as mentioned in Chapter 1.

Figure 4.2 *Clerodendrum kaempferi* in the Hong Kong Zoological and Botanical Garden, one of the plants described by Ji Han in AD 304

Also worth noting is the fact that, although so far no plans to rebuild the Yuanmingyuan outside Beijing have been realised, some of its features have recently been reproduced as the New Yuan Ming Palace on an area of almost 2 square km in Zhuhai, north of Macao. There is a large lake surrounded by various building complexes and 'scenic spots', including at least one of the European-style buildings and the 'Shopping Street'. I have not visited this attraction either but have read a description of it in a Chinese magazine called *The Rail Monthly* (1999, nos 2/3). The photographs accompanying the article show the buildings to have been reproduced with considerable accuracy. Amongst other things, the anonymous author says:

> In the New Yuan Ming Palace there are not only fantastic buildings and scenery, but also gorgeous performances which are arranged to offer the top enjoyment to visitors. "Ceremony of Ascending the Throne" demonstrates a magnificent royal occasion and makes visitors feel as if they were back to the period of Emperor Kangxi and Qianlong in Qing Dynasty. "Royal Wedding Ceremony" will show how funny it was when the emperor choosing his empress and concubines, and how splendid was the Ceremony. A large-scale dance play—The Divine Pearl of China is performed in Central Performance Square at 19.15.

If ever one were nearby, it would be tempting to go.

Guangzhou

Guangzhou, formerly known in the West as Canton, is the capital of Guangdong. It is situated at the northern end of the Pearl River delta, close to the sea but protected from typhoons by its inland position. Also, with three tributaries of the Pearl River converging here, giving it riverine access to the inland and even the north of China, it is not surprising that it developed as a major port. It was reached by Arabs from the Persian Gulf at least 2000 years ago, and it seems probable that the jasmines, *Jasminum sambac* and *J. officinale*, reached China by this route early in the first millennium (Schafer, 1948).

The city has attracted overseas traders ever since. The Portuguese were the first Europeans to appear, reaching the delta early in 1513, and the Dutch arrived about a century later. The British East India Company set up a trading post in Guangzhou in 1684, and other countries followed. China, however, was unwelcoming to Westerners and, as noted in Chapter 1, in 1756 issued an edict allowing them to trade only at Guangzhou, and then only with a small number of accredited merchants. They were confined to a narrow strip of the shoreline outside the city walls, allowed to reside there only during the trading season, and prevented from bringing with them any Western women. Outside the trading season they retreated to the Portuguese colony of Macao, the only place in China where the families of merchants and missionaries could live.

It was the stress caused by these restrictions that led to the outbreak of the Opium Wars and the subsequent opening up of the country to foreigners. Hong Kong was ceded to the British in 1843 and, by 1855, Hong Kong and Shanghai had surpassed Guangzhou as the main centres of China's import-export trade. Nevertheless Guangzhou has remained an important administrative and commercial centre and now exhibits the towering office blocks and modern hotels that characterise most major Chinese cities.

In light of the restrictions placed on foreigners, it may seem remarkable that it was from here in the late 18th and early 19th centuries that the best-known Chinese garden plants reached the rest of the world. Most of them were obtained from the Fa Tee Gardens—a collection of nurseries a few miles upstream from the city on the opposite bank of the river. Foreigners were allowed to visit these nurseries and from them plants were obtained and sent to Europe and elsewhere on the tea clippers.

There are very few records of gardens in Guangzhou, though it seems that Europeans from time to time were able to visit those of the merchants who, prior to the Opium Wars, held a monopoly of foreign trade. Descriptions of these have been noted in Chapter 1 and there are also a few photographs, for example those reproduced in Thomson (1898) and Worswick and Spence (1978). John Thomson photographed 'Pun-shi-Cheng's Garden', including its 'willow pattern bridge', and remarked that '... when I look at my picture, I find it falls far short of the scene on our soup plates'. His photograph certainly indicates that the garden was nothing to write home about. In addition there is a painting of 'Pan Khaqua's garden' reproduced by Titley and Wood (1991), which shows a large number of potted plants displayed on stone tables and balustrades. No doubt there are others.

Figure 4.3 (left) New Year display,
Dongfang Hotel, Guangzhou
Figure 4.4 (below left) New Year
display at a Guangzhou restaurant

in street plantings of banyans (*Ficus microcarpa* and *F. virens*), silk cotton trees (*Bombax ceiba*) and other tropical species. And the displays of peach blossom, mandarins, calamondins, kumquats, chrysanthemums, narcissuses, dahlias, rhapis palms and other plants mounted at New Year in parks, temple grounds, the foyers of hotels and office blocks, and outside restaurants, are unmatched elsewhere in the country (figs 4.3, 4.4).

GUANGXIAOSI (GLORIOUS FILIALITY TEMPLE)

This temple occupies a site in the centre of the old part of the city where there was once a palace of a king of Nanyue. It later became the home of a high official whose family turned it into a temple in the 3rd century. After that and during the Tang many Indian monks came there to preach. The Sixth Patriarch, Hui Neng, who founded the Southern

While I know of no gardens of the types mentioned above in Guangzhou today, there are several modern gardens and parks which are worthy of notice, an important botanical garden and some interesting old temples. And, as might be expected in a frost-free climate, the range of species planted encompasses not only many of the plants associated with classical Chinese gardens but numerous other kinds as well. Hibiscuses, frangipanis, erythrinas, rose apples (*Syzygium jambos*), bougainvilleas, crinums, murrayas, bauhinias and pyrostegias are common, as are codiaeums and other foliage plants. Also the appearance of the city is enhanced by the use

School of Chinese Buddhism, was ordained here in 676.

As is usually the case, the temple now has far fewer buildings than earlier in its history, as is made clear by Felice Beato's photographs of 1860 (fig. 4.5). The enclosure, however, still has a certain grandeur. Beyond the entrance there is a large space occupied by old banyans (*Ficus microphylla*) and displays of pot plants. The imposing main hall, the Mahavira Hall, is on the far side and appears exactly as it does in Beato's photographs, with two small, seven-tiered pagodas standing in front (fig. 4.6). Behind it there are two much older pagodas. The seven-storey Jingfa Pagoda on the

Figure 4.5 (right)
Side view of the
Mahavira Hall,
Guangxiao Temple,
Guangzhou, with the
pagoda of the Liurong
Temple in the back-
ground, April 1860.

ALBUMEN SILVER PHOTOGRAPH
BY FELICE BEATO ENTITLED
*JOSS HOUSE, CANTON—NINE
STOREY PAGODA IN THE
DISTANCE, 1860.* NATIONAL
GALLERY OF AUSTRALIA,
CANBERRA.

Figure 4.6 (below)
Mahavira Hall,
Guangxiao Temple,
in 1999

western side was originally built over a hair of Hui Neng (fig. 4.7). To the east of this is the Dongtie Pagoda, which is about the same size but is made of iron and has 900 niches for Buddha figures. Between them is a much revered bohdi tree (*Ficus religiosa*)—the species under which the Buddha received enlightenment. It is said to have been planted in 502 but, as Schafer (1967) has pointed out, the present tree is an 18th-century replacement. It was commented upon in the 19th century by Sampson (1869), who noted that pictures of flowers, butterflies and suchlike made from the skeletonised leaves of this species were on sale at that time in almost every curio shop in the city.

LIURONGSI (SIX BANYAN TEMPLE)

The Six Banyan Temple, which is not far from the Guangxiao Temple, was originally built in 537 to house some of the ashes of the Buddha which a monk had brought back to China. After several changes of name it got its present one in 1099 after it was visited by the famous poet, painter and calligrapher Su Dongpo who, impressed by the banyans growing there, inscribed the words 'six banyans', which have been carved in his calligraphy on a board hung above the entrance. What the species to which he referred actually were is unclear, but there are still several large banyans (*Ficus microcarpa*) there and also specimens of *Ficus religiosa*.

The most conspicuous feature of the temple is its pagoda (fig. 4.8), now in a much better state than when it was photographed in 1860 by Felice Beato (Harris, 1999), in front of which masses of flowering pot plants are assembled during festivals. Plants such *Cymbidium sinense* and *Cordyline terminalis* are displayed on raised benches in some of the smaller courtyards and there are frangipanis and many other plants of interest in various parts of the grounds.

ZHONGSHAN JINIANTANG (SUN YAT-SEN MEMORIAL HALL)

This imposing octagonal building was completed in 1931 in memory of Dr Sun Yat-sen. In the post-war period it was restored and in 1998 modern seating and stage equipment were installed. It is now a major performance space with seating

Figure 4.7 (left) **Jinfa Pagoda and** *Ficus religiosa*, **Guangxiao Temple**
Figure 4.8 (opposite page) **Banyan and pagoda, Liurong Temple, Guangzhou**

Figure 4.9 Entrance to the Sun
Yat-sen Memorial Hall, Guangzhou

eye-catching were the pagodas, pandas, goldfish and rabbits made of chrysanthemums (fig. 4.11). A huge sphere of double pink azaleas near the entrance was not without impact either. With their auspicious colours and plants, these objects attract huge crowds of admirers. And a visit to such a display provides a wonderful opportunity for seeing the Chinese

for more than 3000 and has become a tourist attraction. The six hectare site has been developed as a semi-Western formal garden with lawns and displays of bedding plants (fig. 4.9).

use of both traditional garden plants and newer arrivals. I must say I thoroughly enjoyed it.

China has a long tradition of making creations such as these, as is evidenced by the observations of Miss Gordon Cumming (1890) when, about this time of year in 1879, she visited the Fa Tee Gardens. She was of the opinion that

YUEXIU GONGYUAN (YUEXIU PARK)

Yuexiu Park, which is immediately north of the Sun Yat-sen Memorial Hall, is Guangzhou's largest park and gets its name from the hill of the same name around which it has been developed. Visitors are usually taken to the Statue of the Five Goats, the symbol of Guangzhou, which was erected in 1959 (fig. 4.10). It is said that long ago five Immortals wearing robes of five colours and riding through the air on male goats arrived in Guangzhou. Each carried a stem of rice which they presented to the people as a sign that the region would always be free from famine. The statue is set in a garden of clipped Chinese box, bedding plants and erythrinas.

Floral displays and temporary gardens are set up at New Year at the northern end of this park. I visited this area at the beginning of the Year of the Rabbit (1999), and was able to view many remarkable compositions. Amongst favourites was a calamondin about 5 m tall, covered with fruit and trained in the shape of a carrot, which was sitting beside an enormous styrofoam rabbit. Also

the predominant feature of these gardens lies in the grotesqueness of the figures produced by training certain shrubs over a framework of wire, so as to exactly take its form … Evergreen dragons, frisky fishes, dolphins with huge eyes of china, and human figures with china or wooden hands, heads, and feet, are among the favourite forms represented. We also saw a very fine vegetable stag, with well-developed antlers; also a long rattan trained into the likeness of a serpent. Different shrubs assume the forms of junks, bridges, houses, flower baskets, fans or birds, and tall evergreen pagodas are adorned with little china bells hanging from each storey.

Figure 4.10 (left) Statue of the Five
Goats, Yuexiu Park, Guangzhou
Figure 4.11 (opposite page) Part of a
New Year display, Yuexiu Park

Figure 4.12

Mannikins

photographed

in Macao.

FROM F.W. CARPENTER
(1927).

plays. In many ways it is the most appealing of Guangzhou's gardens, even though there is nothing particularly Chinese about it apart from the plants. Huge numbers of pots of the traditionally grown *Cymbidium* species are assembled here, both in shade houses and under the trees (fig. 4.13). Further specimens are displayed in an exhibition hall along with foliage plants and ornamental rocks (fig. 4.14). Most of the area, however, is devoted to plants other than orchids, particularly bamboos, and has been developed as an informal garden with ponds, streams and shady walks (fig. 4.15).

LIUHUAHU GONGYUAN (FLOWING WITH FLOWERS LAKE PARK)

This large park was built in 1958 at the time of the Great Leap Forward. It is half a kilometre or so west of Yuexiu Park and contains Guangzhou's largest lake. The lake is of complex design and is broken up by causeways and bridges. The principal causeway running east-west is planted with an imposing avenue of *Livistona chinensis*—one of the plants described by Ji Han in 304—and various islands and peninsulas have been developed as gardens. On one of these there is a small formal garden

A photograph taken in Macao of human figures made in the manner she described was reproduced by Carpenter (1927) (fig. 4.12), and this method of training plants into ornamental shapes has become popular in the West in recent years.

LANYUAN (ORCHID GARDEN)

The Lanyuan is a modern garden built on part of the old Moslem burial ground adjoining Jiefang Beilu, opposite the entrance to the part of Yuexiu Park used for the floral dis-

Figure 4.13 (below) **Cymbidiums in the Orchid Garden, Guangzhou**

Figure 4.14 (right) *Cymbidium sinense* in bloom in the display house, Orchid Garden, Guangzhou

Figure 4.15 (opposite page below) **Modern planting, Orchid Garden, Guangzhou**

Figure 4.16 Copy of Canova's sculpture of Pauline Borghese, Liuhuahu Park, Guangzhou

in which a version of Canova's statue of the reclining Pauline Borghese is given pride of place (fig. 4.16).

Amongst the usual panoply of trees and shrubs there are magnolias, flowering peaches, *Michelia figo* and a group of the American *Taxodium distichum*, which seems largely to have ousted the native but slower-growing *Glyptostrobus pensilis* for waterside planting in China. Amongst the herbaceous plants

there are the usual cannas, liriopes and aspidistras, and extensive use is made of *Crinum asiaticum.*

About halfway along the northern side of the park there is a large area devoted to penjing. Some of these are displayed in a formal manner in a courtyard, while others are displayed on stands arranged along the paths which wind along the waterside under the banyans (fig. 4.17).

LIESHI LINGYUAN (GARDEN CEMETERY OF THE MARTYRS)

This 26 hectare park is on Zhongshan Lu about 4 km east of the city centre. It was laid out in 1957 as a memorial for those who died in the unsuccessful Communist uprising of 11

December 1927. More than 5000 people were shot here by the Guomindang and are buried beneath the tumulus at the end of the main axis. The tombs of other revolutionary heroes have been added from time to time in the grounds on either side.

The chief feature of the park is its central axis, which is in European style with flights of steps, fountains and arrangements of pot plants (fig. 4.18). The area to the west of this has been laid out as an informal park with areas for picnicking, tai chi and general relaxation. On the other side there is a large garden with lakes and many flowering trees and shrubs including peaches and silk cotton trees. And to the

Figure 4.17 (left) **Penjing under a banyan, Liuhuahu Park, Guangzhou**

Figure 4.18 (above) **Garden Cemetery of the Martyrs, Guangzhou**

Figure 4.19 (following pages) **Bamboo garden, Garden Cemetery of the Martyrs, Guangzhou**

west of the entrance a path bordered with simple stone seats of traditional design winds through a garden in which only two kinds of plant have been used—a single species of bamboo and *Syngonium podophyllum*—a striking example of the effectiveness of simplicity (fig. 4.19).

HUANAN ZHIWUYUAN (SOUTH CHINA BOTANICAL GARDEN)

Beginning in 1956 this garden on the outskirts of Guangzhou has gradually increased in size and now covers more than 140 hectares. It is affiliated with the Chinese Academy of Sciences and is the major centre for botanical research in South China. There are lakes and waterways around which are arranged

Figure 4.20 (left)
Cycad and palm collection,
South China Botanical Garden
Figure 4.21 (below left)
Musa coccinea, South China
Botanical Garden
Figure 4.22 (below)
Glyptostrobus pensilis with
developing 'knees', South
China Botanical Garden

many different collections. Amongst the most impressive are the palms, bamboos, conifers, cycads, medicinal plants, orchids, and tropical and sub-tropical economic plants (fig. 4.20). Amongst the orchids I was interested to see *Renanthera coccinea*— a vigorous climber, the brilliant red flowers of which had greatly impressed the early European visitors to this part of the world. And growing against the wall of the orchid house is a clump of *Musa coccinea*, which was bearing its striking inflorescences of a similar colour (fig. 4.21). I was interested, too, to be able to examine a group of the Chinese swamp cypress (*Glyptostrobus pensilis*) growing on the edge of the lake and to observe that some of them had produced small 'knees' (fig. 4.22). Writing in 304, Ji

Han, who described them as a separate parasitic plant, said that they were used to make pattens, and there is a report from the middle of the 20th century recording that they were then used as a substitute for cork and as an insulating material in sun helmets (Li, 1979). In Western botanical and horticultural literature it is often stated that *Glyptostrobus pensilis* does not produce these outgrowths.

Hong Kong

Hong Kong Island was ceded to Britain in 1842 under the Treaty of Nanking at the conclusion of the First Opium War. Prior to that it had been under the jurisdiction of the Governor of Guangdong. As a British colony Hong Kong rapidly developed into one of the great trading centres of the Far East. The mainland area known as Kowloon was ceded in 1860 at the conclusion of the Second Opium War, and the New Territories and a large number of smaller islands were leased to Britain for 99 years in 1898. The whole area was returned to China as a Special Administrative Region in 1997.

As can be seen in old photographs, the island was almost denuded of vegetation at the time the British took over. However the settlers were quick to establish a wide range of Chinese and other garden plants and to take an interest in the natural history of the area. Construction of a botanical garden was commenced in 1860 and it was opened to the public in 1864. In 1975 it was renamed the Hong Kong Zoological and Botanical Garden to reflect the increased presence of zoological exhibits. Also on the island is the Tiger Balm Garden, a very different cup of tea.

On the Kowloon side there are the relatively recent Salisbury Gardens on the waterfront and, a short distance north along Nathan Road, the extensive Kowloon Park. Further north again, in the Mongkok district, there is the Yuen Po Street Bird Garden and the flower and plant market.

Further north still, in the New Territories, is the Kadoorie Experimental and Extension Farm in Lam Tsuen Valley. There is a renowned botanical garden here which I have not visited, but a description is given in *The Oxford Companion to Gardens* (Jellicoe et al., 1986).

HONG KONG ZOOLOGICAL AND BOTANICAL GARDEN

The Hong Kong Zoological and Botanical Garden is situated just above Government House on the lower slopes of Victoria Peak behind the Central district. It is divided by Albany Road but the two sections are connected by a subway. The eastern part, known as the Old Garden, fulfils the role of a botanical garden, whereas the western part, known as the New Garden, is largely devoted to zoological exhibits.

The history of this garden has been documented by Griffiths (1988). The steepness of the site caused many difficulties during construction and on several occasions the garden has been severely damaged by typhoons. It was also badly damaged during the Japanese occupation. It was restored subsequently, though eventually the principal open space, the Fountain Terrace, had to be removed temporarily in order to replace the roof of the reservoir over which it was built. It now has a new fountain and is laid out in formal style with tropical and subtropical trees, shrubs and flowers (fig. 4.23). Amongst these are crepe myrtles, cultivars of *Ixora chinensis*,

Figure 4.23 **The Fountain Terrace, Hong Kong Zoological and Botanical Garden**

and leopard lilies (*Belamcanda chinensis*) (fig. 4.24). It is also in this area at Chinese New Year that a large display is mounted of the plants traditionally associated with this season. Also here are a few plants of the scarlet-flowered *Clerodendrum kaempferi*, another of the plants described in 304 by Ji Han, who said it was planted everywhere in southern China at that time (fig. 4.2). Nowadays, however, it is rarely seen. Nearby there is a clump of *Musa coccinea*, which was also once more popular in China than it is now.

Elsewhere in the Old Garden there are aviaries, a jaguar enclosure, a large greenhouse, a herb garden and a bamboo garden. I was interested to see in the bamboo garden notices condemning the Chinese penchant for carving names and statements on bamboo culms and threatening those transgressing with fines and imprisonment (fig. 4.25).

TIGER BALM GARDEN

I have included this well-known attraction simply because it is there, on the island some distance to the south-east of the Central district. Three hectares ornamented with grotesque statuary, artificial mountains and a pagoda 50 m tall were laid out here in 1935 by Aw Boon Haw, the originator of Tiger Balm ointment, as a gift to Hong Kong. He built another Tiger Balm Garden in similar taste in Singapore. There can be no denying, however, that these areas are Chinese gardens.

SALISBURY GARDENS

The paved area bearing this name is on the Kowloon side immediately to the east of the new Cultural Centre. It is ornamented with tropical trees and contains beds planted principally with azaleas, ixoras, cannas, cassias, *Serissa japonica* and a variety of foliage plants. With its bold foliage and terminal panicles of large mauve flowers, one of the most conspicuous trees here is *Lagerstroemia speciosa* (Pride of India) (fig. 4.26).

KOWLOON PARK

This large area on the western side of Nathan Road serves as the principal recreation area for the densely built-up Kowloon peninsula. It is planted with a variety of trees and is popular with the practitioners of tai chi and similar activities. It contains a swimming pool, a mosque, a museum of local history, playgrounds, a sculpture walk, a Chinese garden, an ornamental garden, a lake and a police station.

Figure 4.24 (opposite page) *Belamcanda chinensis*, Hong Kong Zoological and Botanical Garden
Figure 4.25 (above left) Notice in the bamboo garden, Hong Kong Zoological and Botanical Garden
Figure 4.26 (left) *Lagerstroemia speciosa*, Salisbury Gardens, Hong Kong

FLOWER MARKET

The flower market is in Prince Edward Road West close to the MTR Prince Edward station. Here there are numerous shops selling flowers and plants. At the time of the Chinese New Year they stock a wide range of auspicious plants, including mandarins, cumquats, calamondins, finger citrons, narcissuses (fig. 4.27) and yellow chrysanthemums. As in Guangzhou, these plants also feature prominently at this time of year in the displays mounted in the forecourts and foyers of hotels and office buildings.

Figure 4.27 (left)

Narcissus tazetta trained in 'crab's claw' style, Flower Market, Hong Kong

Figure 4.28 (below)

Cinnamomum cassia and *C. camphora*, Binjiang Lu, Guilin

YUEN PO STREET BIRD GARDEN

The Yuen Po Street Bird Garden is a rectangular garden occupying a raised area opposite the north-eastern corner of the flower market. Stalls selling cages, birds, and everything needed for their care are arranged along the sides of the paths. It is an interesting place to obtain an insight into the Chinese fascination with caged birds, which were traditional occupants of Chinese gardens.

Guangxi

From early times Guangxi has been occupied by a number of non-Han races, predominant amongst which are the Zhuang. As a result it has had a long history of resistance against the Chinese administration and colonisation. It was for this reason that in 1958 the central government set it up as the Guangxi Zhuang Nationality Autonomous Region, one of five such regions for national minorities with a status equivalent to that of a province. While the region does not boast much in the way of gardens, I have included it on account of the famous landscape of karst mountains around Guilin, a landscape which has been greatly admired at least since the Tang and which must surely have influenced both painters and garden builders. Guangxi has also been drawn to the attention of gardeners, from the middle of the 20th century on, by the discovery there of several species of *Camellia* with yellow flowers.

Guilin

Guilin was the capital of Guangxi from the Ming until 1914, when Nanning replaced it. The name Guilin (Cassia Forest) dates back only to the Ming, and was inspired by the trees of *Cinnamomum cassia* which grew there. It is from this city that we have one of the first European descriptions of Chinese gardens, that of Gaspar da Cruz, who spent a few months in southern China in 1556 and whose observations have been mentioned in Chapter 1.

No trace of the sort of garden described by da Cruz remains in Guilin today. The city itself, which is situated on the west bank of the Li River, has comparatively little to interest the visitor, having been largely rebuilt and expanded since 1949. However it is surrounded by what is perhaps China's most famous scenery, a huge area from which rises an enormous number of karst peaks. While the traditional way of viewing this fascinating landscape is to take a cruise down

Figure 4.29 (above) **View of Duxiu Feng (left) from Fubo Shan, Guilin**

Figure 4.30 (right) *Malva sylvestris*, Fubo Shan, Guilin

the river to Yangshuo, there are several peaks in and around the city which can be ascended and which are surrounded by grounds which have been developed as gardens. Seven Star Park on the east bank of the river is similar but on a larger scale.

The street plantings are interesting too. Binjiang Lu, which runs along the western bank of the river, is lined with camphor laurels and *Cinnamomum cassia* (fig. 4.28), and in the middle of Ronghu Beilu, which runs along the northern side of Rong Hu (Banyan Lake) in the southern part of the city, there is an 800-year-old banyan (*Ficus microcarpa*). This is the subject of much veneration and at most times has numerous supplications written on red paper attached to its trunk. This species of fig is amongst the plants described in 304 by Ji Han. As its timber is useless, it is often left to live to a great age, as Ji Han noted. Elsewhere in the city, paulownias, koelreuterias, liquidambars, melias, bamboos and other traditional Chinese garden plants are to be seen here and there, and on the cruise down the Li River plantations of chestnuts (*Castanea mollissima*) and *Cupressus funebris* are conspicuous on the hillsides. There is also the Guilin Botanical Garden, 24 km south of the city, which I have not seen.

CHENGZHONG ZHI SHAN (CITY PEAKS)

The most central of these is Duxiu Feng (Solitary Beauty Peak) (fig. 4.29). It is set in a small wooded park where once there was a Ming palace of which only the gate remains. The climb is very steep but there is a fine view of the town, surrounding peaks and the Li River from the top. To the east of this on the west bank of the Li River is Fubo Shan (Wave-subduing Hill). Although not as tall as Duxiu Feng, its summit offers equally expansive views. The area around its base has been developed as a garden where, at the time of my visit in late February, a bed of *Malva sylvestris* was in bloom (fig. 4.30). Taller than either of these peaks, also close to the river bank, is Diecai Shan (Folded Brocade Hill), the path to the summit of which passes through a cave. This peak is surrounded by a park in which cassia trees have been planted.

These peaks and others in the vicinity have been tourist attractions for well over 1000 years. Although the pavilions and monuments of the past have vanished there are still inscriptions and Buddhist sculptures dating from the Tang and Song in the caves on their slopes.

QIXING GONGYUAN (SEVEN STAR PARK)

This is Guilin's largest park. It is on the east bank of the river and gets its name from its seven peaks which are said to be disposed in a manner similar to the seven stars of the Great Bear constellation. Here there are more caves, inscriptions and famous sights. Amongst the trees in the park there are flowering peaches and close to the Seven Star Cave some enormous old liquidambars (*L. formosana*). There is also a mosque near which is a penjing garden where interesting compositions have been created in cavities let into walls (fig. 4.31).

Yangshuo

This small town on the Li River is where the tour boats end their journey from Guilin. As it happens, it has all the charm that Guilin lacks, even though, like Dali in Yunnan, it has become a legendary destination for backpackers, complete with internet cafés and other establishments catering for their needs. The garden of the Paradise Hotel in the centre of town, although not well cared for, is worth a look for its plants, which include osmanthuses, clumps of the form of *Bambusa*

Figure 4.31 **Penjing landscape, Seven Star Park.**
PHOTOGRAPH: R. CLOUGH.

Figure 4.32 *Bambusa vulgaris* 'Wamin',
Paradise Hotel, Yangshuo

Figure 4.33 (left)   The 1300-year-old banyan (*Ficus microcarpa*) near Yangshuo

Figure 4.34 (above)   Trunk of the banyan with written supplications attached

vulgaris known in the West as 'Wamin' (fig. 4.32), and pots of *Cymbidium sinense*. But it is the countryside which surrounds it which is the real star, with its fields of rice and rape, its orchards of pomelos, other citrus fruits, plums, peaches, pears and chestnuts, all set amongst the fantastic peaks. In early spring the dry rice fields are carpeted with the pink flowers of *Astragalus sinicus*, which is grown as a green manure crop and is the 'pink clover' about which Miss Gordon Cumming (1890) waxed lyrical when she saw it in the fields around Ningbo in the spring of 1879.

There are wonderful panoramas where the road south from the town crosses the Jingbao River on the way to Yueliang Shan (Moon Hill), and nearby is a huge banyan (*Ficus microcarpa*) said to be 1300 years old (figs 4.33, 4.34). Like its counterpart in Guilin it is an object of great veneration. There are further wonderful views north-west of Yangshuo near Baisha from the Longqiao (Dragon Bridge)— an ancient stone bridge on which a stand was made against the Japanese invaders (fig. 4.1). But in this part of the world there are magical scenes wherever you look.

CHAPTER 5

The East

For the purposes of this chapter, 'The East' is taken to
mean the provinces of Jiangsu and Zhejiang, together
with what is now the separate administrative area of
Shanghai. This is the region bordering the sea and the
lower reaches of the Yangtze, which was thought of
by Kangxi and Qianlong as 'the south' and by Robert
Fortune as 'the north'. It is one of the richest parts of
the country, and it is here that China's greatest concentration of private gardens was built. A factor contribut-
ing to this, according to Liu (1993), was the easy availability of good rocks and abundant water. While the
ravages of time, the Taipings, the Cultural Revolution
and redevelopment have swept the majority of them
away, there still remains a surprising number, most of
which have been restored and are open to the public.
Much has already been written about the gardens of
this part of the country. In fact, much of the text
of almost all the more recent books about Chinese
gardens is devoted to them. As mentioned in Chapter 1,

Figure 5.1 Canal scene, Suzhou

the earliest general account of the gardens of this region is that of Tung (1936), who described the situation as it was in the early 1930s. This information was reinforced by the photographs and descriptions of Graham (1938), Powell (1943) and Sirén (1949), who visited the area in the same period. Today these works provide a valuable reference point when looking at the gardens which have survived, and they have provided a most useful background to my own observations, as have more recent works such as Hu Dongchu's *The Way of the Virtuous* (1991), R.S. Johnston's *Scholar Gardens of China* (1991) and Craig Clunas's *Fruitful Sites* (1996).

Most people who have written about the gardens of this region have concentrated on the 'scholar gardens'—the gardens of retired officials who had obtained their position through the traditional examination system. The design of these gardens as we see them today evolved during the Ming. There had earlier appeared gardens in which their owners had attempted to create a feeling of the solitude of the mountains in a situation where, at the same time, the pleasure and convenience of city life could still be enjoyed. In the early Ming such gardens generally contained simple scenery suggesting open country in which a few thatched pavilions and other modest structures were strategically placed. They also contained orchards and vegetable gardens, surplus produce from which was sold (Clunas, 1996). The garden of this type which we know most about is the Zhuozhengyuan (Humble Administrator's Garden) in Suzhou, built early in the 16th century. A description and paintings of it, which have been reproduced by Kate Kerby (1922) (fig. 1.31), have come down to us from Wen Zhengming, who produced them in 1533.

With late Ming prosperity, retired officials, merchants and the local gentry alike indulged in an unprecedented mania for building gardens. This seems to have occurred first in Suzhou, then in other cities of the lower Yangtze, and later in the wider empire. And, beginning in the 16th century, the character of the gardens changed markedly. Increases in population and the availability of less land in the cities meant that gardens became smaller, and everything in them tended to take on a more symbolic character. Rocks, in particular, played an increasingly important part in garden design. The principal garden space usually had a lake in the centre with a rockery to the north and the main building or buildings on the southern side. Buildings came to occupy a greater proportion of the area, forming an integral part of the composition, and architectural types became more diverse, with

halls, pavilions, roofed walkways, and storeyed buildings to take advantage of views. As well as these, stone tables and stools were provided for outdoor activities (Cheng, 1999). Groves of fruit trees gradually became less prominent and were replaced by plants grown for their appearance and symbolic associations. Also the use of penjing for ornamenting gardens and rooms seems to have become popular at this time.

When considering the use of rocks in gardens it is necessary to keep in mind the distinction between single rocks and agglomerations of rock. The two did not have an equally long, nor a continuous history. While, as has earlier been pointed out, the use of individual rocks in gardens began early, the dominance of rocks and rock mountains which we so often see in Chinese gardens today arose only in the 16th and 17th centuries. The building of elaborate artificial mountains made of composite rockwork appears to have begun as a specialty of Suzhou, and to have gone on to become one of the visually dominant features of fashionable gardens elsewhere in China after about 1550 (fig. 5.2). According to Clunas (1996), these creations were still seen as something of a novelty to the Hangzhou writer Lang Ying (1487–c.1566). Lang remarked that, although rich and noble families had taken to making them, they did not have the 'vital air' of real mountains and that they became infested with snakes in spring and summer, so that moonlit nights could not be enjoyed. As far as I know, this drawback is not mentioned by other Ming writers.

By the 17th century the construction of rock mountains had become a highly developed art. It took into account such things as the manner in which rocks and mountains had been depicted by famous painters of earlier times. It was acceptable only to use rock of one kind, and the type chosen, the manner in which the stones were assembled, the texture of the surface, the provision of peaks, grottoes and gorges, and the way it was arranged for shadows to fall were all matters for careful consideration. As well as bringing with them all the symbolism and associations of mountains, these structures were appreciated as works of art in the same way that individual stones were.

The limestone rocks dredged up from Tai Hu (Lake Tai) in Jiangsu were in great demand for gardens, the most desirable specimens being those with tortuous, rugged contours and abundant hollows. Although Wen Zhenheng, writing in the early 17th century, records that the artificial mountains which were valued at Suzhou were all made of Taihu stones,

Figure 5.2 **Rock mountain, Yuyuan, Shanghai**

he gives advice about the use and acceptability of other kinds (Clunas, 1996). One of the most frequently seen is 'huang-shi' (yellow rock), a brownish-yellow limestone which breaks into angular blocks and has veining which suggests the brush-work seen in classical Chinese paintings. Amongst the more unusual stones which are used to ornament gardens are fos-silised tree trunks, upright pieces of fossilised wood, stalag-mites and stalactites. These are often used to represent bam-boo shoots and are arranged amongst living bamboos to sug-gest spring.

In view of the enthusiasm for garden-making in the late Ming, it is perhaps not surprising that it was during this peri-od that the first known manual devoted entirely to garden design and construction in China, should appear. This was Ji Cheng's *Yuanye*, attention to which has already been drawn in Chapter 1. It has been suggested that Ji Cheng's book was intended for merchants and others anxious to improve their position in society, as the old-established scholar class would hardly feel the need for such advice (Hardie, A., in Ji, 1988; Wong, 1997). As has been noted earlier, in the Confucian social hierarchy merchants were at the lowest level—buying

and selling being considered unproductive. Only from the beginning of the 17th century did groups of merchants begin to form trade guilds to defend their interests. Nevertheless, in view of their poor social status and in spite of their wealth, they were not permitted to sit for the civil service examina-tions. Their sons, however, could and thus success in these exams was a way of improving the social status of the fami-ly. In this period, then, it became possible for wealthy fami-lies literally to purchase status by investing in the education of their sons, arranging fortuitous marriages, and acquiring symbols of breeding and culture such as antiques, works of art, and gardens in the approved taste (von Glahn in Shaughnessy, 2000). In the late Ming, pursuance of these ends resulted in an intensification of merchant-literati interaction, and elite culture changed (Handlin Smith, 1992). In the sub-sequent Qing dynasty it was exactly this situation which arose in the city of Yangzhou, where gardens were built by wealthy salt merchants to satisfy their needs both for enjoyment and social recognition (Wong, 1997).

Be all this as it may, one wonders in whose gardens it was that Ji Cheng had observed the lapses in taste he remarked upon and to what extent the scholars actually designed their own gardens and supervised the construction. According to Liu (1993), those who had the real mastery were the artisans who spent their whole lives constructing gardens, but whose names and achievements never appeared in the historical records. Like other luxury items in the late Ming, gardens had become commodities, as Clunas (1996) puts it, and it seems to me unlikely that merchants would have been the only customers.

The late Ming, too, was a time when the literati wrote guides to good taste, carefully distinguishing what was 'ya' (refined) and what was 'su' (vulgar). One of the best known of these is Wen Zhenheng's *Zhangwu zhi* (Treatise on Superfluous Things), which was written around 1615–20 and the contents of which are discussed by Clunas (1996). Amongst other things, Wen has a lot to say about gardens. While he does not present the garden as a coherent site, he does give advice about all the ingredients from which a late Ming aesthetic garden could be assembled.

Amongst the things he cautioned against was the making of bridges with Taihu rocks, though he did not consider this as vulgar as the placing of a pavilion in the centre of a bridge. And I found it interesting that he should have advised the tasteful garden-maker to be wary of roses, particularly those that require a framework to support them—a state of affairs apparently quite intolerable. Ji Cheng, writing just a few years later, agreed, but said that it was acceptable to train them over rocks—a situation in which they are still to be seen in many gardens (fig. 3.49). Another thing Wen considered vulgar was the planting of peaches and willows together at the waterside.

All in all, Wen Zhenheng sounds to have been a frightful snob. How seriously his pronouncements were taken at the time we can probably never know, particularly since many of the things he fulminated against became commonplaces of garden design in the centuries that followed. For instance the building of pavilions on bridges became so common in the Qing that, as Clunas (1996) notes, it was transmitted to Europe as one of the clichés of chinoiserie. And nowadays the planting of peaches and willows together is standard practice, as anyone who has walked along the causeways at the Summer Palace, Hangzhou or Yangzhou will know (figs 3.64, 5.49, 5.82). However, the fact that Wen was moved to write the book at all suggests that there must have been a demand for it.

It is unlikely that any private gardens originally built in the Ming have survived without substantial alteration. Nevertheless, the great legacy of the period has been the development of the scholar garden in the form we know it today. In this regard it is interesting that Clunas should point out that, whereas on Song maps gardens were represented by ponds (often rectangular) and groves of trees, Qing maps of Suzhou indicate the sites of gardens by representations of architecture and piled up rocks. The garden is no longer a place of trees but of rockeries and pavilions, this transition having taken place principally in the 16th century.

The style established in the late Ming, with its emphasis on rockeries, was taken further during the Qing. According to Cheng (1999), the most significant achievement of Qing garden architects was to build rockeries in small gardens to simulate natural cliffs, peaks and deep valleys. The treatment of water also advanced. Islands, mid-lake pavilions, zigzag bridges and short dikes were often used to divide up the water surface. In general it may be said that gardens had become more ornate than in the previous period, and it is principally restored gardens of this type which we see in the lower Yangtze region today.

Presumably as a result of further increases in the population of cities, the private gardens of the period were generally even smaller than those of the Ming. And another factor which must surely have influenced their appearance was the schedule of regulations concerning the building of residences for government officials and aristocrats of different rank and status. Gardens were excepted from these strictures and this may well have been at least partly responsible for an increase in the proportion of buildings to open space which occurred. Buildings were put up in gardens to serve not only as residences but studies, studios, and halls for entertaining guests. These garden buildings thus served a double function, satisfying the material requirements of the owners and at the same time forming an indispensable part of the composition.

As regards the rest of this chapter, it must be pointed out that there are more gardens in Jiangsu and Zhejiang than those which I have visited and described below. One or two others are mentioned by Yoshikawa (1990) in his survey of the gardens of this region, and Tung (1997), in an updating of his earlier work completed just before his death in 1983, mentions examples in Taizhou, Rugao, Changzhou, Qingpu, Jiangyin, Changshu, Kunshan, Pinghu and Jiashan, many of them illustrated with colour photographs.

Shanghai Shi

Shanghai and its surroundings were previously part of Jiangsu province but now, like Beijing, Tianjin and Chongqing, they are part of an independently administered area which extends some distance from the city itself and has a population of almost 17 million. Now included are towns such as Jiading, Nanxiang and Songjiang, where there are interesting gardens, and the municipality stretches west about 60 km to Dianshan Lake, which has become a recreational area for the city.

Shanghai

Although little more than a village on the western shore of the Huangpu River until after the First Opium War, when the foreign powers began establishing trading concessions there, it is not surprising that Shanghai has developed as it has. Situated at the mouth of the Yangtze and connected to most of the country by water, by 1853 it had overtaken all other Chinese ports. In recent times the amount of demolition and construction which has taken place is amazing. Skyscrapers, sports stadiums, museums, theatres and expressways have appeared almost overnight and business has boomed.

A stroll around the city itself is not without horticultural interest. Although the English garden at the northern end of The Bund—once forbidden to dogs and Chinese except those accompanying Europeans—has now gone, the permanent plantings along the riverside are largely of traditional Chinese garden plants such as *Ilex cornuta*, Chinese box, flowering quinces, roses and photinias. Elsewhere in the street plantings there are occasional specimens of the white-flowered *Paulownia fortunei*, and fine avenues of planes are still to be seen in many parts of the city. It seems likely that this tree was first introduced to China, probably to Shanghai, by the international settlers, as its Chinese names 'English Firmiana' and 'French Sycamore' might be taken to suggest.

YUYUAN (GARDEN TO PLEASE)

The Yuyuan is in the centre of the old Chinese city and within walking distance of The Bund. Although it has been much altered over the years, it is a good example of a classical Chinese garden. It was originally built between 1559 and 1577 to please his father by Pan Yunduan, an official who, though a native of Shanghai, had held high office in Sichuan. By the end of the Ming the fortunes of the Pan family had

declined and the garden had fallen into disrepair. It remained derelict until about 1760 when a group of merchants combined to buy it. However it lost its status as a pleasure garden in the first half of the 19th century when businesses were established in its grounds. The garden fell on further hard times during the disturbances of the second half of the 19th century. During the Taiping Uprising it was occupied by imperial troops and sustained further damage. It was damaged again under the Japanese when they invaded the city in 1942 but was restored from 1956 on. It now incorporates the small Neiyuan (Inner Garden) which was built on its eastern side early in the 18th century.

In view of its history it is not clear how closely it now resembles the original garden. Markbreiter (1979), for instance, was of the opinion that after the post-war restoration there were more open spaces and a great deal more rockwork than originally intended. However, shaded by camphor laurels and other trees, and combining pavilions, pools, rockeries, walls and winding walkways, it creates an illusion of space and diversity within a relatively small area. It is approached by means of a zigzag bridge over a pond, which has a tea house in its centre and which was once part of the garden. Many people have referred to this tea house as the Willow Pattern Tea House, perpetuating the fiction that this is the building depicted on willow-pattern porcelain. Included amongst these is A.S. Roe (1910) who visited it during her tour of 1907–09. She thought it 'was picturesque enough, or would have been if only the water round the building with pagoda roofs had been more like water and less like mutton broth'. The present entrance to the garden is on the north side of this pond.

Immediately inside the entrance is the Sansuitang (Three Ears of Grain Hall), a large building which features woodcarvings of cereals, vegetables and fruit—symbols of a good harvest. Attached to its north side is another hall which overlooks a pond, on the far side of which is a rock mountain 12 m high (fig. 5.2). This is made of huangshi stone and is believed to be a surviving example of the rockwork of the Ming master, Zhang Nanyang. A path to the right of this passes beneath a pergola supporting an old *Wisteria sinensis* 'Alba' and leads to a complex of small pavilions, walkways and courtyards planted with pomegranates, camellias, bananas and other traditional plants. Beyond this is a large paved space on the far side of which is a long rockery set against a whitewashed wall. This rockery is home to azaleas, tree peonies and many other plants, and in front of it is a narrow waterway which continues into the preceding space through an archway in a wall. This part of the garden is one of the scenes photographed by Henry Inn (1940) in 1936, and it looks much the same today as it did then. Continuing from the south-east corner of this area one comes to the principal open space of the garden. Here there are, amongst other things, a central pavilion, the garden's largest pond, a water-side pavilion with penjing specimens arranged on its balcony, a hexagonal pavilion reached by a zigzag bridge (fig. 5.3), and several interesting trees, including maples and a pear.

Continuing south, the water is crossed with the aid of stepping stones, on the left of which the pond is home to an enormous number of goldfish (fig. 1.22), and on the right there is a fine form of *Wisteria sinensis* growing over a rockery together with *Jasminum mesnyi*. The path then passes through a wall to the next enclosure where the Yuhuatang (Jade Flower Hall) looks across a pond to a rockery, the chief feature of which is an enormous Taihu stone, Yulinglong (Exquisite Jade), described by Tung (1997) as 'a superb specimen of nature's abstract sculpture' (fig. 5.4). It is said to have been destined originally for the Genyue garden of the Northern Song emperor Huizong in Kaifeng, but to have been shipwrecked in the Huangpu and later dredged up by Pan Yunduan. It is flanked by two lesser specimens—an arrangement which emphasises the analogy with mountains by mimicking the Chinese character 'shan', as has already been mentioned in Chapter 3. Further south is the original

Neiyuan, a charming space completely enclosed by buildings and walkways, and beyond this again are courtyards used for exhibitions, and a restored hall with an external stage, once part of the Temple of the City God. One can return to the street from this region or retrace one's steps, diverging to examine some of the courtyards lying to the sides of the route described above.

A peculiarity of this garden which visitors are sure to notice is the presence of 'dragon walls', the undulating ridges of which are capped with overlapping grey tiles and which are terminated with dragons' heads.

RENMIN GONGYUAN (PEOPLE'S PARK) AND RENMIN GUANGCHANG (PEOPLE'S SQUARE)

Renmin Park is a well-worn space used for recreation principally by the city's older residents. It is planted with a selection of traditional garden plants, so there is something of interest for the horticulturally minded visitor. Renmin Square, on the other hand, is a huge modern showpiece, on opposite sides of which are the new Shanghai Museum and the

Figure 5.3 (opposite page) **Pavilion overlooking a pond, Yuyuan, Shanghai**

Figure 5.4 (left) **The Exquisite Jade Rock and its companions, Yuyuan, Shanghai**

Figure 5.5 (left)
Cultivar of *Rosa multiflora*, Renmin Square, Shanghai

Figure 5.6 (below)
Hostas, Jade Buddha Temple, Shanghai

Shanghai Grand Theatre. The square is ornamented with fountains and beds of annuals and modern roses. Amongst all this, however, are some old China roses, two large, scrambling plants of a double yellow tea rose, and some Chinese cultivars of *Rosa multiflora* (fig. 5.5) and *Nerium oleander*.

YUFOSI (JADE BUDDHA TEMPLE)

The Jade Buddha Temple in the north-west of the city was established in 1882 by a monk from Putuo Shan to house two run-of-the-mill white jade Buddha statues from Burma. While it is incorporated in all tours and hence is usually crowded, some interest can be derived from the plants, which include lohan pines (*Podocarpus macrophyllus*), junipers, cycads, *Magnolia grandiflora*, liriopes and *Hosta ventricosa*

(fig. 5.6). Presumably because of the similarity of its flowers to those of the lotus, *Magnolia grandiflora* has been enthusiastically adopted by Chinese Buddhists and has been given the name Hehua Yulan (Lotus-flower Magnolia). It is one of many plants from the Americas which have become popular in China.

LONGHUASI (LONGHUA TEMPLE)

This temple is in the south-west of the city and is said to date back to the 3rd century, though most of the buildings have been replaced many times. Its famous pagoda was built in 977 during the Northern Song (Qiao & Sun, 1982), and looks now just as it did in John Thomson's (1873–74) photograph taken in 1869. The temple and its environs were once one of the most famous sites for peach blossom in China. Presumably it was here that were to be found the 'celebrated peach gardens near the south and west gates of the city', the destruction of which during the defence of Shanghai against the Taiping rebels in the mid-19th century was so lamented by Robert Fortune (1855).

Figure 5.7 (right) **Tree peonies under-planted with *Oxalis articulata*, Longhua Temple, Shanghai**

Figure 5.8 (above) **A spring display, Shanghai Botanical Garden**

Regrettably there are no peach trees there now but, since the temple is being restored as a tourist attraction, they may well reappear. Meanwhile there are some interesting trees to admire and in a rear courtyard there is a large bed of tree peonies (fig. 5.7) underplanted with *Oxalis articulata*. Prior to the establishment of the People's Republic the temple was used as a prison and execution ground by the Guomindang, and there is now a Memorial Park to the Revolutionary Martyrs next door.

SHANGHAI ZHIWUYUAN (SHANGHAI BOTANICAL GARDEN)

About 12 km south-west of the centre of Shanghai, not far from the Longhua Temple, is the Shanghai Botanical Garden

(fig. 5.8). It was founded in 1974 on the site of the former Longhua Nursery, which specialised in floriculture and penjing. Its finances would appear to allow a slightly better standard of maintenance than that encountered in many Chinese botanical gardens, and amongst the plants to be seen there are collections of magnolias, roses, azaleas, peonies, conifers, maples, osmanthuses and bamboos. While there is much to interest the plantsperson, a visit is likely to be most rewarding in late April, when the tree peonies are flowering, or in autumn when displays of chrysanthemums are mounted. There is also a splendid collection of penjing for which the garden is famous (fig. 5.9).

Nanxiang

Sirén (1949) was able to write of Nanxiang that, when he saw it, it still retained the character of a garden city, with temple grounds and private gardens in idyllic settings. However, this town about 20 km north-west of central Shanghai has now

become part of the Shanghai conurbation and little of its former character remains. Nevertheless it is the site of a recently restored garden, the Guyiyuan.

GUYIYUAN (ANCIENT MAGNIFICENT GARDEN)

Originally built in the 16th century by Zhu Sansong, it was given its present name when it changed hands in 1748. It was donated to a temple in 1788 and later passed into private ownership once more. It was restored in the first half of the 19th century only to be ruined soon after by the Taipings. It was restored again in 1868 and in the 1930s became a public park. Beginning in 1980, it has undergone another restoration. Since the southern half of the area is now more in the nature of a recreation area and the portion of chief interest is in the north, the garden is best entered by the north gate.

The principal feature is a lake with three islands connected to one another and to the shore by bridges. There are rockeries, a waterside pavilion, a land boat (fig. 5.10), and many other buildings, including a Plum Blossom Hall which looks out onto an orchard of *Prunus mume*. There are also flowering peaches, wisterias, jasmines, *Iris tectorum*, bamboos, Chinese quinces and many other plants of interest.

Jiading

Jiading is about 30 km north-west of Shanghai in the same general direction as Nanxiang. Near the centre of the town there is an interesting garden, the Quxiapu, and a park containing a Heilongtan (Black Dragon Pool), one of numerous Black Dragon Pools to be found in China.

QUXIAPU (AUTUMN ROSY CLOUDS GARDEN)

This garden was originally built in the 16th century by Gong Hong, a court minister. In the mid-17th century it passed into

Figure 5.9 (above)
Giant penjing
landscape,
Shanghai
Botanical Garden

Figure 5.10 (right)
Waterside pavilion
and land boat,
Guyiyuan,
Nanxiang

the hands of the Wang family, who donated it to a temple in 1726. Then, 40 years later, it was combined with an adjoining garden which was donated to the temple by the Shen family. It was damaged during the Taiping Uprising, but was repaired in 1886. In the 1930s it was described as being in a very neglected state but it has been recently restored.

In its present form the Quxiapu is a picturesque small garden in the central portion of which the buildings are arranged around a lake shaded by old specimens of *Pterocarya stenoptera* (fig. 5.11). The principal building is the Biwuxuan (Hall of Emerald-green Phoenix Trees), which fronts onto a terrace on the northern side of the lake. A little to the southwest of this hall is the Biguangting (Pavilion of Emerald-green Light). This is open on three sides and built out over the water—an ideal arrangement for viewing the fish and the autumn moon. A white form of *Orychophragmus violaceus* is growing under the trees along with *Iris japonica* and, amongst other things, off to one side there is a mound planted with tree peonies. The principal space of this garden is a particularly charming composition.

Figure 5.11 (above) **Quxiapu, Jiading**

Figure 5.12 (left) **Zuibaichi, Songjiang**

Songjiang

Songjiang, 35 km south-west of Shanghai, is an old town where there were many gardens before the Taiping Uprising. Only one of these, the Zuibaichi, has survived. However, an interesting modern garden, the Fangtayuan, has been constructed nearby around an old pagoda and other relics.

ZUIBAICHI (DRUNKEN BAI POND)

This garden was built in 1650 by Gu Dashen, an official and painter who greatly admired the Tang poet Li Bai, who had a house by the lake in his garden in Luoyang where he drank and wrote poems. In the early 19th century it was used as an orphanage but is now restored and open to the public. The outer area, through which one passes after entering, is park-like and not particularly interesting, though there are some handsome stone bridges over the waterways. However, beyond this, within an inner walled enclosure, are some charming courtyards, in one of which is the actual Zuibai Pond, over-hung by camphor laurels (fig. 5.12). The pond continues beneath one of the buildings behind which it is planted with waterlilies and surrounded by rocks over which a double pink multiflora rose is growing. Another courtyard contains a rectangular lotus pool, rocks have been placed to provide focal points for views through doorways (frontispiece), and amongst the plants I noticed two kinds of yucca, persimmons, crepe myrtles, osmanthuses, bananas, an orchard of *Prunus mume*, and large trees of *Viburnum odoratissimum*.

FANGTAYUAN (SQUARE PAGODA PARK)

This park was designed and built between 1981 and 1984 by a team of architects from Tongji University in Shanghai around three historical relics (Wang, J.C., 1998). These are a pagoda originally built between 1096 and 1094, a Ming screen wall built in 1370, and a Qing temple hall. In addition to these a waterside pavilion in traditional style has been built beside the lake (fig. 5.13). In the park there are two 350-year-old ginkgos and some old junipers. The rest of the planting is modern, although largely of traditional plants such as magnolias, *Cercis chinensis*, *Weigela florida*, *Prunus mume*, *Hypericum monogynum*, *Crataegus* species, daylilies and yuccas. Also of interest is a huge plant of *Jasminum polyanthum*—a Chinese native not often planted in China—and several unusually vigorous examples of *Chimonanthus praecox*, perhaps as much as 6 m tall.

Jiangsu

Jiangsu is one of the most densely populated, productive and affluent areas of the country. Bordering the lower Yangtze, which is intersected here by the Grand Canal, and with a wealth of further natural and artificial waterways, it lies at the centre of China's traditional transport system. This, together with its climate, agricultural abundance and industrialisation, has ensured its prosperity. Over the centuries these circumstances have favoured the building of gardens, and it is in the ancient cities of Nanjing, Yangzhou, Wuxi and Suzhou that many of the country's most famous gardens are to be found.

Suzhou

Renowned as a centre of art and culture, Suzhou lies on the Grand Canal in the south of the province. It dates back to the 6th century BC and in due course became famous for its silk production and its picturesque canals (fig. 5.1). Now, however, most of the old houses have been swept away and many of the canals filled in, so that it has become much less attractive. Nevertheless, it remains China's most famous city for what were once private gardens, since more of them have survived here than anywhere else.

Figure 5.13 Fangtayuan, Songjiang

In 1860 Suzhou was captured by the Taipings and their local leader set himself up there in a mansion, now the Suzhou Museum, next door to the Zhuozhengyuan. Perhaps it is because of this that the city was spared the wholesale destruction which befell Hangzhou at this time and a surprising number of gardens has survived. Several of these were still in private hands and in reasonable condition when Chinese and Western visitors saw, photographed and described them in the 1920s and 30s. Now they have been restored and, for better or worse, are major tourist attractions—a state of affairs which can make visiting them a bit of a bunfight.

This situation has arisen even though few people born in mainland China after 1949 have had an upbringing which would equip them to appreciate the references and nuances to be found in traditional gardens. And, even if they have, they are unlikely to be moved by them in the way the scholars of the past were. None of this, however, seems to have reduced their enthusiasm for visiting them. In fact, the greatest threat to the gardens here and elsewhere in China at the present time is not neglect but people.

The disappearance of the traditional courtyard houses from most Chinese cities means that, apart from the streets, the only places where city dwellers can relax in the open air are parks, gardens and the grounds of a greatly reduced number of temples. Add to this an endless succession of tour groups and there is a danger that the best known of these places will be trampled out of existence.

As well as this, some gardens have undergone changes which can hardly be considered to be improvements. For example, charming garden buildings are sometimes occupied by souvenir sellers, and the eaves of others have been outlined with coloured lights to create 'atmosphere' for those herded in at night to watch 'traditional' entertainments. Elsewhere, too, there are often gaily coloured beach umbrellas sheltering sellers of snacks, drinks and films. And the national obsession for photographing people in front of, and even on, almost everything does not help either. All the same, the fundamental qualities of the gardens remain.

Interestingly, Craig Clunas (1996) claims it can fairly easily be demonstrated that, in the later Qing period, Suzhou was not particularly renowned for its gardens. He quotes an 18th-century source as saying 'Hangzhou is famous for its lakes and hills, Suzhou is famous for its shops and markets, Yangzhou is famous for its gardens'. He also draws attention

Figure 5.14 The lake, Wangshiyuan, Suzhou

to the fact that in the mid-18th century Qianlong saw only two urban gardens in Suzhou, the Canglangting and the Shizilin, both of them now distinguished as much for their lengthy history as for their present condition. And Lin Qing, who saw many of the famous Chinese gardens in the 19th century, does not single out those of Suzhou for any special attention (Lin, 1847–50). Also, Robert Fortune (1847), who went there illegally from Shanghai in 1844, visited nurseries but made no mention of the gardens.

Clunas (1996) suggests that increased Western tourism, boosted by the completion in 1911 of the railway from Shanghai which brought the city within range of day trips, played an important part in bringing about Suzhou's present status as 'The Garden City'. Apparently it first acquired this appellation in 1936 when F.R. Nance gave the title *Soochow, The Garden City* to his guidebook. Earlier than this, however, Matilda Thurston (1931) had written:

Soochow has the finest gardens on a smaller scale and is the best place to visit if one would see gardens after the old pattern, better kept than those of Peiping or in cities like Changsha and Nanking, where the ravages of recent war have worked havoc with such places.

Other writers to have visited and written about Suzhou gardens in this period are Chuin Tung (1936), Dorothy Graham (1938), Henry Inn (1940), Florence Lee Powell (1943) and Osvald Sirén (1949).

Apart from Chuin Tung, the Chinese themselves seem not to have shown any great interest in these gardens until after 1949. Even Liu Dunzhen, who was later to write one of the most important books on the subject, was dismissive of them in his account of the early architectural monuments of the city published in 1936 (Clunas, 1996). Clunas suggests that the Western tourist appropriation of China's cultural heritage, which by then had become so conspicuous, may well have influenced his attitude towards them. However, after

1949 their significance as part of the country's heritage came to be fully recognised, and since then they have come to be the subject of continuously growing enthusiasm and study, both Chinese and Western. Amongst the most comprehensive of the books on the subject is *Chinese Classical Gardens of Suzhou* by Liu Dunzhen (1993), and R.S. Johnston (1991) devotes much space to Suzhou in his *Scholar Gardens of China*. Brief accounts of the gardens that I have visited are given below. I have not included the Heyuan (Crane Garden), which is described in most accounts of the gardens of Suzhou, as it was being used as offices and was not open at the times of my visits.

WANGSHIYUAN (MASTER OF THE NETS GARDEN)

The much admired Wangshiyuan is in the southern part of the old city. A garden was originally built here in the Southern Song by a scholar-official, Shi Zhengzhi, who called

it Yuyin (Fisherman's Retreat), suggesting his love of simple pleasures. It was later abandoned and the present layout is largely that of the second half of the 18th century when it was rejuvenated by Song Zongyuan, an official who retired there and gave it its present name, an allusion to that which it had in the 12th century. In the 18th century it was famous for its herbaceous peonies which were said to rival those of Yangzhou (Tung, 1936). It subsequently passed through various hands and at the time Tung was writing it was one of the few gardens in the city that were still inhabited and in good condition. It belonged then to He Yanong who owned it until the 1950s, when it became public property (Tung, 1997).

The main garden space is a lake bordered with huangshi rock, halls, covered walkways and pavilions—one of the most charming and tranquil garden scenes in China (fig. 5.14). The dominant feature of this space is the much-photographed Yuedao Fenglai Ting (Arrival of the Moon and Coming of

Figure 5.15 (left) **Rocks and ornamental plants in the courtyard of the Five Peaks Study, Wangshiyuan**
Figure 5.16 (below left) **Ornamental windows, Canglangting, Suzhou**
Figure 5.17 (bottom left) **Canglangting, view from outside**
Figure 5.18 (below right) **Confucian Temple, Suzhou**

the Wind Pavilion). Opposite this is a small rock mountain over which a wisteria is growing and *Rosa banksiae* has been trained up the wall behind. From

this central area paths lead to various courtyards in which there are many traditional trees, shrubs and flowering plants, including *Alchornea davidii*, *Ilex cornuta*, camellias and azaleas (fig. 5.15). Also to be seen is a variety of paving and rockwork. On a visit to this relatively small garden it is easy to appreciate the reasons for its fame.

CANGLANGTING (BLUE WAVE PAVILION)

The Canglangting, the name of which recalls an ancient saying advising acceptance of the ups and downs of life, has the longest history of all the surviving gardens in Suzhou. It is a little to the east of the Wangshiyuan on a site where in the early 10th century there was a villa and an imperial flower garden. The actual Blue Wave Pavilion, from which the garden takes its name, was built in the 11th century by Su Shunqin. After various changes of ownership the property was restored in the closing years of the 17th century, when the pavilion was moved from the waterside to its present position on top of a small hill. It was restored again in 1827 and once more in 1873, after its destruction by the Taipings. At this time it was greatly altered when more buildings were added and connected by roofed walkways. In 1927 it was donated to an art school and according to Tung (1936), pseudo-Western buildings were constructed which did nothing to preserve its ancient charm. Eventually

it was restored yet again and reopened to the public in 1954.

The chief features of the garden today are the rocky, tree-shaded hill on which the pavilion is situated and a pool in a deep ravine to its east, above which stands the Yubeiting (Imperial Tablet Pavilion). This area is almost entirely surrounded by walkways and, to its north, there are a series of halls and a two-storey building, from the upper floor of which are distant views. The garden is also notable for the tracery of its windows, no two of which are alike (fig. 5.16).

The Canglangting is unique in that it is quite as picturesque when viewed from the outside as it is within. It is situated on the southern side of a narrow lake across which a zigzag bridge leads to the entrance, and it is bounded not by the usual blank wall but by a roofed double walkway, over which there is a glimpse of the Blue Wave Pavilion. The

walkway has small pavilions at both ends and its central partition is pierced by ornate windows. As a result there are views out from inside the garden and, since the outer side of the walkway can be reached from the inner, it is possible for visitors to stroll along the shore of the lake (fig. 5.17).

KONGMIAO (CONFUCIAN TEMPLE)

This temple is just a short walk across Renmin Lu from the Canlangting. It dates back to the 11th century, when it was built by Fan Zhongyan (989–1052), a renowned Confucian administrator who was responsible for increasing Suzhou's prosperity (Morris, 1983). It was destroyed by the Taipings but rebuilt in 1864 (fig. 5.18). The large courtyard in front of the main hall is laid out as a formal garden and the rear portion is entirely filled with penjing.

Figure 5.20 Lake and rock mountain, Yiyuan

YIYUAN (JOYFUL GARDEN)

The eastern part of this garden, which is entered from Renmin Lu, is the site of a Ming official's residence and consists of a group of courtyards in which displays of azaleas, chrysanthemums and other seasonal flowers are mounted from time to time (fig. 5.19). These spaces lead to a double walkway which winds along the eastern side of the main garden. This garden is an extension made in the late 19th century by Gu Wenbin, a high official who had been a magistrate in eastern Zhejiang where, according to Liu (1993), he had exploited the people cruelly. It is the last large private garden to have been built in Suzhou before the fall of the Qing and incorporates features inspired by the earlier gardens of the city. It is laid out in typical fashion with a lake in the centre, on the southern side of which the principal garden building, the Lotus Fragrance Pavilion, looks across to a large rock mountain on the northern side (fig. 5.20). There are various other spaces, buildings and rockeries, and set into the walls of the walkways are stone tablets carved with the

writings of famous calligraphers from as far back as the Tang and earlier. Amongst the wide selection of trees and shrubs are several wutongs (*Firmiana simplex*) and, close to the double walkway, a tall specimen of the Chinese quince displays its handsome bark.

QUYUAN (SQUARE GARDEN)

The Quyuan is short distance north of the Yiyuan. I have found no reference in the literature to this garden, which was built in 1874 by Yu Yue, a well-known scholar and writer, who retired there after losing his official position. It is both small and L-shaped, like a carpenter's square ('quchi'), and it was ostensibly for this reason that Yu Yue called it the Quyuan. However the character 'qu' can also mean 'stooped', suggesting unjust treatment, or 'crouching', ready as it were to spring up again. Thus the name of this interesting little garden brings with it a number of possible interpretations.

The Quyuan was damaged during the Cultural Revolution but was restored in 1982. It is approached from the street through small courtyards in which there are arrangements of rocks, penjing and potted plants. At its northern and southern ends it is overlooked by single-storeyed halls which have been given names recalling Yu's literary achievements and

Figure 5.19 (previous pages) **Azaleas in the entrance courtyard, Yiyuan, Suzhou**

Figure 5.21 (right) **Quyuan, Suzhou**

Figure 5.22 (below right) **Rock mountain, Huanxiu Shanzhuang, Suzhou**

knowledge. On the south-eastern side there is a small rock mountain complete with a cavern and, in the centre, a rectangular pond. To the north of this is a group of Taihu rocks and tree peonies, the Mudantai (Peony Terrace), and against the eastern wall is a three-sided pavilion. This looks across the pond to a similar structure on the opposite side, sitting in the middle of a roofed walkway which runs along the western wall. One tall tree, a few shrubs and some mondo grass and that is it (fig. 5.21). All the principal features of a classical Chinese scholar's garden have been accommodated effectively in a tiny space.

HUANXIU SHANZHUANG (MOUNTAIN VILLA ENCIRCLED BY ELEGANCE)

This garden, a little to the north-west of the Quyuan, dates back to the 10th century. Since then it has had many owners before being acquired by the Jiang family during the reign of Qianlong (1736–95), from which period the present garden dates. It suffered some damage during the Taiping Uprising but was repaired in 1898. However, by 1949 almost all the buildings had been destroyed, although the rock mountain, said to have been constructed by the famous rockery artist, Ge Yuliang, survived. The garden has now been restored and, although it is small, it is renowned on account of its rock mountain, which is considered by Chinese authors to be the best of the lake-stone rockeries in Suzhou (fig. 5.22).

The principal view of the garden is obtained from a terrace in front of the main hall on its southern side. The rockery

overlooks a pool in which there is small pavilion connected by walkways to the shore and to another pavilion, the Buqiufang (Replenishing-autumn Land Boat), which lies behind and is the only building to date from before 1949 (Liu, 1993). From this another walkway leads up to a small square building which sits at the rear of the rockery which is divided into three by ravines, has a cave at its base, and is shaded by tall Chinese hackberries (*Celtis sinensis*).

YIPU (ART GARDEN)

The Yipu is in a narrow lane in the north-western part of the city. It was first built by Wen Zhenmeng (1574–1636), a great grandson of the scholar and painter Wen Zhengming, who both wrote about and painted the Zhuozhengyuan in the early 16th century. At the time of its founding the Yipu was called the Yaoyuan (Medicine Garden) but was given its present name by its then owner, Jiang Zhenyi, in the early Qing. It is often stated in the modern literature that it retains its Ming and early Qing layout. But if the description given in the family genealogy compiled in the early 18th century and quoted by Clunas (1996) can be relied on, apart from the position of the lake and the mountain made of earth and Taihu stones to its south, little of the original composition survives. While both Liu (1993) and Tung (1997) see faults in the layout of the present garden, I found it tranquil and satisfying.

The main garden is on the southern side of the residential buildings. It is entered through a hall on its south-west corner, beside which there is a small enclosed garden from which a moon gate leads to the principal space. Most of this is occupied by the lake with the main hall on its northern side, the square Ruyuting (Fry Pavilion), the timber frame of which dates back to the Ming, on its eastern shore, and the tree-covered hill and rockery on its southern side. Small arms of the lake, each crossed by a low stone bridge, penetrate the eastern and western sides of this region, suggesting that the

Figure 5.23 (below left) **Yipu, Suzhou,** the lake and artificial mountain, with the Ruyuting on the left

Figure 5.24 (right) **Yipu, courtyard behind main building**

Figure 5.25 (below right) **The waterway, Ouyuan, Suzhou**

water originates in the wilds of the mountains. Paths lead through and around the rockery, towards the rear of which there is another small pavilion (fig. 5.23).

Amongst the trees beside the lake there is a specimen of the Chinese tulip tree (*Liriodendron chinense*), a species rarely seen in Chinese gardens. And in the courtyard to the north of the main hall there is a rock-edged bed containing, amongst other things, *Podocarpus macrophyllus*, tree and herbaceous peonies, *Iris tectorum*, and *Trachelospermum jasminoides* trained over an upright rock (fig. 5.24). Also, as everywhere, the use of pot plants both indoors and out adds to the feeling of unity between the interiors and the garden.

OUYUAN (PAIRED GARDEN)

This, as its name suggests, consists of two small gardens, the East Garden and the West Garden, lying on either side of an old residence. The East Garden was laid out in the north-east of the city in the early Qing but was later abandoned. Then, following the Taiping Uprising, the garden was restored and expanded by Shen Bingcheng who, according to Liu (1993), was one of the people responsible for the massacres of the revolutionaries at the time. During the Republic it was owned by a textile manufacturer and after 1949 was acquired by the local authorities.

The West Garden consists merely of two small courtyards ornamented with rocks, trees and flowers. The East Garden, on the other hand, occupies about a third of a

hectare. It consists of a waterway running north-south overlooked at its north-western end by a much-admired rock mountain made of chunks of huangshi rock and through which a narrow ravine runs (fig. 5.25). Spanning the waterway towards its southern end is the garden's principal building, the two-storeyed Shanshuijian (Study [Amidst] the Mountains and Waters). At the time of my visit only the East Garden was open to the public.

SHIZILIN (LION GROVE)

West of the Ouyuan in the north of the city, the Lion Grove has a long history. It was the site of a deserted Song garden where bamboos and odd-looking rocks were abundant. A temple was built here in 1342 for the monk Tianru Weizi by his followers. According to Liu (1993), a Yuan record states that lying in disorder in part of the wooded grounds there were rocks which looked like lions and wild horses, so it was named Shizilin. Others have suggested that it may have got its name because Tianru Weizi had studied at a place called Lion Cliff on Tianmu Shan in neighbouring Zhejiang (Sensabaugh, 1998). Some idea of its original simple layout can be obtained from paintings which have survived.

The garden became separated from the temple at the end of the Ming and has changed hands and been rebuilt many times. The site was completely ruined by the early Qing, when it was built over for housing. It was rebuilt from scratch for the emperor Qianlong's southern tour of 1762, when its present fame seems to have begun (Clunas, 1996). The rockery built then presumably incorporated the lion-shaped rocks of the original or was adorned with similar replacements. Qianlong must have been impressed as he subsequently had gardens modelled on it built in the Yuanmingyuan and at Chengde. In 1918 it was acquired by the Pei family, who remodelled it between then and 1926, when Florence Lee Powell photographed it (Powell, 1943). It must have been seen around the same time by Tung Chuin, who observed that, apart from the rockery, the garden was all of recent construction and exhibited showy detail that reflected the owner's wealth (Tung, 1997).

As might be expected, the present garden shows none of the restraint and simplicity of its 14th-century antecedent. It is entered at its south-eastern corner and a passageway leads to a small courtyard in front of the Yanyutang (Famed-for-swallows Hall). This contains two magnolias which frame a small rockery planted with tree peonies, behind which stands a Taihu stone. Placed against the background of a white-washed wall, I found this as satisfying a part of the garden as any. Beyond this is the principal garden space with a lake and the famous rockery (fig. 5.26). The lake is surrounded by walkways, buildings and further huge complicated rockeries. Other conspicuous features are a land boat in the north-west corner of the lake and a hexagonal pavilion standing in the water and connected to the shore by zigzag bridges. The former does not appear in Florence Lee Powell's photographs

Figure 5.26 Shizilin, Suzhou, general view with the famous rockery on the right

and is not shown on her plan of the garden, so it may well be a recent addition.

The rockery is, of course, the chief point of interest with its caverns and curiously shaped Taihu stones, which seem to be much the same as those shown in photographs taken in 1918 and 1926 (Powell, 1943; Sirén, 1949). Beside it is a wisteria pergola and the whole scene is softened by tall trees, including ginkgos and specimens of *Pinus bungeana*. But, when all is said and done, I tend to agree with Shen Fu (1809), who said that although it was the most famous place in Suzhou he failed to see anything particularly wonderful about it.

ZHUOZHENGYUAN (HUMBLE ADMINISTRATOR'S GARDEN)

This garden, a short distance north of the Shizilin in the north-eastern part of the city, seems to be the most acclaimed of all Chinese gardens still in existence. A garden was first built here in the early 16th century on the site of a Yuan temple by a retired official, Wang Xianchen. Just as gardens achieve fame today when people write about them and publish carefully taken photographs, the renown of this garden has been enhanced by its history and by the poems, paintings and descriptions of its scenes which were executed soon after its completion by the scholar and painter, Wen Zhengming. His prose description of 1533, along with 31 paintings and poems relating to specific spots within the garden, ensured its place in China's cultural history, as has been noted in Chapter 1. At this time it was relatively simple, with ponds, a few modest buildings, many trees and other ornamental plants, and a considerable

area devoted to fruit trees and vegetables (Clunas, 1996). Clearly it bore little or no resemblance to the garden we see today (fig. 1.31).

The Zhuozhengyuan has changed hands and been rebuilt many times. By the end of the Ming it was almost abandoned but, during Kangxi's reign, there was renewed building and development and subsequently, in Qianlong's time, it became divided into three separate gardens. It escaped damage during the Taiping Uprising as it was occupied by one of the leaders. Then, following the defeat of the Taipings, the central portion, the Zhuozhengyuan proper, was occupied by the provincial administration and later became the home of the Manchu Guild. Under the Republic this part of the garden was opened to the public, though Tung (1936) records that most of the buildings were in danger of collapse—a state of

affairs born out by Osvald Sirén's (1949) photographs from the same period, which also show the ponds to be almost dry. Even so, this situation did not dampen the enthusiasm of F.R. Nance who, in his guidebook of 1936, wrote that this garden 'even in its present state of dilapidation has a lure and beauty all its own' (Clunas, 1996).

The three sections were eventually brought together again and the whole garden was repaired and opened once more in 1952. It is now entered through its eastern section. This is a modern park-like area of comparatively minor interest, to the west of which is the main part of the garden. Much of this central section, which largely retains its Qing appearance, is occupied by a lake in which there are two islands connected to one another and the shore by bridges. The hills in this area are largely made of earth and harmonise well with their

Figure 5.27

(left)

Roofed walkway, Zhuozhengyuan, Suzhou

Figure 5.28

(below left)

Rosa banksiae 'Lutea', Zhuozhengyuan

surroundings. There are pavilions on the islands but the main buildings are arranged along the southern shore. There are more than 25 buildings in this part of the garden and their architecture and their disposition amongst walkways, bridges and extensions of the lake have been greatly praised by various authors (fig. 5.27).

Although the present western part of the garden dates back only to the late 19th century, it continues the style of the main garden, with an extension of the lake overlooked by the Hall of Thirty-six Mandarin Ducks, to the west of which an arm of the lake runs south along a narrow, rocky ravine. To the west of this ravine are a courtyard where pots of seasonal flowers are displayed (fig. 1.23), an enclosure filled with penjing, and a service area. Throughout the whole garden there is a representative selection of traditional garden plants (fig. 5.28) and in summer a collection of lotus cultivars blooms in the lake.

SUZHOU BOWUGUAN (SUZHOU MUSEUM)

This was originally the residence of the adjoining Zhuozhengyuan which was taken over and converted for the local Taiping leader in the mid-19th century. I have included it here as its courtyards contain osmanthuses, Chusan palms, weeping sophoras and other plants which, set against the browns and greys of the old buildings, form satisfying compositions (fig. 5.29).

BEISITA (NORTH TEMPLE PAGODA)

This pagoda at the northern end of the main street, Renmin Lu, was originally built in the 12th century and is all that remains of a temple believed to date back to the Three Kingdoms period. On the land associated with it there are now a couple of large halls in traditional style around which collections of penjing and potted plants are arranged. Amongst these are cultivars of *Hibiscus rosa-sinensis* which are brought out when the weather permits. The adjoining area has been developed as a garden surrounding a lake and is planted with trees, shrubs and herbaceous plants. These include camellias, wutongs, *Viburnum macrocephalum*, hostas and *Iris tectorum*. At the time of my visit the spring foliage of *Alchornea davidii* was particularly striking (fig. 5.30).

Figure 5.29 (below) **A courtyard at the Suzhou Museum**
Figure 5.30 (right) ***Alchornea davidii*, North Temple Pagoda, Suzhou**

LIUYUAN (LINGERING GARDEN)

The Liuyuan is a large garden situated to the east of the boundary of the old city. It occupies the site of the Dongyuan (East Garden), one of a pair of gardens built by a Ming official, Xu Shitai, during the reign of the emperor Jiajing (1522–67), and rebuilt during the reign of Jiaqing (1796–1820) by the Liu family, who named it Hanbizhuang (Cold Emerald Villa). Although it was spared from destruction during the Taiping Uprising, it was largely rebuilt once again in 1876 by the Sheng family, who gave it its present name—a pun on that of its former owners. At this time it was greatly enlarged to the east and west of the central pool and rockery. The garden and its buildings appear to have been in good order when photographed in 1926 by Florence Lee Powell (1943), and Sirén's (1949) photographs from the same period create a similar impression.

After the vicissitudes of the years which followed, the garden was restored and reopened in 1954. On the whole its appearance now is much the same as it was in the 1920s and 30s, though some of the stonework shows evidence of damage or has disappeared, the layout of some of the spaces is simpler, and others have been redeveloped.

Figure 5.31 (left) Liuyuan, Suzhou, wisteria on the rustic bridge leading to the island

Figure 5.32 (above) Liuyuan, the Cloud-capped Peak

there is a hexagonal pavilion on top, over which tower two enormous 200-year-old ginkgos.

In the eastern part of the garden, which was the main residential quarter, there are many interesting courtyards, the most impressive of which is that in which a famous Taihu stone, Guanyun Feng (Cloud-capped Peak), stands in front of a mandarin duck hall. At 6.5 m this is the tallest lake-stone in any Suzhou garden and is said to date from the original Dongyuan (fig. 5.32). From the second storey of the building beyond there is a view of Tiger Hill. And in the western area there are, amongst other things, a collection of penjing and a small orchard of flowering peaches. Throughout the garden there is a wealth of ornamental plants, including azaleas, camellias, tree peonies, bananas, bamboos, *Alchornea davidii* and *Viburnum macrocephalum*.

The Liuyuan came in for particular praise from Dorothy Graham (1938), who considered it to be the most beautiful garden in the Ming tradition. Of the gardens in Suzhou it is my favourite too.

XIYUAN (WEST GARDEN)

This and the adjoining temple stand on the site of the original Xiyuan which Xi Shitai built during the Ming, next door to what is now the Liuyuan. The original Xiyuan was given by his son to a Buddhist community who built a temple there in 1635. This, along with the garden, was destroyed by the Taipings in 1860. The temple was rebuilt subsequently and is now known popularly as the Xiyuan Temple, but the garden area to its west has not so far been fully restored. It consists

From the entrance a winding corridor leads the visitor through a series of spaces of contrasting size and interest until the lake and its surrounds are glimpsed through windows before a full view is obtained. This part of the garden is based on the layout of the Hanbizhuang and, with its surrounding buildings, rockeries and vegetation, it adds up to one of the most satisfying scenes in any Chinese garden. In the lake there is an island, Xiaopenglai (Small Penglai), which is connected to the shore by pergola-like bridges over which wisteria is growing (fig. 5.31), and on the northern side there is an artificial mountain. This is decorated with rockeries and

largely of the Fangshengchi (Setting-free-captive-fish Pond), in the centre of which is the much-photographed Mid-lake Pavilion, which is connected to the shore by zigzag bridges (fig. 5.33). There is also a peninsula projecting into the lake on which stone tables and seats have been arranged under a group of tall camphor laurels. Towering above a wall near these there is an unusually floriferous and well-coloured paulownia.

HANSHANSI (COLD MOUNTAIN TEMPLE)

The Hanshansi stands opposite a picturesque hump-backed bridge, the Fengqiao (Maple Bridge), which spans a canal a short distance west of the Xiyuan. The temple, founded in the 6th century, was destroyed by the Taipings, rebuilt in the late 19th and early 20th centuries, and upgraded in recent times. I have included it here because its courtyards are profusely planted with ginkgos, camellias, Japanese maples (fig. 5.34), bamboos and other plants, and there is some well-executed paving in the plum-blossom pattern. Also

of interest is a stele inscribed in Wen Zhengming's calligraphy of a Tang poem by Zhang Ji entitled 'Anchored at night by the Maple Bridge'.

HUQIU SHAN (TIGER HILL)

Legend has it that this is the burial place of He Lu, founder of Suzhou and King of Wu (reigned 514–496 BC), together with 3000 of his swords. It is said that a white tiger was seen crouching on his grave three days after his interment— hence the name of the hill. An alternative explanation is simply that the shape of the hill resembles a crouching tiger. All that aside, the proximity of this famous scenic spot to the city has long made it a popular resort for all levels of

Suzhou society. It has been the subject of numerous poems and paintings, and seems to have been particularly fashionable during the Ming. There were several private gardens there at this time and it was also the site of a famous flower and plant market, supplied by growers who brought their produce by boat along the canals. It is recorded that penjing were available there in the early 16th century and, a century later, Wen Zhenheng mentions that huge amounts of jasmine were brought there for sale (Clunas, 1996). Shen Fu (1809) admired some of the scenic spots there but felt that others were 'obviously man made and spoiled by decoration so that they had lost the true look of mountains and forests'. It remains a popular recreation area with tea houses, displays of seasonal flowers, and other diversions.

On the lower slope of the hill, not far from the entrance, there is a restored garden, the Yongcui Shanzhuang (Embracing Green Mountain Villa). It was begun in 1884 and consists of a series of

Figure 5.33 The Mid-lake Pavilion, Xiyuan, Suzhou

courtyards and buildings which rise up the hill and from which there are good views. A little higher up the slope there is a large area of rock and a lotus pond, above which a bridge spans a huge cleft. It is in the base of this, under the water, that He Lu is supposed to have been buried with his swords. Above this again, on the summit, is a leaning pagoda, built between 959 and 961. This is all that remains of the Yunyan temple which once dominated the site and it is believed to be the earliest Song pagoda to have survived. It is shown in Thomas Allom's fanciful illustration of the hill (fig. 5.35).

Figure 5.34 (left) **Japanese maples, Hanshansi, Suzhou**
Figure 5.35 (below) **Tiger Hill, Suzhou.**
FROM ALLOM AND WRIGHT (1843).

Below the pagoda, on the eastern side of the hill, there is a large area in which penjing are displayed (fig. 5.36), and beyond this is a wooded area with many interesting old trees, including *Celtis sinensis* and *Zelkova schneideriana*.

LINGYAN SHAN (SPIRIT-CLIFF HILL)

Supposedly the site of the legendary King of Wu's palace, this famous hill south-west of the city, with the Lingyan Temple on its summit, has fared less well than Tiger Hill. There was a travelling palace here used by Kangxi and Qianlong during their visits to the south, but this and the old temple were amongst the buildings destroyed by the Taipings in 1860. The temple was not rebuilt until after 1927, and the halls and pagoda were restored again in 1980 (fig. 5.37). The site, however, remains popular with tourists and pilgrims, who make their way up the hill past bamboo groves, clumps of *Rosa laevigata*, and rocks in which they see resemblances to drums and various animals. The temple courtyards have been planted with trees and shrubs, conspicuous amongst which is a tall specimen of the Chinese Fan Palm (*Livistona chinensis*). This is one of the places described by Shen Fu (1809), who expressed the view that its features were laid out carelessly, 'merely spread out without any organisation', and that it lacked the great beauty of other well-known hills near the city. I imagine he would be even more critical were he to return now.

Tongli

Tongli, about 20 km south-east of Suzhou, became a fashionable place to live during the Ming and Qing. It was in this district that Ji Cheng, the author of the *Yuanye*, was born, and in its heyday there were more than 60 gardens in the town. Almost all of these have disappeared but one, the Tuisiyuan, has been restored and is open to the public.

TUISIYUAN (RETREAT FOR CONTEMPLATION GARDEN)

The Tuisiyuan was built between 1885 and 1887 by Ren Lansheng, a general in charge of Anhui and Jiangsu provinces, who had been dishonourably discharged. The garden was designed by the poet and painter Yuan Long. It is approached through a courtyard surrounded by two-storey buildings and in which there is a rockery. This courtyard, which serves as a prelude to the main garden, is

Figure 5.36 (opposite page) **Tiger Hill, penjing garden and pagoda**
Figure 5.37 (left) **Lingyan Temple near Suzhou**

shaded by a camphor laurel, a tall *Magnolia denudata* and a large *M. grandiflora*.

The central part of the garden consists of a lake surrounded by walkways, rockeries, and buildings of different sizes and styles. Amongst these are a waterside pavilion, a land boat, and two-storeyed pavilions, from the upper levels of which there are views. In spite of its relatively recent date, the principal hall, the Tuisi Caotang (Thatched Cottage for Retreat and Contemplation), which sits on a terrace overlooking the lake, has been described as one of the most beautiful garden buildings in China (fig. 5.38). And amongst the plants there are many of the well-known favourites, including gardenias, *Hypericum monogynum*, *Fatsia japonica*, *Trachelospermum jasminoides*, crabapples, plums, Chusan palms and bamboos.

Wuxi

Now a modern industrial city, Wuxi is situated on the Grand Canal close to the northern end of Lake Tai. It has a long his-tory and was originally called Youxi (Has Tin) because this metal was mined there. However, it was renamed Wuxi (No Tin) during the Han, which suggests that the deposits had become exhausted by this time. Long famous for its trade in rice, in the early 20th century it also became a centre for silk production.

Apart from Xihui Park, in which the Jichangyuan is found, there is little of horticultural interest in the city centre. Wuxi's other attractions are several kilometres to the west on and near the shores of Lake Tai, where there are two other gardens, the Liyuan and the Meiyuan. Also here is the start-ing point for cruises on the lake. This lake is famous for a variety of reasons, though, from a gardener's point of view, it is notable principally for the Taihu stones dredged up from its waters for use as garden ornaments. The most popular cruises go to Yuantou Zhu (Turtle Head Peninsula). This peninsula, which is said to resemble a turtle's head in shape, has been 'improved' with ornamental plantings, including crabapples, *Syringa oblata* and *Jasminum mesnyi*. Although

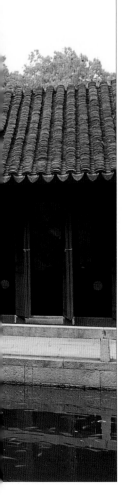

thronged with visitors it is not, however, a particularly exciting place. Nevertheless this cruise provides an opportunity to see the lake and there is a good view of the island known as Taihusanshan (Three Hills on Lake Tai), another popular scenic spot.

XIHUI GONGYUAN (XIHUI PARK)

This park was constructed in 1958 by linking two hills, Xi Shan (Tin Mountain) and Hui Shan (Generosity Mountain). Xi Shan is crowned by the 16th-century Dragon Light Pagoda (Longguangta) from which there is an extensive view of the city and lake. And at the base of Hui Shan is Wuxi's most significant garden, the Jichangyuan, from which a path leads up the hill to a famous spring, the Second Spring under Heaven (fig. 5.39). This spring was so named by Lu Yu (733–804) in his *Chajing* (Classic of Tea), as he considered its waters

the second best in China for making tea. It feeds a pond which is crossed by the Golden Lotus Bridge, thought to have been built in the Tang or Song. A short distance above this is the Huishan Temple, in front of which are beautifully carved Song and Tang pillars and an old ginkgo.

JICHANGYUAN (DELIGHT-CONVEYING GARDEN)

This famous garden was first laid out on the site of a Yuan dynasty monastery during the reign of the emperor Zhengde (1506–21) by Qin Jin, whose descendants remained its owners until at least the 1930s. The rock mountain was added at the beginning of the reign of Kangxi, who saw it when he came south. His grandson Qianlong visited it in 1751 and, as mentioned earlier, built a garden based on its design in the Qingyiyuan, now the Summer Palace outside Beijing.

The original Jichangyuan was destroyed by the Taipings, only the bottle-gourd shaped pond and some of the rockery surviving. It was rebuilt early in the 20th century but no doubt has suffered more recent tribulations. Now, however, it is well maintained, though how great a resemblance it bears to the original is unclear. Nevertheless it shows an overall similarity to the woodcut of it in Lin Qing's mid-19th century autobiography (Lin, 1847–50) (fig. 5.40) and, although it now has fewer buildings than were present originally, and undoubtedly differs in other ways, it retains an air of distinction.

The present entrance is at the opposite end of the garden to that shown in Lin Qing's illustration, and from it a path leads to the southern end of the lake. From here a roofed

Figure 5.38 (left) **Tuisiyuan, Tongli, general view with the Tuisi Caotang on the right**

Figure 5.39 (above) **The Second Spring Under Heaven, Hui Shan, Wuxi**

Figure 5.40 (above right) **Jichangyuan, Wuxi, woodcut in Lin Qing (1847–50).**

FROM SIRÉN (1949).

277

Figure 5.41 (above left) **Jichangyuan, view towards the pagoda and temple on Xi Shan**

Figure 5.42 (left) ***Iris japonica*, Jichangyuan**

Figure 5.43 (above) **Pavilion on the edge of Lake Tai with a walkway leading to the Liyuan (far left) behind**

walkway runs along the eastern bank to the Zhiyujian (Fish-knowing Study), which is built out over the water. Along the western bank there is an elongated and tree-covered rock mountain made of huangshi stone, from which a tiny stream runs into the lake through a narrow ravine. At the northern

end of the lake there is a bridge from which one gets a view across to the pagoda on the top of Xi Shan, an excellent example of the use of 'borrowed scenery' (fig. 5.41).

The principal trees in the garden are camphor laurels and amongst other plants of note are *Iris japonica*, which is used as an extensive ground cover near the entrance (fig. 5.42), and a weeping peach planted in a strategic position on the western bank of the lake.

LIYUAN (WORM-EATEN GARDEN)

According to Wood (1992), this garden gets its name from that of the inlet of Lake Tai on which it lies (fig. 5.43). This was originally known as Li Hu (Worm-eaten Lake) but is now called Wuli Hu (Five-li Lake), a li being an old unit of measurement approximately equivalent to 0.5 km. The present garden was made between 1927 and 1930 out of two gardens, the original Liyuan and the Yuzhuangyuan (Fishing Village Garden). It would appear to have been revived as a tourist attraction, though, as Wood puts it, it is 'not enormously to be recommended'. In spite of the fact that qualities such as restraint and felicitous taste fail to make an appearance here, it is immensely popular and usually crowded. Elaborate and somewhat crude rockwork abounds, as do ponds, hills, bridges, causeways, concrete pavilions and the vendors of distressing souvenirs. For all this it is pleasant taking in the views by walking around the shore of the lake, and the garden contains an interesting collection of plants, including willows, pines, Chinese redbuds (*Cercis chinensis*), peaches, crabapples, roses and an occasional lilac (*Syringa oblata*).

MEIYUAN (PLUM GARDEN)

The Meiyuan is on a hillside west of the city and is a large, roughly maintained park which has been planted with hundreds of plum trees (*Prunus mume*). In the late Qing it was the garden of a scholar named Xu Dian and was called Xiaotaoyuan (Small Peach Garden), but in 1912 it became the garden of the Song family who planted the plum trees. From the entrance a path leads beneath a wisteria pergola past a collection of different crabapples, Chinese quinces (*Pseudocydonia sinensis*) (fig. 5.44) and dwarf flowering almonds (*Prunus glandulosa*), to the top of the hill where there is a three-storey pagoda, built by two of the Song brothers to commemorate their mother's 80th birthday. From here there is a distant view across to the lake.

While a visit to the Meiyuan may not be one of the more exciting experiences China has to offer, it seems likely that it would create an impact in late winter when the plum trees are in bloom.

Zhenjiang

Zhenjiang is an ancient city on the south bank of the Yangtze between Shanghai and Nanjing. It is a busy commercial centre strategically situated where the Grand Canal crosses the river. Its principal tourist attractions are three famous hills, Jin Shan, Beigu Shan, and Jiao Shan, each of which is of significance for those interested in gardens and plants. Amongst other sights are the tomb of the Song artist Mi Fei (1051–1107) and the house where the American writer Pearl Buck, remembered for her novel *The Good Earth*, spent her early years. And it was near here in 1949 that the the British gunboat *Amethyst* was attacked by Communist forces, ran aground, and was trapped for over 14 weeks before making its escape.

JIN SHAN (GOLDEN MOUNTAIN)

Jin Shan, which gets its name from the gold which was found there during the Tang, is west of the city centre close to the banks of the Yangtze. Originally it was a small island but by the end of the Qing silting had joined it to the shore, greatly diminishing its visual impact. It is now some distance from the river (fig. 5.45).

A temple was first built here in the 4th century and, with its pagoda and temple buildings, the island became one of the most picturesque and admired sights on the Yangtze. The Qing emperors Kangxi and Qianlong both stayed here when they travelled down the Grand Canal to visit the cities of the Yangtze delta region, and it was remarked upon, painted, drawn and photographed by Western visitors (fig. 5.46). Lord Macartney saw it on 6 November 1793 (Cranmer-Byng, 1962) and wrote that it was

> built from the water's edge to the top with temples, turrets and belvederes on regular terraces or stories one above the other, intermixed with evergreen trees of various volumes and shades of verdure, contrasted in so happy a taste and distributed in such a manner as to give the whole the air of a fairy edifice suddenly raised upon the river by the magic of an enchanter.

It had earlier so impressed Kangxi that he had the Jade Spring Hill near Beijing remodelled along similar lines and a small replica built on the lake at the Imperial Summer Villa in Chengde. Subsequently it influenced Qianlong's rearrangement of the buildings on Qionghua Island in Beihai Park. There is also a small version in the garden of the Slender West Lake at Yangzhou.

Figure 5.44 (left)

Chinese quince, Meiyuan, Wuxi

Figure 5.45 (opposite page top)

Jin Shan, Zhenjiang

Figure 5.46 (opposite page bottom)

Jin Shan, engraving from a watercolour by William Alexander.

FROM STAUNTON (1796). TAKEN FROM A COPY HELD IN THE RARE BOOK COLLECTION, STATE LIBRARY OF NEW SOUTH WALES.

the summit of the hill a pavilion overlooks the city and the shipping on the Yangtze. The hill is now part of a park in which azaleas (fig. 5.47), wutongs (*Firmiana simplex*) and other ornamental plants have been established.

JIAO SHAN (SCORCHED MOUNTAIN)

Jiao Shan is an island in the Yangtze a little east of Beigu Shan. It is only a short distance from the shore and is reached by ferry or cable car. Although somewhat faded, it is an interesting place which, like Jin Shan, was remarked upon and drawn by early European visitors, who referred to it as the Silver Island—presumably ranking it second to its more picturesque golden neighbour. What the correct translation of the Chinese name of this island is I have been unable to determine with certainty. The version I have given above is the literal one but the same character is also a surname. Baedecker (1994) states that a certain Jiao Guang took refuge here during the Eastern Han (25–220), which suggests that the mountain may have been named after him. Unlike Jin Shan, in its general appearance it looks the same today as it did when photographed by John Thomson (1873–74).

Visitors arrive on the western side of the island close to the Dinghuisi (Settling of Wisdom Temple), which was founded in the Han, although the present buildings are modern. In front of the temple is an 800-year-old ginkgo (fig. 5.48), and a little further along the path there are other old trees, including a 400-year-old *Pterocarya stenoptera*, near which is an enclosure with a display of penjing. From here the path, beside which fortune tellers set up tables, continues amongst the trees to the fortifications on the eastern side, over which the British and Qing forces fought during the First Opium War in 1842. From the fortifications one can climb to take in the view from the Xijiangting (Breathing River Pavilion) on the summit of the hill, from where the path continues down to the vicinity of the ferry wharf.

The buildings on the island were devastated by the Taipings in the middle of the 19th century, but were subsequently restored. John Thomson's (1873–74) photograph of around 1870, when the island had already become attached to the bank, shows the temple buildings to be in excellent order although the pagoda, originally constructed in the Tang, was still in a ruinous state. It was rebuilt in 1900. Jin Shan came under attack again during the Cultural Revolution but has recently been rebuilt once more with the aid of money donated by benefactors anxious to see this famous place restored. While there is little for the plantsperson here, the site is notable on account of its history and because it has served as a model for features ornamenting the great landscape gardens at Yangzhou, Beijing and Chengde. Also there are extensive views of the city and the Yangtze from the summit and the pagoda.

BEIGU SHAN (NORTHERN DEFENCE HILL)

Like Jin Shan, this famous hill on the banks of the Yangtze east of the town centre has a long history. It was here during the Three Kingdoms period that Sun Quan, King of Wu, enticed his rival, Liu Bei, King of Shu, into a trap by pretending to offer him his sister in marriage. This event, whether fact or fiction, was later immortalised in the famous novel *Romance of the Three Kingdoms*, which has long captured the imagination of the Chinese. A recreation of this incident involving life-size models has been installed in one of the buildings forming part of the Ganlusi (Refreshing Dew Temple). There is also the remains of a Song pagoda and on

Yangzhou

As did Zhenjiang, Yangzhou came into prominence when the construction of the Grand Canal linked it with the Sui capital at Luoyang. Situated a short distance to the north of the junction of the canal with the Yangtze, it was in an ideal position to benefit from its connection with most parts of China and also with the ocean. By the time the Song fell in the 13th century the canal had fallen into disrepair and the city's fortunes declined, though Marco Polo, who claims to have been governor of the city late in that century, described it as thriving. Its prosperity returned with the repair of the canal in the Ming, and it became an important cultural and commercial centre once more. With the defeat of the Ming in 1644 the city held out for a time against the Manchu troops, but in 1645 it was captured, most of the population was massacred, and there was much destruction. The city recovered and prospered again during the Qing, becoming the centre of the salt trade. Much of this was controlled by merchants from Anhui, who became enormously rich. As has been mentioned in the introduction to this chapter, these people, in order to improve their social position, became patrons of the arts and built themselves mansions and gardens (Ho, 1954).

Yangzhou was a major stopping-off point for Qianlong's party during his journeys to the south in the 18th century, and the salt merchants undertook landscaping works around the Shouxihu (Slender West Lake) and vied with one another to build elaborate houses and gardens in which to entertain the imperial visitors. Their efforts were admired by Shen Fu, who wrote of the area around the lake that, although the scenery 'was entirely the product of human labour and imagination, it was a natural and idyllic park, and the

residences of the Immortals could not have surpassed it'. He also said that it 'probably should be looked upon as a beautiful woman handsomely dressed, rather than regarded as one would a simple country girl' (Shen, 1809). According to Cheng (1999) there were more than 100 private gardens on the banks of the Slender West Lake at this time, and Tung (1936) says that Yangzhou was transformed into the most stupendous garden city history ever saw. However, after Qianlong's death most of the gardens were neglected and disappeared. Also, Yangzhou suffered badly from the depredations of the Taipings and much of what one now sees dates from the late 19th century and subsequent restorations.

**Figure 5.48 An 800-year-old ginkgo,
Jiao Shan, Zhenjiang**

The gardens of Yangzhou are undoubtedly in a category of their own. The number of buildings used for garden living, enjoyment and entertainment is greater in relation to the overall area than in the scholars' gardens of Suzhou. Also, while the architecture of the city is definitely southern, the gardens show northern influences, as Chen (1983) has noted, particularly in the design of rockeries and the solidity of some of the pavilions.

The gardens of Yangzhou have been documented in detail by Chen Congzhou (1983) in his *Yangzhou yuanlin* (Gardens

Garden), which is simply a collection of picturesque buildings backed by trees and shrubs and overlooking a widened part of the moat. At the time of my visit the moat had been drained here, and the buildings were being refurbished, but no doubt it has been back to normal long since.

A little further along is the Hongyuan (Red Garden) in which there is a large collection of penjing and a nursery area. Beyond this again the moat widens and makes a right-angled bend to the north, becoming the stretch of water known as the Slender West Lake, which was made from old moats and

of Yangzhou). He described the gardens in the park surrounding the Slender West Lake, as Shen Fu (1809) did before him, and 16 others, giving detailed plans of each. How many of these still survive is unclear. The Cuiyuan (Assembly Garden) and the Zhenyuan (Precious Garden), for example, have become hotels and, apart from a few old stones and trees, nothing appears to be left of their original layouts. A few of the larger gardens remain but most of the rest are quite small, some occupying only tiny courtyards. It is not easy to gain access to most of these as they form part of residences or offices. Hence I have included below only those which are open to the public or to which inquiry at the gate enabled me to gain entry.

Figure 5.49 (above) **The Long Embankment with Spring Willows, Slender West Lake, Yangzhou**
Figure 5.50 (right) **The White Dagoba, Wild Duck Villa and Five Pavilion Bridge, Slender West Lake, Yangzhou**

SHOUXIHU (SLENDER WEST LAKE) AND ENVIRONS

A good starting point for visiting the gardens of Yangzhou is Yanfu Road, which runs beside the northern moat of the old city. Walking west from its intersection with Shi Kefa Road one comes first to the Yechunyuan (Enchanting Spring

waterways. The name alludes to the famous West Lake at Hangzhou and thus brings with it notions of similar beauty. Originally there were 24 named scenes here (Qiao, 1982). It is crossed at its southern end by the Dahongqiao (Great Rainbow Bridge), which is one of the original scenes.

The embankment running north from the bridge is lined with willows and flowering peaches and is known as the Long Embankment with Spring Willows (fig. 5.49). There is a pavilion with an inscription halfway along and the path leads to the Xu Garden, built in the early 20th century (Tung, 1936), where there is a pond, rockery and a variety of plants. Here, too, are two huge iron cauldrons which stand in front of the Pavilion for Listening to the Orioles. Across the water to the east is the Misty Rain Pavilion, the design of which, like that of the one in the garden of the Imperial Summer Villa at Chengde, is based on the famous building of the same name at Jiaxing in Zhejiang. To the north a bridge leads to the island called the Little Golden Mountain. This was designed to recall the Golden Mountain at nearby Zhenjiang, but in

would improve the scenery of the lake. The Five Pavilion Bridge (figs 1.28, 5.50), which terminates the principal vista, was built in 1757, the year of Qianlong's second journey to the south, also at the expense of a salt merchant (Hu, 1991; Wood, 1992). The Fuzhuang (Wild Duck Villa), with its variety of wooden buildings, adds interest to the scene in a quieter manner. It is an addition built by the Chen family in 1924 on an island connected to the shore by a bridge. It fell into ruin in the 1930s but has been entirely renewed. All these features add up to an impressive landscape composition.

its present form the resemblance is tenuous. A long causeway extends west from this island and at its end is a small square pavilion, Breezy Terrace, where Qianlong is supposed to have enjoyed fishing. Its moon-shaped windows allow views of the lake's most conspicuous features, the White Dagoba, the Five Pavilion Bridge, and the Wild Duck Villa (fig. 5.50).

The White Dagoba is similar to that in Beihai Park, Beijing, and is said to have been built by a salt merchant to please Qianlong, who had remarked that such a structure

To the west of the Five Pavilion Bridge there are further buildings and gardens. One of these is devoted to herbaceous peonies, a plant for which Yangzhou became famous during the Song (Needham, 1986). Wang Guan's *Yangzhou shaoyao pu* (Treatise on the Herbaceous Peonies of Yangzhou) appeared in 1075, and it is said that in the 12th century the garden of the Zhu family there contained almost 60 000 plants (Li, 1959). Yangzhou continued to be renowned for herbaceous peonies at least up to the 19th century.

Figure 5.51

Xiyuan, Daming

Temple, Yangzhou

Also in the north-western region, not far from the north gate, is a recently constructed 'garden within a garden' in which there is a splendid plant of *Wisteria sinensis* 'Alba' trained over a rock pile. Other wisterias are to be found in various parts of the garden, along with roses and displays of potted plants. Also here are plants of *Viburnum macrocephalum* f. *keteleeri*, the floral emblem of the city.

DAMINGSI (GREAT BRIGHTNESS TEMPLE)

A canal leads north from the Slender West Lake to the foot of the hill on which this temple has been built. It was founded in the 5th century but the surviving buildings all date from the late Qing, the earlier ones presumably having been destroyed during the Taiping Uprising. Apparently Qianlong stayed here, as this temple is included in an album of anonymous 18th-century paintings (*Palaces of the Emperor along the Road from Peking to Suzhou*) held by the Bibliothèque nationale, Paris, and in a similar album in the British Library (*Album of paintings illustrating the stations of the Qianlong emperor's fifth tour of inspection to South China*). Although the buildings are now different and fewer, the position of the axes and that of the garden and its lake remain the same.

To the west of the main axis is the Pingshantang (Level with the Mountains Hall) originally built in 1048 by Ouyang Xiu, a famous Song scholar who at one stage was governor of Yangzhou. In horticultural circles he is best known as the author of the outstanding early book about tree peonies, *Luoyang mudan ji* (Account of the Tree Peonies of Luoyang), which he wrote in 1034 (Needham, 1986). Further back on the same axis is his memorial temple, the Ouyangci.

On the eastern side of the main axis of the Daming Temple is the Jian Zhen Memorial Hall built in Tang style in the late 20th century and financed by Japanese contributions. This building is modelled on the main hall of the Toshodaiji Temple established in 759 at Nara by Jian Zhen, who was a monk of the Daming Temple. He arrived in Japan in 753 with the aim of imposing discipline on the lax Japanese Buddhist community. He is also said to have introduced medicine, architecture, printing and the written language to Japan.

Amongst the temple buildings there is little of horticultural interest apart from a wisteria pergola shading a terrace from which, it is claimed, the Golden Mountain at Zhenjiang can be seen on a clear day. However, to the west of the complex of buildings there is the extensive Xiyuan (West Garden), built around a lake in which there are two islands (fig. 5.51). There are pavilions on the islands and other buildings around the shore. This garden was built during the reign of Qianlong and appears still to correspond roughly with the garden shown in the illustrations mentioned above. It was in poor condition at the time of my visit in 1995 but had clearly been most impressive in the past. It appeared to be being restored and by now may well be in a better state. According to Morris (1983), it contains the Fifth Spring under Heaven, the water of which the Tang author Lu Yu in his *Chajing* considered the fifth best for brewing tea.

A little to the east of this temple, on the same hill, are the ruins of the Tang city wall. These have been partly restored and the flat ground behind has been developed as a small park with flowering peaches and other ornamental plants.

YANGZHOU BOWUGUAN (YANGZHOU MUSEUM)

Back in the city and walking west along Yanfu Road one comes first to the Yangzhou Museum, which occupies the buildings of a former temple (fig. 5.52). Two large ginkgos stand in front of the principal hall and the surrounding area is ornamented with a selection of trees and shrubs both in the ground and in pots. Amongst these is an unusually large loquat (*Eriobotrya japonica*).

SHI KEFA CITANG (SHI KEFA MEMORIAL HALL)

Shi Kefa (1601–45) was an official loyal to the Ming who refused to surrender Yangzhou to the Qing. He was eventually arrested and executed. His body was not found but his belt of 20 pieces of jade was buried here and the temple to his memory erected in 1772.

A bridge over the moat leads to the gate, inside which there is a pair of tall ginkgos on either side of the path leading to the principal hall, behind which is the tomb mound in a white-walled enclosure. On both sides of the principal axis and beyond is a large shady garden in which there are further buildings. Although attention has rarely been drawn to it, this is one of Yangzhou's most interesting gardens. There is much complex rockwork and an earth mountain, at the base of which a cascade runs into a pond edged with rocks of fanciful shape (fig. 5.53). Owing to the sheltered nature of the site, the surface of the water remains calm and reflections add much to the mood of the garden. And in one of the subsidiary courtyards there is a raised stone bed of begonia-blossom shape, planted with tree peonies and ornamented with a Taihu rock.

Figure 5.52 (right) **Yangzhou Museum**

Figure 5.53 (below) **Garden of the Shi Kefa Memorial Hall**

GEYUAN (GE GARDEN)

There is an entrance to this garden on the opposite side of Yanfu Road to the above, but the main entrance is in Dongguan Road which runs parallel further south. It is traditionally said to have been designed by the famous Yangzhou painter Shi Tao (1642–c.1717) for a salt merchant, Huang Zhiyu, but apparently no proof of this has been found. It was remodelled in the 19th century by Huang Yingtai and named after his byname, Geyuan (Tung, 1997). It is also known as the Bamboo Garden because the three strokes which make up the character 'ge' 个 resemble bamboo leaves.

As is often the case, the garden lies to the north of the residential buildings. It is unusual in that it consists largely of scenes representing the four seasons. It is entered between two raised beds of bamboo, amongst which 'stone bamboo shoots' have been arranged to suggest spring (fig. 5.54). There is a pond more or less in the centre of the main garden, which is overlooked by a hexagonal pavilion on its north-east side and by the Osmanthus Hall, the main building in the garden, on its southern side. To the north-west of this is an elaborate mountain of eroded limestone representing summer. This has a pool and grotto at its base and a small square pavilion at the summit, beside which a wisteria grows over the rocks (fig. 5.55). A tortuous path leads up through the interior of this to a veranda on the upper storey of a 7-bayed building

Figure 5.54 (left) **Beds representing spring, Geyuan, Yangzhou**

Figure 5.55 (below) **Mountain representing summer, Geyuan**

which lies across the northern boundary. The eastern end of this veranda gives access to the top of another mountain, the Autumn Mountain, made of blocks of huangshi rock, down through which a narrow path leads to ground level (fig. 5.56). Then in the south-east corner of the garden there is an arrangement of whitish rocks representing a mountain range in winter, the ground in front of which is paved with flat white stones in a 'cracked ice' pattern. Looking west from here through a round window there is a glimpse back to the spring scene, and the circuit is complete (fig. 5.57).

PUHADING MUYUAN (TOMB OF PUHADDIN)

While the present Grand Canal is a little east of the city, its earlier course runs along the eastern and southern sides of the old city. The Tomb of Puhaddin is on the eastern bank of the old canal overlooking a bamboo market. Puhaddin was a Moslem teacher, said to be a 16th-generation descendant of the Prophet. He died in Yangzhou in 1275 and his tomb is in a small rectangular building with a vaulted ceiling. This and other buildings showing a mixture of Chinese and Arab influences are grouped here in a garden setting quite different from any other in Yangzhou (fig. 5.58).

HEYUAN (HE GARDEN)

This garden is named after its late 19th-century owner He Zhidao (Chen, 1983), who enlarged and rebuilt an earlier garden, the Jixiao Shanzhuang (Resounding Roars Mountain Villa). It is entered from the east and in the centre of the first courtyard there is a two-storeyed building to the north of

Figure 5.56 (above left) Geyuan, central courtyard with the autumn mountain of huangshi rock in the background

Figure 5.57 (above right) Geyuan, looking through an opening from the winter scene to that representing spring

Figure 5.58 (below) Entrance to the Tomb of Puhaddin, Yangzhou

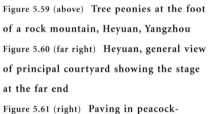

Figure 5.59 (above) Tree peonies at the foot of a rock mountain, Heyuan, Yangzhou

Figure 5.60 (far right) Heyuan, general view of principal courtyard showing the stage at the far end

Figure 5.61 (right) Paving in peacock-feather pattern, Heyuan

which is a rock mountain with a bed of red tree peonies at its base (fig. 5.59). On the top there is a small hexagonal pavilion which overlooks a narrow waterway. The remainder of the area is covered with pebble paving in a wave pattern (fig. 1.35), one of the patterns included by Ji Cheng in his *Yuanye* of 1634 (Ji, 1988). A rock pile, over which *Rosa banksiae* has been trained, occupies the south-eastern corner of this space, and beyond this is the entrance to the principal courtyard. This is filled almost entirely by a large pool on three sides of which there are two-storeyed buildings with open verandas on their upper levels from which there are views down onto the garden and a stage which has been built out over the water at the eastern end (fig. 5.60). A fanciful bridge leading to this is made of foraminate rock, the use of which for such structures was one of the things Wen Zhenheng in the 17th century considered vulgar. The area bordering the pond on the northern side is paved with pebbles in a peacock-feather pattern (fig. 5.61). Growing here are two tall specimens of *Trachycarpus fortunei*.

In the south-western corner of this courtyard is a rock mountain on which *Pinus bungeana* has been planted and which can be ascended by a tortuous path. To the south of this a path leads through a building to another courtyard with trees and rocks, and beyond this is the entrance to the neighbouring garden, the Pianshi Shanfang.

PIANSHI SHANFANG (STONE SLAB MOUNTAIN LODGE)

The Pianshi Shanfang is another late Qing garden and was originally owned by the Wu family. Here most of the features typical of Chinese gardens are grouped in a modest space. It consists of walkways and open pavilions which overlook a pond on the northern side of which fanciful rock mountains pierced with grottoes have been built against the wall of the adjoining property (fig. 5.62). Behind the buildings is a series of small courtyards with white walls pierced with openwork

Figure 5.62
(left)
**Pianshi
Shanfang,
Yangzhou**

windows and doors in the shape of a vase, a begonia blossom
and the new moon (figs 1.6, 5.63).

XIAOPANGU (SMALL WINDING VALLEY)

The Xiaopangu is a short distance north-west of the Heyuan.
At the time of my visit the residential portion had been separated and had become a hotel, and entry to the garden portion was gained only after a lengthy discussion with the caretaker. According to Cheng (1999) it was laid out during the
Guangxu period (1875–1908) and used to be the residence
of Zhou Fu, Governor of Guangdong and Guangxi.

The garden is unique amongst those of Yangzhou in that
it is divided in two longitudinally by a high wall running
north-south. Not far from the entrance a peach-shaped opening in this wall gives access to the eastern half (fig. 5.64). This
is flat and now contains little of inter-
est. However running along the wall
and rising up it towards the north is a
roofed walkway which leads to a
hexagonal pavilion sitting on top of a
rock mountain. This pavilion looks
down onto both parts of the garden
and from it steps lead down into the
western half where there is a winding
pond crossed by a bridge. On the eastern side of the pond there are covered
walkways and garden buildings with
open verandas which look out onto it
(fig. 5.65). The garden is filled with
rocks in the local manner, and
amongst the plants clumps of bananas
are conspicuous.

WEIPU (LUXURIANT GARDEN)

This is another garden to which I gained entry with the permission of the caretaker. It consists of one tiny court-yard of a house which belonged to the Chen family. It is entered through a wall on the western side and on the eastern side is bounded by the former residential quarters, now used as municipal offices. A short, roofed walkway runs along the northern wall to a tiny pavilion built into the north-western corner. This is surrounded on two sides by a narrow pond enclosed by a stone balustrade. Another walkway runs along the southern wall. In the north-east corner of the courtyard there is a small arrangement of rocks and shrubs, and in the south-west, beside the entrance, is a tall rock mountain, honeycombed with large cavities. Over this a white wisteria is growing and in front of it there are weeping sophoras and other plants. The remainder of the area is paved with flat stones in a cracked-ice pattern. The pots of *Buxus microphylla* var. *sinica* lined up in front of the old residential building at the time of my visit seem unlikely to have been part of the original composition (fig. 5.66).

Looking out from their rooms the family would have seen a landscape of mountains, water, trees and shrubs, a notable example of what can be achieved in a small area. Almost all the features typical of the Chinese garden have been incorporated into a space measuring approximately 6×10 m without its seeming overcrowded.

Figure 5.64 (left)

Peach-shaped doorway,

Xiaopangu, Yangzhou

Figure 5.65 (above)

Rock, water and buildings,

Xiaopangu

Figure 5.66 (right)

Weipu, Yangzhou

QIONGHUAGUAN (JADE FLOWER TEMPLE)

This Daoist temple was built in 11 BC and at that time its name was Houtuci. During the Sui, Tang and Northern Song it was renowned for a shrub known as Qionghua (Jade Flower). So admired was this plant that a pavilion was built next to it with the inscription 'Without Peer'. It was even said that the Grand Canal had been dug so that Yangdi, the second emperor of the Sui dynasty, could travel from Luoyang to see it. During the Song the name of the temple was changed to Panliguan but it was destroyed and the plant removed by the Jin when they came south in 1129. In spite of several investigations, beginning later in the 12th century,

its identity has remained uncertain ever since. However it is now generally believed in Yangzhou that it was *Viburnum macrocephalum* f. *keteleeri*, the wild type of the familiar snowball tree (fig. 5.67). It has been adopted as the floral emblem of the city and is widely planted there, including at the temple, which has recently been restored and opened to the public as the Jade Flower Temple, the name by which it has long been known to the local people (fig. 5.68).

Nanjing

Nanjing, the capital of Jiangsu province, has been a city of some importance for at least 2000 years. It was the capital of several regimes during the Three Kingdoms and Six Dynasties periods and later the first capital of the Ming. More recently it was the capital of the Taiping Heavenly Kingdom (1851–64) and of Chiang Kai-shek's Nationalist Government.

In spite of extensive modern developments, Nanjing retains much of the character it developed when it was the capital in the 1920s and 30s. In the central part of the city there are still Western-style buildings dating from that time and the plane trees planted then now arch over the broad streets. And in spite of the devastation it has suffered over the centuries, many interesting relics remain including much of the old city wall. There are several parks, the largest of which is the Xuanwu Lake Park just outside the northwestern part of the wall. The lake itself covers almost 450 hectares and there are five small islands connected by bridges and causeways.

A large scenic area lies immediately to the west of the city on the southern slopes of Zijin Shan (Purple Gold Mountain). Amongst the sights here is the Xiaoling, the tomb of the first Ming emperor, construction of which was completed in 1383, 15 years before he died.

Figure 5.67 (above left) **The Jade Flower (*Viburnum macrocephalum f. keteleeri*)**

Figure 5.68 (left) **Jade Flower Temple, Yangzhou, undergoing restoration in 1995**

Figure 5.69 Stone elephants on the approach to the Ming Tomb, Nanjing

Comparatively little remains of the buildings, though the stone animals and figures lining the approaches to the tomb mound are impressive. These were seen by the Rev. Williamson (1870) in the 1860s, when presumably they were standing in the bare landscape shown in the subsequent photographs of John Thomson (1873–74), Mrs Little (1901) and A.S Roe (1910). Now, however, trees have been planted amongst them (fig. 5.69). Further on are the imposing Sun Yat-sen Mausoleum and the concrete Linggu Pagoda. All of this park-like region is of minor horticultural interest. Also here is the Nanjing Sun Yat-sen Botanical Garden, which is described briefly below along with the principal gardens of the city itself.

ZHANYUAN (LOOK FORWARD GARDEN)

Although it has been altered in recent times, this is the most significant garden in Nanjing. It is in the southern part of the city not far north of the Zhonghua Gate and is entered through the Taiping Museum, which commemorates the uprising of 1850–64. The museum is housed in a residence once used by Yang Xiuqing, one of the 'Heavenly Princes', as the Taiping leaders were known, and Lai Hanying, Vice

Premier at the time. It incorporated this old garden which was said to be the residence of Xu Da, a general who helped the first Ming emperor found the dynasty, though the actual laying out of the garden probably dates from the early 16th century. An early 18th-century handscroll shows that at that time it was notable for its rockeries, caverns and individual rocks. Later in that century it was visited twice by Qianlong, in whose calligraphy the name Zhanyuan is inscribed over the entrance. His admiration for the garden was such that he had a replica made at the Yuanmingyuan near Beijing.

The Zhanyuan was largely destroyed when the Taipings were defeated but was restored in the late 19th century— badly, according to Tung (1936). In the 1930s it was divided between a school and a government ministry, but eventually it was completely renovated and extended in the second half of the 20th century. The main additions have been a new rock mountain at its southern end, designed by Professor Liu Dunzhen, and a new area on the eastern side. Nevertheless the old layout largely remains and the innovations blend in harmoniously.

The garden occupies a narrow site running north-south and is entered on the eastern side opposite the widest part of

(Hall of Superb Tranquillity), on the northern side of which is a pergola covered with *Wisteria sinensis* 'Alba'. On the southern side an open veranda looks across an extension of the lake to the new rock mountain (fig. 5.71). To the east of this is a new extension with a waterway surrounded by rocks, walkways and pavilions (fig. 5.72). The garden is ornamented throughout with traditional plants, including *Kerria japonica*, *Rosa banksiae*, *Iris tectorum*, willows, pines, camellias and *Mahonia bealei*.

XIYUAN (WEST GARDEN)

This garden, sometimes also called the Xuyuan (Warm Garden), is close to the centre of the city and, like the Zhanyuan, dates from the Ming and is on a narrow site running north-south. As is so often the case, the garden has had a complex history and how far it now resembles the original is unclear. It became incorporated in the palace of Hong Xiuquan, the leader of the Taipings, which was destroyed when they were defeated in 1864. Apparently little survived other than the lake and the base of the land boat. Nonetheless, in its present restored form it is an interesting garden in traditional style.

The entrance is in the south-east corner where there are several tall wutongs (*Firmiana simplex*). A small hexagonal pavilion stands on a rockery near the entrance and to the right is a large building, the Sound of the Wutongs Pavilion. Further on is the Mandarin Duck Pavilion, with an unusual design of two interlocking squares. Beyond this the Untied Boat sits in the southern end of the lake (fig. 5.73), the edge of which is overhung

the lake. At the northern end there is a large rock mountain, the lower parts of which are believed to be the remains of a Ming construction (fig. 5.70). There are artificial hills surmounted by pavilions on the western side and a zigzagging roofed walkway along the eastern side. Towards the southern end of the garden is its principal building, the Jingmiaotang

Figure 5.70 (opposite page top)
Old rock mountain, Zhanyuan,
Nanjing
Figure 5.71 (opposite page bottom)
New rock mountain, Zhanyuan
Figure 5.72 (right) A recent
extension at the Zhanyuan
Figure 5.73 (below) Land-boat,
Xiyuan, Nanjing

Figure 5.74 (left) **A multiflora hybrid rose, Xiyuan**

Figure 5.75 (above) **Statue of Lu Mochou, Mochou Lake, Nanjing**

by a multiflora rose (fig. 5.74). There are three other buildings on the edge of the lake, the two-storeyed Beautiful Sunset Pavilion on the western side, the Ripples Pavilion to the north, and the Waterside Pavilion on the eastern shore.

Beyond the northern end of the lake, in a separate area, there is a Western-style building which was used as an office by Sun Yat-sen and in which there is an exhibition of old photographs and mementoes. In front of this a modern formal garden has been laid out.

MOCHOU HU (MOCHOU LAKE)

This lake is named after Lu Mochou, a woman of the Southern Qi kingdom (479–502), who is supposed to have lived here. It is just outside the line of the western wall of the old city and has been a famous scenic spot at least since the Song. It is said that the first Ming emperor played chess here

with his general Xu Da in the Winning Chess Hall, though presumably the present building of that name must do no more than commemorate that alleged event.

After 1949 the area was rejuvenated and is said to have become the city's most admired park, though it may not be everyone's cup of tea. Various buildings are grouped along the southern shore of the lake, rockeries have been constructed, and a statue of Lu Mochou now stands in the middle of a pond in one of the courtyards (fig. 5.75). A wide range of traditional Chinese garden plants has been established, including bananas, lotuses, snowball trees, *Paulownia fortunei*, various crabapples, *Wisteria sinensis* and flowering peaches.

Owing to its popularity this park exhibits the well-worn look which is so often the lot of such places. And from time to time it falls victim to the vagaries of taste. When I visited it, a subsidiary lake, with water so enriched that it was completely covered by floating weeds, had clusters of red and yellow umbrellas distributed over its entire surface (fig. 5.76). I suspect that, with its auspicious colours, this expression of creativity received much approval.

NANJING ZHONGSHAN ZHIWUYUAN
(NANJING SUN YAT-SEN BOTANICAL GARDEN)

This botanical garden, one of the earliest to be established in China, is located at the southern foot of Zijin Shan. It was founded in 1929 in memory of Sun Yat-sen but its development was curtailed by the difficult conditions which followed. It was severely damaged by war but restored in 1954, although it seems likely that it faced further difficulties during the Cultural Revolution. Now, however, it is once more a research centre and has greenhouses for frost-tender plants and collections of coniferous, medicinal, rare and endangered, and ornamental plants. Amongst these is a collection of cultivars of *Prunus mume*, which was chosen as the Chinese national flower by the government of Chiang Kai-shek (fig. 5.77). Now what is perhaps the most renowned of all Chinese flowers has to be content with being merely the floral emblem of Nanjing.

Figure 5.76 (below) **Umbrellas arranged on the weed-covered surface of a pond, Mochou Lake, Nanjing**

Figure 5.77 (right) **A double white cultivar of *Prunus mume*, Nanjing Sun Yat-sen Botanical Garden**

Figure 5.78 Yanyulou, Jiaxing

and wheat, the rice planting was just beginning, the first batches of leaves were being taken from the mulberry plantations, and beside the occasional fields of wild rice (*Zizania aquatica*) people were preparing the stems for market. These stems, which become swollen as a result of infection by a smut fungus, are prized as a vegetable. I ordered some at a restaurant and found them to be excellent.

Zhejiang

Although like Jiangsu it is one of China's smallest provinces, Zhejiang is also one of the most densely populated and affluent. As well as being a leader in tea, silk, ceramic and agricultural production, it has also been one of the great cultural centres of China. It was the site of a number of early kingdoms and after the fall of the Northern Song dynasty in 1126 the court fled south and established the Southern Song dynasty with its capital at Hangzhou (then called Lin'an). Here the West Lake had long been a famous scenic area and it became the focus of the new capital. Both imperial and private gardens were built around its shores and others were built in the countryside and in the towns and cities of the region. The arts, which had reached new heights during the Northern Song, continued to flourish, and poetry, painting, calligraphy and garden-building became intertwined. Several books were written about garden plants in this period, and it was during this time that they accumulated many of the associations and much of the symbolism that they have carried with them to the present day. In particular there was a vogue for the plum (*Prunus mume*), with gardeners, poets, painters and calligraphers all becoming involved.

Jiaxing

Jiaxing is an old town, now much modernised, which is almost exactly halfway between Shanghai and Hangzhou. Immediately to the east of the railway station is the Nan Hu (South Lake), on an island in which stands the Yanyulou, another of the places mentioned by Shen Fu (1809).

At the time of my visit in late May, the surrounding countryside was full of interest. Farmers were harvesting rapeseed

YANYULOU (MISTY RAIN PAVILION)

The Yanyulou was constructed in 1549 on the ruins of a building dating from 940. It was rebuilt early in the Qing dynasty but the entire group of buildings was burnt down by the Taipings. The site was not restored until 1919 and, judging by appearances, it has been renovated in recent years as well. As mentioned earlier, the Yanyulou served as a model for similar buildings at Chengde and beside the Slender West Lake at Yangzhou.

A ferry from the eastern shore of the Nan Hu provides regular access to and from the island, which is a local tourist attraction and usually presents an animated scene. The Yanyulou is framed by a pair of huge old ginkgos (fig. 5.78), and there are fine specimens of *Koelreuteria paniculata*, *Podocarpus macrophyllus*, *Ilex cornuta*, *Cinnamomum camphora*, flowering peaches, loquats, camellias, Chinese box and many other plants in its garden. Behind the pavilion is an elaborate rockery which had children climbing all over it at the time of my visit.

Of interest, moored against the south-eastern shore of the island, is the boat to which the founders of the Chinese Communist Party withdrew in July 1921 to complete their deliberations after their inaugural congress in Shanghai was broken up by the police. Of note, too, are the entrepreneurs who sell water caltrops (*Trapa bicornis*), which they cook in ancient pressure cookers and sell to the tourists. It is claimed they are a product of the lake.

Haiyan

Haiyan is a flourishing town about 30 km south-east of Jiaxing, on the coast of Hangzhou Bay. At the northern end of the town centre there is a restored garden, the Qiyuan.

QIYUAN (BEAUTIFUL GARDEN)

According to Tung (1997) this garden dates back to the early Qing. It was repaired and restored in the 19th century by a scholar-official named Huang who renamed it Zhuoyiyuan (Garden Suitable for the Stupid). After its destruction by the Taipings the site was inherited by his son-in-law, a Mr Feng, who commenced a new garden there in 1871 and named it Qiyuan. According to Tung (1997), the layout suffered from lack of funds and scholarly taste. Nevertheless it has recently been repaired and is open to the public.

Immediately inside the entrance there are displays of penjing and potted annuals, and beyond, through a moon gate, lies the main part of the garden. This is divided in two by a central ridge planted with trees and covered with rockwork, including stone bamboo shoots made of petrified wood. On the eastern side is a large pavilion beside a narrow winding ravine crossed by a zigzag bridge and with further rockwork and grottoes beyond (fig. 5.79). The water in this ravine curves round the northern end of the ridge and widens into an extensive lake on the western side. Here it is crossed by a stone bridge of classical design with a climbing rose with clusters of small single white flowers festooning a dead tree at one end (fig. 5.80). This rose appeared to me to be a wild form of *Rosa multiflora*. On the opposite side of the bridge an

Figure 5.79 (following pages) **Pavilion overlooking the gorge, Qiyuan, Haiyan**

Figure 5.80 (below) **Bridge at the head of the lake, Qiyuan**

enormous wisteria has climbed a camphor laurel and, at the end of the lake nearest the entrance, there is a waterside pavilion now used as a tea house. Shaded by huge ginkgos, koelreuterias and other trees, in which birds were singing, I found walking round this garden a most agreeable experience, regardless of what Tung (1997) thought about it.

Hangzhou

Hangzhou, the capital of Zhejiang province, first came into prominence in the early 7th century after it was reached by the Grand Canal. Subsequently it blossomed when it became the capital of the Southern Song, after the court had been driven from Kaifeng in 1126. The city then became one of the most splendid in the world and there are numerous accounts of its magnificence. By the 13th century it had a population of more than a million and was renowned for the beauty of its lake and for its palaces, temples and gardens. During succeeding regimes it remained an important commercial and cultural centre and, during the Qing, was amongst the sites in the south visited by Kangxi and Qianlong.

The splendours of Hangzhou, no doubt by this time somewhat faded, were wiped out in 1862 when the Taipings destroyed the city and slaughtered most of the population. It gradually recovered, as cities usually do, and most of the temples were rebuilt in the late 19th and early 20th centuries. Even so, photographs taken of the West Lake in this period show a treeless and rather desolate scene (fig. 5.81). And, although the

Figure 5.81 (left) Mrs Little's photograph of the Bai Causeway, West Lake, Hangzhou. FROM MRS LITTLE (1901).

Figure 5.82 (below) Bai Causeway, West Lake, 1996

city continued to attract the well-to-do, Tung (1936) wrote the following unenthusiastic description of it at this time:

> Although a peer of Soochow in scenic beauty since olden times, Hangchow has lost its supremacy in garden craft. The invasion of commercialism and civic improvement, which often takes the form of European monstrosity, have quite rapidly destroyed charming old landmarks to which the city owed its fame. Hangchow, regarding gardens, has little to its credit today save quantity. The ever increasing number of villas smacks more of the parvenu than the literary and artistic.

In spite of everything that has happened, it would be unreasonably harsh to say that things are not much better now. Although many of the city's surviving monuments were damaged once more during the Cultural Revolution they have been restored, there has been much replanting, new public gardens have been developed, and the landscape of the West Lake continues to attract admiration. Tourists pour in, seemingly unaware of the changes which have taken place.

As well as the sites described below there are the Botanical Garden of the Zhejiang Agricultural University and the Zhejiang Bamboo Botanical Garden, upon which I am not in a position to comment as I have not visited them.

XI HU (WEST LAKE)

For convenience, I have described under this heading not only the lake and its islands but gardens and features on or close to its shore. Those further afield are dealt with under separate headings.

The West Lake, surrounded by hills on three sides, has been admired for centuries, and its appearance has greatly improved since Mrs Little saw it (fig. 5.82). It was originally an inlet in the estuary of the Qiantang River. This estuary is famous for its tidal bore which, before the lake became separated by siltation, used to force water inland and cause the city to be flooded. During the Tang the first dike was built with bridges and locks to control the flow of water. The dike was strengthened in the 9th century by the famous poet, Bai Juyi, who was serving as the city's governor at the time, and it was named after him. In the late 11th century a second dike was constructed in the lake when another poet, Su Dongpo, was the governor, and this is named after him.

Liulangwenying (Listening to the Orioles in the Waving Willows), Nanpingwanzhong (Evening Bell at Southern Screen [Hill]), Leifengxizhao (Sunset Glow at Thunder Peak [Pagoda]), Santanyinyue (Three Pools Mirroring the Moon), Huagangguanyu (Observing the Fish at Flower Harbour), Sutichunxiao (Spring Dawn at the Su Causeway), Quyuanfenghe (Lotuses in the Breeze at Crooked Garden), and Shuangfengchayun (Twin Peaks Piercing the Clouds). The last of these is actually some distance to the west of the lake on the road to the Lingyin Temple and others no longer properly exist. All the same, a circuit of the lake still leads visitors past the sites of the 'prospects' and enables a variety of gardens and landscapes to be seen.

The Baochuta (Protect Chu Pagoda), first built in the 10th century, is one of the chief focal points of the scene and stands on a hill at the north-east corner of the lake. At the foot of this hill the Bai Causeway runs across the water to Gushan Island. The causeway is lined with flowering peaches and willows and there are two handsome stone bridges. The first of these, the Broken Bridge, is the site of the prospect known as Melting Snow on Broken Bridge. On the eastern end of Gushan Island, close to where the causeway ends, there is a pavilion and terrace—the site for viewing the Autumn Moon on the Calm Lake. From here a path along the northern side of the island leads to the Crane Pavilion, which stands beneath enormous camphor laurels on the far side of a zigzag bridge (fig. 5.83). This pavilion was first built in the Yuan in memory of the poet Lin Hejing (967–1028), who lived there for 20 years planting plum trees and rearing cranes. On the southern side of the island is the area where Qianlong constructed a palace, including a library, the Wenlan'ge. This was built to hold one of three additional copies of the *Siku quanshu* which he had had made. All this was destroyed by the Taipings and the buildings now there house the Zhejiang Provincial Museum. Nearby is the headquarters of the Seal-engravers' Society of Zhejiang, founded in 1903, which includes a garden which stretches up the hill behind, where there are many plants of the single red *Camellia japonica* (fig. 5.84). Much of this hilly island is now a park, yet another Zhongshan Park, formed from the remains of the old imperial garden. From the path along the southern shore there are views of two picturesque islands

Figure 5.83 (above) Crane Pavilion, Gushan Island, Hangzhou

Figure 5.84 (left) Wild type of *Camellia japonica*, Gushan Island, Hangzhou

The lake has long been a tourist attraction and has been thronged with pleasure boats, as it is now, from early times. In accordance with traditional Chinese practice, 'prospects' around the lake were given names, each of four characters. These 10 scenes, all of which had been completed by the time the Song court arrived in Hangzhou (Chen & Yu, 1986), are Pinghuqiuyue (Autumn Moon on the Calm Lake), Duanqiaocanxue (Melting Snow on Broken Bridge),

Figure 5.85 (opposite page) **Crooked Garden, West Lake**

Figure 5.86 Guozhuang, West Lake

as the Quyuan (Crooked Garden) and has been revived and enlarged in recent years (fig. 5.85). Many traditional garden plants have been established and about 100 lotus varieties are cultivated in the ponds. Close to this, on the western shore, there is a restored private garden of the late Qing, Guozhuang (Guo's Villa) (fig. 5.86). This is laid out in traditional style with pavilions, rockeries and walkways round a pool, in a manner reminiscent of the Tuisiyuan at Tongli.

The Su Causeway, like the Bai, is planted with willows and flowering peaches. However there are also many other plants here and there, including a very pale form of *Wisteria sinensis* and clumps of *Jasminum mesnyi*. Looking west from the northern end there is a good view of the waterside pavilion of Jiangzhuang (Jiang's Villa), a late

which lie further out in the lake and can be reached by ferry. The eastern one is dominated by the Huxinting (Mid-lake Pavilion), first built in 1552. The present structure, with double eaves and a yellow-tiled roof, dates from 1953. The western island, Ruandun Huanbi (Ruan's Mound Encircled by Blue [Water]), was formed from mud dredged from the lake on the instructions of an official named Ruan. Most of the buildings on it are occupied by shops and restaurants.

At the western end of Gushan Island there is a bridge back to the shore near the northern end of the Su Causeway. Close to the lake in this region the garden of the Shangri La Hotel is quite attractive, with rocks, azaleas and other plants arranged under camphor laurels. The Tomb of Yue Fei is in a similar position a little to the west. Yue Fei (1103–42) was a general of the Southern Song who became a popular hero on account of his extreme loyalty. He was buried by the lake and a temple to his memory was erected here in 1221. The temple was destroyed by the Taipings but rebuilt in the late 19th century. There was further damage during the Cultural Revolution but it has been restored once more. The courtyards are of interest for their old trees which obviously did not attract the attention of either the Taipings or the Red Guards. Amongst these are camphor laurels and a specimen labelled *Celtis julianae*, all said to be 700 years old. On the opposite side of the road there is a penjing garden on the edge of the water.

In the north-west corner of the lake is the area where, at the appropriate time of the year, visitors can still view the Lotuses in the Breeze at Crooked Garden. This is still known

Figure 5.87 **View of the garden at Flower Harbour, West Lake**

Figure 5.88 **One of the four pools at**
Xiaoying Zhou, West Lake

Qing garden mentioned by Tung (1936) and Yoshikawa (1990). And, of course, it is from the middle of the causeway that the Spring Dawn at the Su Causeway should be viewed.

On the western side of the causeway, at its southern end, is Huaguang (Flower Harbour) Park, the site of Observing the Fish at Flower Harbour. Lin Qing went to see this sometime in the first half of the 19th century but found that the pond was drying up and was in danger of becoming nothing more than a marsh, so he went to observe the fish at a temple nearby instead (Minford, 1993). The park, reputedly established in the Song, has now been rebuilt and there are plenty of fish once more in the pools and plenty of people observing them. As well as this there are rockeries and a wealth of ornamental plants (fig. 5.87). It is also the site of a display of tree peonies in spring. And it is from the jetty on the causeway here that boats leave for Xiaoying Zhou (Small Seas Islet). This low-lying island was made in 1607 from mud dredged from the lake and consists of four pools separated by narrow banks. Pavilions of various kinds add interest to the scene and the banks are planted with trees and shrubs (fig. 5.88). It is from the southern side of this island that the Three Pools Mirroring the Moon can be viewed. Standing in the water here are three small stone lanterns which were erected in 1621 on the site of three earlier ones, said to have been put there by Su Dongbo to prevent people clogging up the lake by growing aquatic plants. The present lanterns are about 2 m tall and have hollow, bulbous bodies. When the moon is full, lighted candles are placed in them and the circular openings covered with paper so that they seem like small moons, their reflections joining that of the real moon in the lake. A.S. Roe (1910) remarked on these when she went to the island on her tour of 1907–09. And Titley and Wood (1991) have drawn attention to the fact that such stone lanterns are still conspicuous in Japanese gardens and that, here, they survive as an isolated example of what must once have been a fashionable garden feature in China.

Figure 5.89 View in Taiziwan Park, Hangzhou

Not far away, at the foot of Nanping Shan (Southern Screen Mountain), just south of the peninsula, is the Jingcisi (Pure Compassion Temple), where the Sound of the Evening Bell used to be heard. The temple was founded in 954 and has undergone restoration on several occasions. In the middle of a pool near the entrance there is a miniature garden which is a stylised model of the temple and the mountain which lies behind (fig. 1.18). The pool in which this garden now stands can be seen in the left foreground of fig. 5.91. Further up the slope, in the courtyard in front of the main hall, there are specimens of the Chinese horse chestnut (*Aesculus chinensis*), which, as mentioned earlier, is planted in temples as a substitute for *Shorea robusta*, the tree under which the Buddha died.

There is less of interest along the eastern side of the lake. A small park occupies the site known as Listening to the Orioles in the Waving Willows, and the lake shore running north from here has been planted with many different ornamentals. Notable amongst these are *Mahonia fortunei*, *Camellia* × *hiemalis*, and the pink form of *Loropetalum chinense*.

Across the road from the southern end of the Su Causeway is a large modern park, Taiziwan Gongyuan (Crown Prince Cove Park). Here there are ponds, waterways and an interesting selection of trees and shrubs. These include Japanese cherries, Japanese maples, *Michelia maudiae* and forms of *Viburnum macrocephalum* (fig. 5.89). In spring this park is also home to a stupendous display of tulips (fig. 5.90).

Further east is a peninsula on which there are government guesthouses and where, before it collapsed in 1924, the Leifeng (Thunder Peak) Pagoda stood. It was originally built in the 10th century and was an important feature of the lake scenery, though the photograph of it in A.S. Roe's (1910) *China as I Saw It* suggests that it was already well on the way to oblivion at the time of her visit (fig. 5.91). In 2000 the local government decided to rebuild this famous landmark and, when work commenced in March 2001, an iron case was unearthed from its foundations. Amongst its contents was a small silver-gilt pagoda inside which was a small gold vessel believed to contain a hair of the Buddha.

WU SHAN (WU HILL)

This hill to the east of the southern end of the West Lake marked the southern boundary of the state of Wu during the Spring and Autumn Period (722–480 BC). The top of the hill is a public park, the site of another prospect known as Wushantianfeng (Heavenly Breeze over Wu Hill). This park is popular with elderly people and is notable for its camphor laurels which range in age from 400 to 700 years (fig. 5.92).

Figure 5.90 (right) **Tulips, Taiziwan Park, Hangzhou**

Figure 5.91 (right) Thunder Peak Pagoda,
West Lake. FROM A.S. ROE (1910).

Figure 5.92 (above) Tablet beneath an old
camphor laurel, Wu Shan, Hangzhou

Figure 5.93 (top) **View in the garden at the Huanglong Temple, Hangzhou**

Figure 5.94 (above) **Doorways, Huanglong Temple**

HUANGLONGTUCUI
(YELLOW DRAGON SPITTING GREEN)

This name is given to the scenic spot where the Yellow Dragon Cave is situated and it is intended to suggest something along the lines of the creation of exuberant vegetation. The garden here is that of a former Daoist retreat, which was established in the late Qing near the cave. It fell into disrepair but was eventually restored in 1933 (Yoshikawa, 1990). It has been restored again and was opened to the public in 1985. It is set against the north-facing slope of Baoshi Shan (Precious Stone Mountain), the hill which lies across the northern end of the West Lake, and is reached along a path through a small tea plantation, beyond which tall bamboos grow against its whitewashed walls.

I was attracted to this garden by Osvald Sirén's (1949) photographs, which show a pond surrounded by rockeries with an octagonal pavilion beyond and the wooded hill rising behind. The general layout of the area around the pond is much the same today, though the pavilion is new and not quite the same (fig. 5.93). Elsewhere there are courtyards with ornamental planting (fig. 5.94), and beyond this a stepped path leads up the forested slope through fanciful rockeries and past the Yellow Dragon Cave to the hilltop (fig. 5.95). Below, in the main garden, there are various other buildings and courtyards, and amongst the plants there are bananas, wisterias, bamboos, *Ficus pumila*, *Podocarpus macrophyllus* and a 700-year-old *Ilex rotunda* var. *microcarpa*.

When I first visited this garden in 1994 a small orchestra of traditional instruments was playing in the pavilion overlooking the pond and the whole effect was delightful. Since then, however, it has been promoted as a place to visit for those contemplating marriage and special entertainments for them are put on in one of the courtyards. The fundamentals, however, remain intact.

Figure 5.95 (opposite page) **Hillside behind the Huanglong Temple**

Figure 5.96 *Magnolia liliiflora*, Hangzhou Botanical Garden

HANGZHOU ZHIWUYUAN (HANGZHOU BOTANICAL GARDEN)

The Hangzhou Botanical Garden is a little west of the northern end of the lake. It was founded in 1956 on the site of a 5th-century temple and opened to the public in 1965. It covers over 250 hectares and has collections of many different types of plants, including azaleas, camellias, conifers, magnolias (fig. 5.96), bamboos, osmanthuses and medicinal plants. There are pavilions of traditional design in various parts of the garden, a large lake with a waterside pavilion, and greenhouses open to the public. There is also a courtyard complex where displays of seasonal flowers are mounted. When I was there in April 1996 this area was being used for an exhibition of penjing Kurume azaleas.

HANGZHOU HUAYUAN (HANGZHOU FLOWER GARDEN)

In the local tourist literature this is usually referred to in English simply as the 'Flower Nursery'. However this rectangular enclosure, west of the lake a short distance south of the botanical garden, is not a nursery but a collection of penjing and orchids. Just inside the gate there is a famous crepe myrtle which has been trained into the shape of a deer—an auspicious symbol. And growing in the ground a little to the west of this is an unusual camellia, *Camellia grisjii* 'Zhenzhu Cha' ('Pearl Camellia'), which has small, fully double white

flowers. The penjing collection comprises many different tree and shrub species ranging in height from a few centimetres to two or more metres. The orchids, almost all of which are the terrestrial species of *Cymbidium* traditionally favoured by the Chinese, are displayed in a large shade house.

**LINGYINSI
(TEMPLE OF THE SOUL'S RETREAT)**

The Lingyin Temple is a few kilometres west of Hangzhou at the foot of Beigao Feng (Tall North Peak). It was founded by an Indian monk in 326 and is one of the most famous Chan (Zen) temples in China. It is said that in the 10th century there were 3000 monks living here, but the temple has since been through more than its fair share of disasters. It was destroyed during the Taiping Uprising, rebuilt in the early 20th century, damaged by collapses and fire in the 1920s and 30s, restored in 1956, severely damaged during the Cultural Revolution, and repaired once more subsequently.

On the left, immediately inside the entrance is an area where there are modern copies, executed in concrete, of several of China's largest and most famous ancient Buddha statues. Fortunately the principal path avoids this feature and leads directly to the Feilai Feng (Peak that Flew), which apparently is part of an Indian mountain which arrived here miraculously by air sometime before the founding of the temple. The path goes along the far side of a stream which runs along the northern side of this mountain where there are a cliff and caves, on and in which are the most

important group of Buddhist rock carvings south of the Yangtze. There are well over 300 images here, dating from the Five Dynasties to the Yuan (fig. 5.97). The most famous of them is the fat Maitreya popularly known as the Laughing Buddha. Many of the images were defaced by the Red Guards but fortunately many others escaped by being high up and not easily reached.

The principal temple buildings are the huge entrance hall, with a double-eaved roof, and the main hall which is even larger—30 m high with a triple-eaved roof. Between the two is a large courtyard in which there are two stone pagodas said to date from 960 (fig. 5.98). The courtyard is filled with trees, the most impressive of which

Figure 5.97 (left) Buddhist sculptures, Lingyin Temple, Hangzhou
Figure 5.98 (below) Stone pagoda in the principal courtyard, Lingyin Temple

Figure 5.99

Pond dating

from the Song

dynasty,

Shenyuan,

Shaoxing

are a liquidambar (*L. formosana*), which rises above the entrance hall, osmanthuses of considerable stature, and a 500-year-old *Podocarpus macrophyllus*, the lohan pine. The lohan pine is a tree of symbolic significance to Buddhists, the purplish-red seeds of which bear a resemblance to the outer vestments of the lohans. The Lingyin Temple was famous for its collection of 500 ancient statues of lohans which was destroyed by the Taipings. Elsewhere in the grounds there are many kinds of trees, shrubs and bamboos.

LIUHETA (SIX HARMONIES PAGODA)

The Liuhe Pagoda was originally built in 970 on the bank of the Qiantang estuary in the hope of subduing the tidal bore. This landmark, which has been rebuilt or restored on numerous occasions, is one of the famous buildings spared during the Cultural Revolution as a result of the efforts of Zhou Enlai. It now stands surrounded by a modern garden, in which there are wisterias and many other well-known plants.

Shaoxing

Shaoxing, a town of historical significance and renowned for the production of rice wine, is 60 km south-east of Hangzhou. From 770–211 BC it was the capital of the Kingdom of Yue and, much later, it grew rapidly when nearby Hangzhou was the imperial capital during the Southern

Song. It is much praised in guidebooks for its unspoilt character and for the charm of its canals, arched bridges and whitewashed houses. Alas these features are hard to find nowadays, as most of them have been swept away. However, as far as gardens are concerned, there are still the Shenyuan and the Qingteng Shushi in the town itself, and about 3 km to the east is the East Lake, a scenic area formed during the Qing by flooding a quarry. Further afield, 14 km south-west, is the celebrated Lanting.

SHENYUAN (SHEN GARDEN)

The Shenyuan was the garden of the Shen family, originally built in the 12th century. It is now indifferently maintained and only the gourd-shaped pond is original (fig. 5.99). However, this neglected Song pond imposes an air of timelessness on the place, and conspicuous amongst the plants are tree peonies, *Kerria japonica*, *Viburnum macrocephalum* f. *keteleeri* and *Rosa banksiae* 'Lutea', which is not common in Chinese gardens—the double white being the cultivar most frequently planted.

QINGTENG SHUSHI (GREEN VINE STUDIO)

The Qingteng Shushi is a rare surviving example of a Ming house. It was the home of the renowned poet, painter, calligrapher and dramatist, Xu Wei (1521–93). Xu Wei is also remembered for destroying his testicles prior to beating to death his third wife, of whom he had become suspicious. In contrast to his turbulent life, his house and simple garden have a quiet, albeit faded charm. The house has only two main rooms, one of which overlooks a tiny courtyard. The other now houses a small exhibition of paintings, some of them Xu Wei's.

The garden, where the standard of maintenance is similar to that at the Shenyuan, consists merely of a relatively large entrance courtyard and a smaller one on the left of the house. This is separated from the former by a moon gate and contains a few rocks, a rectangular pond and a wisteria (fig. 5.100). In the larger space bamboo has been planted against a whitewashed wall and there are pomegranates, nandinas and osmanthuses. At the time of my visit there were also cymbidiums in pots.

LANTING (ORCHID PAVILION)

The Lanting is a place of pilgrimage for calligraphers, both Chinese and Japanese. It was here, or somewhere nearby, that China's most famous calligrapher, Wang Xizhi, held the famous gathering in 353 at which cups of wine were floated on a stream. Whenever a cup floated in front of a guest, he had to compose a poem at once or forfeit by drinking the wine. In all, 37 poems were written and the collection was

carved in stone with a preface by Wang Xizhi. As a result his calligraphy was preserved and has been treasured and admired ever since.

It was this event, as mentioned in Chapter 2, that inspired others to construct garden pavilions with stone floors carved with sinuous runnels so that groups of friends could play the same game. A more naturalistic open-air version has been re-created outdoors at the Lanting, along the lines of that depicted in paintings of the original gathering (fig. 5.101). Also the present layout of the grounds exhibits a general resemblance to that shown in the woodcut included in Lin Qing's memoirs (Lin, 1847–50).

Figure 5.100 (above right) Tiny courtyard at the Green Vine Studio, Shaoxing

Figure 5.101 (right) Cup-floating stream, Lanting, near Shaoxing

On entering the enclosure a path takes the visitor past a bamboo grove to the Goose Pond, beside which is a small pavilion sheltering a stele with the characters for 'goose' and 'pond' carved on it. It is said that they were written by Wang Xizhi and his son, the father having been interrupted after writing 'goose', leaving the son to write 'pond'. Whatever truth there may be in this, the pool, stocked with white geese and overhung by shrubs through which a wisteria twines, presents a placid scene (fig. 5.102).

Further along from the pool are lotus ponds, pavilions housing steles inscribed by the emperors Kangxi and Qianlong, buildings containing stone slabs carved with the efforts of famous calligraphers, and the re-created cup-floating stream mentioned above. The courtyards are ornamented with various shrubs and pot plants, including *Rohdea japonica* and *Cymbidium goeringii*, both plants heavy with symbolism. I was pleased to find that there were still cymbidiums there, as Wang Xizhi's original Lanting was given this name because it was built on a site where the King of Yue is said to have cultivated orchids hundreds of years earlier.

Ningbo and Environs

From the Song until the end of the Ming, Ningbo was China's most important port, close to the major tea, ceramic and silk-producing areas. To the north of the city centre, across the Xiangjiang Bridge, is the old foreign concession, an area originally occupied by the Portuguese, the first European traders to settle in China. The Portuguese had reached Ningbo about 1517, and by 1533 a trading colony was flourishing there. However, in 1545 a Portuguese adventurer fell foul of the authorities and this triggered off an attack by the imperial forces. More than 1000 Christians were killed, half of them Portuguese, and many ships were burnt (Wood, 1992). After that, in spite of repeated attempts by the British to settle there, it was not until 1842 that the port was opened once more to foreign trade. However, with the rapid development of nearby Shanghai, its importance soon declined.

The old part of Ningbo, where the wealthier officials and merchants lived, lies around Moon Lake, now a recreation area with tea houses and trees, many of them large specimens of *Viburnum odoratissimum*. It is in this district that is found Ningbo's most famous monument, the Tianyige, associated with which is the city's most important garden. From a western horticultural point of view Ningbo is also of interest as it and its environs were the sites of much of the collecting done in China by Robert Fortune, who visited the area during his journeys of 1843–46, 1848–51 and 1852–56. It was in gardens in Ningbo, for instance, that he found the white form of *Wisteria sinensis* and the rose 'Fortune's Yellow' (Fortune, 1846).

Amongst other visitors to record horticultural experiences in and around this city were Miss Gordon Cumming (1890) and Mrs Little (1901). In April 1879 Miss Gordon Cumming went to stay there with Bishop Russell of the English Church Mission. While she was there, a Miss Laurence, who was in charge of the girls' school, was allowed a break from her duties to take her on excursions to temples in the surrounding mountains. Miss Gordon Cumming gave enthusiastic descriptions of the hillsides where there were large white dog-roses (probably *Rosa laevigata*), wisterias, 'thickets of the most gorgeous golden azaleas' (*Rhododendron molle*), an abundance of vividly crimson ones (*R. simsii*) and, on higher levels, 'delicate rose and lilac coloured varieties' (*R. mariesii*). She was also greatly impressed by a paulownia she came across.

Having read what Miss Gordon Cumming had to say about the azaleas, Mrs Little felt that some day she must see them too. The opportunity came some 10 years later when she went on an excursion from Ningbo to

Figure 5.102 The Goose Pond, Lanting, near Shaoxing

Figure 5.103 The Tianyige, Ningbo

neighbouring temples. While she tired of the pink azaleas, preferring the orange and deep red, she revelled in the wisteria, ferns, bamboos and *Cunninghamia sinensis*. All these plants are still there, though not in the abundance they were in earlier times.

TIANYIGE (ONE [ROOM] IN THE SKY PAVILION)

The Tianyige was built between 1561 and 1566 by Fan Qin, an official who had retired to Ningbo with his library of Ming editions. It is the oldest private library in China and, according to the printed guide handed to visitors, the name was derived from an old saying which translates as 'One room in the sky produces water, six rooms on the ground bring peace'. It goes on to say that, in line with this, Fan Qin built a two-storeyed building of six bays, with one large room on the upper floor, and dug pools to protect the books from fire (fig. 5.103). The property subsequently remained in the hands of the Fan family for almost 400 years.

Books were sent from this library to be copied for Qianlong's *Siku quanshu* and, in 1774, an official from Hangzhou was dispatched on the emperor's order to report on the architecture and arrangements of the building, as it was considered that, having survived and to have preserved the books for over two centuries, it must have features worthy of reproduction. As a result of this, as has been mentioned earlier, it became the model for the libraries Qianlong had constructed in various places to house copies of the *Siku quanshu*.

Today the Tianyige looks out onto a pool, on the far side of which is an elaborate rockery shaded by camphor laurels (fig. 5.104). This small garden was constructed in 1665 by Fan Guangwen, a great grandson of Fan Qin, and is notable for its rock arrangements suggesting happiness, wealth and longevity. There are also rocks resembling such things as a lion, a sheep, a goat, an elephant, and a woman looking in a mirror. While this may sound a bit immoderate, in fact the garden presents a charming scene. The rocks are variously clothed with *Ficus pumila* and *Parthenocissus tricuspidata*, and to the left as one looks out from the pavilion there is a

Figure 5.104 (over page) **Garden of the Tianyige**

huge sour orange. At the time of my last visit there were few other visitors, it was drizzling gently, birds were singing, and the orange tree was in bloom, its scent wafting throughout the whole area.

Within the enclosure where the Tianyige stands there is much else to see. Immediately behind the library building is the Zunjingge (Pavilion for Respecting the Classics), a double-eaved pavilion which was originally built at the Ningbo Fuxue (Ningbo Government School), moved to a hilltop in the 19th century, and rebuilt in its present position in 1934 (fig. 5.105). It now stands in its own garden where, amongst other things, there are more orange trees.

Figure 5.105 (below)
The Zunjingge in the grounds of the Tianyige
Figure 5.106 (left)
Iron ox, East Garden, Tianyige

South of the actual Tianyige is the extensive East Garden, opened in 1986. This was begun in 1959 and further developed in the 1980s by Professor Chen Congzhou. Surrounding the lake in this large space are antique buildings, tablets and ornaments brought from elsewhere. Notable amongst these are two large Qing pavilions, an iron ox (fig. 5.106), stone lions in different styles, and the Baie Pavilion (fig. 5.107). This pavilion is a handsome Ming structure of carved stone brought here from Zuguan Mountain in 1959. It originally stood in front of a tomb where it was used for memorial ceremonies.

Also south of the Tianyige and immediately west of the East Garden is the South Garden, completed in 1996. This is similar in style with a lake and rockery, and it contains the Shuibei Pavilion, formerly the library of Xu Shidong, a famous book collector of the late Qing dynasty in eastern Zhejiang.

Beyond the East and South Gardens are further interesting courtyards and buildings, in several of which historical exhibitions have been mounted. Particularly impressive is the ancestral hall of the Fan family, completed in 1925, with its carved and gilded outdoor stage. And throughout the whole area there are interesting examples of penjing (fig. 5.108) and many trees, shrubs and flowers (fig. 5.109).

Figure 5.107 (top) **Baie Pavilion, East Garden, Tianyige,**

Figure 5.108 (right) **Penjing, Tianyige**

Figure 5.109 (above) **Cultivar of *Rosa multiflora*, Tianyige**

Figure 5.110 (above) Lotus pond, Asoka Temple, near Ningbo

Figure 5.111 (left) *Viburnum plicatum*, Asoka Temple

ASOKASI (ASOKA TEMPLE)

This temple, founded in 425 about 20 km east of Ningbo, was named in 522 after Asoka, an Indian king of the 3rd century BC who distributed relics of the Buddha. The Asoka temple has what is said to be one of these, dug up in here in 282 (Strassberg, 1994). The temple is also of interest to Western gardeners as it is one of the sites visited by Robert Fortune. It is likely, too, that, while on her excursion to see the azaleas,

this was the temple at which Mrs Little (1901) stayed before going on to the Tiantongsi the next day. If so, it is where she attended her first Buddhist service and admired the two ginkgos growing outside the hall in which it was held.

The temple complex was most recently restored in 1980. It is extensive and has two large pagodas. The one to the west of the main buildings dates from the 14th century (fig. 5.110). Near the entrance there is a large rectangular lotus pond surrounded by flowering peaches and other trees and shrubs, including *Viburnum plicatum*, now rarely seen in Chinese gardens (fig. 5.111). It was one of the plants which Fortune sent to the Horticultural Society of London from Shanghai.

In the principal courtyard there is a pair of 600-year-old camphor laurels, and in other parts of the temple grounds there are old ginkgos, liquidambars, pines and other large trees. Hydrangeas, gardenias, osmanthuses and many other Chinese garden plants are also to be found.

TIANTONGSI (HEAVENLY CHILD TEMPLE)

This temple, which is about 35 km south-east of Ningbo, was built towards the end of the 3rd century. It became renowned as a centre for Chan Buddhism in the Tang and Song, when it was visited by many famous Japanese monks. On the road from Ningbo the striking Wufo Pagoda is passed, sitting astride a ridge, and a short distance further on an avenue of tall pines leads to the temple.

Robert Fortune stayed here on several occasions and made collections in and around the grounds. It was nearby that he collected *Clematis lanuginosa* in July 1850, and when this plant was introduced to Britain, it became involved in the breeding of the popular large-flowered hybrids. Amongst other visitors were Miss Laurence and Miss Gordon Cumming, who stayed the night here on 1 May 1879. Of her visit Miss Gordon Cumming wrote:

> Everything about this place is venerable and harmonious, especially the colouring of the buildings, the walls of which, like those of the rest houses, are of a rich but faded red, with weather-beaten grey roofs, a background of richly wooded hills, and a quiet pool in the foreground. It is a very large and handsome old monastery, as fine an example as we could wish to see.

After they had settled in, the pair went to explore the surroundings and 'revel in scent and colour on the azalea-covered hills'. And on their way they were interested to find 'the cave home of a genuine old hermit'.

Mrs Little (1901) also stayed the night there while on her excursion to see the azaleas. She admired the approach with its avenues of magnificent trees, the giant trees surrounding the squares, and the lotus ponds. However, she 'did not think much of the temples and the guest-rooms were dark. But the trees behind were beautiful and had enticing paths leading on into the wood.'

While the original altars, statues and interior furnishings of the principal halls suffered the fate of the interiors of most temples during the Cultural Revolution, the scene remains much as Miss Gordon Cumming described it and as it appeared in a photograph taken in the early 20th century by Donald Mennie (1920?). It is still a very large and handsome monastery, beautifully situated against the hillside (fig. 5.112). In front of it, on terraces one above the other, there are two large lotus ponds surrounded by huge old liquidambars and other trees. Climbing the trunk of an old camphor laurel beside the lower pond is an enormous *Trachelospermum jasminoides* (fig. 5.113), and a path to the left of the upper pond leads to the wooded slopes which surround the temple. These are now incorporated in a protected area known as the Tiantong Forest Park, where paths take the visitor past various named rocks, caves and other features and provide an excellent opportunity for observing the native vegetation.

Figure 5.112 Tiantong Temple near Ningbo

Figure 5.113 (left) *Trachelospermum jasminoides* on the trunk of a camphor laurel overhanging the lower lotus pond, Tiantong Temple

Figure 5.114 (above) Miniature landscape, Tiantong Temple

BAOGUOSI (PROTECT THE NATION TEMPLE)
The Baoguo Temple is about 15 km north-west of Ningbo high up in a park-like enclosure on a hillside above the north bank of the Yao River. Its principal claim to fame is the Mahavira Hall built in 1013, which, though restored, is the oldest wooden building in the Yangtze delta region (fig. 5.115). The temple is no longer active and, as the interior of the hall has been stripped of its statues, furnishings and ornaments, there is an unobstructed view of the details of its construction in the Northern Song style.

Nearly all the courtyards of the temple itself are arranged as gardens. Amongst the plants of note are camellias, flowering peaches, sour oranges, pomegranates, *Prunus mume*, *Hibiscus mutabilis* and *H. syriacus*, *Deutzia scabra*, *Michelia maudiae* and a variegated *Serissa japonica*. Also of interest here are several miniature mountains, each standing in a pool, with tiny pavilions here and there and stepped pathways to their summits (fig. 5.114). And from the uppermost levels of the enclosure there are splendid views across to the wooded hillsides, the lower slopes of which support groves of bamboo.

Plants in the temple grounds include *Aesculus chinensis*, *Magnolia denudata*, *M. grandiflora*, *Rohdea japonica*, *Trachycarpus fortunei*, an ancient *Buxus microphylla*, the usual camphor laurels and, at the time of my visit, *Solanum pseudocapsicum* in pots. In the park surrounding the temple are a number of pavilions placed to take in the view, and halfway down to the lower entrance a waterfall emerges from a dragon's head spout.

PUTUO SHAN (MOUNT PUTUO)

This small island, approximately 80 km east of Ningbo, is one of China's four famous Buddhist mountains. Its significance is said to date from 847 when an Indian monk meditating there saw a vision of the bohdisattva Avalokitesvara, who was associated with compassion. The name in Chinese of this bohdisattva is Guanyin, who in China has come to be regarded as feminine and is known generally as the Goddess of Mercy. The significance of Putuo Shan in relation to this bohdisattva was powerfully reinforced in 916 when a Japanese monk was taking a statue of Guanyin from Wutai Shan in Shanxi to Japan and, according to which story you choose to believe, was either shipwrecked there, prevented from continuing by a typhoon, or had his way barred by an iron lotus flower which rose out of the sea. As a result the statue remained on Putuo Shan and the monk retired to a hut in the Zizhulin (Purple Bamboo Grove). This episode was commemorated by the construction of the Bukenqu Guanyinyuan (Temple of Guanyin Unwilling to Depart).

According to another legend Guanyin received enlightenment while meditating on a mountain nearby on the mainland. She then crossed the sea with a single leap, landing on the seashore of Putuo Shan and leaving behind a footprint at a site known as Guanyintiao (Guanyin's Leap) close to the Bukenqu Guanyinyuan and the Purple Bamboo Grove.

These goings on led to the building of more than 200 monasteries and nunneries on the island between the 10th and 12th centuries. However the buildings suffered over the years from pirate attacks, and more recently those which remained were destroyed or seriously damaged during the Cultural Revolution. Nevertheless, many ancient trees have survived (fig. 5.116) and the principal temples have been rebuilt, again attracting crowds both of sightseers and of pilgrims seeking favours from Guanyin.

While a non-believer visiting Putuo Shan can easily overdose on Guanyin, the principal temples and their surroundings have much to attract the attention of those interested in gardens.

Figure 5.115 (above right) Mahavira Hall, Baoguo Temple, near Ningbo

Figure 5.116 (right) Camphor laurel reputedly 1000 years old, Putuo Shan

PUJISI (TEMPLE OF UNIVERSAL SUCCOUR)

The Pujisi, originally built in 1080, is the largest temple on Putuo Shan. In front of it is a series of rectangular lotus ponds crossed by picturesque causeways and bridges (fig. 5.117). The present appearance of this area appears much the same as that shown in John Thomson's (1873–74) photograph taken c.1870 and those of Edwin Howard (1931) taken in 1919 (fig. 5.118). Amongst the trees in this area are some huge old camphor laurels and much younger specimens of the Chinese Tulip Tree (*Liriodendron chinense*), which were in bloom at the time of my visit in May. At this time, too, pots of modern cultivars of *Dianthus chinensis* had been set out to enliven the scene (fig. 5.119).

Within the temple compound itself the buildings are shaded by some magnificent old trees, including 400-year-old camphor laurels (fig. 5.120), a 300-year-old *Juniperus chinensis* and a 200-year-old *Podocarpus macrophyllus*. Also there are edgeworthias, lagerstroemias, hydrangeas, euonymuses and many other ornamental plants. Here, as elsewhere on the island, the branches of many of the trees support a growth of ferns and other epiphytes which are favoured by the frequent showers and fogs to which Putuo Shan is subject.

DACHENG'AN (MAHAYANA NUNNERY)

On a hillside a little to the north of the Puji Temple is the Dacheng Nunnery, the principal feature of which is an undistinguished image of the sleeping Buddha. The path to this passes through small vegetable gardens and orchards of pomelos and mandarins before becoming lined with stalls as the temple is approached. Apart from a century-old

Figure 5.117 (right)   Pavilions and lotus pond, Puji Temple, Putuo Shan

Figure 5.118 (above)   Pavilion and lotus pond, Puji Temple, in 1919. FROM EDWIN HOWARD (1931).

Figure 5.120
(overpage)
Principal
courtyard,
Puji Temple,
Putuo Shan

Figure 5.121
(left)
Dacheng
Nunnery,
Putuo Shan

Figure 5.119
(right)
*Dianthus
chinensis,*
Putuo Shan

osmanthus and some gardenias, nandinas and variegated euonymuses in the principal courtyard (fig. 5.121), there is little of horticultural interest here, though the excursion is pleasant. One can return to the Puji Temple via the Sunrise Viewing Pavilion and Caoyang Cave overlooking the sea, stopping for refreshment at a tea house beside an ancient well overhung by an old tree with the local name of 'hongnan'. Since it had no flowers or fruit I was at a loss to identify it with certainty, though I suspect that it is *Pterocarpus indicus*, the padauk or Burmese rosewood.

FAYUSI (RAIN OF THE DHARMA TEMPLE)

The second largest temple on Putuo Shan and the site with the most to offer those interested in gardens is the Fayu Temple, which overlooks the sea towards the north-east of the island. After crossing a handsome stone bridge over a

Figure 5.122 (right) Entrance to the
Fayu Temple, Putuo Shan

Figure 5.123 (below) *Rhaphiolepis
indica*, Yangzhi Nunnery, Putuo Shan

Figure 5.124 (bottom) Miniature
landscape shrouded in fog, Huiji
Temple, Putuo Shan

lotus pond the pathway to the temple
winds up through a luxuriant forest
of camphor laurels (fig. 5.122). As at
the Puji Temple, the restored buildings
are surrounded by huge trees including,
in addition to the camphor laurels,
liquidambars, junipers, lohan pines,
ginkgos and an ancient hongnan. Also
there is an interesting old specimen of
Camellia japonica, a huge sour orange
which scents the temple grounds when
in bloom, and many other ornamental
plants, including cycads, peaches, plums,
Prunus mume, gardenias, pomegranates,

Figure 5.125

(below)

Hollyhocks,

Bukenqu

Guanyinyuan,

Putuo Shan

HUIJISI (WISDOM ASSISTANCE TEMPLE)

From the Fayu Temple a stepped path leads to the Huiji Temple on top of Foding Shan, at 291 m above sea level the highest point on the island. However, these days most visitors approach this temple from the other side of the island by means of a newly installed cable car. The temple, greatly enlarged between 1793 and 1907, is of no particular distinction but the views are expansive. Amongst the plants in the principal courtyard at the time I was there were pots of *Lilium longiflorum*, which in Chinese gardens now often replaces *L. brownii*, the species previously traditionally grown. There is also a miniature landscape depicting Foding Shan with the temple on its peak (fig. 5.124), and close by is a specimen of the Putuo Hornbeam (*Carpinus putuoensis*), a rare tree indigenous to the island. Also the area around the cable car terminal has been planted with camellias, osmanthuses, *Michelia figo*, Japanese maples and various other trees and shrubs.

BUKENQU GUANYINYUAN (TEMPLE OF GUANYIN UNWILLING TO DEPART)

This temple appears to have been recently restored and occupies a steep site running down to the sea on the end of a small peninsula. The main hall faces the sea and the courtyard in front of it is ornamented with potted plants. From here a path leads down to a small pavilion on a rock overlooking the sea, behind which is another courtyard which, at the time I saw it, was filled with red hollyhocks (fig. 5.125).

As well as this, a large grove of purple bamboo (*Phyllostachys nigra*) has been established on the flat land above the temple and the roadsides nearby have been planted with gardenias, *Euonymus japonica*, *Mahonia bealei*, *Hypericum monogynum* and *Podocarpus neriifolius*. And, a short distance to the south, an astonishing 30 m high statue of Guanyin has recently been built on an elaborate platform overlooking Guanyin's Leap.

oleanders, crepe myrtles, tree peonies, *Buxus microphylla*, hollyhocks and osmanthuses. The sloping site and the luxuriant growth promoted by the damp climate add much to the charm of the place.

YANGZHIAN (POPLAR BRANCH NUNNERY)

To the left of the entrance to the Fayu Temple another path leads beneath enormous liquidambars to the Yangzhi Nunnery, where there are further interesting plants (fig. 5.123) and a Tang stele bearing an incised depiction of Guanyin, which escaped the attention of the Red Guards. And between the Fayu Temple and the sea is a modern park and a Sea Viewing Pavilion into which those so inclined may climb.

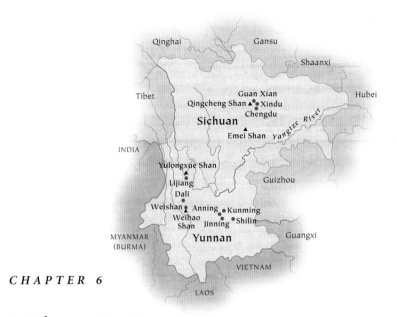

CHAPTER 6

The West

This chapter is devoted to Sichuan and Yunnan. With their remoteness and their populations which include various minority races, these provinces have distinctive characteristics. And, abutting what is in effect the eastern end of the Himalayas, they have the richest floras in China. Thus it is not surprising that from the middle of the 19th century to the present day this region has been a favourite hunting ground of foreign plant collectors. This circumstance seems also to have stimulated Chinese botanists here to take a greater interest in their own flora, with the result that many previously unknown species have been collected, described and brought into cultivation.

Some of the most handsome plants of the region, however, were brought into cultivation by the local inhabitants long ago. It appears that a few of these found their way across to the east and became favourite garden plants in the centres of wealth and power. It seems likely that some of the roses and crabapples,

Figure 6.1 View from Weibao Shan, Yunnan

Figure 6.2 *Michelia yunnanensis*

for instance, originated in the west. But other plants, partic-ularly some of those long cultivated in Yunnan, for example *Magnolia delavayi*, *Michelia yunnanensis* (fig. 6.2), *Prunus cerasoides*, *Cupressus duclouxiana* and most cultivars of *Camellia reticulata* appear not to have been taken to other parts of the country, not even to neighbouring Sichuan. On the other hand, most of the traditional garden plants of other parts of the country have found their way to the west, prob-ably hundreds of years ago.

While there are few traditional gardens in western China, the grounds of many temples in the region are both pic-turesque and horticulturally interesting, as are some of the newer parks. However, little has been written about them, at least in European languages.

I have not been to Tibet so I know nothing of gardens there. However, Qiao (1982) and Qiao and Sun (1982) men-tion and illustrate the Norbu Lingka (Treasure Garden) in Lhasa, calling it the summer palace of the Dalai Lama. They say it dates from the Qing and contains monasteries, lily ponds, pavilions, paths paved in ornamental patterns, and various rare animals and birds.

Sichuan

Sichuan, the second-largest province of China, is located in the western part of the Yangtze valley. Apart from the Yellow River valley, it was the first area of China to be settled by the Han Chinese, an organised migration taking place in the 5th

century BC. As a result it has had a long relationship with the centres of power in the east of the country. Presumably this is why the gardens here reflect this rather than Sichuan's own flora and its proximity to Yunnan. *Camellia reticulata*, for instance, does not appear to be grown, although I have seen young plants of the double Yunnan cherry—presumably a recent introduction.

The name Sichuan means 'Four Streams', and refers to the four large tributaries which flow into the Yangtze within its borders. It is one of the most populous regions of the coun-try, particularly in the eastern basin area, which is surround-ed on all sides by mountains. With its mild humid climate and fertile soils, this is one of the most prosperous and eco-nomically self-sufficient parts of the country. These features, together with its geographical isolation, have from time to time encouraged political separatism. And during the war with Japan, the Japanese failed to penetrate the area and the province served as the seat of the Nationalist government from 1938 to 1946.

Sichuan has a long horticultural history. For instance, as early as the 10th and 11th centuries the city of Tianpeng became famous as a centre of tree peony cultivation. The province has also been paid much attention by the plant hunters, particularly in the mountainous areas of its west.

Chengdu

Chengdu, the provincial capital, was founded during the Spring and Autumn period (475–220 BC) at the time when the remarkable Dujiangyan irrigation system was put in place on the Min River. During the Three Kingdoms it became the capital of the state of Shu, and ever since it has retained its importance as one of China's principal cities. It became known for the production of silk brocade as long ago as the Han, and the major river flowing through the city is known as the Jin Jiang (Brocade River). As well, the city itself has sometimes been called Jincheng (Brocade City). However, it is claimed by some that this name relates also to the bloom-ing of *Hibiscus mutabilis*, the floral emblem of Chengdu. The flowers of this species open white in the morning and change gradually to deep pink as the day wears on. Formerly the walls of the city were covered with it and when it was in bloom the city was said to resemble a piece of pink brocade (Li, 1959). The Chinese name for this hibiscus is 'mufurong' (tree lotus) and Chengdu is also sometimes referred to as Rongcheng (Hibiscus City). These days the street plantings are not particularly imaginative, though in the city centre a purple-leaved form of the cherry plum (*Prunus cerasifera*) with small white flowers is frequently seen. It is unlike any cultivar of this species which I have seen outside China.

In spite of its size and modernity, some ancient and interesting garden sites remain in the city, most of them associated with temples and memorial halls. Others are in the countryside nearby. Chengdu also has an interesting plant market in the narrow street running from Renmin Nan Lu beside the Minshan Hotel. Here, according to the season, all the old and new favourites are for sale. During my visit in early March those of Chinese origin included camellias, magnolias, cycads, kumquats, rhapis palms, roses, and cymbidiums, mostly *C. goeringii*, *C. ensifolium* and their cultivars and hybrids (fig. 6.3). In fact the plants available were much the same as those seen for sale by John Birch (1902) when he went to a temple fair in this city in 1900.

The magnolias in the street market and in most gardens in Chengdu are nearly all white with a faint tinge of purple on the midribs and bases of the petals. Whether this is a variant of *M. denudata* or a form of

M. × *soulangiana* I was unable to decide (fig. 6.4). The typical white *M. denudata* is also seen here and there, flowering at the same time.

WUHOUCI (MEMORIAL TEMPLE OF THE MILITARY MARQUIS)

This temple was founded in the 5th century in honour of Zhuge Liang, a famous military strategist who helped Liu Bei, who proclaimed himself emperor of Shu when the Han were overthrown in 220. Both Zhuge Liang and Liu Bei are regarded as heroes in Sichuan, their exploits having entered the realm of mythology in the famous novel *Romance of the Three Kingdoms*.

Originally there was a temple commemorating Liu Bei beside the Wuhouci, but both were burned down and the complex was rebuilt in 1692. Subsequent restorations and alterations have clearly taken place and, although the temple is still called Wuhouci, the first main hall on the principal axis is devoted to Liu Bei and that which lies behind it to Zhuge Liang.

Figure 6.3 (below) **Cymbidium at the plant market, Chengdu**

Figure 6.4 (right) **Magnolia, Wuhouci, Chengdu**

The courtyards of the temple buildings are attractive (fig. 6.5) and contain, amongst other things, magnolias, cycads, flowering peaches and unusually tall plants of *Chaenomeles speciosa*. There are also displays of penjing and a huge plant of *Rosa banksiae* sprawls across the roof of one of the halls. The surrounding tree-filled grounds are extensive and a walled path overhung by bamboos (fig. 6.6) leads to a grassy mound said to be Liu Bei's tomb.

DU FU CAOTANG (DU FU'S THATCHED COTTAGE)

This park has been laid out on the supposed site of the rustic retreat of Du Fu, the celebrated Tang poet who lived in Chengdu for four years in the mid-8th century. From the entrance a straight path leads to an axially arranged series of buildings where there is a statue of Du Fu and statues of other Tang poets (fig. 6.7). The halls contain displays relating to Du Fu's life, examples of his work, and paintings of scenes from

Figure 6.5 (left) **Principal courtyard, Wuhouci**

Figure 6.6 (below) **Path to the tomb of Liu Bei, Wuhouci**

Figure 6.7 (above) **View of main halls, Du Fu's Thatched Cottage, Chengdu**
Figure 6.8 (right) ***Primula sinensis*, Du Fu's Thatched Cottage**

his poems. The associated courtyards are surrounded by roofed walkways and contain a collection of plum cultivars (*Prunus mume*) planted in a formal arrangement. Further on there is another plum garden and a large informal garden with ponds and rockeries, evergreen and deciduous trees, and shrubs such as camellias, magnolias, flowering quinces and *Jasminum mesnyi*. Also here is a small thatched pavilion representing Du Fu's hut. To the east of this is a large courtyard where there is a two-storeyed hexagonal pavilion and a display of penjing and flowering pot plants.

Amongst these, at the time of my visit, were cultivars of *Primula sinensis*, a plant I have not seen grown in any other province except Yunnan (fig. 6.8). As in Yunnan, however, it seems to be losing out to *P. malacoides* and *P. obconica*, plants which, although native to China, are not known to have been cultivated there in the past.

Also in the park there is a circular walled enclosure devoted to a collection of orchids, mainly the traditional small-flowered terrestrial cymbidiums. However, elsewhere in the grounds there are many pots of a large-flowered cymbidium hybrid with brownish flowers. Cymbidiums of this type are rarely seen in Chinese gardens other than in Sichuan and Yunnan.

WANGJIANGLOU (RIVER-VIEWING PAVILION)

This pavilion is a four-storeyed tower built in the Qing and dedicated to the memory of Xue Tao, a female Tang Poet who greatly admired bamboo. It is unusual in that the lower two storeys are square and the upper two octagonal. It stands overlooking the Brocade River in a park most of which is given over to bamboos of various kinds (fig. 6.9). There are also buildings and courtyards used for displays of penjing and potted plants, including azaleas and *Rohdea japonica*. And close to the pavilion there are cultivars of *Camellia japonica* and a fine *Malus halliana* with single flowers.

QINGYANGGONG (GREEN SHEEP PALACE)

This Daoist temple was founded in the Tang but the surviving buildings date from the Qing. Amongst the statues in the main hall are two bronze 'sheep', one with one horn, the other with two. The former is said to incorporate attributes of all the 12 animals of the Chinese zodiac. It is believed to have

been cast in 1723 and was brought from Beijing to add to relics relating to Laozi who, in the 6th century BC, allegedly wrote one of the principal Daoist texts.

The halls and courtyards of this temple are laid out according to the usual axial plan and contain old ginkgos and lohan pines (*Podocarpus macrophyllus*). Yuccas have been used to striking effect near the entrance (fig. 6.10) and there is the usual array of potted plants.

**Figure 6.9 (left)
Bamboo Garden,
River-viewing
Pavilion, Chengdu
Figure 6.10 (below)
Green Sheep
Palace, Chengdu
Figure 6.11 (right)
Aspidistras and
penjing, Renmin
Park, Chengdu**

RENMIN GONGYUAN (PEOPLE'S PARK)

This relatively modern park is a short distance south-west of the city centre and has been developed on the site of a late Qing private garden. A large lake occupies most of the eastern end and elsewhere there are rockeries, ponds, and areas devoted to different kinds of plants—cycads, penjing, camellias, crepe myrtles and philadelphus, for example. Many of the penjing have *Saxifraga stolonifera* growing in the pots, and in the enclosure where they are displayed there are also many pots of aspidistras (fig. 6.11). There are also many plants of the brownish-flowered cymbidium mentioned above as being present at Du Fu's Thatched Cottage (fig. 6.12). As well there is a long pergola with *Rosa banksiae* growing over it and another onto which *Chaenomeles speciosa* has been trained. There are also free-standing specimens of this

species 4 m and more tall, as there are in many gardens in Sichuan. Amongst the plants in other parts of the park are flowering peaches, *Forsythia viridissima*, *Jasminum mesnyi*, *Prunus glandulosa*, magnolias and single and double forms of *Malus halliana*.

WENSHUYUAN (MANJUSRI MONASTERY)

This ancient temple is in the north of the city. It dates back to the 6th century and is the headquarters of the Sichuan Buddhist Association. The plant-filled courtyards (fig. 1.36) —photographs of which were published by the Danish architect J. Prip-Moller (1937), who was in China from 1929 to 1933—appear no longer to exist. Nowadays the temple holds comparatively little of interest for gardeners but,

nevertheless, it is worth visiting for historical reasons and for its lively atmosphere (fig. 6.13).

ZHAOJUESI (ENLIGHTENMENT TEMPLE)

This temple, a few kilometres north-east of the city centre, is near the Chengdu Zoo. It was founded in the Tang and its layout has served as a model for many temples in Asia. It suffered greatly during the Cultural Revolution, but now has been restored. The entrance pathway, lined with a selection of traditional Chinese garden plants leads to a very large courtyard with a bell tower on one side and a drum tower on the other. On the far side of this space the principal hall stands on a terrace, on which there is also a huge old banyan (*Ficus virens*) (fig. 6.14). Behind the main hall there are

further old trees, including a pair of ginkgos and *Podocarpus macrophyllus*.

Ficus virens is known locally as 'huangguo' (yellow fruit), and Mrs Little (1901) records that, in her day, old specimens were common on hilltops in Sichuan, at the foot of each of which was 'a little stone shrine, showing how at one time reverence was entertained for the spirit of this very beautiful shade tree'. Just such a scene was amongst those photographed by Donald Mennie (1926). Ernest Wilson (1913) also remarked on the prominence of this tree in Sichuan and he, too, published a photograph of an example.

CHENGDU ZHIWUYUAN (CHENGDU BOTANICAL GARDEN)

Founded in 1983, this botanical garden is at Tianhui, 10 km north of the city centre. There is a penjing collection and gardens devoted to plums, camellias, magnolias, osmanthuses and other plants. Unfortunately it is poorly maintained and unlikely to appeal to most Western visitors. However, it is the only place in China outside Yunnan where I have seen the double Yunnan cherry, a cultivar of *Prunus cerasoides*.

Figure 6.12 (above)
Cymbidiums, Renmin Park, Chengdu
Figure 6.13 (right) **Principal courtyard, Wenshu Monastery, Chengdu**
Figure 6.14 (above right)
Banyan (*Ficus virens*), Zhaojue Temple, Chengdu

Xindu

Xindu is a small town about 20 km north of Chengdu which is notable for the presence there of the Baoguangsi.

BAOGUANGSI (MONASTERY OF THE DIVINE LIGHT)

The Monastery of Divine Light was founded in the 9th century but most of the present buildings are of Qing date. It is an active monastery with many buildings and courtyards and is popular with tourists. Its main attraction appears to be the sport of walking towards the spirit wall with one's eyes shut in an attempt to hit its centre. Success apparently ensures good fortune and groups of Chinese dissolve into gales of laughter as their companions miss the wall altogether.

There are, however, other things to see. There is the Arhat Hall containing 500 clay figures, and the entrance courtyard is dominated by a square pagoda of 13 storeys, which appears to be Tang in date and is the oldest structure in the complex. In 1980 this pagoda was surrounded by four mature trees of *Magnolia denudata*, but in 1999 only one remained and did not appear to be in good health.

From a gardener's point of view, however, the most interesting parts of the complex are the two courtyards on either side of the main hall. These have changed little since they were photographed sometime between 1929 and 1933 by Prip-Moller (1937) (fig. 6.15). Nor have they changed between my visits in 1980 and 1999. The one to the west of the hall

Figure 6.15 (above) **Abbot's garden, Baoguang Temple, Xindu.** FROM PRIP-MOLLER (1937).

Figure 6.16 (left) **Abbot's garden, Baoguang Temple, 1999**

contains rectangular beds symmetrically arranged in which osmanthuses and other shrubs are growing. In the centre is a tall container in which there is an arrangement of rocks, nandina and a double pink cultivar of *Prunus glandulosa*. While this is an intriguing space, its companion, reached through a door in the wall to the east of the hall, is the more interesting of the two. It is also laid out in symmetrical fashion and is best viewed from the reception room in which the abbot entertains guests (fig. 6.16). It is dominated by a pair of ginkgos which have been trained into umbrella shapes, in front of which is a large wintersweet (*Chimonanthus praecox*). Around these trees are arranged pots of camellias, *Rhapis humilis*, *Buxus microphylla*, large-flowered cymbidiums, *Primula sinensis*, cinerarias and other plants. Both of my visits were in early March and it seems probable that different plants are used to ornament the courtyard as the seasons progress. All in all this is one of the most appealing small garden spaces in China.

As mentioned above there were formerly small courtyard gardens of this type, with plants in symmetrically arranged raised stone beds, at the Wenshuyuan. Also an example is

shown in Xia Xianggeng's *Shaoyuyuan ershisi xiaozhaotu* (Twenty-four small pictures of [Wu Xinfu's] 'Almost non-existent' garden) of 1815 (Titley & Wood, 1991), so it seems probable that this style of garden has a long history.

Guan Xian

Guan Xian about 60 km north-west of Chengdu is the site of the Dujiangyan irrigation scheme. This remarkable undertaking was begun about 250 BC by the local prefect Li Bing and his son. This project, one of the earliest irrigation schemes in China, involved dividing the Min River into two channels by means of a dike constructed with stones. This enabled water to be diverted to a previously unirrigated area of the plain.

FULONGGUAN (SUBDUED DRAGON TEMPLE)

The Fulongguan was built during the Song to commemorate Li Bing and his son. It is approached from the town through Lidui Park, which contains some interesting trees including magnolias and crepe myrtles. The lower trunk of one of the latter, claimed to be 500 years old, is composed of branches woven into a basket-like structure (fig. 6.17). Perhaps this is a traditional way of training this tree, as there is a youthful example in the Shandong garden at the World Horti-Expo

Figure 6.17
A 500-year-old crepe myrtle, Lidui Park, Guan Xian

Garden in Kunming. Another has had its lower branches trained in a vertical plane.

The entrance to the temple is flanked by a huge ginkgo and several tall nanmu trees (*Persea nanmu*). In the courtyards there are further crepe myrtles said to be more than a century old and a large osmanthus of similar age. Also conspicuous are tall plants of *Chaenomeles speciosa* (fig. 6.18).

In the main hall there is a stone statue of Li Bing carved in 168 and dredged up from the river in 1974. It is speculated that it had been cast into the river in a superstitious gesture to ensure the continued success of the scheme. And at the highest part of the temple there is a pavilion looking out over the division of the waters.

ERWANGMIAO (TWO KINGS TEMPLE)

A short distance upstream from the Fulongguan, this is another temple overlooking the irrigation scheme and commemorating Li Bing and his son. It was founded in the late 5th century but the buildings are all Qing. They contain modern statues of the 'two kings' and mementoes concerning them.

The temple is built on a steep slope and, although the main entrance is beside the river, it can be entered through a gate at its highest point, from which a path leads down through the grounds. Entering from this direction one arrives in an area planted with tall evergreen and deciduous trees, including nanmus and junipers. Then, just before reaching the temple buildings, there is a terrace on which stands a rustic wooden pavilion sheltering a tree stump excavated from a river bed nearby and reputed to be 3500 years old (fig. 6.19). From this terrace steps descend to a space between the buildings where there are flowering quinces, camellias, *Podocarpus macrophyllus* and the largest *Magnolia denudata* I have seen—a wonderful sight when covered with what must be thousands of flowers (fig. 6.20). In a courtyard nearby is one of those curious miniature gardens that one finds here and there in temples. This one is a romantic representation of the

Figure 6.18 (above) *Cycas revoluta, Chaenomeles speciosa* and *Osmanthus fragrans*, Fulongguan

Figure 6.19 (left) Ancient tree stump, Erwangmiao

Figure 6.20 (opposite page) *Magnolia denudata*, Erwangmiao

temple grounds and is planted with *Jasminum mesnyi*, *Pittosporum tobira* and *Nandina domestica*, amongst which ferns and *Primula sinensis* have become naturalised (fig. 6.21).

A.S. Roe (1910), who visited the Erwangmiao during her tour of 1907–09, provided the earliest Western description of this temple which I have found. She described it as 'one of the finest in China' and must have gone there at about the same time of year as I did. She walked up through the various courtyards rather than down and remarked that 'here and there green and leafy gardens hovered in stray nooks, where, in spite of the inclement weather, primulas and camellias were in full flower'.

QINGCHENG SHAN (GREEN CITY MOUNTAIN)

During the Han the 'Heavenly Master' Zhang Daoling built a thatched hut for himself on Qingcheng Shan and since then it has been a Daoist centre, though most of the present buildings are relatively recent. The mountain rises to 1600 m not far from the Fulongguan and Erwangmiao and, in view of its modest altitude, its ascent is an easier option than that of Emei Shan, the Buddhist holy mountain near Leshan.

As is so often the case with mountains in China these days, it is hardly necessary to walk at all. From the temple at the base an electric trolley goes up to the edge of a lake. A ferry ride across the lake then takes you to a chairlift which ends not far from the uppermost temple, the Shangqinggong. From there you can walk to a pavilion on the mountaintop from which there are wonderful views, as there are from the

Figure 6.21 (above) **Miniature landscape, Erwangmiao**
Figure 6.22 (right) ***Magnolia denudata*, Qingcheng Shan**

chairlift. By avoiding the walk, however, one misses out on various sites of Daoist significance. The most important of these is the Tianshidong (Cave of the Heavenly Master), where Zhang Daoling is believed to have delivered his sermons. Here there is a huge ginkgo which he is said to have planted, together with pines and other trees to which great antiquity is attributed. Also along the way there are rustic shelters of unpainted timber and thatch, which harmonise with the scenery and accord with the Daoist view of nature.

The journey up the mountain starts amongst tall nanmu trees, cunninghamias and cryptomerias. The 'motorised' route has been ornamented with garden plants, including camellias, flowering quinces, magnolias (fig. 6.22) and *Prunus mume*. And from the chairlift there are good views of the native flora, which appears similar to that on the lower slopes of Emei Shan—plants such as cherries, *Lindera* species and *Stachyurus chinensis* being conspicuous in early spring. Beside the path leading from the top of the chairlift to the Shangqing Temple there is a small tea plantation in which

Chinese gooseberries (I cannot bring myself to call them kiwi fruit when they are in their native country) are also being grown. In the garden of the adjoining farmhouse there are plants of *Rhododendron davidii*. This species is native to this district and the specimens in this garden appear to have been transplanted from the wild (fig. 6.23).

The temple itself is not particularly interesting, though there are a few plants of a red cultivar of *Camellia japonica* in the main courtyard. However, there are several Daoist monks in residence who, with their black robes, hats and topknots, add character to the scene.

Figure 6.23 *Rhododendron davidii* in a farmer's garden, Qingcheng Shan

EMEI SHAN (LOFTY EYEBROW MOUNTAIN)

With its temples, pavilions and stairways, Emei Shan is, like Qingcheng Shan, yet another example of a modified landscape. At 3099 m, it is the highest and westernmost of China's nine famous sacred mountains. It lies approximately 160 km south-west of Chengdu, on the edge of the great mass of mountains which rise in western Sichuan. The establishment of Emei Shan as a Buddhist holy mountain dates back at least to the Six Dynasties period. It is reputed to have been the abode of the Bodhisattva Samantabhadra who went there on the back of a white elephant to meditate. A stepped path was constructed to the summit and it is estimated that by the 14th century there were several thousand monks living on the mountain in more than 100 temples.

The first European to ascend the mountain was E.C. Baber, a British consular official stationed at Chongqing, who went there in 1877. Because of its height, accessibility and diverse flora, Emei Shan has long been a favourite site for plant hunters, beginning with Dr Ernst Faber, a German missionary who went there in 1887. In 1897 it was climbed by Mr and Mrs Archibald Little, who spent a fortnight on the summit, where most of the temples had been destroyed by fire a few years previously. From their reports it appears that these had been rebuilt with 'rough pine-wood'. The most famous building on the summit, the Golden Temple, had earlier been burned down in 1466, following which, according to the Littles, a bronze temple had been completed there in 1474. This in turn was largely destroyed in a fire of 1544, and all that remained of it at the time of their visit were the 'beautiful fragments' which Mrs Little photographed (Little, A.J., 1901; Little, Mrs A., 1901).

Many of the monastery buildings went up in flames once more during the Cultural Revolution and little remains of their past glory today. Even so, much reconstruction has taken place in recent years and the mountain is once more thronged with pilgrims and tourists. The arduous ascent and descent can take several days if undertaken entirely on foot. However, you can now cheat by driving or taking a bus to the Jieyin Hall at 2540 m, from where it is a manageable climb to the summit. But even this can be avoided by using a cable car.

Presumably it is as a result of the visits of botanists and plant collectors that the horticultural potential of the flora of this mountain has been brought to the notice of those in charge of temple gardens, in which a selection of local plants

Figure 6.24 (far left) Bronze pagoda and *Magnolia denudata*, Baoguo Temple, Emei Shan

Figure 6.25 (left) Mixed planting, Baoguo Temple, Emei Shan.

PHOTOGRAPH: T. SMYTH.

Figure 6.26

Modern garden,

Wannian

Temple,

Emei Shan.

PHOTOGRAPH:
T. SMYTH.

has been added to the usual temple favourites. The most notable of these gardens are at the Baoguosi (Protect the Nation Temple) at the base of the mountain and at the Wanniansi (Ten Thousand Year Temple) at about 1000 m.

The Baoguo Temple was the traditional place for pilgrims to commence their ascent of the mountain. It was founded in the Ming, restored during the Qing, and again more recently. The name of the temple is inscribed over the gate in the calligraphy of the emperor Qianlong and in one of the courtyards is a Ming bronze pagoda beside which is a plant of *Magnolia denudata* (fig. 6.24). Nearby is a collection of penjing and in the courtyards there are many other plants including palms, cycads, tree ferns, *Rosa banksiae* and formal double cultivars of *Camellia japonica* (fig. 6.25).

Although most of its buildings are of recent construction, the Wannian Temple is the most important surviving temple on the mountain. It dates from the Six Dynasties Period, was rebuilt during the late Ming, and now consists largely of recently constructed buildings. The only Ming building to have survived is the square brick pavilion housing an enormous statue, cast in 980, of the Bodhisattva on his white, six-tusked elephant.

While the Littles did not find much to comment on by way of a garden here other than to mention the lohan pines (*Podocarpus macrophyllus*), the temple now has a modern garden (fig. 6.26) which contains a selection of plants not usually seen in Chinese gardens, including *Rhododendron* species in pots, *Pinus armandii*, *Lagerstroemia faurei*, and various others used for topiary and penjing.

Yunnan

With its mixed population and its borders with Myanmar (Burma), Laos and North Vietnam, Yunnan has a character all its own. It is a mountainous province, the highest peaks being in the north-west where the Salween, Mekong and Yangtze run parallel to one another. By contrast, the southernmost region, Xishuangbanna, is at a low altitude in the valley of the Mekong and is tropical.

Not surprisingly, Yunnan remained geographically isolated until relatively recent times, and it retained varying degrees of independence for much longer than was the case in neighbouring Sichuan. It was the seat of the Nanzhao kingdom, which in 751 defeated the invading Tang imperial army and for five centuries, until its overthrow by the Mongols in 1253, controlled most of the province as it now exists. The name Yunnan (Cloudy South) was first applied at the time of its domination by the Mongols. However, it was not until the Ming dynasty that the Chinese began seriously to colonise the province.

Figure 6.27 Cultivars of *Camellia reticulata* in a courtyard at Dali

in Yunnan, however, are rare until the Ming, when closer contact was established between Yunnan and the central administration. One of the most interesting is Zhang Zhichun's *Yongchang erfang ji* (Notes on Two Ornamentals from Yongchang) of 1495, in which he describes 20 rhododendrons and 36 camellias from what is now Baoshan in the west of the province (Needham, 1986).

The best known Yunnanese ornamental plants are undoubtedly the forms of *Camellia reticulata* (fig. 6.27). There are references to this species said to date from the 11th century on (Feng, Xia & Zhu, 1986; Yu, 1950), and it seems probable that it has been grown since at least the Sui or Tang dynasties. Curiously enough, it seems to have gone unnoticed by any of the foreign plant collectors to visit the region in the 19th and early 20th centuries. This seems surprising since the flowers rival those of the tree peonies in sumptuousness. It remained for H.H. Hu (1938) to draw the attention of the West to these plants, and the first detailed description in English of a selection of cultivars did not appear until 1950 (Yü, 1950).

Also frequently encountered are *Cymbidium* species not usually seen in gardens elsewhere in China, as are old plants of *Michelia yunnanensis*, *Magnolia delavayi* and *Cupressus duclouxiana*. The last mentioned seems often to take the place of the junipers and thujas so widely planted in temple gardens in the rest of the country. These plants, along with many others from eastern China, appear to have moved throughout the province along the trade routes mentioned above.

Also notable are the cherry cultivars with large carmine flowers which are conspicuous in many parts of the province in early spring. These produce single, semi-double or double flowers in sessile umbels in early March (figs 6.28, 6.77, 6.89). Chinese botanists place these plants in *Prunus cerasoides*, but this species, as it generally occurs, produces smaller and paler flowers in stalked umbels a few weeks earlier. Perhaps the later-flowering cherries are forms of the enigmatic *P. cerasoides* var. *rubea* which Ingram (1948) described, as Kingdon Ward noted that it flowered considerably later

It was the war against Japan that brought modernisation. Except for a brief incursion in the far west, Yunnan remained unoccupied by the Japanese, and factories, universities and government agencies were transplanted there from the east. Supplies for allied bases flowed through the province along the Burma Road, and a major United States Air Force base was set up in Kunming.

In more recent times Yunnan's reputation as a floral kingdom has been given a boost by the holding in Kunming of the 1999 International Horticultural Exposition. In preparation for this roads were improved, airports and hotels built, gardens and temples renovated and extended, and tourist facilities upgraded throughout the province.

From the point of view of the movement of cultivated plants, the old trade routes through the province appear to have had a marked effect. Firstly there was the route from India through Burma to Baoshan in the west of the province, on to Dali and Kunming, and then north-east to Yibin on the Yangtze in southern Sichuan. Then from Dali another route ran north as far as Chengdu. Minor routes from Dali ran north to Lijiang and south to Weishan. It has been pointed out, for instance, that most of the ancient specimens of cultivars of *Camellia reticulata* are to be found in temples and villages close to these routes (Pang et al., 1995).

The gardens and temples of Yunnan are interesting from the point of view both of their layout and the plants they contain. It is clear that plants native to the province have been cultivated here for hundreds of years, plants not cultivated, at least until very recently, in other parts of the country. References in the literature to horticulture and gardens

than the form with paler flowers. On the other hand perhaps they are derived from the cherry described as *P. majestica* by Koehne (Sargent, 1913), which has been collected by Augustine Henry, George Forrest and others in the province, where it has been recorded as being cultivated (Ingram, 1948). Until someone sorts all this out it seems simplest for me to follow various Chinese authors and to refer to it as the 'Yunnan cherry', a form of *P. cerasoides*. Considering its widespread presence in temple gardens and elsewhere it seems surprising that it has been remarked upon so rarely. And, since there are cultivated trees of great age, it seems clear that it and its variants must have been brought into cultivation long ago.

A more recent introduction to the gardens of Yunnan is the extraordinary *Musa lasiocarpa*, a banana considered by Chinese botanists to belong to a separate genus, *Musella* (Wu, 1978; Zhang et al., 1988). This produces its broad, yellow, upwardfacing inflorescences on stout stems, usually less than 1 m tall, and remains in bloom for months on end (fig. 6.29). It is endemic to Yunnan where it is known locally as 'diyong jinlian' (golden lotus bursting from underground). It did not attract attention as an ornamental plant until the 1970s but is now widely planted.

Figure 6.28 (above right) **The double cultivar of the Yunnan cherry**

Figure 6.29 (right) *Musa lasiocarpa*, **Cuihu Park, Kunming**

Kunming and Environs

Kunming, the capital of the province, is now a large modern city. It lies at 1890 m above sea level at the northern end of Lake Dian. As Chinese cities go it has a great deal to offer the garden visitor, much of it quite unlike what is to be found elsewhere in the country. For a start a tour of the flower and bird market provides an overview of the garden plants at present available in this city. And then there is much variety in the street plantings, which include planes, deodars, *Magnolia grandiflora*, *Grevillea robusta*, eucalypts, *Cupressus duclouxiana* and paulownias, to which in recent times have been added *Magnolia delavayi*, the double form of *Prunus cerasoides*, and other plants native to the province. This state of affairs seems to have resulted from the work of the Kunming Botanical Institute, which has done much to record, introduce to cultivation, and popularise many of the region's indigenous plants.

The parks, gardens and temples which I have visited in and around Kunming are described below.

Figure 6.30 (left) **The lake, Kunming Zoo**

Figure 6.31 (far left) **Double Yunnan cherries, Kunming Zoo**

Figure 6.33 (below right) ***Rhododendron arboreum*** ssp. ***delavayi*, Yuantong Temple, Kunming**

Figure 6.34 (below) **Yuantong Temple, Kunming**

KUNMING DONGWUYUAN (KUNMING ZOO)

This zoo has been built on Yuantong Hill in the northern part of the city (fig. 6.30). When I first came here at the end of February 1980 I was astonished by the avenue of a double carmine form of *Prunus cerasoides* in full bloom (fig. 6.31). Stands had been erected between the trees, as they still are, so that visitors could be photographed amongst the blossom. At the time I could find no reference to this double-flowered cherry in the literature and I did not see it anywhere else in Kunming. Now it is widely planted in the city.

The zoo is also notable for a long avenue of a double form of *Malus halliana*, amongst which occasional plants with single flowers are to be found (fig. 6.32). And, although the whole area has not been designed in a particularly exciting manner, there are many other plants which attract attention.

YUANTONGSI (TEMPLE OF UNIVERSAL PENETRATION)

This temple is at the foot of the hill now occupied by the zoo. It was founded in the Tang and, as is usually the case, has undergone numerous restorations. From the gate a path, lined with osmanthuses, camellias, cherries, azaleas, crab-apples, *Rhododendron arboreum* ssp. *delavayi* (fig. 6.33) and a selection of potted plants, leads down a slope to the principal courtyard. This is constructed in a style not uncommon in Yunnan but which is unusual elsewhere in China. It is occupied by a large rectangular pool surrounded by buildings

and walkways. In the centre of the pool is an octagonal pavilion connected to the shore by two stone bridges built on the central axis of the complex. Facing opposite sides of the pool, two flights of steps lead down from the pavilion to the water. At the time of my visit a collection of cultivars of *Camellia reticulata* were arranged on these steps (fig. 6.34). And on the right-hand side of the pool as you face the main hall there is an elaborate rockery. Overall this is a fascinating space.

Figure 6.32 (following pages) **Avenue of *Malus halliana*, Kunming Zoo**

Figure 6.35

(above left) Cuihu Park, Kunming

Figure 6.36

(above) *Ligustrum sinense* and *Camellia reticulata* 'Liuye Yinhong', East Pagoda, Kunming

Figure 6.37

(left) Entrance of the Tanhua Temple, Kunming

CUIHU GONGYUAN (GREEN LAKE PARK)

This park is also in the northern part of the city and consists principally of a large lake with islands connected by bridges and causeways. It is one of the chief recreational areas of the city, with tea houses, boats for hire, and children's play areas. Willows, crabapples, peaches and other trees and shrubs make up the permanent planting, and there are seasonal displays, largely of potted plants (fig. 6.35). There are also buildings in which a collection of narcissus and other flowers associated with the New Year is mounted during the Spring Festival, along with penjing and flower arrangements. But, apart from the interest generated by some of the plants, there is not a lot to cause one to linger in this park.

DONGSITA AND XISITA (EAST TEMPLE PAGODA AND WEST TEMPLE PAGODA)

Two square pagodas, thought to date from the Nanzhao period, have survived not far from one another in downtown Kunming. They are all that remain of the temples of which they once formed part. Little ground remains around the

West Pagoda, but the East Pagoda stands in a larger space which has recently been planted with a collection of camellias—largely cultivars of *Camellia reticulata*. Also conspicuous there are the potted privets which line one of the paths (fig. 6.36).

TANHUASI (TANHUA TEMPLE)

Apart from those already mentioned, most sites of horticultural interest in and around Kunming are found on the hills which surround the city. This temple, however, is on flat ground in the eastern suburbs (fig. 6.37). It gets its name from that of an old tree of *Magnolia delavayi* which grows there and which has the popular name of 'tanhua', which translated literally means 'covered-with-clouds flower'. The Chinese, however, choose to give its name in English as 'broad-leaved epiphyllum', since tanhua is also the name given to *Epiphyllum oxyphyllum*, the well-known cactus which blooms at night, as does this magnolia. The tree concerned in this instance is said to be 350 years old and grows in an inner courtyard where its history is outlined on a tablet set in the wall (fig 6.38).

There are several courtyards in this temple complex, including one devoted to bamboos and intricate rockwork. The garden has recently been extended considerably and contains most of the plants typical of Kunming gardens, both in the ground and in pots.

HEILONGTAN GONGYUAN
(BLACK DRAGON POOL PARK)

The Black Dragon Pool Park is 12 km north of the city and is reached along a road that passes several large nurseries. The park has an area of just over 90 hectares, much of it covered with oaks. Near the entrance is a group of ancient trees—a juniper, a lohan pine (*Podocarpus macrophyllus*) and a pair of crepe myrtles. In addition to these there is much modern planting and the entrance path is lined with pot plants. At the time of my visits in early March these included cultivars of *Camellia reticulata*

and specimens of *Rhododendron arboreum* ssp. *delavayi* and *R. irroratum*. The actual Black Dragon Pool is in two sections separated by a dike. One of these is said to be turbid and the other clear, symbolising the yin and yang. At the time I viewed them neither appeared especially limpid, though steam was rising from the smaller of the two, suggesting it was warmer than the larger one. Nearby in the park a new garden has been made for a collection of cultivars of *Prunus mume*, the largest in south-western China.

Beside and above the pool are two Daoist temples. The lower one, the Xiaguan (Lower Temple) or Heilonggong (Black Dragon Palace) was first built in 1394. Its courtyard contains plants, but none of particular note. Of much greater interest is the Heishuiguan (Black Water Temple) or Shangguan (Upper Temple) on the hilltop beyond the pool, which dates from the Han. Here there are some truly wonderful old trees. Beside the steps leading up to this

Figure 6.38 *Magnolia delavayi,* **Tanhua Temple**

Figure 6.39 (left) An ancient *Cryptomeria japonica* towering over the Upper Temple, Black Dragon Pool Park, Kunming

Figure 6.40 (above) Azaleas in slate containers, Upper Temple, Black Dragon Pool Park

Figure 6.41 (below) View into the principal courtyard of the Upper Temple, Black Dragon Pool Park, with an old *Prunus mume* on the left and *Cupressus duclouxiana* said to date from the Song on the right

temple is a *Magnolia delavayi*, and in the entrance courtyard are two gigantic cryptomerias, said to date from the Yuan (fig. 6.39). Beneath these in early March were many pink and purple azaleas in pots each made from four pieces of slate (fig. 6.40). Then in the principal courtyard there is a huge cypress (*Cupressus duclouxiana*) which, according to tradition, was planted in the Song (fig. 6.41). On either side of this are two cultivars of *Camellia reticulata*. The one on the left as you face the main hall is 'Zaotaohong' ('Early Crimson') and is claimed to date from the Ming,

though Feng, Xia and Zhu (1986) are more cautious and say 'estimated to be 200 years old'. Flanking the entrance are two old plums (*Prunus mume*) and close to the camellia on the right-hand side is the trunk of a plum said to date from the Tang, which is now dead but has been retained. Elsewhere in the temple complex are the usual double Yunnan cherries, *Malus halliana* and penjing. Amongst the less frequently encountered plants of Chinese gardens is what is commonly called *Camellia × hiemalis*, in this instance growing here in pots lining a path.

KUNMING ZHIWUYUAN (KUNMING BOTANICAL GARDEN)

This garden adjoins the Black Dragon Pool Park. Founded in 1938, it is one of China's leading botanical gardens and is affiliated with the Kunming Institute of Botany of the Chinese Academy of Sciences, the headquarters of which are located within the grounds. It is a centre famous for its research and for its leading role in the botanical exploration of the province. The garden itself is in two parts, the East Garden and the West Garden, on opposite sides of a road. It has become famous for collecting together all the old cultivars of *Camellia reticulata* and for introducing many new ones. There are also important collections of Magnoliaceae, rhododendrons, orchids and many other plant groups. Amongst the traditional garden plants which caught my attention were *Bambusa ventricosa* (Buddha's Belly Bamboo) (fig. 6.42) and *Edgeworthia papyrifera*, grown in the time-honoured fashion with its stems tied in knots (fig. 6.43).

Figure 6.42 (right) Buddha's Belly Bamboo (*Bambusa ventricosa*), Kunming Botanical Garden

Figure 6.43 (above) *Edgeworthia papyrifera* grown in the traditional fashion with its stems tied in knots, Kunming Botanical Garden

JINDIAN (GOLDEN TEMPLE)

This Daoist temple is on a mountaintop about about 7 km north-east of the city. It is entered along an avenue of crabapples (*Malus halliana*) (fig. 6.44), at the far end of which a stairway leads to a terrace on which is a specimen of *Camellia reticulata* 'Shizitou' ('Lion Head') planted in 1602. Beyond this is an enclosure surrounded by a crenellated wall of grey bricks in which stands the square pavilion which gives the temple its name. This building, dating from the Ming, faithfully reproduces timber architecture in cast bronze. On either

side of it are crepe myrtles which, like the camellia, were planted in 1602 (fig. 6.45). To the right as you face the pavilion is another courtyard which creates a dignified impression as it is planted with nothing but osmanthus bushes (fig. 6.46). And to the left is a courtyard with some mixed planting which overlooks a new garden containing cycads and other plants. This garden also contains reproductions of other famous Chinese bronze pavilions—those at Wutai Shan in Shanxi, Wudang Shan in Hubei, and Wanshou Shan, the hill at the Summer Palace on the outskirts of Beijing (fig. 6.47).

Figure 6.44 (top) **Entrance to the Golden Temple, Kunming**

Figure 6.45 (above) **Crepe myrtle planted in 1602, Golden Temple**

Figure 6.46 (right) **The osmanthus courtyard, Golden Temple**

On the occasions that I have visited them, the gardens at the Golden Temple have had displays of *Primula sinensis*, the only place in Yunnan where I have seen this grown (fig. 6.48). As in Sichuan, however, it seems to be losing out to *P. malacoides* and *P. obconica*. Modern strains of polyanthus also seem to be gaining a foothold.

Leaving the main temple by the opening in the wall behind the bronze pavilion and passing a large oak (*Quercus variabilis*), said to be at least 250 years old, an area known as the Kunming Horticultural Landscape Botanical Garden is reached. This was begun in 1983 in the park surrounding the temple and is principally devoted to plant collections of various types. The largest

of these is the camellia garden in which it is claimed all the famous camellias of Yunnan have been gathered together (fig. 1.44). There are also a rhododendron and azalea garden, a magnolia garden, a bamboo garden, a fern garden, a rose garden, a collection of rare and endangered plants, display greenhouses (fig. 6.49), and a bell tower built to house a 14 tonne bronze bell cast in 1423.

Figure 6.47 (above) **Garden with replicas of famous bronze temples, Golden Temple**

Figure 6.48 (top) ***Primula sinensis* at the Golden Temple arranged around a stone tortoise with a snake coiled on its back. It was once believed that all tortoises were female and that in order to reproduce they mated with snakes.**

Figure 6.49 (left) **Cacti in the conservatory, Kunming Horticultural Landscape Botanical Garden**

SHIJIE YUANYI BOLANYUAN (WORLD HORTI-EXPO GARDEN)

This is the name now given to the site of the 1999 International Horticultural Exposition. After the exposition closed in October of that year the site was sold to a private company and is now run as a business. Almost all the gardens, displays and features have been retained, so, in effect, the exposition continues.

The garden occupies an extensive site in a valley at the foot of the mountain on which the Golden Temple is situated and is connected with it by a cable car. At the main entrance visitors are greeted by the mascot of the exposition, the Yunnan Golden Monkey, executed in the style favoured nowadays for such objects by the organisers of extravaganzas such as this and the Olympic Games. Passing through the turnstiles one comes to an enormous floral clock featuring the yin-yang symbol of Daoism—no doubt a reference to the Golden Temple. A stupendous display of bedding plants follows, the centrepiece of which is a huge junk in full sail, entirely covered at the time of my visit with pansies (fig. 6.50)—an echo perhaps of the land boats of classical Chinese gardens and the floral dragons, phoenixes, butterflies and peacocks popular in public gardens elsewhere in the country.

Beyond this things calm down somewhat, though the presence of a huge artificial tree momentarily diverts the attention (fig. 6.51). Just past this is a large area devoted to gardens contributed by the various Chinese provinces. Some of these are very good (figs 6.52, 6.53), while others

Figure 6.50 (left) **Floral display at the entrance to the World Horti-Expo Garden, Kunming**

Figure 6.51 (below right) **Giant artificial tree, World Horti-Expo Garden**

Figure 6.52 (bottom left) **Jiangsu garden, World Horti-Expo Garden**

Figure 6.53 (below) **Shandong garden, World Horti-Expo Garden**

Figure 6.54 (bottom right) **Australian garden, World Horti-Expo Garden**

may perhaps best be described as interesting. The same applies to the international gardens laid out nearby. As an Australian I was pleased to see the contribution of my country. This had been provided by Wagga Wagga, a sister city of Kunming. Prior to my visit, countrypersons of my acquaintance had been less than enthusiastic about it, but I thought it was good, conjuring up well the atmosphere of rural Australia (fig. 6.54).

Also to be seen are a tea plantation, a bamboo garden, a Chinese vegetable garden, a garden of medicinal plants, a huge conservatory and various other gardens and indoor displays. Presumably, however, the continued success of this huge venture will depend on its financial viability and the ability of its owners to keep up the standard of maintenance.

QIONGZHUSI (BAMBOO TEMPLE)

This temple lies 10 km west of the city on top of a mountain largely covered with eucalypts, peach and plum orchards, and, at the higher levels, graves. It is believed to date back to the Tang or Song and to be the first place in Yunnan to which Chan Buddhism was introduced. According to legend, two princes of the Nanzhao kingdom were hunting here and through a cloud saw a monk holding a bamboo staff. Soon afterwards the staff grew into a clump of bamboo and this gave the temple its name (Wood, 1992). Its present fame rests largely on its collection of 500 painted clay figures of lohans made in the late 19th century.

As at the Upper Temple in the Black Dragon Pool Park, there are two huge old cryptomerias in the entrance courtyard.

The central path of the main courtyard which follows is lined with pot plants and there are two trees of *Malus halliana* framing the entrance to the principal hall (fig. 6.55). Also in this courtyard are old plums (*Prunus mume*), cultivars of *Camellia reticulata* (fig. 6.56) and *C. japonica*, two ancient pears

Figure 6.56 (left)
Camellia reticulata 'Hentiangao', Bamboo Temple

Figure 6.57 (below)
Magnolia delavayi, Bamboo Temple, Kunming

Figure 6.55 (left)
Main courtyard, Bamboo Temple, Kunming

and two trees of *Magnolia delavayi*. These are said by Sun et al. (1998) to be 300 years old, although a notice beside them declares that they were planted in the Yuan dynasty (fig. 6.57). In the next courtyard there is a double Yunnan cherry and an exceptionally tall loquat, along with further potted plants of various kinds.

DAGUANLOU GONGYUAN (GRAND VIEW TOWER PARK)

This park is at the foot of the Western Hills, south of the Qiongzhu Temple on the western shore of the northern end of Lake Dian. It has been a popular scenic spot since the Ming, with views across the lake to the Western Hills (fig. 6.58). It attracted further attention after the construction of the Daguanlou (Grand View Tower) in 1690, and its fame increased in the 18th century during the reign of Qianlong, when the tower was decorated with

a pair of long couplets extolling the virtues of the site. The park was renovated and extended out into the lake just prior to the 1999 International Horticultural Exposition and is now the scene of massed displays of tulips, stocks and other plants in season (fig. 6.59). There is also a new garden accommodating a collection of penjing.

HUATINGSI (MAGNIFICENT PAVILION TEMPLE)

Further south than the Daguan Park and about halfway up the Western Hills, this country temple of the Nanzhao kingdom is believed to have been founded in the 11th century. It has been rebuilt and extended several times and is pic-

turesquely set against a forested hillside. There is an unusually large entrance courtyard in the centre of which is a pond, around which have been planted cherries, contorted willows, and cultivars of *Camellia reticulata*. A flight of steps leads up from this space to the principal courtyard of the complex where there is a fine collection of old trees, including pairs of ginkgos, *Magnolia delavayi*, crepe myrtles, and double white plums (*Prunus mume*), symmetrically arranged. There is also a pair of beds surrounded by stone balustrades and containing arrangements of rocks (fig. 6.60). As well there are mature plants of *Malus halliana* and *Cupressus funebris* (fig. 6.61), along with cultivars of *Camellia reticulata* (fig. 6.62) and

Figure 6.58 (above)
View of the Western
Hills from the
Daguanlou, Kunming

Figure 6.59 (far left)
Tulips, Daguanlou
Park, Kunming

Figure 6.60 (over page)
Main courtyard,
Huating Temple,
Western Hills,
Kunming

Figure 6.61 (right)
Cupressus funebris
and *Malus
halliana*, Huating
Temple

Figure 6.62 (above left)
*Camellia
reticulata* 'Juban',
Huating Temple

masses of potted plants. In a higher courtyard behind the main hall there are more plants of interest, including potted *Chaenomeles* cultivars, *Prunus triloba*, and clivias, which have become popular in Chinese gardens. In keeping with the traditional role of temples in providing travellers with accommodation, part of this temple is now a small hotel.

TAIHUASI (TAIHUA TEMPLE)

This temple is a little higher up in the Western Hills than the Huatingsi and is named after the Taihua (Most Magnificent) Hill on which it stands. It was founded in the Yuan, rebuilt in the Qing, and has been restored and extended in recent years. To the right of the entrance is an old ginkgo, which an inscription announces to have been planted by the Ming emperor Jianwen (reigned 1399–1402). He is also said to have planted a camellia which grew here but, when it died in 1961, a count of its growth rings revealed it to have been only 129 years old (Feng et al., 1986). If it has not already become clear, this confirms that the claims of great age made for many trees in China need to be treated with caution.

As at the Huating Temple, there is a splendid view from the entrance to the principal courtyard across to the main hall and the hill behind (fig. 6.63). On either side of the central path are several plants of *Magnolia denudata* and *M. × soulangiana*, underplanted with a collection of tree peonies. There are also several cultivars of *Camellia reticulata*, including 'Shizilin', 'Juban' and a tall specimen of 'Zipao' (fig. 6.64), estimated to be more than a century old (Feng et al., 1986).

Figure 6.63 (below left)

Main courtyard,

Taihua Temple,

Western Hills,

Kunming

Figure 6.64 (right)

Century-old

Camellia reticulata

'Zipao', Taihua

Temple

Figure 6.65

(below right)

Lake garden,

Taihua Temple

The courtyard is surrounded by roofed walkways, as are those to either side of it. That to the right as you face the main hall contains a rock mountain, bamboos, *Cercis chinensis* and other plants. That to the left consists almost entirely of a small lake from the surface of which intricate rockeries protrude (pre-title pages and fig. 6.65). There are also clumps of bamboo. A walk around this peaceful space provides ever changing views, including glimpses of the principal courtyard through the surrounding open-sided walkways.

The road beyond the Taihua Temple leads to the Longmen (Dragon Gate). Here a path, cut out of the cliff by a Daoist monk and his assistants, leads past caves containing sculptures. From this path there are extensive views of Lake Dian and botanical interest is provided by a tiny primula growing on the rocks. This is *Primula duclouxii*, which flowers in March and is like a diminutive *P. malacoides*. Other plants flower at the same time in the surrounding vegetation, including *Cercis yunnanensis*, *Michelia yunnanensis*, *Berberis wilsoniae*, *Rhododendron spinuliferum*, *R. spiciferum*, a white cherry and a pale mauve buddleja.

Anning

This town is 40 km south-west of Kunming. A few kilometres to its east are the Anning Hot Springs, where a resort has been developed which is popular with Chinese tourists. Close to this is the Caoxisi, a temple worth visiting for its garden.

CAOXISI (CAOXI TEMPLE)

This temple takes its name from that of the stream near which it stands. The temple was founded in the Tang and, although in its present form it is small, the main courtyard has some interesting features. These include a plum, which it is claimed dates from the Tang and around which an intricate rockery has been built, and an ancient *Magnolia delavayi*, which is

Jinning

A few kilometres east of this town on the south-western tip of Lake Dian is the Panlongsi, another temple worth visiting for its plants.

PANLONGSI (INTERTWINED DRAGON TEMPLE)

This old temple is built on a steep slope and is of horticultural interest on account of the presence of two trees said to have been planted in 1347. One is a plum in the main courtyard close to the entrance at the bottom of the hill. The other is a plant of *Camellia reticulata* 'Songzilin', which grows in the courtyard of a separate building complex at the top of the hill, for which there is an additional admission charge. It is 10 m tall and the oldest known plant of this cultivar (fig. 6.67). It is surrounded by potted plants of this and other cultivars (fig. 6.68). Elsewhere there are many other ornamental plants amongst which I saw some attractive double hollyhocks (fig. 6.69).

Shilin (Stone Forest)

The Stone Forest, 120 km southeast of Kunming, is one of the major tourist attractions of the area and visiting it can be a bit of

Figure 6.66 Ancient *Magnolia delavayi*, Caoxi Temple, Anning

said to be 700–800 years old, and hence the oldest known example in cultivation (fig. 6.66). According to the tablet erected beside it, the flowers appear from May to August each year and the buds begin to open about 7 pm each night, the blooms being fully expanded 10 minutes later. In the courtyard there are also cypresses, camellias and the usual array of pot plants. Outside the walls are many interesting trees, including a huge specimen of *Pistacia chinensis*.

a free-for-all. However, I have included it here as in many ways it can be seen as a garden, or at least a much modified landscape. It is a collection of grey limestone pillars which have been eroded into fanciful shapes, much like the mountains depicted in Chinese paintings, though the tallest of them rises only to about 30 m (fig. 6.70).

The Stone Forest covers a very large area, but the portion developed as a tourist attraction has lakes, walkways, pavil-

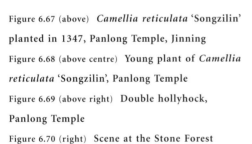

Figure 6.67 (above) *Camellia reticulata* 'Songzilin' planted in 1347, Panlong Temple, Jinning

Figure 6.68 (above centre) Young plant of *Camellia reticulata* 'Songzilin', Panlong Temple

Figure 6.69 (above right) Double hollyhock, Panlong Temple

Figure 6.70 (right) Scene at the Stone Forest

ions, and introduced plants such as crabapples and climbing roses. Many interesting plants native to the area are also found among the rocks, including spiraeas, thujas (*Platycladus orientalis*) and cypresses (*Cupressus duclouxiana*). As well as this some of the principal peaks are inscribed in Chinese characters with poetic inscriptions or their names, which are usually related to their resemblance to something else. Thus it is a site in which Chinese tourists, with their penchant for seeing, in the shapes of rocks and mountains, resemblances to animals, birds, people and so on, have a field day photographing one another. All the same the landscape is fascinating.

Dali and Environs

Dali is 250 km north-west of Kunming. Something in the order of 70 per cent of the population of the district belong to the Bai minority, whose characteristic architectural style dominates most scenes. The present walled town was built in 1382 near the site of the ancient capital of the Nanzhao Kingdom. It is picturesquely situated at an altitude of 1990 m on the shore of Erhai Lake, with the imposing Cangshan Range rising to 4000 m behind. A chairlift to the Zhonghe Temple on the eastern slope affords wonderful views of the town and lake and, also, an opportunity for seeing with a minimum of effort a little of the vegetation which has attracted plant collectors for well over a century.

A walk along the walls of the town allows glimpses into courtyard gardens (fig. 6.27) in which peaches, plums, flowering quinces, camellias, azaleas, cycads and bougainvillea are prominent. Also widely planted nowadays are a semi-double form of the Yunnan cherry and *Rhododendron arboreum* ssp. *delavayi*. In the case of the latter the plants appear to have been dug from the wild. Some of the principal streets are planted with *Prunus cerasoides*, which bears single pink flowers in stalked umbels a few weeks earlier than the Yunnan cherry which, as mentioned earlier, is also considered by Chinese botanists to be a form of this species.

A little to the north-west are the famous Three Pagodas, once part of the Chongsheng Monastery. With the snow-capped mountains rising behind them, these pagodas form a picturesque composition (fig. 6.71). The central and oldest of the three was built in the 9th century, is square, and stands over 69 m tall. The other two are about 42 m tall, are round, and were probably built slightly later. The site has recently been restored and as a result has lost much of its ancient atmosphere. The principal pagoda now looks almost new and a huge temple hall has recently been built beyond it. The same fate, however, has not yet befallen the Single Pagoda, a little to the south. This is also square and, although in the Tang style, was built in the Song.

Described briefly below are gardens in the Dali district which I have visited. I have not been to the 3240 m high Jizu Shan, a famous Buddhist holy mountain to the east of Erhai Lake, so I do not know whether the temples there have interesting gardens. During the Qing there were per-

Figure 6.71 Southernmost of the Three Pagodas, Dali

Figure 6.72 (left) Courtyard at the Museum of Dali Bai Autonomous Prefecture, Xiaguan

Figure 6.73 (below) Penjing apricot, Museum of Dali Bai Autonomous Prefecture

haps 100 temples on this mountain and thousands of monks. Also, to the north and south of Dali on the western shore of Erhai Lake are several sites which, although not gardens, are of interest to gardeners. For a start at Xiaguan, the principal town of the district a few kilometres away on the southern tip of the lake, there is a flower and bird market. Here many plants are offered for sale including azaleas, cymbidiums, *Primula denticulata*, osmanthuses, cycads, cultivars of *Camellia reticulata*, and even large plants of *Rhododendron arboreum* ssp. *delavayi*. And in the market place at Zhoucheng, a Bai village north of Dali, there are two ancient banyans (*Ficus virens*). On the lower side of this market place there is also an old stage, upon which travelling theatrical groups performed. Perhaps they still do.

ERHAI GONGYUAN (ERHAI PARK)

This park on the shore of the lake at Xiaguan contains a number of pavilions in typical Chinese style. Amongst the plantings is a collection of cultivars of *Camellia reticulata*, usually at their best in February and early March.

DALI BAIZU ZIZHIZHOU BOWUGUAN (MUSEUM OF DALI BAI AUTONOMOUS PREFECTURE)

Also at Xiaguan, this museum is housed in a building of traditional style. The two main courtyards are particularly attractive. Each has a tree of *Michelia alba* in the centre and, at the time of my visit in early March, they were ornamented with pots of *Camellia reticulata*, cymbidiums, and dwarfed peaches, apricots and *Jasminum mesnyi* (figs 6.72, 6.73). These courtyards differ from those of houses and temples in having a tree in the centre, and thus are designed to be walked around rather than through. Elsewhere in the compound are azaleas, *Magnolia liliiflora*, and other ornamental shrubs.

GUANYINTANG (GUANYIN HALL)

This temple is about halfway between Xiaguan and Dali. At the time of writing it is undergoing extensive renovations and additions, but the old part of the temple retains its character and interest. Like all the temples near Dali, it faces east, away from the snow-capped mountains which rise abruptly in the background.

The first courtyard is laid out like that at the Yuantong Temple in Kunming, with a pavilion sitting in the middle of a pool and connected to its shore by two bridges. Here, however, the pavilion sits on a huge rock said, according to one tradition, to have been placed there by Guanyin to block the advance of an invading army. In another version of this story Guanyin enabled one of the defending soldiers to carry the rock on his back, so that when the invaders saw this they fled, thinking the locals were too strong for them. Anyway, as a result of whatever it was that happened, the temple was built around the rock as a token of thanks to Guanyin for driving off the enemy.

The pool in the first courtyard is surrounded by a bed containing cultivars of *Camellia reticulata* (fig. 6.74) and, in the second courtyard, in front of the main hall, there are more camellias, enormous old crepe myrtles (fig. 6.75), *Rhododendron arboreum* ssp. *delavayi*, bougainvillea and a clump of the recently popular *Musa lasiocarpa*.

HUDIEQUAN (BUTTERFLY SPRING)

This spring is at the foot of the Yunlong Peak of the Cangshan Range, about 30 km north of Dali between the villages of Zhoucheng and Shangguan. It has been mentioned in Chinese guidebooks as early as the Ming (Wood, 1992).

Legend has it that a young woman and her lover threw themselves into the pool to escape a despotic prince who wanted to make her his wife. On drowning they were transformed into a pair of butterflies. The pool which is fed by the spring is surrounded by a marble balustrade and overhung by an ancient silk tree (*Albizia mollis*), whose branches sweep down to the water (fig. 6.76). Other large trees surround the pond, including an old *Erythrina variegata*.

It is said that, when the silk tree flowers in the fourth lunar month, 20 or so different kinds of butterfly converge on it, linking themselves head to tail into numerous colourful ribbon-like strings which dangle down to the surface of the water. There may be something to this seemingly unlikely story, as Roy Lancaster (1989), who saw *Albizia mollis* in flower elsewhere in Yunnan, recorded that the air above 'was filled with large blackish butterflies attracted to the glistening nectar'.

Figure 6.74 **Pool at the Guanyintang between Xiaguan and Dali**

Figure 6.75 *Camellia reticulata* **and old crepe myrtles, Guanyintang**

I suspect that the charm of this interesting spot has not been enhanced by its recent promotion as a tourist attraction. Not only has a butterfly museum been added but it has also been given an excessively long and straight approach, planted with more silk trees, *Cupressus funebris, C. duclouxiana*, thujas, acacias and bamboo, amongst which sit groups of Bai women preparing cotton material for tie-dyeing. Presumably this has been arranged to create the impression that the fabric of this type now on sale here is hand made.

Weishan

Weishan lies some 80 km south of Dali in the valley which was the cradle of the Nanzhao State, where in 730 Pi Luoge declared himself king and began to build a capital city. The capital was later moved close to the present town of Dali.

The city of Weishan was founded in 1389 and, like Dali, is laid out on a grid pattern with a tower in the central square. The main north-south street is lined with interesting old wooden shops, restaurants and other businesses and ornamented with large pots of *Hibiscus rosa-sinensis*.

From a garden point of view there is little to see in the city, though a few metres to the west of the central tower and opposite the courthouse there is a park. This appears to have been developed in the grounds of a temple of which a pavilion remains, as well as some old cypresses, apricots and

Figure 6.76 The Butterfly Spring, north of Dali

Figure 6.77 (above) **Single form of the Yunnan cherry, Weishan**

Figure 6.78 (right) **Longtan Temple, Weibao Shan**

peaches. Notable amongst more recent planting is a short avenue of the Yunnan cherry, a form with flowers predominantly single (fig. 6.77).

Of greater interest from a garden point of view is Weibao Shan, a mountain south of the city on the uppermost part of which is a group of Daoist temples situated in what is now a forest park, itself of botanical interest.

WEIBAO SHAN

This is one of China's lesser Daoist mountains. Even so, it would require a lengthy walk and a whole day to visit all 18 temples which still exist here. I had the time to visit only the three closest to the end of the road. The second, the Longtan (Dragon Pool) Temple, is in the style of other temples in Yunnan, the principal courtyard having a rectangular pool with a pavilion in its centre connected to the shore by two bridges aligned with the central axis of the complex (fig. 6.78). Overhanging this is an old weeping cypress (*Cupressus funebris*) and the courtyard is ornamented with plants in pots, including cymbidiums and flowering quinces.

A short walk further up the mountain is the Zhujunge (Sovereign Lord's Pavilion). As soon as the buildings of this temple come into view an enormous camellia is seen towering above the principal courtyard. At the time of my visit this was covered with rose pink flowers and was an astonishing

sight (fig. 6.79). It is the cultivar 'Guiye Yinhong' of *C. reticulata*, and at 17.5 m is the tallest cultivated camellia recorded in China. It is said locally to date from the Ming dynasty but, since the temple was not built until the 18th century, it seems likely that Pang et al. (1995), who say it is more than 200 years old, are nearer the mark.

In a courtyard above that in which the camellia stands are two trees of *Magnolia denudata* which flower two or three weeks apart, the earlier one being the finest, according to those living at the temple.

Pang et al. (1995) record another ancient camellia on Weibao Shan, a specimen of 'Zhusha Zipao' ('Cinnabar Purple Gown') which is 8 m tall and has deep red flowers, but give no location. Unfortunately I did not have the time to

In view of its position close to the first bend of the Yangtze, the Tiger Leaping Gorge, and the Jade Dragon Snow Mountain, Lijiang has become a popular tourist destination. With the aid of a chairlift visitors can now reach a point 3200 m above sea level on the Jade Dragon Snow Mountain with ease and, this excursion, like the ascent of Emei Shan in Sichuan, provides an easy way of seeing something of the flora of the mountains of western China. The Kunming Botanical Institute in collaboration with the Royal Botanic Garden Edinburgh has recently begun the development of a new garden here with the aim of assembling a representative collection of plants from the area, and it is hoped that conservation projects will be initiated.

Plants in the old part of Lijiang include upright, weeping and contorted willows, semi-double Yunnan cherries, a single white cherry, and occasional plants of *Rhododendron arboreum* ssp. *delavayi*. As far as gardens are concerned,

Figure 6.79 *Camellia reticulata* '**Guiye Yinhong**' **towers above the Zhujunge, Weibao Shan**

search for it, as it would surely be worth seeing. It may be that there is much else of horticultural interest in the temples on this mountain.

Lijiang and Environs

Lijiang is the home of the Naxi people and was made well known to both plant lovers and ethnologists by Joseph Rock, who lived there for many years in the 1920s and 30s. It is around 150 km north of Dali and is situated about 2400 m above sea level near the southern end of the Yulong Xueshan (Jade Dragon Snow Mountain), which rises to over 5500 m. The attractive 800-year-old Naxi town has been preserved, but a modern city with more than a million inhabitants has now sprung up around it.

Figure 6.81 (left) The Five Phoenix Tower, Black Dragon Pool Park, Lijiang
Figure 6.82 (below left) Courtyard with penjing, Black Dragon Pool Park, Lijiang

the grounds surrounding this one have been developed as a public park. The pool itself is of the proportions of a lake, complete with bridge, willow-lined dikes and ornamental pavilions. These, together with the 'borrowed view' of the Jade Dragon Snow Mountain, make up a striking landscape composition (fig. 6.80).

The most significant architectural feature is the Wufenglou (Five Phoenix Tower) which was moved here in 1977 from the nearby Fuguo Temple. The Wufenglou was originally built in 1601 but, like many famous structures in China, has undergone repeated rebuilding and restoration. It has been reinstated here in a temple courtyard setting (fig. 6.81). In this courtyard are a pair of *Michelia yunnanensis*, a semi-double form of the Yunnan cherry, a dark red, double flowering quince, and numerous plants in pots, including plums (*Prunus mume*), peaches, a forsythia and clivias.

visits to the Black Dragon Pool Park and the grounds of various lamaseries in the vicinity are rewarding. There are, as you might expect, places in the vicinity other than those mentioned below, for example the Wenbi and Wenteng temples south of the city, which might prove to be worth visiting from a gardener's point of view.

HEILONGTAN GONGYUAN (BLACK DRAGON POOL PARK)

As must have already become clear, Black Dragon Pools are to be found in many parts of China and, like that at Kunming,

In a building complex a little to the south of this are further courtyards with interesting plants. In the principal one are more Yunnan cherries along with penjing specimens of various sorts (fig. 6.82). An adjoining courtyard is dominated by a large *Michelia yunnanensis* and a bright red cultivar of *Camellia japonica*. At the time of my visit there were also numerous pots of what appeared to be *Cymbidium wilsonii*, a species native to Yunnan (fig. 6.83). This is known locally as Tiger's Head Orchid and is one of the few large-flowered cymbidiums to be found in Chinese gardens. Another is *C. lowianum* (fig. 6.84), also native to this province.

Elsewhere in the park, small-flowered cymbidiums of the *C. goeringii* and *C. ensifolium* types are to be seen, as are

Figure 6.80 (previous pages) **Black Dragon Pool Park, Lijiang**

Magnolia denudata, *M.* × *soulangiana*, flowering peaches and apricots, and cultivars of *Camellia reticulata*.

ZHIYUNSI (POINTING AT THE CLOUDS TEMPLE)

This lamasery is a few kilometres south-west of Lijiang near the village of Lashi. Until recently it was difficult to reach but there is now a well-made road leading to it from the main Lijiang–Shigu road. Like most other surviving temples in the district, it dates from the 18th century.

Outside the entrance there are a few old trees including *Magnolia delavayi* and, in the entrance courtyard, a pair of thujas. The central axis of the principal courtyard is flanked

Figure 6.83 (right) **Tiger's Head Orchid (*Cymbidium wilsonii*), Black Dragon Pool Park, Lijiang**

Figure 6.84 (far right) ***Cymbidium lowianum*, Lijiang Grand Hotel**

Figure 6.85 (below) **A pair of old plums in raised beds on either side of the central axis of the Zhiyun Temple, Lashi, with an ancient Yunnan cherry beyond**

by a pair of gnarled old plums (*Prunus mume*) and, at the steps up to the principal hall, by a Yunnan cherry, and a pine which has had its trunk and branches trained in a contorted manner. In defiance of the symmetry otherwise prevailing, there is on the left as you enter an ancient Yunnan cherry most of the flowers of which are single. As well as these plants there is the usual assortment of penjing, including plums, pines and wisterias (fig. 6.85).

Figure 6.86
(opposite page)
*Michelia
yunnanensis,*
Zhiyun Temple,
Lashi, with
small plants for
sale arranged
beneath it
Figure 6.87
(right)
View over the
Puji Temple,
looking towards
Lijiang

Of particular note in this temple is a side courtyard in which grows the largest specimen of *Michelia yunnanensis* I have seen, an indication that it has been cultivated in this part of the country for many years (fig. 6.86). The temple propagates this *Michelia* and the verandas and ledges are crowded with potted plants for sale. Elsewhere in the temple grounds the Chinese Lantern (*Physalis alkekengi*) appears to grow in a self-sown manner. Surprisingly for this part of the world, there are no camellias.

PUJISI (PUJI TEMPLE)

This lamasery, which dates from 1771, takes its name from that of the peak on the lower slopes of which it is situated. It is one of three on the lower eastern slopes of the Jade Dragon Snow Mountain and the nearest to Lijiang (fig. 6.87). There is no road to it but it is reached from the nearest village by a relatively easy walk up through old walnut orchards and a pine forest.

Outside the entrance are a pair of enormous cypresses (*Cupressus duclouxiana*), a loquat, a single specimen of *Magnolia delavayi*, clumps of *Jasminum mesnyi*, and a tall Tasmanian Blue Gum (*Eucalyptus globulus*)—one of the trees most commonly planted in western China.

The axis of the main courtyard is flanked by a pair of Yunnan cherries (fig. 6.88), a form with semi-double flowers

Figure 6.88 **Old Yunnan cherries, Puji Temple**

(fig. 6.89), and in front of the copper-roofed main hall are another cherry, a large osmanthus and mature specimens of *Camellia reticulata* 'Juban' and *Wisteria sinensis*. A large slate box containing a tree peony sits on the central axis and various potted plants, including hydrangeas, roses, azaleas, flowering quinces and plums are arranged on stands. As at the Zhiyun Temple, there is a *Michelia yunnanensis* in a side courtyard along with *Magnolia liliiflora* and an old plum with a tree peony growing beneath it.

FUGUOSI (HAPPY NATION TEMPLE)

A few kilometres north of the Puji Temple, this temple, founded in 1601, was once the largest temple in the Lijiang district. It was given its name at the time of its founding when Ming officials came to Lijiang and saw how well the various minority races were getting along with one another. It was badly damaged during the Cultural Revolution and as a result of this and the removal of its most important building, the Wufenglou, to the Black Dragon Pool Park, it is only a shadow of its former self, as the saying goes. Now there is little to see apart from a tall, storm-blasted cypress and some penjing pines and plums, amongst which *Primula malacoides* has seeded itself.

YUFENGSI (YUFENG TEMPLE)

This lamasery takes its name from the Yu Feng (Jade Peak) at the base of which it lies, close to the village of Xiehou, where Joseph Rock lived for many years. As a result of its being promoted as a tourist attraction, a road has recently been made up to it and a long arcade of shops selling local produce and souvenirs has been built along its approaches. It can also be reached by walking up the slope behind the Fuguo Temple, where *Primula denticulata* blooms in damp places in March (fig. 6.90) and where an occasional plant of *Rhododendron decorum* can be seen.

Outside the main temple complex is a huge, three-trunked *Magnolia delavayi*, the largest I have come across. The notice beside it declares it to be 500 years old but, since the temple was not founded until the third quarter of the 18th century, I reserve my judgement. At the most it is probably the same age the temple, as Sun et al. (2000) suggest. Anyway, whatever its age, it is a fine old tree.

While the courtyard of the temple itself is not particularly interesting, further up the hill in the courtyard of a smaller complex of buildings is the temple's main attraction, the Wanduocha (Ten-thousand-flower Camellia). In spite of the date of the founding of the temple, this is said to have been planted in 1465. Perhaps to add to its mystique, it is also put about that, at a risk to his own well being, an old lama kept this tree alive during the Cultural Revolution by regularly watering it. This may, of course, be so, but the old camellias and other plants in temples everywhere else seem to have got by without being afforded any particular attention. All the same it is an interesting plant and, when it is in bloom in February and March, a continuous stream of tourists line up to be photographed in front of it. In the face of this and a series of snow flurries, that I managed to take the photograph reproduced opposite (fig. 6.91) could be regarded as a miracle.

This camellia is unusual in that its trunk and main branches have been trained in one vertical plane—an informal espalier if you like. By some authors (Feng, Xia and Zhu, 1986; Savige, 1993) it has been given the cultivar name 'Wanduocha', which is described as having double pink flowers. However the flowers are bright red (fig. 6.92) and

Figure 6.89 (far left) A semi-double cultivar of the Yunnan cherry, Puji Temple

Figure 6.90 (left) *Primula denticulata* on the hillside below the Yufeng Temple, near Xiehou

I am happy to agree with Pang et al. (1995) that it is 'Shizitou'. It is also interesting that the flowers on some branches, while not exactly single, have a central boss of stamens. So either this is the stock upon which 'Shizitou' was grafted or the original stock must have been grafted with two different varieties, a practice long popular in China with many plants.

A terrace below this courtyard has recently been planted with a selection of other *Camellia reticulata* cultivars and to one side of this is what is labelled the 'Michelia Garden'. This is a small building in the courtyard of which is a pair of old plants of *Michelia yunnanensis*, the trunks of which have been trained in the same manner as that of the Ten-thousand-flower Camellia. Sun et al. (2000) say these are 120–200 years old. Elsewhere in the temple grounds there are plums, tree peonies, hydrangeas and other ornamental plants.

Figure 6.91 (above) The 'Ten-thousand-flower Camellia', Yufeng Temple

Figure 6.92 (right) A close view of part of the "Ten-thousand-flower Camellia'

BIBLIOGRAPHY AND REFERENCES

Abel, C. 1819. *Narrative of a Journey in the Interior of China and of a Voyage to and from that Country in the Years 1816 and 1817.* Longman, Hurst, Rees, Orme and Brown, London.

Allom, T., and Wright, G.N. 1843. *China, in a series of views, displaying the scenery, architecture, and social habits of that ancient empire.* 4 vols. Fisher, Son, & Co., London & Paris.

André, E. 1892. Le Narcise Sacré de Chine. *Revue Horticole* 1892: 198–9.

Arlington, L.C. 1931. *Through the Dragon's Eyes.* Constable & Co. Ltd, London.

_____ and Lewisohn, W. 1935. *In Search of Old Peking.* Paragon Book Reprint Corp., New York, 1967.

Attiret, J.-D. 1752. *A Particular Account of the Emperor of China's Gardens near Pekin.* Trans. by 'Sir Harry Beaumont' (pseudonym of Joseph Spence) of Attiret's letter of 1st Nov. 1743 orig. publ. in Paris in *Lettres édifiantes et curieuses*, vol. 27, 1749. Dodsley & Cooper, London. Reprinted in Hunt, J.D. (ed.) 1982. *The English Landscape Garden*, Garland Publishing, Inc., New York & London.

Baber, E.C. 1882. *Travels and Researches in Western China.* John Murray, London. Reprint by Ch'eng Wen Publishing Company, Taipei, 1971.

Backhouse, E., and Bland, J.O.P. 1914. *Annals & Memoirs of the Court of Peking (from the 16th to the 20th century).* William Heinemann, London.

Baker, D.C. 1925. *T'ai Shan: An Account of the Sacred Eastern Peak of China.* Commercial Press Ltd, Shanghai.

Barnhart, R. 1972. *Wintry Forests, Old Trees: Some Landscape Themes in Chinese Painting.* China Institute in America, New York.

Barnhart, R.M. 1983. *Peach Blossom Spring: Gardens and Flowers in Chinese Painting.* Metropolitan Museum of Art, New York.

Barrow, J. 1804. *Travels in China.* T. Cadell & W. Davies, London.

Béguin, G., and Morel, D. 1997. *The Forbidden City: Heart of Imperial China.* Trans. by Ruth Taylor. Thames & Hudson, London.

Bell, J. 1763. *Travels from St. Petersburgh in Russia to Various Parts of Asia.* William Creech, Edinburgh.

Berliner, N. 1990. The Rosenblum Collection of Chinese Rocks. *Orientations* 21(11): 68–75.

Birch, J.G. 1902. *Travels in North and Central China.* Hurst and Blackett, Ltd, London.

Blofield, J. 1961. *City of Lingering Splendour.* Hutchinson & Co., London.

Boerschmann, E. 1982. *Old China in Historic Photographs.* Dover Publications, New York.

Borel, H. 1912. *The New China.* Trans. from the Dutch by C. Thieme. T. Fisher Unwin, London.

Bouillard, G. 1929. Note Succincte sur l'Historique du Territoire de Peking et sur les Diverses Enceintes de Cette Ville. Reprinted from *The Bulletin of the Museum of Far Eastern Antiquities, Stockholm*, No. 1.

_____ 1931a. *Le Temple des Lamas.* Albert Nachbauer, Peking.

_____ 1931b. *Les Tombeaux Impériaux, Ming et Tsing.* Albert Nachbauer, Peking.

Box, E. 1902. Shanghai Folk-Lore. *Journal of the China Branch of the Royal Asiatic Society* 34: 101–35.

Boxer, C.R. (ed.). 1953. *South China in the Sixteenth Century. Being the narratives of Galeote Pereira, Fr. Gaspar da Cruz, O.P., Fr. Martínde Rada, O.E.S.A. (1550–1575).* Reprint, The Hakluyt Society, London.

Bredon, J. 1931. *Peking: a historical and intimate description of its chief places of interest.* 3rd edn. First published 1919. Kelly and Walsh Ltd, Shanghai.

_____ and Mitrophanov, I. 1927. *The Moon Year.* Paragon Book Reprint Corp., New York, 1966.

Bretschneider, E. 1879. *Recherches archéologiques et historiques sur Pékin et ses Environs.* Traduction française par V. Collin de Plancy. Ernest Leroux, Paris.

_____ 1880. Early European Researches into the Flora of China. *Journal of the North China Branch of the Royal Asiatic Society* n.s. 15: 1–194.

_____ 1881. Botanicon Sinicum. Part 1. Ibid. n.s.16: 18–230.

_____ 1893. Botanicon Sinicum. Part 2. Ibid. 25: 1–468.

_____ 1895. Botanicon Sinicum. Part 3. Ibid. 29: 1–623.

_____ 1898. *History of European Botanical Discoveries in China.* Sampson Low, Marston & Co. Ltd, London.

Bridge, A. 1932. *Peking Picnic.* Little, Brown, & Co., Boston.

Brinkley, Captain F. 1904. *Japan and China.* Vol. 12. T.C. & E.C. Jack, London.

Brown, C. 1998. Where Immortals Dwell: Shared Symbolism in Painting and Scholars' Rocks. *Oriental Art* 44 (1): 11–17.

Bushell, S.W. 1904. *Chinese Art.* Vol. 1. His Majesty's Stationery Office, London.

Cantoniensis. 1867. Grafting. *Notes and Queries on China and Japan* 1(11): 157–8.

Cao, X. 1973–86. *The Story of the Stone.* Orig. publ. in this form 1792. Vols 1–3 trans. by David Hawkes, vols 4, 5 by John Minford. Penguin Books, Harmondsworth, England.

Carpenter, F.W. 1927. *China.* Doubleday, Page & Co., New York.

Chambers, W. 1757. *Designs of Chinese Buildings, Furniture, Dresses, Machines and Utensils.* Reprint 1968, B. Blom, New York.

_____ 1772. *A Dissertation on Oriental Gardening.* Reprint 1972, Gregg International Publishers Ltd, Farnborough, England.

Chen, C. 1956. *Suzhou yuanlin.* Tongji Daxue Jiaocaike, Shanghai.

_____ 1983. *Yangzhou yuanlin.* Joint Publishing Company, Hong Kong.

_____ 1984. *On Chinese Gardens.* Tongji University Press, Shanghai.

Chen, L., and Yu, S. 1986. *The Garden Art of China.* Timber Press, Portland.

Ch'ên, H.-S., and Kates, G.N. 1940. Prince Kung's Palace and its adjoining Garden in Peking. *Monumenta Serica* 5: 1–80.

Cheng, L. 1998. *Ancient Chinese Architecture: Imperial Gardens.* Trans. by Zhang Long. Springer-Verlag, Wien & New York.

_____ 1999. *Ancient Chinese Architecture: Private Gardens.* Trans. by Zhang Long. Springer Verlag, Wien & New York.

Chiu, C.B. 2000. *Yuanming yuan: Le Jardin de la Clarté parfaite.* Les Éditions de l'Imprimeur, Paris.

Chung, W.N. 1982. *The Art of Chinese Gardens.* Hong Kong University Press.

Cibot, P.M. 1778. Serres Chinoises. *Mémoires concernant l'Histoire, les Sciences, les Arts, les Moeurs, les Usages, etc. des Chinois par les Missionaires de Pé-kin* 3: 423–37.

_____ 1782. Essai sur les jardins de plaisance des Chinois. Ibid. 8: 301–26.

Cloud, F.D. 1906. *Hangchow, the "City of Heaven", with a Brief Historical Sketch of Soochow.* Reprint 1971, Ch'eng Wen Publishing Company, Taipei.

Clunas, C. 1991. *Superfluous Things—Material Culture and Social Status in Early Modern China.* University of Illinois Press, Urbana & Chicago.

_____ 1995. The Gift and the Garden. *Orientations* 26(2): 38–45.

_____ 1996. *Fruitful Sites: Garden Culture in Ming Dynasty China.* Reaktion Books, London.

Conner, P. 1986. The 'Chinese Garden' in Regency England. *Garden History* 14(1): 42–9.

Cook, T., & Son. 1924. *Cook's Guide to Peking, North China, South Manchuria, Korea.* 5th edn. T. Cook & Son, Peking.

Cooper, J.C. 1977. The Symbolism of the Taoist Garden. *Studies in Comparative Religion* Autumn 1977: 224–34.

Cotton, R. 1999. In pursuit of human harmony. *Landscape Design* 277: 33–6.

Couling, S. 1917. *The Encyclopaedia Sinica.* Kelly and Walsh, Shanghai.

Cranmer-Byng, J.L. (ed.). 1962. *An Embassy to China, Being the Journal kept by Lord Macartney during his embassy to the Emperor Ch'ien Lung 1793–1794.* Longmans, Green and Co. Ltd, London.

Cranz, G. 1979. The Useful and Beautiful: Urban Parks in China. *Landscape* 23(2): 3–10.

Crombie, I. 1987. China, 1860: A Photographic Album by Felice Beato. *History of Photography* 11(1): 25–37.

Daedess, J.W. 1989. A Ming Landscape: Settlement, Land Use, Labor, and Estheticism in T'ai-ho County, Kiangsi. *Harvard Journal of Asiatic Studies* 498(2): 295–364.

Danby, H. 1950. *The Garden of Perfect Brightness.* Williams & Norgate Ltd, London.

Davis, A.R. 1983. *T'ao Yüan-ming (AD 365–427): His Works and Their Meaning.* 2 vols. Cambridge University Press.

DeFrancis, J. (ed.). 1997. *ABC Chinese-English Dictionary.* Allen & Unwin, St Leonards, NSW.

Dennys, N.B. 1866. *Notes for Tourists in the North of China.* Printed by A. Shortrede & Co., Hongkong.

Der Ling, Princess. 1911. *Two Years in the Forbidden City.* Moffat, Yard & Co., New York.

Doolittle, J. 1866. *Social Life of the Chinese.* 2 vols. Sampson Low, Son, & Marston, London.

Dorsett, P.H. 1928. Chinese Sacred Lilies in Pekin. *National Horticultural Magazine* 7(4): 147–8.

_____ 1931. Glimpses of the white-barked pine in Peiping. Ibid. 10(4): 237–9.

Du Halde, J.B. 1736. *Description Géographique, Historique, Chronologique, Politique, et Physique de l'Empire de la Chine et de la Tartarie Chinoise.* 4 vols. The Hague.

Du Puy, D., and Cribb, P. 1988. *The Genus Cymbidium.* Christopher Helm, London.

Eberhard, W. 1986. *A Dictionary of Chinese Symbols.* Trans. from the German by G.L. Campbell. Routledge & Keegan Paul, London & New York.

Ebrey, P.B. 1996. *The Cambridge Illustrated History of China.* Cambridge University Press.

Edkins, Rev. J. 1870. Peking. In Williamson, Rev. A. *Journeys in North China, Manchuria, and Eastern Mongolia; with Some Account of Corea.* Vol. 2, 313–92. Smith, Elder & Co., London.

Elwood, P.H. Jr. 1930. Impressions of Garden Art in China and Japan. *Landscape Architecture* 20(3): 192–200.

Engel, D.H. 1986. *Creating a Chinese Garden.* Timber Press, Portland.

The Face of China—As Seen by Photographers & Travelers, 1860–1912. Gordon Fraser, London.

Fang-Tu, L.-c. 1980. Ming Gardens. *Papers on Far Eastern History* 22: 1–15.

Farrer, R. 1916. Report of Work in 1914 and 1915 in Kansu and Tibet. *Journal of the Royal Horticultural Society* 42(1): 47–114.

Favier, A. 1902. *Péking: Histoire et Description.* Desclée, de Brouwer et Cie, Paris & Lille.

Feng, G., Xia, L., and Zhu, X. 1986. *Yunnan Camellias of China.* Science Press, Beijing.

Feng, J., and Tan, L. 1986. *Qingdai neiting gongyuan* (Gardens in the Forbidden City). Tianjin Daxue Chubanshe, Tianjin.

Fischer, E.S. (Fei-shi). 1924. *Guide to Peking and its Environs Near and Far.* Revised edn. Tientsin Press Ltd, Tientsin & Peking.

Fleming, P. 1934. *One's Company—A Journey to China.* Jonathan Cape, London & Toronto.

Forêt, P. 1995. The Manchu landscape enterprise: political, geomantic and cosmological readings of the Bishu shanzhuang imperial residence at Chengde. *Ecumene* 2(3): 325–34.

Fortune, R. 1846. Sketch of a Visit to China in search of New Plants. *Journal of the Horticultural Society of London* 1: 208–24.

_____ 1847. *Three Years' Wanderings in the Northern Provinces of China.* John Murray, London.

_____ 1850. Notes of a Traveller. XII. *Gardeners' Chronicle* 1850: 372.

_____ 1852. *A Journey to the Tea Countries of China.* John Murray, London.

_____ 1853. Leaves from my Chinese Notebook. I. *Gardeners' Chronicle* 1853: 230–1.

_____ 1855. Leaves from my Chinese Notebook. X. Ibid. 1855: 502–3.

_____ 1857. *A Residence among the Chinese.* London, John Murray.

_____ 1863. *Yedo and Peking.* John Murray, London.

_____ 1864. Note on a New Forsythia from Peking. *Gardeners' Chronicle* 1864: 412.

Fox, H.M. 1949. *Abbe David's Diary.* Harvard University Press, Cambridge, Mass.

Freeman-Mitford, A.B. 1900. *The Attache at Peking.* Macmillan, London.

Fung, S. 1998a. The interdisciplinary prospects of reading *Yuan ye. Studies in the History of Gardens & Designed Landscapes* 18(3): 211–31.

_____ 1998b. Guide to secondary sources on Chinese gardens. Ibid. 18(3): 269–86.

_____ 1999. Here and there in *Yuan ye.* Ibid. 19(1): 33–6.

Geil, W.E. 1911. *Eighteen Capitals of China.* J.B. Lippincot Co., Philadelphia & London.

Genest, G. 1984. Les Palais européens du Yuanmingyuan: essai sur la végétation dans les jardins. *Arts Asiatiques* 49: 82–90.

Gerbillon, J.-F. 1736. In Du Halde, J.B. *Description Géographique, Historique, Chronologique, Politique, et Physique de l'Empire de la Chine et de la Tartarie Chinoise.* 4 vols. The Hague.

_____ 1780. In Moyriac de Mailla, P.J.-A.-M. de. *Histoire Générale de la Chine.* Vol. XI. Chez Ph.-D. Pierres et Clousier, Paris.

Goodrich, L.C. 1935. *The Literary Inquisition of Ch'ien Lung.* Reprint 1986, Paragon Book Reprint Corp., New York.

Gordon Cumming, C.F. 1890. *Wanderings in China.* Cheaper Edition. William Blackwood & Sons, Edinburgh & London.

Graham, D. 1938. *Chinese Gardens.* Dodd, Mead & Co., New York.

Griffiths, D.A. 1988. A Garden on the Edge of China: Hong Kong, 1848. *Garden History* 16(2): 189–98.

Hall, D.L., and Ames, R.T. 1998. The cosmological setting of Chinese gardens. *Studies in the History of Gardens & Designed Landscapes* 18(3): 175–86.

Halphen, J. 1900. *Miroir des fleurs: guide pratique du jardinier amateur en Chine au XVIIe siècle.* Librairie Plon, Paris.

Handlin Smith, J.F. 1992. Gardens in Ch'i Piaochia's Social World: Wealth and Values in Late Ming Kiangnan. *The Journal of Asian Studies* 51(1): 55–81.

Hargett, J.M. 1988–89. Huizong's Magic Marchmount: The Genyue Pleasure Park of Kaifeng. *Monumenta Serica* 38: 1–48.

Harris, D. 1999. *Of Battle and Beauty: Felice Beato's Photographs of China.* Santa Barbara Museum of Art.

Harrist, R.E. Jr. 1993. Site names and their meanings in the Garden of Solitary Enjoyment. *Journal of Garden History* 13(4): 199–212.

Hay, J. 1985. *Kernels of Energy, Bones of Earth: The Rock in Chinese Art.* The China Institute in America, New York.

Hedin, S. 1932. *Jehol, City of Emperors.* Keegan Paul, Trench, Trubner & Co. Ltd, London.

Hildebrand, H. 1897. *Der Tempel Ta-chüeh-sy (Tempel des grossen Erkennens) bei Peking.* A. Asher, Berlin.

Ho, P.-t. 1954. The Salt Merchants of Yang-chou: A Study of Commercial Capitalism in Eighteenth-century China. *Harvard Journal of Asiatic Studies* 17: 130–68.

Honour, H. 1990. In Sirén, O. *China and Gardens of Europe in the Eighteenth Century.* Reprint 1990, Dumbarton Oaks Research Library and Collection, Washington, D.C.

Hookham, H. 1972. *A Short History of China.* The New American Library, Inc., New York.

Howard, E.L. 1931. *Chinese Garden Architecture.* Macmillan, New York.

Hu, D. 1991. *The Way of the Virtuous: the Influence of Art and Philosophy on Chinese Garden Design.* New World Press, Beijing.

Hu, H.H. 1938. Recent Progress in Botanical Exploration in China. *Journal of the Royal Horticultural Society* 63(8): 381–9.

Hubbard, G.E. 1923. *The Temples of the Western Hills visited from Peking.* La Librairie Francaise, Peking & Tientsin.

Huc, M. 1855. *A Journey Through The Chinese Empire.* 2 vols. Harper & Brothers, New York.

Hummel, A.W. 1943. *Eminent Chinese of the Ch'ing Period (1644–1912).* United States Government Printing Office, Washington, D.C. Reprint 1970, Chen Wen Publishing Company, Taipei.

Ingram, C. 1948. *Ornamental Cherries.* Country Life, London.

Inn, H. 1940. *Chinese Houses and Gardens.* Edited by Shao Chang Lee. Fong Inn's Ltd, Honolulu.

Ip, B. W.-B. 1986. The expression of nature in traditional Suzhou gardens. *Journal of Garden History* 6(2): 125–40.

Ishida, H.-m. S. 1990. Wang Fu and His Depiction of the Bamboo Garden, Zhu Shen Chu. *Oriental Art* 36(3): 138–46.

Jacques, D. 1990. On the Supposed Chineseness of the English Landscape Garden. *Garden History* 18(2): 180–91.

Jellicoe, G. and Jellicoe, S. (consultant eds), Goode, P., and Lancaster, M. (executive eds). 1986. *The Oxford Companion to Gardens.* Oxford University Press.

Ji, C. 1988. *The Craft of Gardens.* Trans. by Alison Hardie of the *Yuan Ye* written between 1631 and 1634. Yale University Press, New Haven & London.

Johnston, R.F. 1934. *Twilight in the Forbidden City.* Victor Gollancz Ltd, London.

Johnston, R.S. 1991. *Scholar Gardens of China.* Cambridge University Press.

Kates, G.N. 1952. *The Years That Were Fat: the last of old China.* Harper & Brothers, New York. Reprinted by M.I.T. Press, Cambridge, Mass., 1967.

Kerby, K. 1922. *An Old Chinese Garden.* Chung Hwa Book Co., Shanghai.

Keswick, M. 1978. *The Chinese Garden.* Academy Editions, London.

Koster, H. 1936. The Palace Museum of Peiping. *Monumenta Serica* 2: 167–90.

Kramer, P. 1967. *The Last Manchu: The Autobiography of Henry Pu Yi, Last Emperor of China.* Trans. by Kuo Ying Paul Tsai. Arthur Baker Ltd, London.

Lai, T.C. 1978. *A Wild Swan's Trail: The Travels of a Mandarin.* Wing Tai Cheung Printing Company, Hongkong.

Lauffer, B. 1912–13. The Wang Ch'uan T'u, a Landscape of Wang Wei. *Ostasiatische Zeitschrift* 1: 28–55.

Lay, G.T. 1846. Outlines of a Natural History Calendar at Foo-chow-foo, the capital of the Chinese province of Fokien. *Journal of the Horticultural Society of London* 1: 119–26.

Le Rougetel, H. 1982. The Fa Tee Nurseries of South China. *Garden History* 10(1): 70–3.

Li, H.-L. 1956. *Chinese Flower Arrangement.* Hedera House, Philadelphia.

_____ 1959. *The Garden Flowers of China.* Ronald Press, New York.

_____ 1979. *Nan-fang Ts'ao-mu Chuang.* The Chinese University Press, Hong Kong.

Li, S. (ed.). 1991. *Botanical Gardens of China: A Traveller's Guidebook.* Jindun Publishing House, Beijing.

Liang, E.J. 1988. Qiu Ying's Depiction of Sima Guang's Duluo yuan and the View from the Chinese Garden. *Oriental Art* 33(4): 375–80.

Lin, J.-x., Hu, Y.-s., and Wang, X.-p. 1996. Old Ginkgo trees in China. *International Dendrology Society Yearbook* 1995: 32–7.

Lin, Q. 1847–50. *Hongxue yinyuan tuqi.*

Little, A.J. 1888. *Through the Yang-tse Gorges or Trade and Travel in Western China.* Sampson Low, Marston, Searle, & Rivington, London.

_____ 1901. *Mount Omi and Beyond.* William Heinemann, London.

_____.1910. *Gleanings from Fifty Years in China.* Edited by Mrs Archibald Little. Sampson Low, Marston & Co., Ltd, London.

Little, Mrs A. 1901. *Intimate China.* Hutchinson & Co., London.

_____ 1902. *The Land of the Blue Gown.* T. Fisher Unwin, London.

_____ 1905. *Round About My Peking Garden.* T. Fisher Unwin, London.

Liu, D. 1980. *La Maison Chinoise.* Bibliothèque Berger-Levrault, Paris. Trans. of *Zhongguo Zhuzhai Gaisho.* Peking, 1957.

_____ 1982. The Traditional Gardens of Suzhou. Abridged trans. by Frances Wood. *Garden History* 10(2): 108–41.

_____ 1993. *Chinese Classical Gardens of Suzhou.* Trans. by Chen Lixian. McGraw Hill, New York.

Liu, J. 1982. *Beijing, China's Ancient and Modern Capital.* Foreign Languages Press, Beijing.

Liu, S. 1982. The Chinese Views of Nature, Naturalness, and Understanding of Nature. *Journal of the Institute of Chinese Studies* 13: 237–48.

Livingstone, J. 1822. Account of the Method of Dwarfing Trees and Shrubs, as practised by the Chinese, including their Plan of Propagation from Branches. *Transactions of the Horticultural Society of London* 4: 224–31.

_____ 1824. On the State of Chinese Horticulture and Agriculture; with an Account of several Esculent Vegetables used in China. Ibid. 5: 49–56.

Loehr, G.R. 1940. *Giuseppe Castiglione (1688–1766), Pittore di Corte di Ch'ien-Lung, Imperatore della Cina.* Instituto Italiano per il Medio ed Estremo Oriente, Roma.

Loti, Pierre. 1902. *Les Derniers Jours de Pékin.* Calman-Levy, Paris. Reprint, Editions Juillard, 1991.

Makeham, J. 1998. The Confucian role of names in traditional Chinese gardens. *Studies in the History of Gardens & Designed Landscapes* 18(3): 187–210.

Malone, C.B. 1934. *History of the Peking Summer Palaces under the Ch'ing Dynasty.* University of Illinois Press, Urbana. Reprint 1966, Paragon Book Reprint Corp., New York.

Markbreiter, S. A Garden for a Mandarin. *Country Life* September 4, 1969: 530–2.

_____ 1979. Yu Yuan: A Shanghai Garden. *Arts of Asia* (6): 99–110.

Martin, W.A.P. 1900. *A Cycle of Cathay.* Fleming H. Revell Co., New York, Chicago, & Toronto. Reprint 1966, Ch'eng-Wen Publishing Co., Taipei.

Mayers, W.F., Dennys, N.B., and King, C. 1867. *The Treaty Ports of China and Japan: a complete guide to the open ports of those countries, together with Peking, Yedo, Hong Kong and Macao: forming a guide book and vade mecum for travellers, merchants, and residents in general.* Trubner & Co., London; A. Shortrede & Co., Hong Kong.

Mendoza, J. Gonzalez de. 1588. *The History of the Great and Mighty Kingdom of China.* Originally publ. Rome 1585. Original trans. by R. Parke. Reprinted by Hakluyt Society 1854, with intro. by R.H. Major. Republ. 1970, Lenox Hill, New York.

Mennie, D. 1920. *The Pageant of Peking.* Text by Putnam Weale. A.S. Watson & Co., Shanghai.

_____ 1920? *China North & South.* 2nd revised edn. A.S. Watson & Co., Shanghai.

_____ 1926. *The Grandeur of the Gorges.* A.S. Watson & Co., Shanghai.

Métailié, G. 1998. Some hints on 'Scholar Gardens' and plants in traditional China. *Studies in the History of Gardens & Designed Landscapes* 18(3): 248–56.

Meyer, F.N. 1916. China a Fruitful Field for Plant Exploration. *US Dept Agriculture Yearbook* 1915: 205–24.

Minford, J. (ed.). 1993. Tracks in the Snow—episodes from an autobiographical memoir by the Manchu Bannerman Lin-ch'ing (1791–1846) with illustrations by leading contemporary artists. *East Asian History*: 105–42.

_____ 1998. The Chinese garden: death of a symbol. *Studies in the History of Gardens & Designed Landscapes* 18(3): 257–68.

Morris, E.T. 1983. *The Gardens of China: History, Art, and Meanings.* Charles Scribner's Sons, New York.

Morrison, H., and Eberhard, W. 1974. *Hua Shan: the Taoist sacred mountain in west China, its scenery, monasteries, and monks.* Vetch & Lee Ltd, Hong Kong.

Morrison, R. 1822. *A Dictionary of the Chinese Language.* The Honorable East India Company's Press, Macao. Vol. 3: 172–4.

Mowry, R.D. 1988. Chinese Scholars' Rocks: An Overview. *Oriental Art* 44(1): 2–10.

Moyriac de Mailla, J.-A.-M. de. 1780. *Histoire Générale de La Chine.* Vol. XI. Chez Ph.-D. Pierres et Clousier, Paris.

Mullikin, M.A., and Hotchkis, A.M. 1973. *The Nine Sacred Mountains of China.* Vetch & Lee Ltd, Hong Kong.

Murray, C. 1998. Sharawadgi Resolved. *Garden History* 26(2): 208–13.

Naquin, S. 2000. *Peking: Temples and City Life, 1400–1900.* University of California Press, Berkeley, Los Angeles & London.

Naumkin, V. (series ed.) 1993. *Caught in Time: Great Photographic Archives—China.* Garnet Publishing Ltd, Reading, UK.

Needham, J. 1956. *Science and Civilisation in China.* Vol. 2. *History of Scientific Thought.* With research assistance by Wang Ling. Cambridge University Press.

_____ 1986. Ibid. Vol. 6. *Biology and Biological Technology.* Pt. 1. Botany. With the collaboration of Lu Gwei-djen, special contribution by Huang Hsing-tsung. Cambridge University Press.

Nelson, S.E. 1986. On Through to the Beyond: The Peach Blossom Spring as Paradise. *Archives of Asian Art* 39: 23–47.

Nieuhof, J. 1665. *L'ambassade de la compagnie orientale des provins unies vers le grand cham Tartarie ou empereur de la Chine faite par les Srs. Pierre de Goyer & Jacob de Keyser.* Jacob de Meurs, Amsterdam.

Paludan, A. 1981. *The Imperial Ming Tombs.* Yale University Press, New Haven & London.

_____ 1998. *Chronicle of the Chinese Emperors.* Thames & Hudson, London.

Pang, J., Feng, Z., Zhu, B., and Guo, S. 1995. *Camellias of China.* China Esperanto Press, Beijing.

Pearce, N. 1998. Photographs of Beijing in The Oriental Museum, Durham. *Apollo* n.s. 147 (433): 33–9.

Peking: A Tourist Guide. 1960. Foreign Languages Press, Peking.

Perckhammer, H. von. 1928. *Peking.* Albertus-Verlag, Berlin.

Petit, K. 1982. *Le monde des symboles dans l'art de la Chine.* 2e éd. Editions Thanh-Long, Bruxelles.

Phelps, D.L. 1974. *Mount Omei Illustrated Guide.* Hong Kong University Press.

Plaks, A.H. 1976. *Archetype and Allegory in the Dream of the Red Chamber.* Princeton University Press.

Polo, M. 1958. *The Travels of Marco Polo.* J.M. Dent & Sons Ltd, London; E.P. Dutton & Co. Inc., New York.

Powell, F.L. 1943. *In the Chinese Garden.* The John Day Company, New York.

Powers, M.J. 1998. Garden Rocks, Fractals, and Freedom. *Oriental Art* 44(1): 28–38.

Prip-Moller, J. 1937. *Chinese Buddhist Monasteries.* G.E.C. Gads Forlag, Copenhagen.

Qiao, Y. (ed.). 1982. *Classical Chinese Gardens.* Joint Publishing Company, Hong Kong; China Building Industry Press, Beijing. Reprinted 1984.

_____ and Sun, D. (eds). 1982. *Ancient Chinese Architecture.* Trans. by Wong Chi Kui and Chung Wah Nan. Joint Publishing Company, Hong Kong; China Building Industry Press, Beijing.

Rambach, P., and Rambach, S. 1987. *Gardens of Longevity in China and Japan: The Art of the Stone Raisers.* Rizzoli, New York.

Rennie, D.F. 1865. *Peking and the Pekingese during the First Year of the British Embassy at Peking.* 2 vols. John Murray, London.

Ripa, M. 1712. A copy of the Kangxi emperor's poems describing the summer resort, an illustrated copper engraved edition by Matteo Ripa, postface dated 1712, held by the British Library.

_____ 1844. *Memoirs of Father Ripa, during thirteen years of residence at the court of Peking in the service of the Emperor of China.* Selected and translated from the Italian by Fortunato Prandi. John Murray, London.

Robinson, F.B. 1939. Gardens of Old China. *Country Life* (N.Y.) April 1939: 84, 92, 94, 96, 98, 100.

Roe, A.S. 1910. *China as I Saw It: A woman's letters from the celestial empire.* Hutchinson & Co., London.

Ru, J., and Peng, H. 1998. *Ancient Chinese Architecture: Palace Architecture.* English translation by Zhang, E., Cui, S., Ling, Y., and Liu, H. Springer-Verlag, Wien & New York.

Sampson, T. 1869. In *Notes and Queries on China and Japan* 2: 52–3; 3: 18–22, 50–4, 72–3, 100–5, 115–17, 129–30, 147–50, 170–2.

Sargent, C.S. (ed.). 1913. *Plantae Wilsonianae.* Vol. 1. Cambridge University Press. Repr. 1988, Dioscorides Press, Portland.

Savige, T.J. 1993. *The International Camellia Register.* 2 vols. The International Camellia Society.

Schafer, E.H. 1948. Notes on a Chinese Word for Jasmine. *Journal of the American Oriental Society* 68(1): 60–5.

_____ 1961. *Tu Wan's Stone Catalogue of Cloudy Forest: A commentary and synopsis.* University of California Press, Berkeley & Los Angeles.

_____ 1963a. *The Golden Peaches of Samarkand.* University of California Press, Berkeley & Los Angeles.

_____ 1963b. Cosmos in Miniature: The Tradition of the Chinese Garden. *Landscape* 12(3): 24–6.

_____ 1965. Li Te-Yü and the Azalea. *Asiatische Studien* 18–19: 105–13.

_____ 1967. *The Vermilion Bird.* University of California Press, Berkeley & Los Angeles.

_____ 1968. Hunting Parks and Animal Enclosures in Ancient China. *Journal of the Economic and Social History of the Orient* 11: 318–43.

Sekino, T. 1935. *Summer Palace and Lama Temples in Jehol.* Kokusai Bunka Shinkokai, Tokyo.

Sensabaugh, D.A. 1998. Fragments of Mountain and Chunks of Stone: The Rock in the Chinese Garden. *Oriental Art* 44(1): 18–27.

Shao, T.T. 2000. Update on China Congress in 2003. *International Camellia Journal* 2000(32): 21–2.

Shaughnessy, E.L. 2000. *China: The Land of the Heavenly Dragon.* Duncan Baird Publishers Ltd, London.

Shen, F. 1809. *Six Records of a Floating Life.* Trans. from the orig. with intro. and notes by Leonard Pratt and Chiang Su-hui. Penguin Books, 1983.

Sirén, O. 1926. *The Imperial Palaces of Peking.* 3 parts. Librairie Nationale d'Art et d'Histoire, G. Van Oest, Publisher, Paris & Brussels.

_____ 1948. Architectural Elements of the Chinese Garden. *Architectural Review* June 1948: 251–8.

_____ 1949. *Gardens of China.* Ronald Press, New York.

_____ 1950. *China and Gardens of Europe of the Eighteenth Century.* Ronald Press, New York.

Sitwell, O. 1935. *Penny Foolish.* Macmillan, London.

_____ 1939. *Escape with Me!* Macmillan, London.

_____ 1974. *Queen Mary and Others.* Michael Joseph, London.

Staunton, Sir G. 1797. *An Authentic Account of an Embassy from the King of Great Britain to the Emperor of China.* 2 vols. G. Nicol, London.

_____ 1796. A folio of plates to accompany the above. G. Nicol, London.

Stein, R. 1990. *The World in Miniature: Container Gardens and Dwellings in Far Eastern Religious Thought.* Trans. by Phyllis Brooks. Stanford University Press.

Storey, R., Goncharoff, N., Harper, D., Cambon, M., Huhti, T., Liou, C., and English, A. 1998. *China.* Lonely Planet Publications, Hawthorn, Victoria, Australia.

Strassberg, R.E. 1994. *Inscribed Landscapes: Travel Writing from Imperial China.* University of California Press, Berkeley, Los Angeles & Oxford.

Stuart, J. 1990a. A Scholar's Garden in Ming China: Dream and Reality. *Asian Art* 3(4): 31–51.

_____ 1990b. Ming dynasty gardens reconstructed in words and images. *Journal of Garden History* 10(3): 162–72.

Sun, W., Kong, F., and Yue, Z. 1998. Magnoliaceae in Kunming Botanical Garden, Yunnan, China. In Hunt, D. (ed.). *Magnolias and their allies.* The International Dendrology Society and The Magnolia Society, 1998.

Sun, W.-b., Kong, F.-c., and Luo, G.-f. 2000. *Magnolia delavayi* and its natural forms. In *Proceedings of the International Symposium on the Family Magnoliaceae.* Science Press, Beijing.

Temple, Sir W. 1690. Upon the Gardens of Epicurus: or, Of Gardening, in the Year 1685. *Miscellanea,* The Second Part. In Four Essays. 2nd edn. Printed by J.R. for Ri. and Ra. Simpson, London.

Thiriez, R. 1998. *Barbarian Lens: Western Photographers of the Qianlong Emperor's European Palaces.* Gordon & Breach, Amsterdam.

Thomson, J. 1873–74. *Illustrations of China and its People.* 4 vols. Sampson Low, Marston, Low, and Searle, London.

_____ 1898. *Through China with a Camera.* A. Constable & Co., London.

Thurston, M.C. 1931. Beauty in Chinese Garden Courts. *Asia* 31(8): 514–21, 529–30.

Tianjin University, Bureau of Relics of Chengde (compilers). 1982. *Chengde Gu Jianzhu* (Ancient Architecture of Chengde). China building Industry Press, Beijing; Joint Publishing Company, Hong Kong.

Titley, N., and Wood, F. 1991. *Oriental Gardens.* The British Library, London.

Tokiwa, D., and Sekino, T. 1926. *Buddhist Monuments in China.* Bukkyo-Shiseki Kenkyu-Kwai, Tokyo.

Toshiro, I. 1998. *The Garden as Architecture.* Orig. publ. in Japanese, 1990. Trans. by Pamela Virgilio. Kodansha International, Tokyo, New York & London.

Townley, Lady S. 1904. *My Chinese Notebook.* Methuen & Co., London.

Tsu, F. Y.-s. 1988. *Landscape Design in Chinese Gardens.* McGraw-Hill, New York.

Tu, W.-M. 1984. The Continuity of Being: Chinese Visions of Nature. In Leroy S. Rouner (ed.). *On Nature.* University of Notre Dame Press, Indiana.

Tun, L.-c. 1965. *Annual Customs and Festivals in Peking.* As recorded in the *Yen-ching Sui shih-chi* by Tun Li-Ch'en, c.1901, trans. and annotated by Derek Bodde. 2nd edn (orig. publ. 1936). Hong Kong University Press.

Tung, C. 1936. Chinese Gardens, Especially in Kiangsu and Chekiang. *T'ien Hsia Monthly* 3(3): 220–44.

_____ 1997. *Glimpses of Gardens in Eastern China.* China Architecture & Building Press, Beijing.

Valder, P. 1995. *Wisterias: A Comprehensive Guide.* Florilegium, Sydney.

———— 1999. *The Garden Plants of China.* Florilegium, Sydney.

Van Braam, A.E. 1798. *An authentic account of the Embassy of the Dutch East India Company to the court of the Emperor of China in the years 1794 and 1795.* 2 vols. London.

Vance, M. 1980. *Gardens of China: Books in English.* Vance Bibliographies, Monticello, Illinois.

Van Hecken, J.L., and Grootaers, W.A. 1959. The Half Acre Garden, Pan-mou Yüan. *Monumenta Serica* 18: 360–87.

Von Erdberg, E. 1985. *Chinese Influence on European Garden Structures.* Hacker Art Books, New York.

Wang, D. 1988. The History of ornamental Plants in China. *Camellia News* 107: 14–16.

Wang, J.C. 1998. *The Chinese Garden.* Oxford University Press.

Wang, L. et al. 1998. *Chinese Tree Peony.* China Forestry Publishing House, Beijing.

Wang, Y. 1998. Interior display and its relation to external spaces in traditional Chinese gardens. Trans. by Bruce Doar and John Makeham. *Studies in the History of Gardens & Designed Landscapes* 18(3): 232–47.

Warner, M. 1972. *The Dragon Empress: Life and times of Tz'u-Hsi 1835–1908 Empress Dowager of China.* Weidenfeld & Nicolson, London.

Waugh, T. 1984. *The Travels of Marco Polo.* Sidgwick & Jackson, London.

Weng, W.H.C. 1968. *Gardens in Chinese Art.* The China Institute in America, New York.

Whiten, F., and Whiten, G. 1988. *Chinese Garden Style.* Unwin Hyman Ltd, London.

Who's Who in China 1918–1950. (1982–83). Chinese Materials Center, Hong Kong.

Williams, C.A.S. 1975. *Outlines of Chinese Symbolism and Art Motives.* 3rd edn. Charles E. Tuttle Company, Rutland, Vermont & Tokyo, Japan.

Williamson, Rev. A. 1870. *Journeys in North China, Manchuria, and Eastern Mongolia; with Some Account of Corea.* 2 vols. Smith, Elder & Co., London.

Wilson, E.H. 1913. *A Naturalist in Western China.* 2 vols. Methuen & Co., London.

———— 1929. *China Mother of Gardens.* The Stratford Company, Boston, Mass.

Wonderful Attraction In Zhuhai. 1999. *The Rail Monthly* 1999 (2/3): 34–5.

Wong, K.K.C. 1997. The Influence of Merchant Patronage on Yangzhou Gardens in the Quing Dynasty. In Pickersgill, S., and Scriver, P. (eds). *On what Ground(s)?* Society of Architectural Historians, Australia and New Zealand, Adelaide.

Wood, F. 1992. *Blue Guide: China.* A.& C. Black, London.

Worswick, C., and Spence, J. 1978. *Imperial China: Photographs 1850–1912.* Penwick Publishing, New York.

Wu, C.Y. 1978. *Musella lasiocarpa* (Fr.) C.Y. Wu. *Acta Phytotaxonomica Sinica* 16(3): 56.

Wu, S.-c. 1935. Notes on the Origin of the Chinese Private Garden. *China Journal* 23: 17–22.

Wu, S.H.L. 1979. *Passage to Power: K'ang-hsi and His Heir Apparent, 1661–1722.* Harvard University Press, Cambridge, Mass., & London, England.

Yang, H. 1982. *The Classical Gardens of China.* Trans. by Wang Hui Min. Van Nostrand Reinhold, New York.

Yang, H.-c. 1984. *A Record of Buddhist Monasteries in Lo-yang.* Translated by Yi-t'ung Wang from the original of c. AD 547. Princeton University Press, Princeton, New Jersey.

Yeung, W.L. 1998. *The Yellow Emperor Myth and the Concept of a Unified Chinese Nation.* Ph.D. thesis, University of Sydney.

Yoshikawa, I. 1990. *Chinese Gardens.* English trans. by Jay W. Thomas. Graphic-sha Publishing Company Ltd, Tokyo.

Yu, D. (chief compiler). 1983. *The Botanical Gardens of China.* Science Press, Beijing.

Yu, T.-t. 1950. *Camellia reticulata* and its garden varieties. In Synge, P.M., (ed.). *Camellias and Magnolias.* Royal Horticultural Society, London.

Zhang, J. 1997. *Zhongguo yuanlin yishu dacidian* (Chinese Landscape Art Dictionary). Shanxi Education Press, Taiyuan.

Zhang, Q., Feng, Z., and Yang, Z. 1988. *Rare Flowers and Unusual Trees: A Collection of Yunnan's Most Treasured Plants.* Trans. by Z.R. Xiong. China Esperanto Press, Beijing.

Zhou, S. 1995. *Beijing Old and New.* 2nd edn. New World Press, Beijing.

Zhu, J. 1992. *Chinese Landscape Gardening.* Foreign Languages Press, Beijing.

CHINESE DYNASTIES

XIA	c.2000 BC	to	c.1600 BC	
SHANG	c.1600 BC	to	c.1050 BC	
ZHOU	c.1050 BC	to	221 BC	
QIN	221 BC	to	207 BC	
HAN	206 BC	to	AD 220	
THREE KINGDOMS	AD 220	to	AD 280	
SIX DYNASTIES	AD 265	to	AD 589	
SUI	AD 581	to	AD 618	
TANG	AD 618	to	AD 907	
FIVE DYNASTIES	AD 907	to	AD 960	
NORTHERN SONG	AD 960	to	AD 1126	
SOUTHERN SONG	AD 1127	to	AD 1279	
YUAN	AD 1279	to	AD 1368	
MING	AD 1368	to	AD 1644	
QING	AD 1644	to	AD 1911	

INDEX

Entries consist principally of general topics and the names of individuals, provinces, towns, mountains and sites of horticultural interest mentioned in the text. As far as plants are concerned, most are remarked upon in the text repeatedly or incidentally and to have incorporated every mention of these would have rendered the index unwieldy. Hence only those that are illustrated or are of particular interest, rarity or great age have been included. Page numbers in **bold** refer to illustrations.

In order to assist with the use of this index I have provided the following list of the meanings of Pinyin transliterations commonly used as prefixes, suffixes or individual words:

bei: north
bowuguan: museum
caotang: thatched cottage
chi: pool
daxue: university
dian: palace; temple, usually Daoist
dong: east
dongwuyuan: zoo
feng: peak
fu: mansion
ge: pavilion, usually two-storeyed
gong: palace; temple, usually Daoist
gongyuan: park
guan: hall; temple, usually Daoist
guangchang: square
guju: former residence
hai: sea or large lake
hu: lake
jian: college
lin: forest; grove
ling: tomb
lou: building of two or more storeys
miao: temple, usually dedicated to a person or deity
nan: south
pu: garden
qingzhensi: mosque
quan: spring
shan: mountain
si: temple, usually Buddhist
ta: pagoda
tang: hall
ting: pavilion
xi: west
yuan: garden; temple (occasionally)
zhiwuyuan: botanical garden

Wooden panel on the stele pavilion, Zhougongmiao, Qufu

Azalea, Upper Temple, Black Dragon Pool Park, Kunming